BARRON'S

HOW TO PREPARE FOR THE

AP®

Advanced Placement Exam

PSYCHOLOGY

2ND EDITION

Robert McEntarffer
AP Psychology Teacher
Lincoln Southeast High School
Lincoln, Nebraska

Allyson J. Weseley, Ed.D.
AP Psychology Teacher
Roslyn High School
Roslyn, New York

BARRON'S

I thank all my teachers: Kristin Krohn, Kerstin Vandervoort, my parents and grandparents, my brother, my friends, and my students.—R.M.

To my family and friends for their support and to my students who make the study of psychology an adventure every day.—A.W.

About the Authors

Allyson Weseley has been teaching AP Psychology at Roslyn High School in Roslyn, NY for 8 years. All of her students have passed the AP Exam, and over 80% of them have scored "5's." She earned her undergraduate degree in Psychology at Princeton University and then went on to get a masters degree from the Harvard Graduate School of Education and a doctorate from Columbia University's Teachers College. Dr. Weseley has published a number of psychology-related articles, led numerous psychology teacher workshops, and currently serves on the board of Teachers of Psychology in the Secondary Schools.

Rob McEntarffer has been teaching AP Psychology at Lincoln Southeast High School in Lincoln, NE for 10 years and Introductory Psychology at Nebraska Wesleyan University for 3 years. He earned his B.S. in teaching of psychology at the University of Nebraska and is currently working on a master's degree in educational assessment and measurement. He is past-chair of the national organization Teachers of Psychology in Secondary Schools, works with the committee on National Standards for the Teaching of High School Psychology, and recently wrote the test bank for an introductory psychology textbook.

© Copyright 2004, 2000 by Barron's Educational Series, Inc.

All inquiries should be addressed to:
Barron's Educational Series, Inc.
250 Wireless Boulevard
Hauppauge, New York 11788
http://www.baronseduc.com

Library of Congress Catalog Card No. 2003056001

ISBN-13 (book): 978-0-7641-2349-8
ISBN-10 (book): 0-7641-2349-1

ISBN-13 (package w/CD-ROM): 978-0-7641-7909-9
ISBN-10 (package w/CD-ROM): 0-7641-7909-8

Library of Congress Cataloging-in-Publication Data

McEntarffer, Robert.
   Barron's how to prepare for the AP psychology advanced placement examination / Robert McEntarffer, Allyson J. Weseley.
       p. cm.
   Includes index.
   ISBN 0-7641-2349-1
       1. Psychology—Examinations, questions, etc. 2. Psychology—Examinations—Study guides. 3. Advanced placement programs (Education) I. Title: How to prepare for the AP psychology advanced placement examination. II. Title: AP psychology. III. Weseley, Allyson. IV. Title.

BF78.M34 2004
150'.76—dc21
                                                                                    2003056001

Printed in the United States of America
13 12 11 10 9 8 7

Contents

Introduction: Using This Book

The purpose of this book is to provide you with the best-possible preparation for the Advanced Placement Examination in Psychology. Becoming familiar with the structure of a test is an essential part of preparation. Therefore, this book begins with an overview of the Advanced Placement exam.

We devoted most of the book to a topical review of the main areas of psychology. We organized the psychology content in such a way that it mirrors the format of the exam. These areas and their relative coverage on the AP exam are listed below:

History and Approaches	2–4 percent
Methods	6–8 percent
Biological Bases of Behavior	8–10 percent
Sensation and Perception	7–9 percent
States of Consciousness	2–4 percent
Learning	7–9 percent
Cognition	8–10 percent
Motivation and Emotion	7–9 percent
Developmental Psychology	7–9 percent
Personality	6–8 percent
Testing and Individual Differences	5–7 percent
Abnormal Psychology	7–9 percent
Treatment of Psychological Disorders	5–7 percent
Social Psychology	7–9 percent

Since this is a review book, our aim was to include only that information you need to know for the exam. Nonetheless, some of this information is particularly important and we have tried to convey that fact by highlighting such material as *Hints* wherever applicable. Important terms and people are set in italics in the text and can be found in the index.

At the end of each section appears a series of multiple-choice practice questions and an explanation of the correct answers. We recommend that you first review the material in the chapter and then answer all the review questions in order to test your comprehension.

Because the essays on the AP exam generally transcend any single topic area, we have dealt with them in a separate chapter at the end of the book. We have included both a discussion of how best to approach such essays and a number of examples of the kinds of essay questions likely to appear on the exam. Model essay answers are also included.

We have also included two full practice exams. In order to use them to your full advantage, take these exams after you have completed the curriculum and use them to help you study for the AP exam. Taking a practice exam under actual testing conditions (all at once and within the time limit) is always best.

In addition to providing you with an explanation of the correct answers, we have included a work sheet you can use to identify the topics with which you need the most practice.

Finally, the book contains an index that will be helpful to you anytime you come across a term or person you know is important, but do not remember. It will refer you to page(s) that discuss that term or person.

Overview of the AP Psychology Exam

The Advanced Placement Psychology Test has two parts: a multiple-choice section and an essay section. You will have two hours in which to complete the whole test. The multiple-choice portion of the exam contains 100 five-choice (*A* to *E*) questions. You will have 70 minutes to complete this section, and most students find that to be a sufficient amount of time. Overall, the questions in the latter part of the test are a little more difficult than the early ones.

Like the SAT and other AP tests, this test has a guessing penalty. That is, you lose points ($1/4$ of a point each) for wrong answers. Nonetheless, whenever you can eliminate one or more of the answer choices, you ought to guess. Since you earn a point for each correct answer and lose only a quarter of a point for each incorrect answer, one correct guess will cancel out four incorrect ones.

The essay section of the test consists of two questions, and you must answer them both. Unlike most other AP exams, you have no choice in the essay section of this exam. You will have 50 minutes to complete this portion of the exam. Some students find writing two full essays in such a short amount of time to be difficult. The section of this book about how to prepare for the essay section has some helpful suggestions.

Your score (ranging from 1 to 5) on this exam will take into account your performance on both the multiple-choice and essay sections, with the multiple-choice section counting for twice as much as the essays. Thus, two-thirds of your score depends on your performance on the multiple-choice questions, and the other one-third of your score is based on the quality of your essays.

Each year, the exact breakdown of the percentage of people who earn each score differs. More information is available from the College Board about score breakdowns for various years (see the College Board web site: www.collegeboard.org/ap).

Important Names to Study for the Exam

The AP exam will not require you to be familiar with the work of many psychologists on the exam, but it may ask about a few. To prepare you, we have assembled a "Top 25" list of psychologists, the chapters in which they are discussed, and brief descriptions of the psychologists' best-known work.

Mary Ainsworth—Developmental Psychology
  Placed human infants into a "strange situation" in order to examine attachment to parents
Solomon Asch—Social Psychology
  Conformity experiment—people incorrectly reported lengths of lines
  Impression formation study—professor was warm or cold
Albert Bandura—Learning and Personality
  Social-learning theory (modeling)
  Reciprocal determinism (triadic reciprocality)
  Self-efficacy
Alfred Binet—Developmental Psychology, and Testing and Individual Differences
  Creator of the first intelligence test
Noam Chomsky—Cognition
  Theorized the critical-period hypothesis for language acquisition
Erik Erikson—Developmental Psychology
  Psychosocial stage theory of development (eight stages)
  Neo-Freudian
Sigmund Freud—Personality and States of Consciousness
  Psychosexual stage theory of personality (oral, anal, phallic, and adult genital)
  Stressed importance of unconscious and sexual drive
  Psychoanalytic therapy
  Theory of dreaming
Carol Gilligan—Developmental Psychology
  Challenged the universality of Kohlberg's moral development theory
Harry Harlow—Developmental Psychology
  Experimented with infant monkeys and attachment
David Hubel and Torsten Wiesel—Sensation and Perception
  Discovered feature detectors, groups of neurons in the visual cortex that respond to different types of visual images

William James—Methods, Approaches, and History
  Published *The Principles of Psychology,* psychology's first textbook
  Functionalism
Lawrence Kohlberg—Developmental Psychology
  Stage theory of moral development (preconventional, conventional, and postconventional)
Elizabeth Loftus—Cognition
  Demonstrated the problems with eyewitness testimony and constructive memory
Abraham Maslow—Motivation and Emotion, and Treatment of Psychological Disorders
  Humanistic psychologist
  Hierarchy of needs, self-actualization
Stanley Milgram—Social Psychology
  Obedience studies—participants think they are shocking a learner
Ivan Pavlov—Learning
  Classical conditioning studies with dogs and salivation
Jean Piaget—Developmental Psychology
  Stage theory of cognitive development (sensorimotor, preoperational, concrete operations, and formal operations)
Robert Rescorla—Learning
  Revised the Pavlovian contiguity model of classical conditioning
Carl Rogers—Treatment of Psychological Disorders and Personality
  Humanistic psychologist—person-centered therapy and unconditional positive regard
  Self theory of personality
Stanley Schacter—Motivation and Emotion
  Two-factor theory for emotion
B. F. Skinner—Learning
  Operant conditioning
  Invented Skinner box
John Watson—Learning
  Father of behaviorism
  Baby Albert experiment—classically conditioned fear
Benjamin Whorf—Cognition
  The linguistic relativity hypothesis
Willhelm Wundt
  Set up the first psychological laboratory in an apartment near the university at Leipzig, Germany
  Theory of structuralism

CHAPTER 1
History and Approache

History of Psychology
Psychological Perspectives
Practice Questions
Answers to Practice Questions

History of Psychology

One way to think about the history of psychology is to organize the various theorists and theories into "waves" (or schools of thought). Each wave is a way of thinking about human thought and behavior that dominated the field for a certain period of time until a new way of looking at psychology started to dominate the field.

Wave One—Introspection

Archaeologists and historians find evidence that humans have always thought about our thought and behavior, so in a way, the study of psychology is as old as our species. Archaeologists find evidence of *trephination*—Stone Age humans carving holes through the skull to release evil spirits. Greek philosophers such as *Plato* and *Democritus* theorized about the relationship between thought and behavior. However, thinking about psychology is different than studying it scientifically. Many psychologists specializing in the history of the science date the beginning of scientific psychology to the year 1879. In that year, *Wilhelm Wundt* (1832–1920) set up the first psychological laboratory in an apartment near the university at Leipzig, Germany. Wundt trained subjects in *introspection*—the subjects were asked to record accurately their cognitive reactions to simple stimuli. Through this process, Wundt hoped to examine basic cognitive structures. He eventually described his theory of *structuralism*—the idea that the mind operates by combining subjective emotions and objective sensations. In 1890, *William James* (1842–1910) published *The Principles of Psychology,* the science's first textbook. James examined how these structures Wundt identified function in our lives (James's theory is called *functionalism*). Introspective theories were important in establishing the science of psychology, but they do not significantly influence current psychological thinking.

Wave Two—Gestalt Psychology

While Wundt and James were experimenting with introspection, another group of early psychologists were explaining human thought and behavior in a very different way. *Gestalt psychologists* like *Max Wertheimer* (1880–1943) argued against dividing human thought and behavior into discrete structures. *Gestalt psychology* tried to examine a person's total experience because the way we experience the world is more than just an accumulation of various perceptual experiences. Gestalt theorists demonstrated that the whole experience is often more than just the sum of the parts of the experience. A painting can be represented as rows and columns of points of color, but the experience of the painting is much more than that. Therapists later incorporated gestalt thinking by examining not just a client's difficulty but the context in which the difficulty occurs. Like the introspective theories, other than the contribution to specific forms of therapy and the study of perception, Gestalt psychology has relatively little influence on current psychology.

Wave Three—Psychoanalysis

If you ask a random person to name a famous psychologist, he or she will most likely name *Sigmund Freud* (1856–1939). Freud revolutionized psychology with his psychoanalytic theory. While treating patients for various psychosomatic complaints, Freud believed he discovered the *unconscious mind*—a part of our mind over which we do not have conscious control that determines, in part, how we think and behave. Freud believed that this hidden part of ourselves builds up over the years through *repression*—the pushing down into the unconscious events and feelings that cause so much anxiety and tension that our conscious mind cannot deal with them. Freud believed that to understand human thought and behavior truly, we must examine the unconscious mind through dream analysis, word association, and other psychoanalytic therapy techniques. While many therapists still use some of Freud's basic ideas in helping clients, Freud has been criticized for being unscientific and creating unverifiable theories. Freud's theories were and are widely used by various artists. Many of Freud's terms moved from being exclusively used by psychologists to being used in day-to-day speech (for example, *defense mechanism*).

Wave Four—Behaviorism

John Watson (1878–1958) studied the pioneering conditioning experiments of *Ivan Pavlov* (1849–1936). Watson then declared that for psychology to be considered a science, it must limit itself to observable phenomena, not unobservable concepts like the unconscious mind. Watson along with others wanted to establish *behaviorism* as the dominant paradigm of psychology. Behaviorists maintain that psychologists should look at only behavior and causes of behavior—*stimuli* (environmental events) and *responses* (physical reactions)—and not concern themselves with describing elements of consciousness. Another behaviorist, *B. F. Skinner* (1904–1990), expanded the basic ideas of behaviorism to include the idea of *reinforcement*—environmental stimuli that either encourage or discourage certain responses. Skinner's intellectual influence lasted for decades. Behaviorism was the dominant school of thought in psychology from the 1920s through the 1960s.

Wave Five—Multiple Perspectives

Currently, there is no one way of thinking about human thought and behavior that all or even most psychologists share. Many psychologists describe themselves as *eclectic*—drawing from multiple perspectives. As psychology develops in the new century, perhaps one way of thinking will become dominant. For now, though, psychologists look at thought and behavior from multiple perspectives.

Psychological Perspectives

As described in the section about the history of psychology, different contemporary psychologists look at human thought and behavior from different perspectives. Contemporary perspectives can be placed into seven broad categories.

Humanist Perspective

Partially in reaction to the perceived reductionism of the behaviorists, some psychologists tried to describe some mysterious aspects of consciousness again. The *humanists,* including theorists *Abraham Maslow* (1908–1970) and *Carl Rogers* (1902–1987), stressed individual choice and free will. This contrasts with the *deterministic* behaviorists, who theorized that all behaviors are caused by past conditioning. *Humanists* believe that we choose most of our behaviors and these choices are guided by physiological, emotional, or spiritual needs. A humanistic psychologist might explain that an introverted person may choose to limit social contact with others because he or she finds that social needs are better satisfied by contact with a few close friends rather than large groups. Humanistic theories are not easily tested by the scientific method. Some psychological historians view it as more of a historical perspective than a current one. However, some therapists find humanistic ideas helpful in aiding clients to overcome obstacles in their lives.

Psychoanalytic Perspective

The *psychoanalytic* perspective, as described previously, continues to be a part, if a controversial one, of modern psychology. Psychologists using this perspective believe that the *unconscious* mind—a part of our mind that we do not have conscious control over or access to—controls much of our thought and action. Psychoanalysts would look for impulses or memories pushed into the unconscious mind through *repression*. This perspective thinks that to understand human thought and behavior, we must examine our *unconscious* mind through dream analysis, word association, and other psychoanalytic therapy techniques. A psychoanalytic psychologist might explain that an introverted person avoids social situations because of a repressed memory of trauma in childhood involving a social situation, perhaps acute embarrassment or anxiety experienced (but not consciously remembered) at school or a party.

Biopsychology (or Neuroscience) Perspective

Biopsychologists explain human thought and behavior strictly in terms of biological processes. Human *cognition* and reactions might be caused by effects of our *genes, hormones,* and *neurotransmitters* in the brain or by a combination of all three. A biopsychologist might explain a person's tendency to be *extroverted* as caused by genes inherited from their parents and the genes' effects on the abundance of certain neurotransmitters in the brain. Biopsychology is a rapidly growing field. Some scientists wonder if the future of psychology might be a branch of the science of biology. (Also see the chapter "Biological Bases of Behavior.")

Evolutionary (or Darwinian) Perspective

Evolutionary psychologists (also sometimes called *sociobiologists*) examine human thoughts and actions in terms of *natural selection*. Some psychological traits might be advantageous for survival, and these traits would be passed down from the parents to the next generation. A psychologist using the evolutionary perspective might explain a person's tendency to be extroverted as a survival advantage. If a person is outgoing, he or she might make friends and allies. These connections could improve the individual's chances of survival, which increases the person's chances for passing this trait for extroversion down to his or her children.

Behavioral Perspective

Behaviorists explain human thought and behavior in terms of *conditioning*. Behaviorists look strictly at observable behaviors and what reaction organisms get in response to specific behaviors. A behaviorist might explain a person's tendency to be extroverted in terms of reward and punishment. Was the person rewarded for being outgoing? Was the person punished for withdrawing from a situation or not interacting with others? A behaviorist would look for environmental conditions that caused an extroverted response in the person (see also the "Learning" chapter).

Cognitive Perspective

Cognitive psychologists examine human thought and behavior in terms of how we interpret, process, and remember environmental events. In this perspective, the rules that we use to view the world are important to understanding why we think and behave the way we do. A cognitive psychologist might explain a person's tendency to be extroverted in terms of how he or she interprets social situations. Does the individual interpret others' offers for conversation as important ways to get to know someone or important for his or her own life in some way? To a cognitive psychologist, an extroverted person sees the world in such a way that being outgoing makes sense.

Social-Cultural (or Sociocultural) Perspective

Social-cultural psychologists look at how our thoughts and behaviors vary from people living in other *cultures*. They emphasize the influence culture has on the way we think and act. A social-cultural psychologist might explain a person's tendency to be extroverted by examining his or her culture's rules about social interaction. How far apart do people in this culture usually stand when they have a conversation? How often do people touch each other while interacting? How much value does the culture place on being part of a group versus being an individual? These cultural norms would be important to a sociocultural psychologist in explaining a person's extroversion.

If you ask psychologists which of these perspectives they most agree with, they might say that each perspective has valid explanations depending on the specific situation. This point of view, sometimes called *eclectic,* claims that no one perspective has all the answers to the variety of human thought and behavior. Psychologists use various perspectives in their work depending on which point of view fits best with the explanation. In the future, some perspectives might be combined or new perspectives might emerge as research continues.

Practice Questions

> *Directions:* Each of the questions or incomplete statements below is followed by five suggested answers or completions. Select the one that is best in each case.

1. You are at a lecture about the history of psychology and the speaker states that Wilhelm Wundt's theory of structuralism was the first scientific psychological theory. On what historical fact might the speaker be basing her or his argument?
    (A) Wundt was internationally known at the time, and this lent credence to his theory in the scientific community.
    (B) Wundt studied under Ivan Pavlov for his graduate training, and Pavlov required scientific methods to be used.
    (C) Structuralism was based on the results of his introspection experiments, so it is, at least in part, empirical.
    (D) Structuralism was based on careful anecdotes gathered from Wundt's extensive clinical career.
    (E) Wundt was the first person to study psychology in an academic setting.

2. Sigmund Freud's theory of the unconscious mind
    (A) was revolutionary because it was the first comprehensive explanation of human thought and behavior.
    (B) resulted from discoveries about the human brain obtained by cadaver dissection.
    (C) is outdated and has no relevance for modern psychology.
    (D) focused entirely on human males' sex drive.
    (E) depends on the idea that humans can remember events but not be consciously aware of the memory.

3. In what way might a behaviorist disagree with a cognitive psychologist about the cause of aggression?
    (A) A behaviorist might state that aggression is caused by memories or ways we think about aggressive behavior, while a cognitive psychologist might say aggression is caused by a past repressed experience.
    (B) A behaviorist might state that aggression is a behavior encouraged by our genetic code, while a cognitive psychologist might state that aggression is caused by memories or ways we think about aggressive behavior.
    (C) A behaviorist might state that aggression is caused by past rewards for aggressive behavior, while a cognitive psychologist might believe aggression is caused by an expressed desire to fulfill certain life needs.
    (D) A behaviorist might state that aggression is caused by past rewards for aggressive behavior, while a cognitive psychologist might believe aggression is caused by memories or ways we think about aggressive behavior.
    (E) A behaviorist would not disagree with a cognitive psychologist about aggression because they both believe that aggressive behavior is caused by the way we cognitively process certain behaviors.

4. Dr. Marco explains to a client that his feelings of hostility toward a coworker are most likely caused by the way the client interprets the coworker's actions and the way he thinks that people should behave at work. Dr. Marco is most likely working from what perspective?
    (A) behavioral
    (B) cognitive
    (C) psychoanalytic
    (D) humanist
    (E) social-cultural

5. The research methodology Wilhelm Wundt used is called
    (A) introspection.
    (B) structuralism.
    (C) naturalistic observation.
    (D) inferential.
    (E) scientific.

6. Which of the following psychologists wrote the first psychology textbook?
    (A) William James
    (B) Wilhelm Wundt
    (C) B. F. Skinner
    (D) John Watson
    (E) Albert Bandura

7. Which of the following psychologists was part of the Gestalt group of psychologists?
    (A) Carl Rogers
    (B) Wilhelm Wundt
    (C) B. F. Skinner
    (D) John Watson
    (E) Max Wertheimer

8. Which of the following concepts is most integral to Sigmund Freud's psychoanalytic theory?
    (A) trephining
    (B) structuralism
    (C) the unconscious mind
    (D) the concept of Gestalt
    (E) behaviorism

9. Sigmund Freud's psychoanalytic theory has been criticized for being
    (A) appropriate for female patients, but not male patients.
    (B) only applicable to research settings, not therapy settings.
    (C) based on large groups, not individual cases.
    (D) unscientific and unverifiable.
    (E) too closely tied to behavioristic thought.

10. John Watson relied on the pioneering work of _____ in establishing behaviorism as a paradigm of psychology.
     (A) B. F. Skinner
     (B) Wilhelm Wundt
     (C) William James
     (D) Ivan Pavlov
     (E) Sigmund Freud

11. B. F. Skinner introduced the idea of _____ to the paradigm of behaviorism.
     (A) unconscious thinking
     (B) reinforcement
     (C) conditioning
     (D) defense mechanisms
     (E) introspection

12. Which of the following psychologists might have described himself as a humanist?
     (A) B. F. Skinner
     (B) William James
     (C) Abraham Maslow
     (D) John Watson
     (E) Ivan Pavlov

13. Symbolic dream analysis might be an important research technique to a psychologist from which of the following perspectives?
     (A) behaviorist
     (B) biopsychologist
     (C) psychoanalytic
     (D) evolutionary
     (E) structuralist

14. Behaviorists explain human thought and behavior as a result of
     (A) past conditioning.
     (B) unconscious behavioral impulses.
     (C) natural selections.
     (D) biological processes.
     (E) individual choice.

15. A therapist who says that she uses whatever psychological perspective "works best" for each patient might be best described as
     (A) social-cultural.
     (B) humanist.
     (C) eclectic.
     (D) psychoanalytic.
     (E) functionalist.

Answers to Practice Questions

1. **(C)** Scientific research is empirical by nature, and Wundt based the theory of structuralism on results of experimentation. Wundt's reputation and the academic setting are not relevant to the scientific nature of his theory. Wundt did not study under Pavlov nor was he a clinical psychologist.

2. **(E)** The unconscious mind contains memories of events or feelings of which we are not consciously aware. It was not the first comprehensive theory. Freud did not use cadaver dissection to formulate the theory. While the sex drive figures prominently in the theory, the theory is not focused entirely on sex. While some psychologists would dispute much of Freud's theory, many therapists still find the idea of the unconscious mind relevant.

3. **(D)** Behaviorists look at what behaviors we are rewarded for, and cognitive psychologists explain our behavior through the way we interpret events. The rest of the answers are explanations of other psychological perspectives incorrectly applied to behaviorism or cognitive theory.

4. **(B)** The cognitive perspective emphasizes the role of interpretation of others' actions and best fits the given scenario. The other perspectives would emphasize other types of explanations.

5. **(A)** Wundt used the technique of introspection to research his theory of structuralism. He did not use naturalistic observation and inferential and scientific are general terms that might be applied to many different types of research.

6. **(A)** William James wrote the first psychology textbook, *The Principles of Psychology*, in 1890.

7. **(E)** Wertheimer is the only psychologist in this list that was included as part of the gestalt group in the text.

8. **(C)** The unconscious mind is an integral concept in Freudian theory. Memories and impulses are repressed into the unconscious mind and this drives our later behaviors. The other concepts mentioned do not relate to psychoanalytic theory.

9. **(D)** Freud did not use the scientific method and many of his conclusions cannot be proven or disproven through experimentation. The theory was based on individual male and female cases in therapeutic settings, and is not tied closely to behaviorism.

10. **(D)** Watson referred to the conditioning experiments Ivan Pavlov did with dogs. B. F. Skinner came after Watson chronologically, and the other psychologists mentioned are not part of the behaviorist paradigm.

11. **(B)** Skinner added the idea of reinforcing events, such as rewards and punishments, to the basic idea of behaviorism. Unconscious thinking and defense mechanisms are concepts from the psychoanalytic perspective. Conditioning is a general term used before Skinner did his research. Introspection was a technique used by Wundt.

12. **(C)** Maslow is the only psychologist in this list included in the section on humanism in the text. Skinner, Pavlov, and Watson are behaviorists.

13. **(C)** The idea that dreams contain symbols is central to the psychoanalytic perspective, and not any of the other perspectives listed.

14. **(A)** Behaviorists explain human thought and behavior as a result of conditioning in our pasts, either classical conditioning or operant conditioning. This conditioning restricts (or eliminates) the idea of personal choice, and behaviorists do not usually refer to biological causes and

evolutionary theory (like natural selection). The unconscious mind is a concept from psychoanalytic theory.

15. **(C)** The eclectic perspective claims that no one perspective can best explain all human behaviors and a therapist who works with many different perspectives to help individual patients is in some sense eclectic, not any of the other specific perspectives listed.

CHAPTER 2

Methods

Research Methods

An understanding of research methods is fundamental to psychology. Because of that, you are more likely to see a free-response (or essay) question on this topic than on any other.

Sometimes psychologists conduct research in order to solve practical problems. For instance, psychologists might compare two different methods of teaching children to read in order to determine which method is better or they could design and test the efficacy of a program to help people quit smoking. This type of research is known as *applied research* because it has clear, practical applications. Other psychologists conduct *basic research*. Basic research explores questions that are of interest to psychologists but are not intended to have immediate, real-world applications. Examples of basic research would include studying how people form their attitudes about others and how people in different cultures define intelligence.

Terminology

Validity and Reliability

Good research is both valid and reliable. Research is *valid* when it measures what the researcher set out to measure; it is accurate. Research is *reliable* when it can be replicated; it is consistent. If the researcher conducted the same research in the same way, the researcher would get similar results.

Hypotheses and Variables

Although some research is purely descriptive, most psychological research is guided by hypotheses. A *hypothesis* expresses a relationship between two variables. Variables, by definition, are things that can vary among the participants in the research. For instance, religion, stress level, and height are variables. According to an experimental hypothesis, the *dependent variable* depends on the *independent variable*. In other words, a change in the independent variable will produce a change in the dependent variable. For instance, consider the hypothesis that watching violent television programs makes people more aggressive. In this hypothesis, watching television violence is the independent variable since the hypothesis suggests that a change in television viewing will result in a change in behavior. In testing a hypothesis, researchers manipulate the independent variable and measure the dependent variable. Hypotheses often grow out of theories. A *theory* aims to explain some phenomenon and allows researchers to generate testable hypotheses with the hope of collecting data that support the theory.

Researchers not only need to name the variables they will study, they need to *operationalize* them. When you operationalize a variable, you explain how you will measure it. For instance, in the hypothesis above, what programs will be considered violent? What behaviors will be considered aggressive? These and many other questions need to be answered before the research commences. The operationalization of the variables raises many issues about the validity and reliability of the research.

Hint: When writing about research, students often describe the goal as proof of the hypothesis. However, proving a hypothesis is impossible. Rather, research aims to gather data that either supports or disproves a hypothesis.

Sampling

Before one can begin to investigate a hypothesis, one needs to decide who or what to study. The individuals on which the research will be conducted are called *subjects* (or participants), and the process by which subjects are selected is called *sampling*. In order to select a *sample* (the group of subjects), one must first identify the *population* from which the sample will be selected. The population includes anyone or anything that could possibly be selected to be in the sample.

The goal in selecting a sample is that it be *representative* of a larger population. If I conduct my research about television violence using only my own psychology students, I cannot say much about how viewing violent television affects other people. My students may not be representative of a larger population. I would be better off specifying a larger and more diverse population, the whole student body of 1,000, for example, and then randomly selecting a sample of 100. *Random selection* increases the likelihood that the sample represents the population.

Hint: Using representative samples and random samples allows researchers to generalize about their results.

Note—and this is important—that psychologists use the term *random* differently than laypeople. If I choose my sample by standing in front of the library on a Wednesday morning and approaching people in a way I feel is random, I have not used random sampling. Perhaps, without realizing it, I was less likely to approach people I did not know or people wearing college sweatshirts. Since they would not stand an equal chance of being selected for the study, the selection process is not random. In addition, the method just described would not yield a representative sample of the school's population. Not everybody will walk past the library on Wednesday morning. People who do not will have no chance of being selected for the study and therefore are not part of the population. Random selection is best done using a computer, a table of random numbers, or that tried-and-true method of picking names out of a hat.

Even if I randomly select a sample of 100 people from the school's population of 1,000, clearly the sample will probably not perfectly reflect the composition of the school. For instance, if the school has exactly 500 males and 500 females in it, what are the chances that my random sample will have the same 1:1 ratio? Although we could compute those odds, that is not necessary. Clearly, the larger the sample, the more likely it is to represent the population. A sample of all 1,000 students guarantees that it is perfectly representative, and a sample of 1 person guarantees that it is far from representative. So why not use all 1,000 students? The downside of a large sample is time and money. Also, realizing that the populations psychologists study are often much larger than 1,000 people is important. Therefore, for research to use large, but not prohibitively large, samples is considered optimum. Statistics can be used to determine how large a sample should be in order to represent a population of any particular size. If asked on the Advanced Placement Examination to design your own research, you should specify the size of your sample and avoid using samples of extreme sizes.

One additional action can be taken to increase the likelihood that a sample will represent the larger population from which it was chosen. *Stratified sampling* is a process that allows a researcher to ensure that the sample represents the population on some criteria. For instance, if I thought that subjects of different racial groups might respond differently, I would want to make sure that I represented each race in my sample in the same proportion that it appears in the overall population. In other words, if 500 of the 1,000 students in a school are Caucasian, 300 are African American, and 200 are Latino, in a sample of 100 students I would want to have 50 Caucasians, 30 African Americans, and 20 Latinos. To that end, I could first divide the names of potential participants into each of the three racial groups, and then I could choose a random subsample of the desired size from each group.

Experimental Method

Experiments can be divided into laboratory experiments and field experiments. *Laboratory experiments* are conducted in a lab, a highly controlled environment, while *field experiments* are conducted out in the world. The extent to which laboratory experiments can be controlled is their main advantage. The advantage of field experiments is that they are more realistic.

Hint: Students often equate research with experiments. As described below, many different kinds of research can be conducted, but only experiments can identify cause and effect relationships.

Psychologists' preferred method of research is the *experiment* because only through a carefully controlled experiment can one show a causal relationship. An experiment allows the researcher to manipulate the independent variable and control for *confounding variables*. A confounding variable is any difference between the experimental and control conditions, except for the independent variable, that might affect the dependent variable. In order to show that the violent television programs cause the subjects' aggression, I need to rule out any other possible cause. An experiment can achieve this goal by randomly assigning subjects to conditions and by using various methods of control to eliminate confounding variables.

Assignment is the process by which subjects are put into a group, experimental or control. *Random assignment* means that each subject has an equal chance of being placed into any group. The benefit of random assignment is that it limits the effect of *subject-relevant confounding variables*. If subjects were given the opportunity to choose whether to be in the group watching the violent television or not, it is highly unlikely that the two groups would be comprised of similar people. Perhaps violent people prefer violent television and would therefore select the experimental group. Even if one were to assign people to groups based on a seemingly random criterion (when they arrived at the experiment or where they were sitting in the room), one might open the door to confounding variables. Using random assignment diminishes the chance that subjects in the two groups differ in any meaningful way, or, in other words, it *controls* for subject-relevant variables.

Hint: *Random assignment controls for subject-relevant confounding variables.*

Note that when we talk about differences between groups, we are referring to the group average. A single very aggressive subject will not throw off the results of the entire group. The idea behind random assignment is that, in general, the groups will be equivalent.

If one wanted to ensure that the experimental and control groups were equivalent on some criterion (for example, sex, IQ scores, age), one could use *group matching*. If one wanted to group match for sex, one would first divide the sample into males and females and then randomly assign half of each group to each condition. Group matching would not result in the same number of males and females within each group. Rather, half of the males and half of the females would be in each of the groups.

Situation-relevant confounding variables can also affect an experiment. For the subjects to be equivalent is not enough. The situations into which the different groups are put must also be equivalent except for the differences produced by the independent variable. If the experimental group watches violent television in a large lecture hall while the control group watches other programs in a small classroom, their situations are not equivalent. Therefore, any differences found between the groups may possibly be due not to the independent variable, as hypothesized, but rather to the confounding variables. Other situation-relevant variables include the time of day, the weather, and the presence of other people in the room. Making the environments into which the two groups are placed as similar as possible *controls* for situation-relevant confounding variables.

Hint: *Equivalent environments control for situation-relevant confounding variables.*

Experimenter bias is a special kind of situation-relevant confounding variable. Experimenter bias is the unconscious tendency for researchers to treat members of the experimental and control groups differently to increase the chance of confirming their hypothesis. Note that experimenter bias is not a conscious act. If researchers purposely distort their data, it is called fraud, not experimenter bias.

Experimenter bias can be eliminated by using a *double-blind procedure*. A double blind occurs when neither the subjects nor the researcher are able to affect the outcome of the research. A double blind can be accomplished in a number of ways. The most common way is for the researcher to have someone blind to the subjects' condition interact with the subjects. A single blind occurs when only the subjects do not know to which group they have been assigned; this strategy minimizes the effect of *demand characteristics* as well as certain kinds of *response* or *subject bias*. Demand characteristics are cues about the purpose of the study. Subjects use such cues to try to respond appropriately. Response or subject bias is the tendency for subjects to behave in certain ways (for example, circle the midpoint on a scale or pick the right-hand option more than the left-hand one). One kind of response bias, the tendency to try to give politically correct answers, is called *social desirability*.

Hint: Double blinds eliminate both experimenter and subject bias.

Experiments typically involve at least one *experimental group* and a *control group*. The experimental group is the one that gets the treatment operationalized in the independent variable. The control group gets none of the independent variable. It serves as a basis for comparison. Without a control group, knowing whether changes in the experimental group are due to the experimental treatment or simply to any treatment at all is impossible. In fact, merely selecting a group of people on whom to experiment has been determined to affect the performance of that group, regardless of what is done to those individuals. This finding is known as the *Hawthorne effect*.

Continuing along with the television example, the experimental group would be the participants who view violent television while the control group would view some other type of television, perhaps a comedy. If I were really designing an experiment, I would have to be much more specific in operationalizing my independent variable. For instance, the experimental group might be shown the film *Die Hard* while the control group viewed *When Harry Met Sally*. Many experiments involve much more complicated designs. In our example, additional groups would view other types of films or groups would view differing amounts of violent content.

One important method of control is known as the *placebo method*. Whenever subjects in the experimental group are supposed to ingest a drug, participants in the control group are given an inert but otherwise identical substance. This technique allows researchers to separate the physiological effects of the drug from the psychological effects of people thinking they took a drug (called the *placebo effect*).

Sometimes using subjects as their own control group is possible, a procedure known as *counterbalancing*. For instance, if I wanted to see how frustration affected performance on an IQ test, I could have my subjects engage in a task unlikely to cause frustration, test their IQ, and then give them a frustrating task and test their IQs again. However, this procedure creates the possibility of *order effects*. Subjects may do better on the second IQ test simply by virtue of having taken the first IQ test. This problem can be eliminated by using *counterbalancing*. I can counterbalance by having half the subjects do the frustrating task first and half the subjects do the not-frustrating task first and then switching.

Hint: Students sometimes believe that a control group is the only possible method of control. Remember that although it is an extremely important and obviously named type of control, using control groups is but one of many such methods.

Correlational Method

A correlation expresses a relationship between two variables without ascribing cause. Correlations can be either positive or negative. A positive correlation between two things means that the presence of one thing predicts the presence of the other. A negative correlation means that the presence of one thing predicts the absence of the other. Correlations may be either strong or weak. The strength of a correlation is expressed by a number between −1 and +1 where −1 is a perfect, negative correlation and +1 is a perfect, positive correlation. Correlations of −1 and +1 are equally strong. The number 0 denotes the weakest possible correlation—no correlation—which means that knowing something about one variable tells you nothing about the other. See the statistics section for more information about correlations.

Hint: Correlation does not imply causation.

Sometimes psychologists elect not to use the experimental method. Sometimes testing a hypothesis with an experiment is impossible. Suppose, for example, I want to test the hypothesis that boys are more likely to call out in class than girls. Clearly, I cannot randomly assign subjects to conditions. Boys are boys, and girls are girls. The assignment of the independent variable, in this case, has been predetermined. As a result, I will never be able to isolate the cause of the calling out behavior. It could be a biological difference or one of many social influences that act differently upon the sexes from birth onward. If I seek to control all other aspects of the research process, as I would in an experiment, I will have conducted an *ex post facto study*.

An even more popular research design is the *survey method*. The survey method, as common sense suggests, involves asking people to fill out surveys. To contrast the survey method with the experimental method, return to the question about whether there is a relationship between watching violence on television and aggressive behavior. The original hypothesis, that *"watching violent television programs makes people more aggressive,"* cannot be tested using the survey method, because only an experiment can reveal a cause-effect relationship. However, one could use the survey method to investigate whether there is a relationship between the two variables, watching violence on television and aggressive behavior. In the survey method, neither of the variables can be manipulated. Therefore, while there are two variables, there is no independent or dependent variable.

Using the survey method means that one can no longer control for subject-relevant confounding variables. Some people watch a lot of violent television, and others do not. In all likelihood, these two groups of people would differ in a number of other ways as well. The survey method does not enable the researcher to determine which of these differences cause a difference in violent behavior.

Although controlling for situation-relevant confounding variables using the survey method is possible (by bringing all the subjects to one place at one time to fill out the survey), it is rarely done. One of the advantages of the survey method is that conducting research by mailing surveys for people to fill out at their convenience is easy. However, if people fill out the surveys in different places, at different times of day, by taking different amounts of time, and so on, the research will be plagued by confounding variables. Thus, again, determining what causes a difference in violent behavior becomes impossible. In addition, obtaining a random sample when one sends out a survey is difficult because relatively few people will actually send it back (low *response rate*), and these people are unlikely to make up a representative sample.

Hint: Students often confuse the use of surveys to measure the dependent variable in an experiment with the survey method. While surveys can be used as part of the experimental method, the survey method, as described above, is a kind of correlational research in which the researcher does not manipulate the independent variable.

Naturalistic Observation

Sometimes researchers opt to observe their subjects in their natural habitats without interacting with them at all. Such unobtrusive observation is called *naturalistic observation*. The goal of naturalistic observation is to get a realistic and rich picture of the subjects' behavior. To that end, control is sacrificed.

Hint: Students often confuse naturalistic observation with field experiments. Both involve doing research out in the world. However, in naturalistic observation, the researchers do not impact on the behavior of the participants at all. In contrast, in field experiments, as in all experiments, the researcher has manipulated the independent variable and attempted to eliminate as many confounding variables as possible.

Case Studies

One final research method we will mention is the case study method. The case study method is used to get a full, detailed picture of one subject or a small group of subjects. For instance, clinical psychologists often use case studies to present information about a person suffering from a particular disorder. While case studies allow researchers to get the richest possible picture of what they are studying, the focus on a single individual or small group means that the findings cannot be generalized to a larger population.

Statistics

Descriptive Statistics

Descriptive statistics, as the name suggests, simply describe a set of data. For instance, if you were interested¯in researching what kinds of pets your schoolmates have, you might summarize that data by creating a *frequency distribution* that would tell you how many students had dogs, cats, zebras, and so on. Graphing your findings is often helpful. Frequency distributions can be easily turned into line graphs called *frequency polygons* or bar graphs known as *histograms.* The y-axis (vertical) always represents frequency, while whatever you are graphing, in this case, pets, is graphed along the x-axis (horizontal).

You are probably already familiar with at least one group of statistical measures called measures of *central tendency.* Measures of central tendency attempt to mark the center of a distribution. Three common measures of central tendency are the *mean, median,* and *mode.* The mean is what we usually refer to as the average of all the scores in a distribution. To compute the mean, you simply add up all the scores in the distribution and divide by the number of scores. The median is the central score in the distribution. To find the median of a distribution, simply write the scores down in ascending (or descending) order and then, if there are an odd number of scores, find the middle one. If the distribution contains an even number of scores, the median is the average of the middle two scores. The mode is the score that appears most frequently. A distribution may, however, have more than one mode. A distribution is bimodal, for instance, if two scores appear equally frequently and more frequently than any other score.

The mean is the most commonly used measure of central tendency, but its accuracy can be distorted by *extreme scores* or *outliers.* Imagine that 19 of your 20 friends drive cars valued at $12,000 but your other friend has an Acura NSX valued at $100,000. The mean value of your cars is $16,400. However, since that value is in excess of everyone's car except one person's, you would probably agree that it is not the best measure of central tendency in this case. When a distribution includes outliers, the median is often used as a better measure of central tendency.

Unless a distribution is symmetrical, it is skewed. Outliers skew distributions. When a distribution includes an extreme score (or group of scores) that is very high, as in the car example above, the distribution is said to be *positively skewed.* When the skew is caused by a particularly low score (or group of scores), the distribution is *negatively skewed.* A positively skewed distribution contains more low scores than high scores; the skew is produced by some aberrantly high score(s). Conversely, a negatively skewed distribution contains more high scores than low scores. In a positively skewed distribution, the mean is higher than the median because the outlier(s) have a much more dramatic effect on the mean than on the median. Of course, the opposite is true in a negatively skewed distribution (see Fig. 2.1).

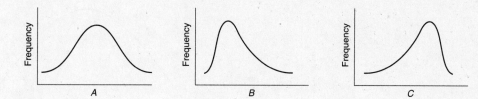

Figure 2.1. *A,* symmetrical distribution; *B,* positively skewed distribution; *C,* negatively skewed distribution.

Another type of descriptive statistical measures is known as measures of variability. Again, you may be familiar with some of these measures, such as the *range, variance,* and *standard deviation.* Measures of variability attempt to depict the diversity of the distribution. The range is the distance between the highest and lowest score in a distribution. The variance and standard deviation are closely related; standard deviation is simply the square root of the variance. Both measures essentially relate the average distance of any score in the distribution from the mean. The higher the variance and standard deviation, the more spread out the distribution.

Sometimes, being able to compare scores from different distributions is important. In order to do so, you can convert scores from the different distributions into measures called *z scores.* Z scores measure the distance of a score from the mean in units of standard deviation. Scores below the mean have negative *z* scores, while scores above the mean have positive *z* scores. For instance, if Clarence scored a 72 on a test with a mean of 80 and a standard deviation of 8, Clarence's *z* score would be –1. If Maria scored an 84 on that same test, her *z* score would be +0.5.

Often in psychology you will see reference to the *normal curve.* The normal curve is a theoretical bell-shaped curve for which the area under the curve lying between any two *z* scores has been predetermined. Approximately 68 percent of scores in a normal distribution fall within one standard deviation of the mean, approximately 95 percent of scores fall within two standard deviations of the mean, and almost 99 percent of scores fall within three standard deviations of the mean. Knowing that the normal curve is symmetrical, and knowing the three numbers given above will allow you to calculate the approximate percentage of scores falling between any given *z* scores. For instance, approximately 47.5 percent (95/2) of scores fall between the *z* scores of 0 and +2 (see Fig. 2.2).

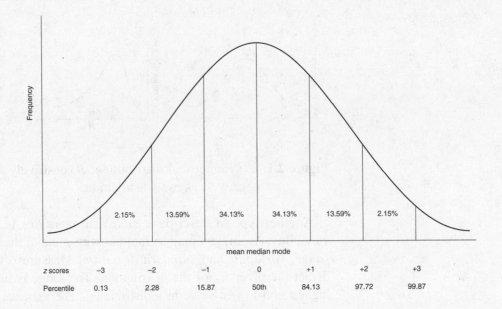

Figure 2.2. The normal distribution.

While *z* scores measure the distance of a score away from the mean, *percentiles* indicate the distance of a score from 0. Someone who scores in the 90th percentile on a test has scored better than 90 percent of the people who took the test. Similarly, someone who scores at the 38th percentile scored better than only 38 percent of the people who took the test. A clear relationship exists between percentiles and *z* scores when dealing with the normal curve. Someone who scores at the 50th percentile has a *z* score of 0, and someone who scores at the 98th percentile has an approximate *z* score of +2.

Correlations

A *correlation* measures the relationship between two variables. Correlations can be either positive or negative. If two things are positively correlated, the presence of one thing predicts the presence of the other. In contrast, a negative correlation means that the presence of one thing predicts the absence of the other. When no relationship exists between two things, no correlation exists. As an example, one would suspect that a positive correlation exists between studying and earning good grades. Conversely, one would suspect that a negative correlation might occur between cutting classes and earning good grades. Finally, it is likely that there is no correlation between the number of stuffed animals one owns and earning good grades.

Correlations may be either strong or weak. The strength of a correlation is expressed by a number called a *correlation coefficient*. Correlation coefficients range from –1 and +1 where –1 is a perfect, negative correlation and +1 is a perfect, positive correlation. Both –1 and +1 denote equally strong correlations. The number 0 denotes the weakest possible correlation—no correlation—which means that knowing something about one variable tells you nothing about the other.

Correlations may be graphed using a *scatter plot*. A scatter plot graphs pairs of values, one on the y-axis and one on the x-axis. For instance, the number of hours a group of people study per week could be plotted on the x-axis while their GPAs could be plotted on the y-axis. The result would be a series of points called a scatter plot. The closer the points come to falling on a straight line, the stronger the correlation. The *line of best fit* is the line drawn through the scatter plot that minimizes the distance of all the points from the line. When the line slopes upward, from left to right, it indicates a positive correlation. A downward slope evidences a negative correlation. The scatter plot depicting the data set given in Table 2.1 below is graphed in Fig. 2.3.

Table 2.1. The Relationship Between Hours Studied and GPA.

Name	Hours Studied	GPA
Teresa	15	3.8
Raoul	17	3.8
Todd	4	1.3
Lucy	11	3.1
Aaron	8	2.4
Pam	12	3.3
Laticia	14	3.9
Greg	9	2.5
Megan	5	0.6

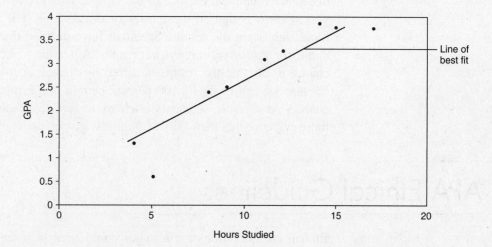

Figure 2.3. Scatter plot showing the correlation between hours studied and GPA.

Inferential Statistics

Whereas descriptive statistics provide a way to summarize information about the sample studied, the purpose of *inferential statistics* is to determine whether or not findings can be applied to the larger population from which the sample was selected. Remember that one of the primary goals in selecting a sample is that the sample represent the population from which it was picked. If a sample does not represent the larger population, one cannot infer anything about the larger population from the sample. Guaranteeing that a sample is representative of a population is impossible. The extent to which the sample differs from the population is known as *sampling error*.

Say that you ran an experiment testing the effects of sugar consumption on short-term memory. You randomly assigned your 20 subjects to either a control group that was given a sugarfree lollipop or to the experimental group that was given a seemingly identical lollipop that contained sugar. You then tested the subjects' ability to recall 15 one-syllable nouns. If the experimental group remembered an average of 7 words and the control group remembered an average of 6.9 words, would you be comfortable concluding that sugar does, in fact, enhance short-term memory? Your gut reaction is probably to say that the 0.1 difference in the example is too small to allow us to draw such a conclusion. What if the experimental group consisted of just one person who recalled all 15 words while the control group contained one person who remembered only 5 words? You would probably be similarly reluctant to draw any conclusions even given this enormous difference in the number of words recalled due to the tiny sample size.

In both cases, you would be correct to be skeptical. The differences between the groups are likely due to sampling error and chance. The purpose of inferential statistics is to help psychologists decide when their findings can be applied to the larger population. Many different inferential statistical tests exist such as t-tests, ANOVAs, and MANOVAs. They all take into account both the magnitude of the difference found and the size of the sample. However, what is most important for you to know is that all these tests yield a *p value*. The smaller the *p* value, the more significant the results. Scientists have decided that a *p* value of .05 is the cutoff for *statistically significant* results. A *p* value of .05 means that a 5 percent chance exists that the results occurred by chance. A *p* value can never equal 0 because we can never be 100 percent certain that results did not happen due to chance. As a result, scientists often try to replicate their results, thus gathering more evidence that their initial findings were not due to chance.

APA Ethical Guidelines

Ethical considerations are a major component in research design. You should know and understand the ethical guidelines established by the APA (American Psychological Association) for human and animal research and be prepared to apply the concepts to specific research designs. Any type of academic research must first propose the study to the ethics board or *institutional review board (IRB)* at the institution. The IRB reviews research proposals for ethical violations and/or procedural errors. This board ultimately gives researchers permission to go ahead with the research or requires them to revise their procedures.

Animal Research

Groups advocating the ethical treatment of animals are focusing more and more attention on how animals are treated in laboratory experiments. The APA developed strict guidelines about what animals and how animals can be used in psychological research. Ethical psychological studies using animals must meet the following requirements.

1. They must have a clear scientific purpose.
   The research must answer a specific, important scientific question.
   Animals are chosen because they are best-suited to answer the question at hand.

2. They must care for and house animals in a humane way.

3. They must acquire animal subjects legally. Animals must be purchased from accredited companies. If wild animals must be used, they need to be trapped in a humane manner.

4. They must design experimental procedures that employ the least amount of suffering feasible.

Human Research

Research involving human subjects must meet the following standards:

1. *Informed consent*—Participants must know that they are involved in research and give their consent. If the participants are deceived in any way about the nature of the study, the deception must not be so extreme as to invalidate the *informed consent*. The research the participants thought they were consenting to must be similar enough to the actual study to give the informed consent meaning. Also, researchers must be very careful about the trauma deception may cause (see *Risk,* below).

2. *Coercion*—Participation must be voluntary.

3. *Anonymity/Confidentiality*—Participants' privacy must be protected. Their identities and actions must not be revealed by the researcher. Participants have *anonymity* when the researchers do not collect any data that enables them to match a person's responses with his or her name. In some cases, such as interview studies, a researcher cannot promise *anonymity* but instead guarantees *confidentiality*, that the researcher will not identify the source of any of the data.

4. *Risk*—Participants cannot be placed at significant mental or physical risk. This clause requires interpretation by the review board. Some institutions might allow a level of risk other boards might not allow. This consideration was highlighted by Stanley Milgram's obedience studies in the 1970s in

which participants thought they were causing significant harm or death to other participants (see the "Social Psychology" chapter).

5. *Debriefing procedures*—Participants must be told the purpose of the study and provided with ways to contact the researchers about study results.

Practice Questions

> *Directions:* Each of the questions or incomplete statements below is followed by five suggested answers or completions. Select the one that is best in each case.

1. Psychologists generally prefer the experimental method to other research methods because
   (A) experiments are more likely to support psychologists' hypotheses.
   (B) experiments can show cause-effect relationships.
   (C) it is easier to obtain a random sample for an experiment.
   (D) double blind designs are unnecessary in an experiment.
   (E) experiments are more likely to result in statistically significant findings.

2. Theoretically, random assignment should eliminate
   (A) sampling error.
   (B) the need to use statistics.
   (C) concerns over validity.
   (D) many confounding variables.
   (E) the need for a representative sample.

3. Karthik and Sue are lab partners assigned to research who is friendlier, girls or boys. After conversing with their first 10 participants, they find that their friendliness ratings often differ. With which of the following should they be most concerned?
   (A) reliability   (C) ethics   (E) assignment
   (B) confounding variables (D) validity

4. Which of the following hypotheses would be most difficult to test experimentally?
   (A) People exposed to the color red will be more aggressive than those exposed to the color blue.
   (B) Exercise improves mood.
   (C) Living with cats makes people more intelligent.
   (D) Studying leads to better grades.
   (E) Divorce makes children more independent.

5. Professor Ma wants to design a project studying emotional response to date rape. He advertises for participants in the school newspaper, informs them about the nature of the study, gets their consent, conducts an interview, and debriefs them about the results when the experiment is over. If you were on the IRB, which ethical consideration would you most likely have the most concern about in Professor Ma's study?
   (A) coercion   (D) anonymity
   (B) deception   (E) clear scientific purpose
   (C) confounding variables

6. Some psychologists consider Stanley Milgram's obedience studies to be unethical because of which ethical consideration?
   (A) improper sampling procedure
   (B) risk of long-term harm
   (C) clear scientific purpose
   (D) debriefing
   (E) anonymity

7. One of the principal differences between the ethical guidelines for human and animal research is:
   (A) Human subjects can be deceived for experimental purposes and animals cannot.
   (B) Animal subjects can be placed at much greater physical risk than human subjects can.
   (C) Human subjects must be chosen much more carefully than animal subjects.
   (D) If humans might physically suffer because of the study, the suffering must be minimal, in contrast to animal studies where any amount of suffering is ethical if it helps to further a clear scientific purpose.
   (E) Environmental conditions for human studies must be monitored much more closely than they are in an animal study.

8. Tamar scored 145 on an IQ test with a mean of 100 and a standard deviation of 15. What is her *z* score?
   (A) −3
   (B) −1.5
   (C) +0.67
   (D) 1.5
   (E) 3

9. What is the median of the following distribution: 6, 2, 9, 4, 7, 3?
   (A) 4
   (B) 5
   (C) 5.5
   (D) 6
   (E) 6.5

10. Sandy scores a perfect 100 on a test that everyone else fails. If we were to graph this distribution, it would be
    (A) symmetrical.
    (B) normal.
    (C) positively skewed.
    (D) negatively skewed.
    (E) a straight line.

11. Jose hypothesizes that a new drug he has just invented will enhance mice's memories. He feeds the drug to the experimental group and gives the control group a placebo. He then times the mice as they learn to run through a maze. In order to know whether his hypothesis has been supported, Jose would need to use
    (A) scatter plots.
    (B) descriptive statistics.
    (C) histograms.
    (D) inferential statistics.
    (E) means-end analysis.

12. Which of the following is an example of random sampling?

    I. Picking out of a hat to assign each of three classes to an experimental condition.
    II. Having a computer generate a random list of 100 high school students.
    III. Approaching any 50 students during sixth-period lunch.

    (A) I only
    (B) II only
    (C) III only
    (D) I and II
    (E) I, II, and III

13. Vincenzo conducts an experiment to see whether fear makes mice run through mazes faster. He assigned his sample of 60 mice to a control group or experimental group. Which cannot be a confounding variable?
    (A) How fast the mice are at the start.
    (B) When the mice run the maze.
    (C) The population from which he selected his subjects.
    (D) How frightened the mice are before the experiment.
    (E) Where the mice run the maze.

14. Charlotte, a nursery school student, hypothesizes that boys have fights with the finger paints more than girls do. She tests her hypothesis by casually watching the finger-painting table for three days of nursery school. What method is she using?
    (A) field experiment
    (B) informal survey
    (C) case study
    (D) naturalistic observation
    (E) ethnography

15. Jen collects survey data that indicates that students who spend more time preparing for the AP test tend to do better than other students. Jen can now conclude that
    (A) studying improves exam grades.
    (B) a relationship exists between studying and exam grades.
    (C) a significant correlation exists between studying and exam grades.
    (D) anyone who does not study will do poorly on the exam.
    (E) better students tend to study more.

Answers to Practice Questions

1. **(B)** Psychologists generally prefer the experimental method to other research methods because experiments can show cause-effect relationships. The hallmarks of an experiment are the ability to manipulate the independent variable, randomly assign subjects to conditions, and eliminate (control for) differences between the conditions. When these steps are taken, disparities between the experimental and control groups can be attributed to the independent variable, the only thing that differed between the groups. No other research method allows for the control necessary to make such an attribution. None of the other statements are true.

2. **(D)** Random assignment should eliminate subject-relevant confounding variables (e.g., conscientiousness, IQ, hair color). Since it would be impossible to match participants on every possible dimension, many psychologists use random assignment. By taking advantage of the laws of probability, random assignment makes it likely that participants in the different conditions of an experiment will be equivalent. Random assignment does not relate to sampling or validity and has no impact on the need for statistics.

3. **(A)** Karthik and Sue's way of measuring friendliness is not reliable. Reliability refers to the consistency of a measure. Since they disagree so often, their measure is not consistent. In all likelihood, they need to operationalize their dependent variable more clearly. Reliability is sometimes confused with validity. Validity refers to the accuracy of a measure, which in this case is whether they are actually measuring friendliness.

4. **(E)** It would be extremely difficult to test whether parental divorce causes children to become more independent because it is essentially impossible to manipulate the independent variable, divorce. If we tried to recruit parents to be in our experiment and told them that half would be assigned to divorce and the other half to stay married, it is unlikely that any would consent to participate. It also might be a little difficult to find people willing to be in an experiment about whether living with cats makes people more intelligent; such people would have to be willing to accept or give up a pet. Nonetheless, there are surely more people who would consent to participate in this study than the one about divorce. The other three examples are relatively easy to study experimentally as the independent variables (color, exercise, and studying) are not difficult to manipulate.

5. **(D)** Professor Ma would need to be particularly careful to ensure the participants' anonymity in this study since it deals with a controversial and possibly embarrassing subject. There is no indication that Professor Ma coerced the participants or deceived them in any way. Confounding variables are a concern for the validity of the study but not an ethical consideration. The study does have a clear scientific purpose.

6. **(B)** Milgram's experiments involved considerable risk of long-lasting stress and anxiety for his subjects. The scientific purpose of Milgram's study is not disputed, and he obtained informed consents, debriefed participants, and provided for anonymity of individual results.

7. **(B)** Within the limits imposed by the guidelines, researchers can physically harm animals if the harm is justified by the nature of the experiments.

Deception is obviously not an issue applicable to animal research. Researchers must keep suffering to a minimum, so "any amount" is not an appropriate response (choice D). Animal subjects must be chosen carefully (from accredited commercial sources) and their environment must follow strict guidelines, so choices C and E are also incorrect.

8. **(E)** Tamar's *z* score is +3. *z* scores measure the distance of a score from the mean in units of standard deviation. Since the mean is 100 and the standard deviation is 15, Tamar's score is 3 standard deviations above the mean.

9. **(B)** The median of the distribution is 5. The problem is easier if you put the scores in order: 2, 3, 4, 6, 7, 9. Since the distribution has an even number of scores, there is no middle score and you must average the two middle scores, 4 and 6.

10. **(C)** Sandy's perfect score is an outlier and will therefore skew the distribution. Since it is a high score in a distribution of low scores, the distribution will be positively skewed.

11. **(D)** Jose needs to compare the performances of the two groups using inferential statistics to determine whether or not the experimental group's performance was significantly better. Scatter plots are used to graph correlations. Jose would certainly be interested in descriptive statistics as well, but he would not know whether or not his hypothesis had been supported until he used inferential statistics. Histograms are bar graphs, and means-end analysis is a problem-solving technique.

12. **(B)** Of the three methods presented, only having a computer generate a random list of names is an example of random sampling. The first example illustrates random assignment and not random sampling. Sampling is the process of choosing a group of participants from a population. Once sampling has been completed, one might assign the participants to conditions as described in I. Finally, approaching 50 students during a lunch period does not constitute random sampling even if the person who picks the people tries to do so randomly. Remember that the word *random* has a very specific meaning in the context of research. Random sampling means that all members of the population had an equal chance of being selected, and people are unable to be so scrupulously unbiased.

13. **(C)** A confounding variable is anything that differs between the control and experimental group besides the independent variable. How fast and frightened the mice are at the onset of the experiment are potential subject-confounding variables. When and where the experiment takes place are possible situation-relevant confounding variables. However, the population from which Vincenzo selected his mice cannot be a confounding variable, because it cannot differ for the two groups of mice; they all came from the same population. True, the population can be flawed. For instance, it can be very homogeneous and thus fail to reflect how other mice would perform under similar conditions. However, such a flaw is not a confounding variable.

14. **(D)** Charlotte is using naturalistic observation. As a student herself, she can observe the finger-painting table unobtrusively. She does not interact with the finger painters; she merely observes. Since Charlotte does not manipulate an independent variable nor attempt to control any aspect of her study, she is not using any kind of experiment. She did not ask the

participants questions as she would have if she were conducting a survey. She did not focus on a single participant or a small group of participants as she would have if she had been interested in putting together a case study. Finally, Charlotte has not conducted ethnographic research. Ethnography is a type of research in which the researcher immerses himself or herself in another culture and then describes it. Ethnography is a method most commonly employed by anthropologists.

15. **(B)** Jen has established a relationship, or correlation, between the two variables she is studying. However, since she has not conducted an experiment, Jen does not know whether a cause and effect relationship occurs between studying and earning high grades on the exam. Therefore, Jen does not know if studying improves exam grades. Although Jen has found a correlation between studying and exam grades, whether or not that correlation is significant can be determined only through the use of inferential statistics. Even if the correlation were significant, it would not guarantee that if someone did not study, he or she would do poorly on the test. Finally, Jen's correlation does not tell us that better students study more. In fact, it tells us nothing about better students, not even what is meant by that term.

CHAPTER 3
Biological Bases of Behavior

Overview

The influence of biology (sometimes called the *neuroscience or biopsychological* perspective) is growing. Some researchers predict that someday psychology will be a specialty within the field of biology. An understanding of the biological principles relevant to psychology is not needed only for the AP exam but for any understanding of current psychological thinking.

Neuroanatomy

Neuroanatomy refers to the study of the parts and function of neurons. *Neurons* are individual nerve cells. These cells make up our entire nervous system, from the brain to the neurons that fire when you stub your toe. Every neuron is made up of discrete parts (see Fig. 3.1).

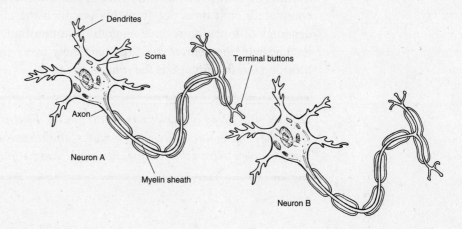

Figure 3.1. A neuron.

Dendrites—rootlike parts of the cell that stretch out from the cell body. Dendrites grow to make synaptic connections with other neurons (see *Synapse,* below).

Cell body (also called the soma)—contains the nucleus and other parts of the cell needed to sustain its life.

Axon—wirelike structure ending in the terminal buttons that extends from the cell body.

Myelin sheath—a fatty covering around the axon that speeds neural impulses.

Terminal buttons (also called end buttons, terminal branches of axon, and synaptic knobs)—the branched end of the axon that contains neurotransmitters.

Neurotransmitters—chemicals contained in terminal buttons that enable neurons to communicate. Neurotransmitters fit into receptor sites on the dendrites of neurons like a key fits into a lock.

Synapse—the space between the terminal buttons of one neuron and the dendrites of the next neuron.

How a Neuron "Fires"

All of the different parts of the neuron work in sequence when a neuron transmits a message. In its resting state, a neuron has an overall slightly negative charge because mostly negative ions are within the cell and mostly positive ions are surrounding it. The cell membrane of the neuron is selectively permeable and prevents these ions from mixing. Visualize a two-neuron chain (see Fig. 3.1). The reaction begins when the terminal buttons of neuron A are stimulated and release neurotransmitters into the synapse. These neurotransmitters fit into receptor sites on the dendrites of neuron B. If enough neurotransmitters are received (this level is called the threshold), the cell membrane of neuron B becomes permeable and positive ions rush into the cell. The change in charge spreads down the length of neuron B like a bullet from a gun. This electric message firing is called an *action potential*. It travels quickly: 120 meters per second. When the charge reaches the terminal buttons of neuron B, the buttons release their neurotransmitters into the synapse. The process may begin again if enough neurotransmitters are received by that next cell to pass the threshold. Notice that a neuron either fires completely or it does not fire; this is called the all-or-none principle. If the dendrites of a neuron receive enough neurotransmitters to push the neuron past its threshold, the neuron will fire completely every time. A neuron cannot fire a little or a lot; the impulse is the same every time.

Hint: Neural firing is an electrochemical process. Electricity travels within the cell (from the dendrites to the terminal buttons), and chemicals (neurotransmitters) travel between cells in the synapse. Electricity does not jump between the neurons.

Neurotransmitters

You already know that neurotransmitters are chemicals held in the terminal buttons that travel in the synaptic gap between neurons. It is important to understand that different types of neurotransmitters exist. Some neurotransmitters are excitatory, meaning that they excite the next cell into firing. Other neurotransmitters are inhibitory, meaning that they inhibit the next cell from firing. Each synaptic gap at any time may contain many different kinds of inhibitory and excitatory neurotransmitters. The amount and type of neurotransmitters received on the receptor sites of the neuron determine whether it will pass the threshold and fire. Researchers are identifying different types and functions of neurotransmitters every year. This ongoing research makes generalizing about what each neurotransmitter does difficult. However, Table 3.1 indicates some of the more important types and functions of neurotransmitters to psychologists.

Table 3.1. Neurotransmitters Important to Psychologists.

Neurotransmitter	Function	Problems Associated with an Excess or Deficit
Acetylcholine	Motor movement	Lack of acetylcholine is associated with Alzheimer's disease
Dopamine	Motor movement and alertness	Lack of dopamine is associated with Parkinson's disease, an overabundance is associated with schizophrenia
Endorphins	Pain control	Involved in addictions
Serotonin	Mood control	Lack of serotonin is associated with clinical depression

Nervous System

We can sense the world because our nervous system brings information from our senses to our brain. Since a neuron fires in only one direction (from dendrite to terminal buttons), our body needs two sets of wires: one to take information to the brain and one to take instructions back from the brain to the muscles.

Afferent Neurons (or Sensory Neurons)

Afferent neurons take information from the senses to the brain. (You can think of *a*fferent nerves as taking information in *a*t the brain.)

Interneurons

Once information reaches the brain or spinal cord, interneurons take the messages and send them elsewhere in the brain or on to efferent neurons.

Efferent Neurons (or Motor Neurons)

Efferent neurons take information from the brain to the rest of the body. (You can think of *e*fferent nerves as carrying information that *e*xits the brain.)

Organization of the Nervous System

Our nervous system is divided into different categories based on function. The two main divisions are the central nervous system and the peripheral nervous system. These are then subdivided further (see Fig. 3.2).

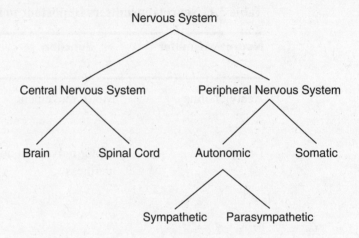

Figure 3.2. The nervous system.

The Central Nervous System

The central nervous system (CNS) consists of our brain and spinal cord—all the nerves housed within bone (the skull and vertebrae). Information about the structure and function of different parts of the brain is available in a later section. The spinal cord is a bundle of nerves that run through the center of the spine. It transmits information from the rest of the body to the brain.

The Peripheral Nervous System

The peripheral nervous system (PNS) consists of all the other nerves in your body—all the nerves not encased in bone. The peripheral nervous system is divided into two categories: the somatic and the automatic nervous systems.

Somatic Nervous System

The somatic nervous system controls our voluntary muscle movements. The motor cortex of the brain sends impulses to the somatic nervous system, which controls the muscles that allow us to move.

Autonomic Nervous System

The autonomic nervous system controls the automatic functions of our body—our heart, lungs, internal organs, glands, and so on. These nerves control our responses to stress—the fight or flight response that prepares our body to respond to a perceived threat. The autonomic nervous system is divided into two categories: the sympathetic and parasympathetic nervous systems.

Sympathetic Nervous System

The sympathetic nervous system mobilizes our body to respond to stress. This part of our nervous systems carries messages to the control systems of the organs, glands, and muscles that direct our body's response to stress. This is the alert system of our body. It accelerates some functions (such as heart rate, blood pressure, and respiration) but conserves resources needed for a quick response by slowing down other functions (such as digestion).

Parasympathetic Nervous System

The parasympathetic nervous system is responsible for slowing down our body after a stress response. It carries messages to the stress response system that causes our body to slow down. Think of the parasympathetic nervous system as the brake pedal that slows down the body's autonomic nervous system.

Normal Peripheral Nervous System Transmission

Let us use an example to demonstrate how sensory information gets to our brain. While on a late-night quest for a snack, you stub your toe on a cast-iron coffee table. Sensory neurons in your toe are activated, and this message is transmitted up a neuron that runs from your toe to the base of your spine (afferent nerves). The message continues up your spinal cord on more afferent nerves until it enters your brain through the brain stem and is transmitted to the brain's sensory cortex (see the next section, "Brain") and you know you have stubbed your poor little toe. Your motor cortex now sends impulses down the spinal cord to the muscles controlling your leg and foot (efferent nerves), causing you to hop up and down holding your damaged limb, muttering under your breath.

Reflexes: An Important Exception

Most sensory information and muscle movements are controlled by the process described above. However, humans have a few reflexes that work differently. Certain reactions occur the moment sensory impulses reach the spinal cord. If you stimulate the correct area just below your kneecap, your leg will jerk without your conscious control. This sensory information is processed by the spine, and the spine tells your leg to move. The information reaches your brain and you realize your knee has been stimulated but only after this reflex has occurred. Another important reflex occurs in response to intense heat or cold. If we touch an object that is very hot or cold, our spine will send back a message jerking us away from that object. This might help keep us from harming ourselves, so it has adaptive value (it might help us survive, and therefore this trait is passed on to our children).

Brain

Possibly the most relevant part of biology to psychologists is the brain. As far as we can tell, the brain controls most of human thought and behavior. Researchers know quite a bit about brain anatomy and function, but many mysteries still remain about how the brain functions. Studying how the brain works is challenging because we cannot simply observe brain function the way we might observe a heart beating. To our eyes, a brain thinking looks exactly like a brain not thinking. Researchers are discovering many new details about how the brain works through experimentation and the use of technology. However, we still have a long way to go before we really understand how the brain controls our thoughts and behavior.

Ways of Studying the Brain

As mentioned previously, the first challenge of brain research is creating a way of detecting brain function. The following describes some of the methods researchers use.

Accidents

In 1848, a railroad worker named Phineas Gage was involved in an accident that damaged the front part of his brain. Gage's doctor took notes documenting the brain damage and how Gage's behavior and personality changed after the accident. Accidents like this give researchers clues about brain function. Gage became highly emotional and impulsive after the accident. Researchers concluded that the parts of the brain damaged in the accident are somehow involved in emotional control.

Lesions

Lesioning is the removal or destruction of part of the brain. This is, of course, never done purely for experimental purposes. Sometimes doctors decide that the best treatment for a certain condition involves surgery that will destroy or incapacitate part of the brain. For example, a person may develop a brain tumor that cannot be removed without removing part of the surrounding brain. When these types of surgeries are performed, doctors closely monitor the patient's subsequent behavior for changes. Any time brain tissue is removed (lesioning), researchers can examine behavior changes and try to infer the function of that part of the brain.

A famous historical example of lesioning is the frontal lobotomy. In the past, this surgery was used (many historians say overused) to control mentally ill patients with no other treatment options. Researchers knew that lesioning part of the frontal lobe would make the patients calm and relieve some serious symptoms. Drug treatments have now replaced frontal lobotomies.

Electroencephalogram

An electroencephalogram (EEG) detects brain waves. Researchers can examine what type of waves the brain produces during different stages of consciousness and use this information to generalize about brain function. The EEG is widely used in sleep research to identify the different stages of sleep and dreaming.

Computerized Axial Tomography

A computerized axial tomography (CAT) scan is a sophisticated X ray. The CAT scan uses several X-ray cameras that rotate around the brain and combine all the pictures into a detailed three-dimensional picture of the brain's structure. Note that the CAT scan can show only the structure of the brain, not the functions or the activity of different brain structures. A doctor could use a CAT scan to look for a tumor in the brain but would not get any information about how active different parts of the brain are.

Magnetic Resonance Imaging

The magnetic resonance imaging (MRI) is similar to a CAT scan in a way: both scans give you detailed pictures of the brain. The MRI, however, uses different technology to create those pictures. An MRI uses magnetic fields to measure the density and location of brain material. Since the MRI does not use X rays like the CAT scan does, the patient is not exposed to carcinogenic radiation. Like the CAT scan, the MRI gives doctors information about only the structure of the brain, not the function.

Positron Emission Tomography

The positron emission tomography (PET) scan lets researchers see what areas of the brain are most active during certain tasks. A PET scan measures how much of a certain chemical (glucose, for example) parts of the brain are using. The more used, the higher the activity. Different types of scans are used for different chemicals such as neurotransmitters, drugs, and oxygen flow.

Functional MRI

Functional MRI (fMRI) is a new technology that combines elements of the MRI and PET scans. An fMRI scan can show details of brain structure with information about blood flow in the brain, tying brain structure to brain activity during cognitive tasks.

Brain Structure and Function

All the different methods of studying the brain give researchers different types of information about brain structure and function. The brain is the most complicated organ in the body (in some ways, it is the most complex object we know of). Researchers categorize hundreds of different parts and functions of different parts of the brain. Because of this complexity, we need to divide the brain into separate categories in order to keep track of the information. When you study and think about the brain, think about three separate major categories or sections: the hindbrain, midbrain, and forebrain.

Hint: Some of the descriptions of brain function may seem vague or redundant when you read about the functions of other structures. Remember that some of the ways in which the brain works are still being investigated and the functions are just summarized here for our purposes. Keep the areas and general functions in mind instead of spending your time trying to figure out exact specific functions and locations.

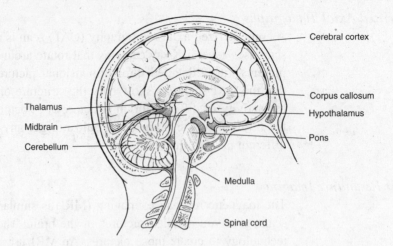

Figure 3.3. The brain.

Hindbrain

The hindbrain consists of structures in the top part of the spinal cord. The hindbrain is our life support system; it controls the basic biological functions that keep us alive. Some of the important specific structures within the hindbrain are the medulla, pons, and cerebellum (refer to Fig. 3.3 for locations of these structures).

Medulla

The medulla is involved in the control of our blood pressure, heart rate, and breathing. It is also known as the medulla oblongata and is located above the spinal cord.

Pons

The pons (located just above the medulla and toward the front) connects the hindbrain with the midbrain and forebrain. It is also involved in the control of facial expressions.

Cerebellum

The cerebellum (located on the bottom rear of the brain) looks like a smaller version of our brain stuck onto the underside of our brain. *Cerebellum* means little brain. The cerebellum coordinates fine muscle movements, such as tracking a target with our eyes or playing the saxophone.

Midbrain

The midbrain (located just above the spinal cord but still below areas categorized as the forebrain) is very small in humans, but this area of the brain controls some very important functions. In general, your midbrain coordinates simple movements with sensory information. For example, if you turn your head right now, your midbrain coordinates with muscles in your eyes to keep them focused on this text. Different parts of the midbrain are important in various muscle coordinations. For purposes of the AP test, though, you should remember that this area is between the hindbrain and the forebrain and integrates some types of sensory information and muscle movements. One specific structure in the midbrain you should be familiar with is the reticular formation. It is a netlike collection of cells throughout the hindbrain that controls general body arousal and the ability to focus our attention. If the reticular formation does not function, we fall into a deep coma.

Forebrain

The various areas of the forebrain are very important to psychologists (and to students taking the AP psychology test). Areas of the forebrain control what we think of as thought and reason. Notice in Figure 3.3 how large the forebrain is in comparison with the other areas. The size of our forebrain makes humans human, and most psychological researchers concentrate their efforts in this area of the brain. Specific areas of interest to us in the forebrain are the thalamus, hypothalamus, amygdala, and hippocampus (the amygdala and hippocampus are not illustrated in Fig. 3.3).

Thalamus

The thalamus is located on top of the brain stem. It is responsible for receiving the sensory signals coming up the spinal cord and sending them to the appropriate areas in the rest of the forebrain (see the specific areas listed in the section about the cerebral cortex for specific examples of where some of these messages end up).

Hypothalamus

The hypothalamus is a small structure right next to the thalamus. The small size of the hypothalamus belies the importance of its functions. The hypothalamus controls several metabolic functions, including body temperature, sexual arousal (libido), hunger, thirst, and the endocrine system (see "Endocrine System" section on pg. 42). If you consider yourself a morning person or a night person, the hypothalamus might be involved since it controls our biological rhythms.

Amygdala and Hippocampus

There are two arms surrounding the thalamus. These are called the hippocampus. Structures near the end of each hippocampal arm are called the amygdala. Both these areas are important in how we process and perceive memory and emotion. Memories are not permanently stored in this area of the brain, however. Memories are processed through this area and then sent to other locations in the cerebral cortex for permanent storage. Researchers now know that memories must pass through this area first in order to be encoded because individuals with brain damage in this area are unable to retain new information.

Hint: These parts of the brain (thalamus, hypothalamus, amygdala, and hippocampus) are grouped together and called the limbic system because they all deal with aspects of emotion and memory. When you study the parts of the brain, grouping structures together according to function should help you remember them.

Cerebral Cortex

When most people think of the human brain, they think of and picture the cerebral cortex. The gray wrinkled surface of the brain is actually a thin (0.039-inch [1-mm]) layer of densely packed neurons. This layer covers the rest of the brain, including most of the structures we have described. When we are born, our cerebral cortex is full of neurons (more than we have now, actually) but the neurons are not yet well connected. As we develop and learn, the dendrites of the neurons in the cerebral cortex grow and connect with other neurons. This process forms the complex neural web you now have in your brain. The surface of the cerebral cortex is wrinkled (the wrinkles are called *fissures*) to increase the available surface area of the brain. The more wrinkles, the more surface area contained within our skull. If our cerebral cortex were not wrinkled, our skull would have to be 3 square feet (0.3 m^2) to hold all those neural connections!

Hemispheres

The cerebral cortex is divided into two hemispheres: left and right. The hemispheres look like mirror images of one another, but they exert some differences in function. The left hemisphere gets sensory messages and controls the motor function of the right half of the body. The right hemisphere gets sensory messages and controls the motor function of the left half of the body (this is called *contralateral control*). Researchers are currently investigating other differences between the hemispheres, such as the possibility that the left hemisphere may be more active during logic and sequential tasks and the right during spatial and creative tasks. However, these generalizations need to be researched further before conclusions are drawn. This specialization of function in each hemisphere is called *brain lateralization* or *hemispheric specialization*. Most of this research in differences between the hemispheres is done by examining *split-brain patients—*patients whose *corpus callosum* (the nerve bundle that connects the two hemispheres, see Fig. 3.3) has been cut to treat severe epilepsy. Split brain patients also cannot orally report information only presented to the right hemisphere, since the spoken language centers of the brain are usually located in the left hemisphere.

Areas of the Cerebral Cortex

When you study the cerebral cortex, think of it as a collection of different areas and specific cortices. Think of the cerebral cortex as eight different lobes, four on each hemisphere: frontal, parietal, temporal, and occipital. Some of the major functions of these parts of the brain that are relevant to the AP test are mentioned here. Any area of the cerebral cortex that it is not associated with receiving sensory information or controlling muscle movements is labeled as an *association area*. Although specific functions are not known for each association area, these areas are very active in various human thoughts and behaviors. For example, association areas are thought to be responsible for complex, sophisticated thoughts like judgment and humor.

Frontal Lobes

The frontal lobes are large areas of the cerebral cortex located at the top front part of the brain behind the eyes (see Fig. 3.4). Researchers believe this part of the brain is responsible for abstract thought and emotional control. The story of Phineas Gage mentioned previously exemplifies one of the functions of the frontal lobe. Phineas Gage's limbic system was separated from his frontal lobes in an accident. Doctors reported that he lost control of his emotions and became impulsive and animalistic. In most people, the frontal lobe in the left hemisphere contains one of the two special areas responsible for language processing (some left-handed people's language centers are in the right hemisphere). *Broca's area* is in the frontal lobe and is responsible for controlling the muscles involved in producing speech. Damage to Broca's area might leave us unable to make the muscle movements needed for speech. (The other area is *Wernicke's area* and is located in the temporal lobe—see that section for more information.)

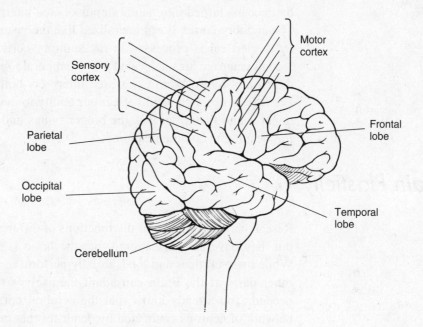

Figure 3.4. The lobes of the cerebral cortex.

A thin vertical strip at the back of the frontal lobe (farthest from the eyes, see Fig. 3.4) is called the motor cortex. This part of the cerebral cortex sends signals to our muscles, controlling our voluntary movements. The top of the body is controlled by the neurons at the bottom of this cortex (by the ears), progressing down the body as you go up the cortex. So the top of the motor cortex controls the feet and toes of the body.

Parietal Lobes

The parietal lobes are located behind the frontal lobe but still on the top of the brain (see Fig. 3.4). The parietal lobes contain the *sensory cortex* (also known as the *somato-sensory cortex*), which is located right behind the motor cortex in the frontal lobe. The sensory cortex is a thin vertical strip that receives incoming touch sensations from the rest of our body. The sensory cortex is organized similarly to the motor cortex. The top of the sensory cortex receives sensations from the bottom of the body, progressing down the cortex to the bottom, which processes signals from our face and head.

Occipital Lobes

Our occipital lobes are at the very back of our brain, farthest from our eyes. This is somewhat anti-intuitive since one of the major functions of this lobe is to interpret messages from our eyes in our visual cortex. (Study hint: the term *occipital* looks like the word *optical* to some students.) Impulses from the retinas in our eyes are sent to the visual cortex to be interpreted. Impulses from the right half of each retina are processed in the visual cortex in the right occipital lobe. Impulses from the left part of each retina are sent to the visual cortex in our left occipital lobe.

Temporal Lobes

The temporal lobes process sound sensed by our ears. Sound waves are processed by the ears, turned into neural impulses, and interpreted in our auditory cortices. The auditory cortex is not lateralized like the visual cortices are. Sound received by the left ear is processed in the auditory cortices in both hemispheres. The second language area is located in the temporal lobe (the first was Broca's area in the frontal lobe). Wernicke's area interprets both written and spoken speech. Damage to this area would affect our ability to understand language. Our speech might sound fluent but lack the proper syntax and grammatical structure needed for meaningful communication.

Brain Plasticity

Researchers know some of the functions of different areas of the cerebral cortex, but they have also discovered that the brain is somewhat plastic or flexible. While these cortices and lobes usually perform the functions already mentioned, other parts of the brain can adapt themselves to perform other functions if needed. You already know that the cerebral cortex is made up of a complex network of neurons connected by dendrites that grow to make new connections. Since dendrites grow throughout our lives, if one part of the brain is damaged, dendrites might be able to make new connections in another part of the brain that would be able to take over the functions usually performed by the damaged part of the brain. Dendrites grow most quickly in younger children. Researchers know that younger brains are more plastic and are more likely to be able to compensate for damage.

Endocrine System

Another part of human biology relevant to psychology (and the AP test) is the endocrine system. This is a system of glands that secrete hormones that affect many different biological processes in our bodies. As mentioned previously, the endocrine system is controlled in the brain by the hypothalamus. The endocrine system is complex, but a few elements of the entire process are especially relevant to psychologists.

Adrenal Glands

The adrenal glands produce adrenaline, which signals the rest of the body to prepare for fight or flight. This response was mentioned earlier in connection with the autonomic nervous system—the part of our nervous system that controls involuntary responses, such as heart rate and blood pressure.

Ovaries and Testes

Women's ovaries and men's testes produce our sex hormones, estrogen for women and testosterone for men. Research shows that levels of these hormones in men and women may partially explain gender differences demonstrated in certain experiments and situations. See the chapter "Developmental Psychology" for examples of these differences.

Genetics

Besides the functioning of the brain and nervous system, another biological factor that affects human thought and behavior is genetics. Most human traits, like body shape, introversion, or temper, result from the combined effects of nature (our genetic code) and nurture (the environment where we grow up and live). Psychological researchers attempt to determine how much nature and nurture contribute to human traits.

Basic Genetic Concepts

Every human cell contains 46 chromosomes in 23 pairs. The genetic material that makes up chromosomes is DNA—deoxyribonucleic acid. Certain segments of DNA control the production of specific proteins that control some human traits. These discrete segments are called genes. Genes can be dominant or recessive. If we inherit two recessive genes for a particular trait, that trait will be expressed. In any other combination of genes, the dominant trait is expressed. Psychological researchers investigate how different combinations of genes create tendencies for physical and behavioral traits.

Twins

Since identical twins (called monozygotic twins since they develop from one fertilized egg called a zygote) share all the same genetic material, researchers study them in order to examine the influence of genes on human traits. In one famous study, Thomas Bouchard found more than 100 identical twins who were given up for adoption and raised in different families. The study compared hundreds of traits and concluded about the relative influences of genetics and the environment on specific traits. For example, the study found a correlation coefficient of 0.69 on the IQ test for identical twins raised apart and a 0.88 for identical twins living together. This shows that the environment has some effect on IQ score since twins raised in the same family have more similar IQs. However, the IQs of twins raised apart are still highly correlated, demonstrating that IQ is also heavily influenced by genetics. Twin studies like this one have been criticized in one important way, however. Even twins raised in separate families obviously share very similar physical appearances. This physical similarity may cause others to treat them in similar ways, creating the same *effective psychological environment* for both twins. This similarity in environment might explain the high correlations that Bouchard attributed to genetic influence.

Chromosomal Abnormalities

Our gender is determined by our twenty-third pair of chromosomes. Men have an X and Y chromosome, and women have two X chromosomes. Usually a man will contribute either an X chromosome to a child (resulting in a girl) or a Y (resulting in a boy). Occasionally, chromosomes will combine (or fail to) in an unusual way, resulting in a chromosomal abnormality. For example, babies with *Turner's syndrome* are born with only a single X chromosome in the spot usually occupied by the twenty-third pair. Turner's syndrome causes some physical characteristics, like shortness, webbed necks, and differences in physical sexual development. Babies born with *Klinefelter's syndrome* have an extra X chromosome, resulting in an XXY pattern. The effects of this syndrome vary widely, but it usually causes minimal sexual development and personality traits like extreme introversion.

Other chromosomal abnormalities may cause mental retardation. The most common type is *Down's syndrome*. Babies with Down's syndrome are born with an extra chromosome on the twenty-first pair. Some physical characteristics are indicative of Down's syndrome: rounded face, shorter fingers and toes, slanted eyes set far apart, and different extents of mental retardation.

Practice Questions

> Directions: Each of the questions or incomplete statements below is followed by five suggested answers or completions. Select the one that is best in each case.

1. Blindness could result from damage to which cortex and lobe of the brain?
    (A) Visual cortex in the frontal lobe.
    (B) Visual cortex in the temporal lobe.
    (C) Sensory cortex in the parietal lobe.
    (D) Visual cortex in the occipital lobe.
    (E) Cerebral cortex in the occipital lobe.

2. Paralysis of the left arm might be explained by a problem in the
    (A) motor cortex in the frontal lobe in the left hemisphere.
    (B) motor cortex in the frontal lobe in the right hemisphere.
    (C) sensorimotor cortex in the temporal lobe in the left hemisphere.
    (D) motor cortex in the parietal lobe in the left hemisphere.
    (E) motor cortex in the occipital lobe in the right hemisphere.

3. Deafness can result from damage to the inner ear or damage to what area of the brain?
    (A) Connections between the auditory nerve and the auditory cortex in the frontal lobe.
    (B) Connections between the auditory nerve and the auditory cortex in the temporal lobe.
    (C) Connections between the areas of the sensory cortex that receive messages from the ears and the auditory cortex.
    (D) Connections between the hypothalamus and the auditory cortex in the temporal lobe.
    (E) Connections between the left and right sensory areas of the cerebellum.

4. According to the theory of evolution, why might we call some parts of the brain the old brain and some parts the new brain?
    (A) Old brain parts are what exist in very young children, and the new brain develops later.
    (B) The old brain developed first according to evolution.
    (C) The old brain becomes more active as we grow older.
    (D) The new brain deals with new information, while the old brain deals with information gathered when we were children.
    (E) The old brain is most affected by age deterioration (dementias) while the new brain remains unaffected.

5. Which chemicals pass across the synaptic gap and increase the possibility the next neuron in the chain will fire?
   (A) synaptic peptides
   (B) inhibitory neurotransmitters
   (C) adrenaline-type exciters
   (D) excitatory neurotransmitters
   (E) potassium and sodium

6. You eat some bad sushi and feel that you are slowly losing control over your muscles. The bacteria you ingested from the bad sushi most likely interferes with the use of
   (A) serotonin.
   (B) dopamine.
   (C) acetylcholine.
   (D) thorazine.
   (E) adrenaline.

7. The three major categories researchers use to organize the entire brain are the
   (A) old brain, new brain, and cerebral cortex.
   (B) lower, middle, and upper brain.
   (C) hindbrain, midbrain, and forebrain.
   (D) brain stem, limbic system, and cerebral cortex.
   (E) neurons, synapses, and cerebral cortex.

8. A spinal reflex differs from a normal sensory and motor reaction in that
   (A) a spinal reflex occurs only in response to extremely stressful stimuli.
   (B) in a spinal reflex, the spine moves the muscles in response as soon as the sensory information reaches the spine while usually the impulse must reach the brain before a response.
   (C) in a normal sensory/motor reaction, the spine transmits the information through afferent nerve fibers, while reflex reactions are transmitted along special efferent nerves.
   (D) spinal reflexes are part of the central nervous system response, while normal sensory/motor reactions are part of the peripheral nervous system.
   (E) spinal reflexes occur only in animals because humans are born without instinctual responses.

9. Antidepressant drugs like Prozac are often used to treat mood disorders. According to what you know about their function, which neurotransmitter system do these types of drugs try to affect?
   (A) serotonin
   (B) adrenaline
   (C) acetylcholine
   (D) endorphins
   (E) morphine

10. Which sentence most closely describes neural transmission?
 (A) An electric charge is created in the neuron, the charge travels down the cell, and chemicals are released that cross the synapse to the next cell.
 (B) A chemical change occurs within the cell, the change causes an electric charge to be produced, and the charge jumps the gap between the nerve cells.
 (C) The electric charge produced chemically inside a group of neurons causes chemical changes in surrounding cells.
 (D) Neurotransmitters produced in the hindbrain are transmitted to the forebrain, causing electric changes in the cerebral cortex.
 (E) Neural transmission is an electrochemical process both inside and outside the cell.

11. Dr. Dahab, a brain researcher, is investigating the connection between certain environmental stimuli and brain processes. Which types of brain scans is he most likely to use?
 (A) MRI and CAT
 (B) CAT and EKG
 (C) PET and EEG
 (D) EKG and CAT
 (E) lesioning and MRI

12. Split-brain patients are unable to
 (A) coordinate movements between their major and minor muscle groups.
 (B) speak about information received exclusively in their right hemisphere.
 (C) speak about information received exclusively in their left hemisphere.
 (D) solve abstract problems involving integrating logical (left-hemisphere) and spatial (right-hemisphere) information.
 (E) speak about information received exclusively through their left ear, left eye, or left side of their bodies.

13. When brain researchers refer to *brain plasticity,* they are talking about
 (A) the brain's ability to regrow damaged neurons.
 (B) the surface texture and appearance caused by the layer known as the cerebral cortex.
 (C) the brain's versatility caused by the millions of different neural connections.
 (D) our adaptability to different problems ranging from survival needs to abstract reasoning.
 (E) new connections forming in the brain to take over for damaged sections.

14. Mr. Spam is a 39-year-old male who has been brought into your neurology clinic by his wife. She has become increasingly alarmed by her husband's behavior over the last four months. You recommend a CAT scan to look for tumors in the brain. Which two parts of the brain would you predict are being affected by the tumors?

    List of symptoms: vastly increased appetite, body temperature fluctuations, decreased sexual desire, jerky movements, poor balance when walking and standing, inability to throw objects, and exaggerated efforts to coordinate movements in a task
    (A) motor cortex and emotion cortex
    (B) motor cortex and hypothalamus
    (C) hypothalamus and cerebellum
    (D) cerebellum and medulla
    (E) thalamus and motor cortex

15. In most people, which one of following is a specific function of the left hemisphere that is typically not controlled by the right hemisphere?
    (A) producing speech
    (B) control of the left hand
    (C) spatial reasoning
    (D) hypothesis testing
    (E) abstract reasoning

Answers to Practice Questions

1. **(D)** The visual cortex is located in the occipital lobe. The other locations are incorrect for the visual cortex. The sensory cortex interprets touch stimuli, and the cerebral cortex is the term for the entire wrinkled surface of the brain, so those items are incorrect.

2. **(B)** The motor cortex (which is located in the frontal lobe) in the right hemisphere controls the left side of the body. No such thing as the sensorimotor cortex exists, and the other locations for the motor cortex are incorrect.

3. **(B)** The auditory cortex is located in the temporal lobe and is connected to the inner ear by the auditory nerve. Other locations given for the auditory cortex are incorrect. The sensory cortex, hypothalamus, and cerebellum are not involved in hearing.

4. **(B)** The old or reptilian brain exists in all mammals and is thought to have developed first. As humans evolved into primates, the cerebral cortex developed and grew larger, allowing us to solve more complex problems. All brain structures are present in children from birth. All parts of the brain might deal with new or old information. Dementia is not more likely to affect the old or new brain.

5. **(D)** Excitatory neurotransmitters increase the likelihood that the next neuron will fire. Inhibitory neurotransmitters actually decrease the chance the next neuron will fire when received by the cells' dendrites. Synaptic peptides and adrenaline-type exciters are not relevant to neuroanatomy (or any other anatomy—they are nonsense terms!). Potassium and sodium are integral in the process of depolarization but are not secreted from terminal buttons into the synaptic gap.

6. **(C)** Acetylcholine is the neurotransmitter involved in muscle control. Serotonin and dopamine are also neurotransmitters, but they would not be responsible for losing control over your muscles. Thorazine is an antipsychotic drug prescribed by psychiatrists. Adrenaline is a hormone released by the adrenal glands in response to stressful situations.

7. **(C)** The hindbrain, midbrain, and forebrain are three of the traditional categories of brain structures. The new brain is synonymous with the cerebral cortex. The brain stem, limbic system, and cerebral cortex are divisions of the brain but not overall categories that include the entire brain. Neurons and synapses are parts of neuroanatomy, not major divisions of the brain.

8. **(B)** Spinal reflexes, such as the reflex that causes your leg to move when a doctor strikes your leg just below your kneecap, are controlled by the spine, not the brain. Stress is not relevant to the process, nor are afferent and efferent nerves. All spinal reflexes involve the peripheral nervous system. Humans do have some spinal reflexes; they are not limited to animals.

9. **(A)** Serotonin is the only neurotransmitter on the list that is identified as being involved in mood disorders. Adrenaline is a hormone released by the adrenal glands in response to stressful situations. Acetylcholine is a neurotransmitter that controls muscle movements. Endorphins are painkillers in the brain that might temporarily elevate mood but would not be responsible for long-term mood disorders. Morphine is a drug that interacts with our endorphins to alleviate pain.

10. **(A)** Neural firing involves an electric charge within the cell and chemical transmission between cells (across the synapse). It is electric within the cell

and chemical between the cells. The electric charge does not jump the gap between neurons. The question refers to an individual neuron firing, not a group of neurons. Neurotransmitters are not confined to the hindbrain or the forebrain.

11. **(C)** The PET and EEG scans both give information about brain function (the PET measures brain activity, and the EEG measures brain waves). The MRI and CAT scans give information about brain structure, not function. An EKG is a medical test for heart function. Lesioning involves destroying brain tissue and would not be used in this type of research.

12. **(B)** Since the left hemisphere typically controls speech, split-brain patients are usually unable to talk about information exposed to only the right hemisphere. Their muscle coordination is usually normal (possible after a short adjustment period). Their ability to solve abstract problems is not affected. Visual information from the left part of each eye is transmitted to the right hemisphere, not the entire left eye. Both hemispheres receive auditory information from the left ear

13. **(E)** Plasticity refers to the brain's ability to rewire itself to recover functions lost through some type of brain damage. This process occurs most quickly in children but can happen to a limited extent in adults. The brain does not regrow neurons, it reconnects existing neurons in new ways. Plasticity has little to do with the texture and appearance of the cerebral cortex. The adaptability referred to in choice D is related to plasticity, but the correct answer E is a much more specific explanation.

14. **(C)** A tumor on the hypothalamus would explain the first three symptoms since the hypothalamus controls (at least in part) body temperature, libido, and hunger. The cerebellum coordinates some types of movements, including throwing objects and our sense of balance. The motor cortex controls voluntary muscle movements, but the specific movements described in the question are controlled by the cerebellum. The medulla controls our life-support functions, like heart rate and respiration. The thalamus directs signals coming in from the spinal cord to different parts of the brain.

15. **(A)** As mentioned previously in the analysis of split-brain patients, the left hemisphere typically controls speech. The left hand is controlled by the motor cortex in the right hemisphere. Some evidence indicates that the right hemisphere is more active in spatial reasoning. Both hemispheres are involved in hypothesis testing and abstract reasoning.

CHAPTER 4
Sensation and Perception

Overview

Right now as you read this, your eyes capture the light reflected off the page in front of you. Structures in your eyes change this pattern of light into signals that are sent to your brain and interpreted as language. The sensation of the symbols on the page and the perception of these symbols as words allow you to understand what you are reading. All our senses work in a similar way. In general, our sensory organs receive stimuli. These messages go through a process called *transduction,* which means the signals are transformed into neural impulses. These neural impulses travel first to the thalamus then on to different cortices of the brain (you will see later that the sense of smell is the one exception to this rule). Constant stimulation of a sense can produce adaptation, a process that results in decreasing responsiveness to a stimuli. For example, you probably feel your socks when you put them on in the morning, but you stop feeling them after a while because of sensory adaptation. What we sense is determined by attention or what we focus on perceiving. We can voluntarily attend to stimuli in order to perceive them, as you are doing right now, but paying attention can also be involuntary. If you are talking with a friend and someone across the room says your name, your attention will probably involuntarily switch across the room (this is sometimes called the *cocktail-party phenomenon*). These processes are our only way to get information about the outside world. The exact distinction between what is sensation and what is perception is debated by psychologists and philosophers. For our purposes, though, we can think of sensation as activation of our senses (eyes, ears, and so on) and perception as the process of understanding these sensations. We will review the structure and functions of each sensory organ and then explain some concepts involved in perception.

Hint: *One of the ways to organize the different senses in your mind is by thinking about what they gather from the outside world. The first three senses listed here, vision, hearing, and touch, gather energy in the form of light, sound waves, and pressure, respectively. Think of these three senses as energy senses. The next two, taste and smell, gather chemicals. Think of these as chemical senses. The last two senses described, vestibular and kinesthetic, help us with body position and balance.*

Energy Senses

Vision

Vision is the dominant sense in human beings. Sighted people use vision to gather information about their environment more than any other sense. The process of vision involves several steps.

Step One: Gathering Light

Vision is a complicated process, and you should have a basic understanding of the structures and processes involved for the AP test. First, light is reflected off objects and gathered by the eye. Visible light is a small section of the electromagnetic spectrum that you may have studied in your science classes. The color we see depends on two factors. First is light intensity. It describes how much energy the light contains. This factor determines how bright the object appears. The second factor, light wavelength, determines the particular hue we see. Wavelengths longer than visible light are infrared waves, microwaves, and radio waves. Wavelengths shorter than visible light include ultraviolet waves and X rays. We see different wavelengths within the visible light spectrum as different colors. Colors in order from shortest to longest wavelengths are violet, indigo, blue, green, yellow, orange, and red. When we look at something, we turn our eyes toward the object and the reflected light coming from the object enters our eye.

Step Two: Within the Eye

To understand the following descriptions, refer to Fig. 4.1 for structures in the eye. The reflected light first enters the eye through the *cornea,* a protective covering. The cornea also helps focus the light. Then the light goes through the *pupil.* The pupil is like the shutter of a camera. The muscles that control the pupil (called the *iris*) open it (dilate) to let more light in and also make it smaller to let less light in. Light that enters the pupil is focused by the *lens,* which is curved and flexible in order to focus the light. Try this: Hold up one finger and focus on it. Now, change your focus and look at the wall behind your finger. Then look at the finger again. You can feel the muscles changing the shape of your lens as you switch your focus. As the light passes through the lens, the image is flipped upside down and inverted. The focused inverted image projects on the *retina,* which is like a screen on the back of your eye. On this screen are specialized neurons that are activated by the different wavelengths of light.

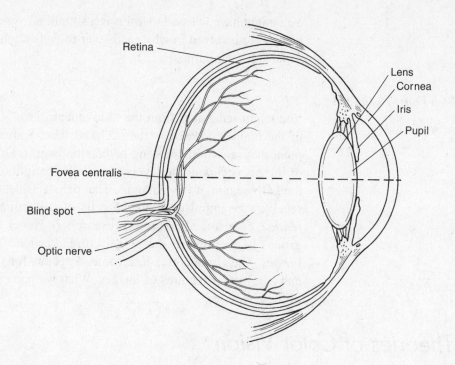

Figure 4.1. Cross section of the eye.

Step Three: Transduction

The term transduction refers to the translation of incoming stimuli into neural signals. This term applies not only to vision but to all our senses. In vision, transduction occurs when light activates the neurons in the retina. Actually several layers of cells are in the retina.

The first layer of cells is directly activated by light. These cells are *cones,* cells that are activated by color, and *rods,* cells that respond to black and white. These cells are arranged in a pattern on the retina. Rods outnumber cones (the ratio is approximately twenty to one) and are distributed throughout the retina. Cones are concentrated toward the center of the retina. At the very center of the retina is an indentation called the *fovea* that contains the highest concentration of cones. If you focus on something, you are focusing the light onto your fovea and see it in color. Your peripheral vision, especially at the extremes, relies on rods and is mostly in black and white. Your peripheral vision may seem to be full color, but controlled experiments prove otherwise. (You can try this yourself. Focus on a spot in front of you and have a friend hold different colored pens in your peripheral vision. You will find you cannot determine the color of the pens until they get close to the center of your vision.) If enough rods and cones fire in an area of the retina, they activate the next layer of bipolar cells. If enough bipolar cells fire, the next layer of cells, *ganglion cells,* is activated. The axons of the ganglion cells make up the optic nerve that sends these impulses to a specific region in the thalamus called the *lateral geniculate nucleus* (LGN). From there, the messages are sent to the visual cortices located in the occipital lobes of the brain. The spot where the optic nerve leaves the retina has no rods or cones, so it is referred to as the *blind spot*. The optic nerve is divided into two parts. Impulses from the left side of each retina go to the left hemisphere of the brain. Impulses from the right side of each retina go to the right side of our brain. The spot where the nerves cross each other is called the *optic chiasm*.

You might have guessed that this is a simplified version of this process. Different factors are involved in why each layer of cells might fire, but this explanation is suitable for our purposes.

Step Four: In the Brain

You might remember from the "Biological Bases" chapter that the visual cortex of the brain is located in the occipital lobe. Some researchers say it is at this point that sensation ends and perception begins. Others say some interpretation of images occurs in the layers of cells in the retina. Still others say it occurs in the LGN region of the thalamus. That debate aside, the visual cortex of the brain receives the impulses from the cells of the retina, and the impulses activate *feature detectors*. Perception researchers Hubel and Weisel discovered that groups of neurons in the visual cortex respond to different types of visual images. The visual cortex has feature detectors for vertical lines, curves, motion, and many other features of images. What we perceive visually is a combination of these features.

Theories of Color Vision

Trichromatic Theory

Competing theories exist about how and why we see color. The oldest and most simple theory is *trichromatic theory*. This theory hypothesizes that we have three types of cones in the retina: cones that detect the different colors blue, red, and green. These cones are activated in different combinations to produce all the colors of the visible spectrum. While this theory has some research support and makes sense intuitively, it cannot explain some visual phenomena, such as *afterimages* and *color blindness*. If you stare at one color for a while and then look at a white or blank space, you will see a color afterimage. If you stare at green, the afterimage will be red, while the afterimage of yellow is blue. Color blindness is similar. Individuals with dichromatic color blindness cannot see either red/green shades or blue/yellow shades. (The other type of color blindness is monochromatic, which causes people to see only shades of gray.) Another theory of color vision is needed to explain these phenomena.

Opponent-Process Theory

The opponent-process theory states that the sensory receptors arranged in the retina come in pairs: red/green pairs, yellow/blue pairs, and black/white pairs. If one sensor is stimulated, its pair is inhibited from firing. This theory explains color afterimages well. If you stare at the color red for a while, you fatigue the sensors for red. Then when you switch your gaze and look at a blank page, the opponent part of the pair for red will fire, and you will see a green afterimage. The opponent-process theory also explains color blindness. If color sensors do come in pairs and an individual is missing one pair, he or she should have difficulty seeing those hues. People with dichromatic color blindness have difficulty seeing shades of red and green or of yellow and blue.

Hearing

Our auditory sense also uses energy in the form of waves, but sound waves are vibrations in the air rather than electromagnetic waves. Sound waves are created by vibrations, which travel through the air, and are then collected by our ears. These vibrations then finally go through the process of transduction into neural messages and are sent to the brain. Sound waves, like all waves, have *amplitude* and *frequency*. Amplitude is the height of the wave and determines the loudness of the sound, which is measured in decibels. Frequency refers to the length of the waves and determines pitch, measured in megahertz. High-pitched sounds have high frequencies, and the waves are densely packed together. Low-pitched sounds have low frequencies, and the waves are spaced apart.

Hint: *One way to remember amplitude and frequency is to imagine you are watching waves go by. Frequency is how frequently the waves come by. If they speed by quickly, the waves are high in frequency. Amplitude is how tall the waves are. The taller the waves, the more energy and the louder the noise.*

Sound waves are collected in your outer ear (see Fig. 4.2 for structures in the ear). The waves travel down the *ear canal* (also called the auditory canal) until they reach the *eardrum* or tympanic membrane. This is a thin membrane that vibrates as the sound waves hit it. Think of it as the head of a drum. This membrane is attached to the first in a series of three small bones. The eardrum connects with the *hammer* (or malleus), which is connected to the *anvil* (or incus), which connects to the *stirrup* (or stapes). The vibration of the eardrum is transmitted by these three bones to the *oval window,* a membrane very similar to the eardrum. The oval window membrane is attached to the *cochlea,* a structure shaped like a snail's shell filled with fluid. As the oval window vibrates, the fluid moves. The floor (lower membrane) of the cochlea is lined with hair cells connected to the *organ of Corti,* which are neurons activated by movement of the hair cells. When the fluid moves, the hair cells move and transduction occurs. The organ of Corti fires, and these impulses are transmitted to the brain via the auditory nerve.

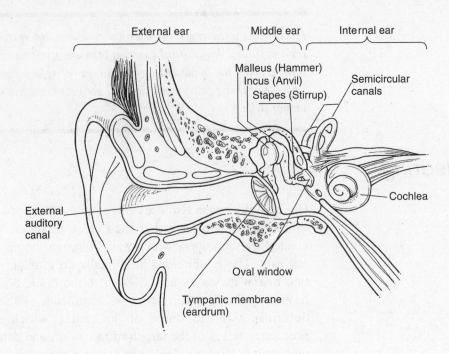

Figure 4.2. Cross section of the ear.

Pitch Theories

The description of the hearing process above explains how we hear in general, but how do we hear different pitches or tones? As with color vision, two different theories describe the two processes involved in hearing pitch: place theory and frequency theory.

Place Theory

Place theory holds that the hair cells in the cochlea respond to different frequencies of sound based on where they are located in the cochlea. Some bend in response to high pitches and some to low. We sense pitch because the hair cells move in different places in the cochlea.

Frequency Theory

Research demonstrates that place theory accurately describes how hair cells sense the upper range of pitches but not the lower tones. Lower tones are sensed by the rate at which the cells fire. We sense pitch because the hair cells fire at different rates (frequencies) in the cochlea.

Deafness

An understanding of how hearing works explains hearing problems as well. *Conduction deafness* occurs when something goes wrong with the system of conducting the sound to the cochlea (in the ear canal, eardrum, hammer/anvil/stirrup, or oval window). For example, my mother-in-law has a medical condition that is causing her stirrup to deteriorate slowly. Eventually, she will need surgery to replace that bone in order to hear well. *Nerve* (or *sensorineural*) *deafness* occurs when the hair cells in the cochlea are damaged, usually by loud noise. If you have ever been to a concert, football game, or other event loud enough to leave your ears ringing, chances are you came close to or did cause permanent damage to your hearing. Prolonged exposure to noise that loud can permanently damage the hair cells in your cochlea, and these hair cells do not regenerate. Nerve deafness is much more difficult to treat since no method has been found that will encourage the hair cells to regenerate.

Touch

When our skin is indented, pierced, or experiences a change in temperature, our sense of touch is activated by this energy. We have many different types of nerve endings in every patch of skin, and the exact relationship between these different types of nerve endings and the sense of touch is not completely understood. Some nerve endings respond to pressure while others respond to temperature. We know that our brain interprets the amount of indentation (or temperature change) as the intensity of the touch, from a light touch to a hard blow. We also sense placement of the touch by the place on our body where the nerve endings fire. Also, nerve endings are more concentrated in different parts of our body. If we want to feel something, we usually use our fingertip, an area of high nerve concentration, rather than the back of our elbow, an area of low nerve concentration. If touch or temperature receptors are stimulated sharply, a different kind of nerve ending called pain receptors will also fire. Pain is a useful response because it warns us of potential dangers.

Gate-control theory helps explain how we experience pain the way we do. Gate-control theory explains that some pain messages have a higher priority than others. When a higher priority message is sent, the gate swings open for it and swings shut for a low priority message, which we will not feel. Of course, this gate is not a physical gate swinging in the nerve, it is just a convenient way to understand how pain messages are sent. When you scratch an itch, the gate swings open for your high-intensity scratching and shut for the low-intensity itching, and you stop the itching for a short period of time (but do not worry, the itching usually starts again soon!). Endorphins, or pain-killing chemicals in the body, also swing the gate shut. Natural endorphins in the brain, which are chemically similar to opiates like morphine, control pain.

Chemical Senses

Taste (or Gustation)

The nerves involved in the chemical senses respond to chemicals rather than to energy, like light and sound waves. Chemicals from the food we eat (or whatever else we stick into our mouths) are absorbed by taste buds on our tongue (see Fig.

4.3). Taste buds are located on *papillae,* which are the bumps you can see on your tongue. Taste buds are located all over the tongue and some parts of the inside of the cheeks and roof of the mouth. Humans sense four different types of tastes: sweet, salty, sour, and bitter. Some taste buds respond more intensely to a specific taste and more weakly to others. People differ in their ability to taste food. The more densely packed the taste buds, the more chemicals are absorbed, and the more intensely the food is tasted. You can get an idea of how densely packed taste buds are by looking at the papillae on your tongue. If all the bumps are packed tightly together, you probably taste food intensely. If they are spread apart, you are probably a weak taster. What we think of as the flavor of food is actually a combination of taste and smell.

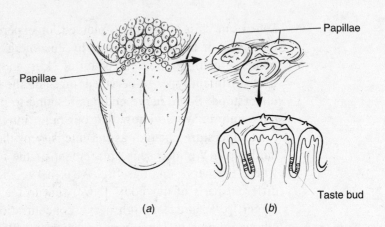

Figure 4.3. Taste sensors.

Smell (or Olfaction)

Our sense of smell also depends on chemicals emitted by substances. Molecules of substances, hot chocolate for example, rise into the air. Some of them are drawn into our nose. The molecules settle in a mucous membrane at the top of each nostril and are absorbed by receptor cells located there. The exact types of these receptor cells are not yet known, as they are for taste buds. Some researchers estimate that as many as 100 different types of smell receptors may exist. These receptor cells are linked to the *olfactory bulb* (see Fig. 4.4), which gathers the messages from the *olfactory receptor cells* and sends this information to the brain. Interestingly, the nerve fibers from the olfactory bulb connect to the brain at the amygdala and then to the hippocampus, which make up the limbic system—responsible for emotional impulses and memory. The impulses from all the other senses go through the thalamus first before being sent to the appopriate cortices. This direct connection to the limbic system may explain why smell is such a powerful trigger for memories.

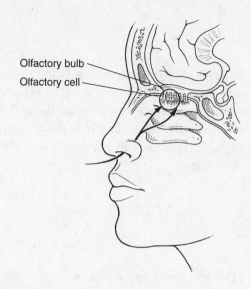

Olfactory bulb
Olfactory cell

Figure 4.4. Cross section of the olfactory system.

Body Position Senses

Vestibular Sense

Our vestibular sense tells us about how our body is oriented is space. Three semicircular canals in the inner ear (see Fig. 4.2) give the brain feedback about body orientation. The canals are basically tubes partially filled with fluid. When the position of your head changes, the fluid moves in the canals, causing hair cells in the canals to move. The movement of these hair cells activate neurons, and their impulses go to the brain. You have probably experienced the nausea and dizziness caused when the fluid in these canals is agitated. During an exciting roller coaster ride, the fluid in the canals might move so much that the brain receives confusing signals about body position. This causes the dizziness and nauseous reaction.

Kinesthetic Sense

While our vestibular sense keeps track of the overall orientation of our body, our kinesthetic sense gives us feedback about the position and orientation of specific body parts. Receptors in our muscles and joints send information to our brain about our limbs. This information, combined with visual feedback, lets us keep track of our body. You could probably reach down with one finger and touch your kneecap with a high degree of accuracy because your kinesthetic sense provides information about where your finger is in relation to your kneecap.

Perception

As stated before, perception is the process of understanding and interpreting sensations. Psychophysics is the study of the interaction between the sensations we receive and our experience of them. Researchers who study psychophysics try to uncover the rules our minds use to interpret sensations. We will cover some of the basic principles in psychophysics and examine some basic perceptual rules for vision.

Thresholds

Research shows that while our senses are very acute, they do have their limits. The *absolute threshold* is the smallest amount of stimulus we can detect. For example, the absolute threshold for vision is the smallest amount of light we can detect, which is estimated to be a single candle flame about 30 miles (48 km) away on a perfectly dark night. Most of us could detect a single drop of perfume a room away. Actually, the technical definition of absolute threshold is the minimal amount of stimulus we can detect 50 percent of the time, because researchers try to take into account individual variation in sensitivity and interference from other sensory sources. Stimuli below our absolute threshold is said to be *subliminal*. Some companies claim to produce subliminal message media that can change unwanted behavior. Psychological research does not support their claim. In fact, a truly subliminal message would not, by definition, affect behavior at all because if a message is truly subliminal, we do not perceive it! Research indicates some messages called subliminal (because they are so faint we do not report perceiving them) can sometimes affect behavior in subtle ways, such as choosing a word at random from a list after the word was presented subliminally. Evidence does not exist, however, that more complex subliminal messages such as "lose weight" or "increase your vocabulary" are effective. If these tapes do change behavior, the change most likely comes from the *placebo effect* rather than from the effect of the subliminal message.

So if we can see a single candle 30 miles (48 km) away, would we notice if another candle was lit right next to it? In other words, how much does a stimulus need to change before we notice the difference? The *difference threshold* defines this change. The difference threshold, sometimes called *just-noticeable difference,* is the smallest amount of change needed in a stimulus before we detect a change. This threshold is computed by *Weber's law,* named after psychophysicist Ernst Weber. It states that the change needed is proportional to the original intensity of the stimulus. The more intense the stimulus, the more it will need to change before we notice a difference. You might notice a change if someone adds a small amount of cayenne pepper to a dish that is normally not very spicy, but you would need to add much more hot pepper to five-alarm chili before anyone would notice a difference. Further, Weber discovered that each sense varies according to a constant, but the constants differ between the senses. For example, the constant for hearing is 5 percent. If you listened to a 100-decibel tone, the volume would have to increase to 105 decibels before you noticed that it was any louder. Weber's constant for vision is 8 percent. So 8 candles would need to be added to 100 candles before it looked any brighter.

Perceptual Theories

Psychologists use several theories to describe how we perceive the world.

Hint: These perceptual theories are not competing with one another. Each theory describes different examples or parts of perception. Sometimes a single example of the interpretation of sensation needs to be explained using all of the following theories.

Signal Detection Theory

Real-world examples of perception are more complicated than controlled laboratory perception experiments. After all, how many times do we get the opportunity to stare at a single candle flame 30 miles (48 km) away on a perfectly clear, dark night? *Signal detection theory* investigates the effects of the distractions and interference we experience while perceiving the world. This area of research tries to predict what we will perceive among competing stimuli. For example, will the surgeon see the tumor on the CAT scan among all the irrelevant shadows and flaws in the picture? Will the quarterback see the one open receiver in the end zone despite the oncoming lineman? Signal detection theory takes into account how motivated we are to detect certain stimuli and what we expect to perceive. These factors together are called *response criteria* (also called *receiver operating characteristics*). For example, I will be more likely to smell a freshly baked rhubarb pie if I am hungry and enjoy the taste of rhubarb. By using factors like response criteria, signal detection theory tries to explain and predict the different perceptual mistakes we make. A *false positive* is when we think we perceive a stimulus that is not there. For example, you may think you see a friend of yours on a crowded street and end up waving at a total stranger. A *false negative* is not perceiving a stimulus that is present. You may not notice the directions at the top of a test that instruct you not to write on the test form (do not do this on the AP exam!). In some situations, one type of error is much more serious than the other, and this importance can alter perception. In the surgeon example mentioned previously, a false negative (not seeing a tumor that is present) is a more serious mistake than a false positive (suspecting a tumor that is there), although both mistakes are obviously important.

Top-Down Processing

When we use *top-down processing,* we perceive by filling in gaps in what we sense. For example, try to read the following sentence:

I _ope yo_ _et a 5 on t_ _ A_ e_am.

You should be able to read the sentence as "I hope you get a 5 on the AP exam." You perceived the blanks as the appropriate letters by using the context of the sentence. Top-down processing occurs when you use your background knowledge to fill in gaps in what you perceive. Our experience creates *schemata,* mental representations of how we expect the world to be. Our schemata influence how we perceive the world. Schemata can create a *perceptual set,* which is a predisposition to perceiving something in a certain way. If you have ever seen images in the clouds, you have experienced top-down processing. You use your background knowledge (schemata) to perceive the random shapes of clouds as organized shapes. In the 1970s, some parent groups were very concerned about *backmasking:* supposed hidden messages musicians recorded backward in their music. These parent groups would play song lyrics backward and hear messages, usually threatening messages. Some groups of parents demanded an investigation about the effects of the backmasking. What was happening? Lyrics played backward are basically random noise. However, if you expect to hear a threatening message in the random noise, you probably will, much like expecting to see an image in the clouds. People who listened to the songs played backward and had schemata of this music as dangerous or evil perceived the threatening messages due to top-down processing.

Bottom-Up Processing

Bottom-up processing, also called *feature analysis,* is the opposite of top-down processing. Instead of using our experience to perceive an object, we use only the features of the object itself to build a complete perception. We start our perception at the bottom with the individual characteristics of the image and put all those characteristics together into our final perception. Bottom-up processing can be hard to imagine because it is such an automatic process. The feature detectors in the visual cortex allow us to perceive basic features of objects, such as horizontal and vertical lines, curves, motion, and so on. Our mind builds the picture from the bottom up using these basic characteristics. We are constantly using both bottom-up and top-down processing as we percieve the world. Top-down processing is faster but more prone to error, while bottom-up processing takes longer but is more accurate.

Principles of Visual Perception

The rules we use for visual perception are too numerous to cover completely in this book. However, some of the basic rules are important to know and understand for the AP psychology exam. One of the first perceptual decisions our mind must make is the *figure-ground relationship.* What part of a visual image is the figure and what part is the ground or background? Several optical illusions play with this rule. One example is the famous picture of the vase that if looked at one way is a vase but by switching the figure and the ground can be perceived as two faces (see Fig. 4.5).

Figure 4.5. Optical illusion.

Gestalt Rules

At the beginning of the twentieth century, a group of researchers called the Gestalt psychologists described the principles that govern how we perceive groups of objects. The Gestalt psychologists pointed out that we normally perceive images as groups, not as isolated elements. They thought this process was innate and inevitable. Several factors influence how we will group objects.

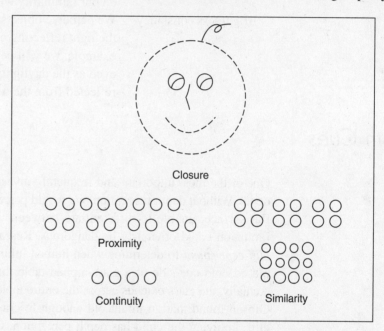

Proximity	Objects that are close together are more likely to be perceived as belonging in the same group.
Similarity	Objects that are similar in appearance are more likely to be perceived as belonging in the same group.
Continuity	Objects that form a continuous form (such as a trail or a geometric figure) are more likely to be perceived as belonging in the same group.
Closure	Similar to top-down processing. Objects that make up a recognizable image are more likely to be perceived as belonging in the same group even if the image contains gaps that the mind needs to fill in.

Constancy

Every object we see changes minutely from moment to moment due to our changing angle of vision, variations in light, and so on. Our ability to maintain a constant perception of an object despite these changes is called *constancy*. There are several types of constancy.

Size constancy	Objects closer to our eyes will produce bigger images on our retinas, but we take distance into account in our estimations of size. We keep a constant size in mind for an object (if we are familiar with the typical size of the object) and know that it does not grow or shrink in size as it moves closer or farther away.
Shape constancy	Objects viewed from different angles will produce different shapes on our retinas, but we know the shape of an object remains constant. For example, the top of a coffee mug viewed from a certain angle will produce an elliptical image on our retinas, but we know the top is circular due to shape constancy. Again, this depends on our familiarity with the usual shape of the object.
Brightness constancy	We perceive objects as being a constant color even as the light reflecting off the object changes. For example, we will perceive a brick wall as brick red even as the daylight fades and the actual color reflected from the wall turns gray.

Depth Cues

One of the most important and frequently investigated parts of visual perception is depth. Without depth perception, we would perceive the world as a two-dimensional flat surface, unable to differentiate between what is near and what is far. This limitation could obviously be dangerous. Researcher E. J. Gibson used the *visual cliff experiment* to determine when human infants can perceive depth. An infant is placed onto one side of a glass-topped table that creates the impression of a cliff. Actually, the glass extends across the entire table, so the infant cannot possibly fall. Gibson found that an infant old enough to crawl will not crawl across the visual cliff, implying the child has depth perception. Other experiments demonstrate that depth perception develops when we are about three months old. Researchers divide the cues that we use to perceive depth into two categories: *mononcular cues* (depth cues that do not depend on having two eyes) and *binocular cues* (cues that depend on having two eyes).

Monocular cues

If you have taken a drawing class, you have learned monocular depth cues. Artists use these cues to imply depth in their drawings. One of the most common cues is *linear perspective*. If you wanted to draw a railroad track that runs away from the viewer off into the distance, most likely you would start by drawing two lines that converge somewhere toward the top of your paper. If you added a drawing of the train, you might use the *relative size cue*. You would draw the boxcars closer to the viewer as larger than the engine off in the distance. A water tower blocking our view of part of the train would be seen as closer to us due to the *interposition cue;* objects that block the view to other objects must be closer to us. If the train were running through a desert landscape, you might draw the rocks closest to the viewer in detail, while the landscape off in the distance would not be as detailed. This cue is called *texture gradient;* we know that we can see details in texture close to us but not far away. Finally, your art teacher might teach you to use *shadowing* in your picture. By shading part of your picture, you can imply where the light source is and thus imply depth and position of objects.

Binocular Cues

Other cues for depth result from our anatomy. We see the world with two eyes set a certain distance apart, and this feature of our anatomy gives us the ability to perceive depth. The finger trick you read about during the discussion of the anatomy of the eye (see page 52) demonstrates the first binocular cue—*binocular disparity* (also called *retinal disparity*). Each of our eyes sees any object from a slightly different angle. The brain gets both images. It knows that if the object is far away, the images will be similar, but the closer the object is, the more disparity there will be between the images coming from each eye. The other binocular cue is *convergence*. As an object gets closer to your face, our eyes must move toward one another to keep focused on the object. The brain receives feedback from the muscles controlling eye movement and knows that the more the eyes converge, the closer the object must be.

Effects of Culture on Perception

One area of psychology cross-cultural researchers are investigating is the effect of culture on perception. Research indicates that some of the perceptual rules psychologists once thought were innate are actually learned. For example, cultures that do not use monocular depth cues (such as linear perspective) in their art do not see depth in pictures using these cues. Also, some optical illusions are not perceived the same way by people from different cultures. For example, below is a representation of the famous Muller-Lyer illusion. Which of the following straight lines, *A* or *B*, appears longer to you?

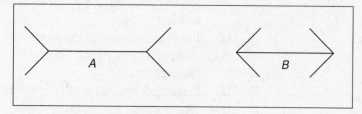

Line A should look longer, even though both lines are actually the same length. People who come from noncarpentered cultures that do not use right angles and corners often in their building and architecture are not usually fooled by the Muller-Lyer illusion. Cross-cultural research demonstrates that some basic perceptual sets are learned from our culture.

Practice Questions

Directions: Each of the questions or incomplete statements below is followed by five suggested answers or completions. Select the one that is best in each case.

1. Our sense of smell may be a powerful trigger for memories because
   (A) we are conditioned from birth to make strong connections between smells and events.
   (B) the nerve connecting the olfactory bulb sends impulses directly to the limbic system.
   (C) the receptors at the top of each nostril connect with the cortex.
   (D) smell is a powerful cue for encoding memories into long-term memory.
   (E) strong smells encourage us to process events deeply so they will most likely be remembered.

2. The cochlea is responsible for
   (A) protecting the surface of the eye.
   (B) transmitting vibrations received by the eardrum to the hammer, anvil, and stirrup.
   (C) transforming vibrations into neural signals.
   (D) coordinating impulses from the rods and cones in the retina.
   (E) sending messages to the brain about orientation of the head and body.

3. In a perception research lab, you are asked to describe the shape of the top of a box as the box is slowly rotated. Which concept are the researchers most likely investigating?
   (A) feature detectors in the retina
   (B) feature detectors in the occipital lobe
   (C) placement of rods and cones in the retina
   (D) binocular depth cues
   (E) shape constancy

4. The blind spot in our eye results from
   (A) the lack of receptors at the spot where the optic nerve connects to the retina.
   (B) the shadow the pupil makes on the retina.
   (C) competing processing between the visual cortices in the left and right hemisphere.
   (D) floating debris in the space between the lens and the retina.
   (E) retinal damage from bright light.

5. Smell and taste are called _____ because _____
   (A) energy senses; they send impulses to the brain in the form of electric energy.
   (B) chemical senses; they detect chemicals in what we taste and smell.
   (C) flavor senses; smell and taste combine to create flavor.
   (D) chemical senses; they send impulses to the brain in the form of chemicals.
   (E) memory senses; they both have powerful connections to memory.

6. What is the principal difference between amplitude and frequency in the context of sound waves?
   (A) Amplitude is the tone or timbre of a sound, while frequency is the pitch.
   (B) Amplitude is detected in the cochlea, while frequency is detected in the auditory cortex.
   (C) Amplitude is the height of the sound wave, while frequency is a measure of how frequently the sound waves pass a given point.
   (D) Both measure qualities of sound, but frequency is a more accurate measure since it measures the shapes of the waves rather than the strength of the waves.
   (E) Frequency is a measure for light waves, while amplitude is a measure for sound waves.

7. Weber's law determines
   (A) absolute threshold.
   (B) focal length of the eye.
   (C) level of subliminal messages.
   (D) amplitude of sound waves.
   (E) just-noticeable difference.

8. Gate control theory refers to
   (A) which sensory impulses are transmitted first from each sense.
   (B) which pain messages are perceived.
   (C) interfering sound waves, causing some waves to be undetected.
   (D) the gate at the optic chiasm controlling the destination hemisphere for visual information from each eye.
   (E) how our minds choose to use either bottom-up or top-down processing.

9. If you had sight in only one eye, which of the following depth cues could you NOT use?
   (A) texture gradient
   (B) convergence
   (C) linear perspective
   (D) interposition
   (E) shading

10. Which of the following sentences best describes the relationship between sensation and perception?
    (A) Sensation is a strictly mechanical process, while perception is a cognitive process.
    (B) Perception is an advanced form of sensation.
    (C) Sensation happens in the senses, while perception happens in the brain.
    (D) Sensation is detecting stimuli, perception is interpreting stimuli detected.
    (E) Sensation involves learning and expectations, and perception does not.

11. What function does the retina serve?
    (A) The retina contains the visual receptor cells.
    (B) The retina focuses light coming in the eye through the lens.
    (C) The retina determines how much light is let into the eye.
    (D) The retina determines which rods and cones will be activated by incoming light.
    (E) The retina connects the two optic nerves and sends impulses to the left and right visual cortices.

12. Color blindness and color afterimages are best explained by what theory of color vision?
    (A) trichromatic theory
    (B) visible hue theory
    (C) opponent-process theory
    (D) dichromatic theory
    (E) binocular disparity theory

13. You are shown a picture of your grandfather's face, but the eyes and mouth are blocked out. You still recognize it as a picture of your grandfather. Which type of processing best explains this example of perception?
    (A) bottom-up processing
    (B) signal detection theory
    (C) top-down processing
    (D) opponent-process theory
    (E) gestalt replacement theory

14. What behavior would be difficult without our vestibular sense?
    (A) integrating what we see and hear
    (B) writing our name
    (C) repeating a list of digits
    (D) walking a straight line with our eyes closed
    (E) reporting to a researcher the exact position and orientation of our limbs

15. Which of the following sentences best describes the relationship between culture and perception?
    (A) Our perceptual rules are inborn and not affected by culture.
    (B) Perceptual rules are culturally based, so rules that apply to one culture rarely apply to another.
    (C) Most perceptual rules apply in all cultures, but some perceptual rules are learned and vary between cultures.
    (D) Slight variations in sensory apparatuses among cultures create slight differences in perception.
    (E) The processes involved in perception are genetically based, so genetic differences among cultures affect perception.

Answers to Practice Questions

1. **(B)** A nerve connects the olfactory bulb directly to the amygdala and hippocampus. This connection may explain why smell may be a powerful trigger for emotions and memories. This connection has nothing to do with learning, long-term memory, or deep processing. Smells are eventually communicated to the cortex, but that does not explain the special connection to memory.

2. **(C)** Hair cells inside the cochlea change the mechanical vibrations received at the oval window into neural signals that are transmitted to the brain. The cochlea is part of the ear, not the eye, so choices A and D are incorrect. The hammer, anvil, and stirrup transfer vibrations to the cochlea, not the other way around. The semicircular canals send messages to the brain about the orientation of the head and body.

3. **(E)** According to shape constancy, we know shapes remain constant even when our viewing angle changes. This experiment would not be investigating feature detectors, because the equipment required to measure the firing of feature detectors is not described. Placement of rods and cones in the retina would not affect perception of the top of the box. Binocular depth cues are probably not the target of the research because the researchers are not asking questions about depth.

4. **(A)** The spot where the optic nerve connects to the retina lacks rods and cones and is thus called the blind spot. Choices B and C are distracter items and are not true. Floating debris and retinal damage could cause blind spots. However, these do not occur in everyone, and the question implies the blind spot present in everyone's eyes.

5. **(B)** We sense tastes and smells by absorbing chemicals. Energy senses are hearing, sight, and touch. Flavor senses and memory senses are not valid terms. Choice D is incorrect because all nerve impulses are sent by an electrochemical process.

6. **(C)** Amplitude is a measure of the height of the wave, creating the volume of the sound. Frequency is the measure of how quickly the waves pass a point, causing the pitch of the sound. The other choices are incorrect distractions.

7. **(E)** Weber's law calculates the difference threshold or the just-noticeable difference. It has nothing to do with sight, subliminal messages, or amplitude.

8. **(B)** Gate control theory explains why some pain messages are perceived while others are not. This theory is specific to the sense of touch, so choices A, C, and D are incorrect. Choice E is incorrect because gate control theory has to do with the perception of pain, not how we interpret sensations in general.

9. **(B)** All the other choices are monocular cues for depth, so they could be used by a person sighted in only one eye. Convergence is a binocular cue and would not work without two functioning eyes. When an object is close to our face and our eyes have to point toward each other slightly, our brain senses this convergence and uses it to help gauge distance.

10. **(D)** Sensation is the activation of our senses by stimuli, and perception is how we organize and interpret sensations. Choice A is incorrect because some sensation processes are more than mechanical. Choice B is too vague—advanced in what sense? Some researchers think part of perception

may happen in the senses themselves, so choice C is incorrect. Choice E is false; perception involves learning and expectations.

11. **(A)** Visual receptors, rods and cones, are embedded in the retina, which is the back part of the eye. The rest of the items are incorrect because they describe functions the retina does not perform.

12. **(C)** The opponent-process theory explains these two phenomena, which the trichromatic theory cannot do. Visible hue is not a color vision theory. Dichromatic is a type of color blindness, not a theory of color vision. Binocular disparity is a depth cue.

13. **(C)** Your mind filled in the information from the picture by drawing on your experience. This is top-down processing. The example does not reflect bottom-up processing because information is being filled in, instead of an image being built from the elements present. Signal detection theory has to do with what sensations we pay attention to, not filling in missing elements in a picture. Opponent-process theory explains color vision. Gestalt theory might relate to this example because you are trying to perceive the picture as a whole, but there is no such term as gestalt replacement theory.

14. **(D)** Our vestibular sense helps with our sense of balance and orientation in space. Our vestibular sense has little to do with our sense of sight or hearing. Repeating digits would not be affected by the vestibular sense. Our kinesthetic sense gives us information about the position of our limbs.

15. **(C)** Most perceptual principles apply in all cultures. However, some perceptual sets are learned and will vary, so choices A and B are incorrect. Sensory apparatuses do not vary among cultures, and perception is not genetically based as implied in choice E.

CHAPTER 5

States of Consciousness

Overview

While you are reading this text, you can probably become aware of your sense of consciousness. Early psychologists were very interested in consciousness. However, since no tools existed to examine it scientifically, the study of consciousness faded for a time. Currently, consciousness is becoming a more common research area due to more sophisticated brain imaging tools and an increased emphasis on cognitive psychology.

The historical discussion about consciousness centers on the competing philosophical theories of *dualism* and *monism*. Dualists believe humans (and the universe in general) consist of two materials: thought and matter. Matter is everything that has substance. Thought is a nonmaterial aspect that arises from, but is in some way independent of, a brain. Dualists argue that thought gives humans free will. Some philosophers maintain that thought is eternal and continues existing after the brain and body die. Monists disagree and believe everything is the same substance, and thought and matter are aspects of the same substance. Thought is a by-product of brain processes and stops existing when the body dies.

Psychology does not try to address these metaphysical questions directly. However, psychologists are trying to examine what we can know about consciousness and to describe some of the processes or elements of consciousness. Psychologists define consciousness as our level of awareness about ourselves and our environment. We are conscious to the degree we are aware of what is going on inside and outside ourselves.

Hint: This psychological definition implies that consciousness is not like an on/off switch. We are not conscious or unconscious. Psychologists refer to different levels and different states of consciousness.

Levels of Consciousness

Ironically, we experience different levels of consciousness in our daily life without being consciously aware of the experience. While you are reading this text, you might be tapping your pen or moving your leg in time to the music you are listening to. One level of consciousness is controlling your pen or leg, while another level is focused on reading these words. Research demonstrates other more subtle and complex effects of different levels of consciousness. The *mere-exposure effect* (also see page 215) occurs when we prefer stimuli we have seen before over novel stimuli, even if we do not consciously remember seeing the old stimuli. For example, say a researcher shows a group of research participants a list of nonsense terms for a short period of time. Later, the same group is shown another list of terms and asked which terms they prefer or like best. The mere-exposure effect predicts that the group will choose the terms they saw previously, even though the group could not recall the first list of nonsense terms if asked. On some level, the group knows the first list.

A closely related concept is *priming*. Research participants respond more quickly and/or accurately to questions they have seen before, even if they do not remember seeing them. Another fascinating phenomenon that demonstrates levels of consciousness is *blind sight*. Some people who report being blind can nonetheless accurately describe the path of a moving object or accurately grasp objects they say they cannot see! One level of their consciousness is not getting any visual information, while another level is able to "see" as demonstrated by their behavior.

The concept of consciousness consisting of different levels or layers is well established. Not all researchers agree about what the specific levels are, but some of the possible types offered by researchers are shown in the following.

Conscious level	The information about yourself and your environment you are currently aware of. Your conscious level right now is probably focusing on these words and their meanings.
Nonconscious level	Body processes controlled by your mind that we are not usually (or ever) aware of. Right now, your nonconscious is controlling your heartbeat, respiration, digestion, and so on.
Preconscious level	Information about yourself or your environment that you are not currently thinking about (not in your conscious level) but you could be. If I asked you to remember your favorite toy as a child, you could bring that preconscious memory into your conscious level.
Subconscious level	Information that we are not consciously aware of but we know must exist due to behavior. The behaviors demonstrated in examples of priming and mere-exposure effect suggest some information is accessible to this level of consciousness but not to our conscious level.
Unconscious level	Psychoanalytic psychologists believe some events and feelings are unacceptable to our conscious mind and are repressed into the unconscious mind. Many psychologists object to this concept as difficult or impossible to prove. See the personality unit (Chapter 9) for more information about the unconscious.

Sleep

As a student, sleep is most likely a subject near and dear to your heart. Many studies show that a large percentage of high school and college students are sleep deprived, meaning they do not get as much sleep as their body wants. To a psychologist, referring to being asleep as being unconscious is incorrect. Sleep is one of the states of consciousness.

Hint: According to the psychological definition of consciousness, sleep is a state of consciousness because, while we are asleep, we are less aware of ourselves and our environment than we are when we are in our normal awake state. Other states of consciousness—drug-induced states, hypnosis, and so on—are states of consciousness for similar reasons.

Sleep Cycle

You may be familiar with the term *circadian rhythm*. During a 24-hour day, our metabolic and thought processes follow a certain pattern. Some of us are more active in the morning than others, some of us get hungry or go to the bathroom at certain times of day, and so on. Part of our circadian rhythm is our sleep cycle. Our sleep cycle is our typical pattern of sleep. Researchers using EEG (see page 36) machines can record how active our brains are during sleep and describe the different stages of sleep we progress through each night. Refer to Fig. 5.1 for a graphic representation of the stages of a typical sleep cycle.

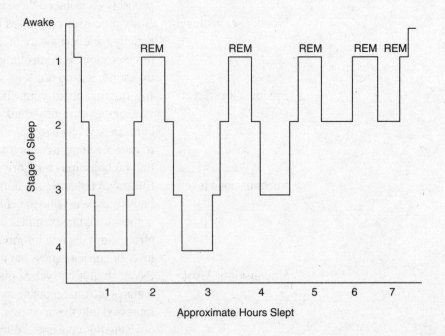

Figure 5.1. Stages of sleep.

As you can see in Fig. 5.1, sleep is far from being a time of unconsciousness. We cycle through different stages of sleep during the night. Our brain waves and level of awareness change as we cycle through the stages. The period when we are falling asleep is called *sleep onset*. This is the stage between wakefulness and sleep. We might experience mild hallucinations (such as falling or rising) before actually falling asleep and entering stage 1. While we are awake and in stages 1 and 2, our brains produce alpha waves, which are relatively high-frequency, low-amplitude waves. However, the alpha waves get progressively slower and higher in amplitude as we go from wakefulness and through stages 1 and 2. In stage 2, the EEG starts to show sleep spindles, which are short bursts of rapid brain waves. From there, we move into stages 3 and 4, which are sometimes called delta sleep (also called slow-wave sleep) because of the delta waves that exist during these stages. The slower the wave, the deeper the sleep and less aware we are of our environment. A person in delta sleep is very difficult to wake up. If you are awakened out of delta sleep, you may be very disoriented and groggy. Delta sleep seems to be very important in replenishing the body's chemical supplies, releasing growth hormones in children, and fortifying our immune system. A person deprived of delta sleep will be more susceptible to illness and will feel physically tired. Increasing exercise will increase the amount of time we spend in stages 3 and 4.

After a period of time in delta sleep, our brain waves start to speed up and we go back through stages 3 and 2. However, as we reach stage 1, our brain produces a period of intense activity, our eyes dart back and forth, and many of our muscles may twitch repeatedly. This is *REM—rapid eye movement*. This sleep stage is sometimes called *paradoxical sleep* since our brain waves appear as active and intense as they do when we are awake. The exact purposes of REM are not clear, but some effects are known. Dreams usually occur in REM sleep. (Dreams can occur in any stage of sleep, but it is far more likely that any detailed dream occurs in REM.) REM sleep deprivation interferes with memory. Individuals deprived of REM sleep will experience REM rebound—experiencing more and longer periods of REM—the next time they are allowed to sleep normally. The more stress we experience during the day, the longer our periods of REM sleep will be.

Notice in Fig. 5.1 that not only do we cycle through these stages during the night, the cycle itself varies during the night. As we get closer to morning (or whenever we naturally awaken), we spend more time in stages 1 and 2 and in REM sleep and less in stages 3 and 4. Also, age affects the pattern. Babies not only spend more total time sleeping than we do (up to 18 hours), they also spend more time in REM sleep. As we age, our total need for sleep declines as does the amount of time we spend in REM sleep. Although research has not answered all the questions about sleep, details about our sleep cycle provide clues as to why we spend so much of our life in this altered state of consciousness.

Sleep Disorders

Many of us will experience a night, or perhaps a series of nights, of sleeplessness. These isolated periods of disruption in our sleep pattern give us an idea of the inconvenience and discomfort true sleep disorders can cause in people's lives. Sleep researchers identify and diagnose several sleep disorders.

Insomnia is far and away the most common sleep disorder, affecting up to 10 percent of the population. An insomniac has persistent problems getting to sleep or staying asleep at night. Most people will experience occasional bouts of insomnia, but diagnosed insomniacs have problems getting to sleep more often than not. Insomnia is usually treated with suggestions for changes in behavior: reduction of caffeine or other stimulants, exercise at appropriate times (not right before bedtime) during the day, and maintaining a consistent sleep pattern. Doctors and researchers encourage insomniacs to use sleeping pills only with caution, as they disturb sleep patterns during the night and can prevent truly restful sleep.

Narcolepsy occurs far more rarely than insomnia, occurring in less than 0.001 percent of the population. Narcoleptics suffer from periods of intense sleepiness and may fall asleep at unpredictable and inappropriate times. Narcoleptics may suddenly fall into REM sleep regardless of what they are doing at the time. One of my students suffered from narcolepsy from the time he was a preadolescent up until his graduation from high school. After he was finally diagnosed, he estimated that before his treatment he was drowsy almost his entire day except for two to three hours in the late afternoon. Narcolepsy can be successfully treated with medication and changing sleep patterns (usually involving naps at certain times of the day).

Sleep apnea may occur almost as commonly as insomnia and in some ways might be more serious. Apnea causes a person to stop breathing for short periods of time during the night. The body causes the person to wake up slightly and gasp for air, and then sleep continues. This process robs the person of deep sleep and causes tiredness and possible interference with attention and memory. Severe apnea can be fatal. Since these individuals do not remember waking up during the night, apnea frequently goes undiagnosed. Overweight men are at a higher risk for apnea. Apnea can be treated with a respiration machine that provides air for the person as he or she sleeps.

My mother tells me that I experienced *night terrors* as a child. I would sit up in bed in the middle of the night and scream and move around my room. Night terrors usually affect children, and most do not remember the episode when they wake up. The exact causes are not known, but night terrors are probably related in some way to *somnambulism* (sleep walking). They occur more commonly in children, and both phenomena occur during the first few hours of the night in stage 4 sleep. Most people stop having night terrors and episodes of somnambulism as they get older.

Dreams

Dreams are the series of storylike images we experience as we sleep. Some people remember dreams frequently, sometimes more than one per night, while others are not aware of whether we dream or not. Some of us even report lucid dreams in which we are aware that we are dreaming and can control the storyline of the dream. Dreams are a difficult research area for psychologists because they rely almost entirely on self-reports. As mentioned previously, researchers know that if people are awakened during or shortly after an REM episode, they often report they were dreaming. Researchers theorize about the purposes and meanings of dreams. However, validating these theories is difficult with the limited access researchers currently have to dreams.

Sigmund Freud considered dreams an important tool in his therapy. Freudian psychoanalysis emphasizes dream interpretation as a method to uncover the repressed information in the unconscious mind. Freud said that dreams were wish fulfilling, meaning that in our dreams we act out our unconscious desires. This type of dream analysis emphasizes two levels of dream content. *Manifest content* is the literal content of our dreams. If you dream about showing up at school naked, the manifest content is your nudity, the room you see yourself in at school, the people present, and so on. More important to Freud was the *latent content,* which is the unconscious meaning of the manifest content. Freud thought that even during sleep, our ego protected us from the material in the unconscious mind (thus the term *protected sleep*) by presenting these repressed desires in the form of symbols. So showing up naked at school would represent a symbol in this type of analysis, perhaps of vulnerability or anxiety. This type of dream analysis is common. Check any bookstore, and you will find multiple dream interpretation books based on this theory. However, popularity does not imply validity. Researchers point out that this theory is difficult to validate or invalidate. How do we know which are the correct symbols to examine and what they mean? The validity of the theory cannot be tested. Consequently, this analysis is mostly used in psychoanalytic therapy and in pop psychology rather than in research.

The *activation-synthesis theory* of dreaming looks at dreams first as biological phenomena. Brain imaging proves that our brain is very active during REM sleep. This theory proposes that perhaps dreams are nothing more than the brain's interpretations of what is happening physiologically during REM sleep. Researchers know that our minds are very good at explaining events, even when the events have a purely physiological cause. *Split-brain patients* (see page 40) sometimes make up elaborate explanations for behaviors caused by their operation. Dreams may be a story made up by a literary part of our mind caused by the intense brain activity during REM sleep. According to this theory, dreams, while interesting, have no more meaning than any other physiological reflex in your body.

The *information-processing theory* of dreaming falls somewhere in between the Freud and activation-synthesis theories. This theory points out that stress during the day will increase the number and intensity of dreams during the night. Also, most people report their dream content relates somehow to daily concerns. Proponents of information processing theorize that perhaps the brain is dealing with daily stress and information during REM dreams. The function of REM may be to integrate the information processed during the day into our memories. Babies may need more REM sleep than adults because they process so much new information every day.

Hypnosis

The high school where I teach usually hires a stage hypnotist to entertain at the postprom party. The day after students see the hypnotist's show, I can expect dozens of questions about the process of hypnosis and whether it is a valid psychological phenomenon or some sort of trick. Many of the questions concern some of the curious powers hypnotism seems to have. One of these is *posthypnotic amnesia,* when people report forgetting events that occurred while they were hypnotized. The hypnotists may also implant a *posthypnotic suggestion,* a suggestion that a hypnotized person behave in a certain way after he or she is brought out of hypnosis. Like many other topics regarding consciousness, many questions about hypnosis are not completely answered. However, at least three theories attempt to explain what goes on during hypnosis.

Role theory states that hypnosis is not an alternate state of consciousness at all. This theory points out that some people are more easily hypnotized than others, a characteristic called *hypnotic suggestibility.* People with high hypnotic suggestibility share some other characteristics as well. They tend to have a richer fantasy life, follow directions well, and are able to focus intensely on a single task for a long period of time. These factors may indicate that hypnotism is a social phenomenon. Perhaps during hypnosis, people are acting out the role of a hypnotized person and following the suggestions of the hypnotist because that is what is expected of the role.

Other researchers use *state theory* to explain hypnosis. They point out that hypnosis meets some parts of the definition for an altered state of consciousness. Hypnotists seem to be able to suggest that we become more or less aware of our environments. In addition, some people report dramatic health benefits from hypnosis, such as pain control and reduction in specific physical ailments.

Researcher Ernest Hilgard explained hypnosis in a different way in his *dissociation theory.* According to Hilgard, hypnosis causes us to divide our consciousness voluntarily. One part or level of our consciousness responds to the suggestions of the hypnotist, while another part or level retains awareness of reality. In an experiment investigating hypnotism and pain control, Hilgard asked hypnotized participants to put their arm in an ice water bath. Most of us would feel this intense cold as painful after a few seconds, but the hypnotized participants reported no pain. However, when Hilgard asked them to lift their index finger if any part of them felt the pain, most participants lifted their finger. This experiment demonstrated the presence of a hidden observer, a part or level of our consciousness that monitors what is happening while another level obeys the hypnotist's suggestions.

Drugs

Psychoactive drugs are chemicals that change the chemistry of the brain (and the rest of the body) and induce an altered state of consciousness. Some of the behavior and cognitive changes caused by these drugs are due to physiological processes, but some are due to expectations about the drug. Research shows that people will often exhibit some of the expected effects of the drug if they think they ingested it, even if they did not (this is similar to the placebo effect).

All psychoactive drugs change our consciousness through similar physiological processes in the brain. Normally, the brain is protected from harmful chemicals in the bloodstream by thicker walls surrounding the brain's blood vessels. This is called the *blood-brain barrier.* However, the molecules that make up psychoactive drugs are small enough to pass through the blood-brain barrier. These molecules either mimic or block naturally occurring neurotransmitters in the brain. The drugs that mimic neurotransmitters are called *agonists*. These drugs fit in the receptor sites on a neuron that normally receive the neurotransmitter and function as that neurotransmitter normally would. The drugs that block neurotransmitters are called *antagonists*. These molecules also fit into receptor sites on a neuron. However, instead of acting like the neurotransmitter, they simply prevent the natural neurotransmitters from using that receptor site. Other drugs prevent natural neurotransmitters from being reabsorbed back into a neuron, creating an abundance of that neurotransmitter in the synapse. No matter what mechanism they use, drugs gradually alter the natural levels of neurotransmitters in the brain. The brain will produce less of a specific neurotransmitter if it is being artificially supplied by a psychoactive drug.

This change causes *tolerance*, a physiological change that produces a need for more of the same drug in order to achieve the same effect. Tolerance will eventually cause *withdrawal* symptoms in users. Withdrawal symptoms vary from drug to drug. They range from the headache I might get if I do not consume any caffeine during the day to the dehydrating and potentially fatal night sweats (sweating profusely during sleep) a heroin addict experiences during withdrawal. Dependence on psychoactive drugs can be either psychological or physical or can be both. Persons psychologically dependent on a drug feel an intense desire for the drug because they are convinced they need it in order to perform or feel a certain way. Persons physically dependent on a substance have a tolerance for the drug, experience withdrawal symptoms without it, and need the drug to avoid the withdrawal symptoms. Different researchers categorize psychoactive drugs in different ways, but four common categories are stimulants, depressants, hallucinogens, and opiates.

Caffeine, cocaine, amphetamines, and nicotine are common *stimulants*. Stimulants speed up body processes, including autonomic nervous system functions such as heart and respiration rate. This dramatic increase is accompanied by a sense of euphoria. The more-powerful stimulants, such as cocaine, produce an extreme euphoric rush that may make a user feel extremely self-confident and invincible. All stimulants produce tolerance, withdrawal effects, and other side effects (such as disturbed sleep, reduced appetite, increased anxiety, and heart problems) to a greater or lesser degree that corresponds with the power of the drug.

Depressants slow down the same body systems that stimulants speed up. Alcohol, barbiturates, and anxiolytics (also called tranquilizers or antianxiety drugs) like Valium are common depressants. Obviously, alcohol is by far the most commonly used depressant and psychoactive drug. A euphoria accompanies the depressing effects of depressants, as does tolerance and withdrawal symptoms. In addition, alcohol slows down our reactions and judgment by slowing down brain processes. The inhibition of different brain regions causes behavioral changes. For example, when enough alcohol is ingested to affect the cerebellum, our motor coordination is dramatically affected, eventually making it difficult or impossible for the user to even stand. Because it is so widespread, more research has been done on alcohol than on any other psychoactive drug.

Hint: *Alcohol is categorized as a depressant because of its effect on our nervous system, even though some people report feeling more energized after ingesting a small amount of alcohol. This energizing effect is due to expectations about alcohol and because alcohol lowers inhibitions. Similarly, nicotine is a stimulant because it speeds up our nervous system, but some smokers smoke to relax.*

Hallucinogens (also sometimes called *psychedelics*) do not necessarily speed up or slow down the body. These drugs cause changes in perceptions of reality, including sensory hallucinations, loss of identity, and vivid fantasies. Common hallucinogens include LSD, peyote, psilocybin mushrooms, and marijuana. One notable feature of hallucinogens is their persistence. Some amount of these drugs may remain in the body for weeks. If an individual ingests the hallucinogen again during this time period, the new dose of the chemical is added to the lingering amount, creating more profound and potentially dangerous effects. This effect is sometimes called *reverse tolerance* because the second dose may be less than the first but cause the same or greater effects. Effects of hallucinogens are less predictable than those of stimulants or depressants.

Opiates such as morphine, heroin, methadone, and codeine are all similar in chemical structure to opium, a drug derived from the poppy plant. The opiates all act as agonists for endorphins and thus are powerful painkillers and mood elevators. Opiates cause drowsiness and a euphoria associated with elevated endorphin levels. The opiates are some of the most physically addictive drugs because they rapidly change brain chemistry and create tolerance and withdrawal symptoms.

Practice Questions

> *Directions:* Each of the questions or incomplete statements below is followed by five suggested answers or completions. Select the one that is best in each case.

1. Agonists are psychoactive drugs that
   - (A) produce tolerance to the drug without the associated withdrawal symptoms.
   - (B) mimic and produce the same effect as certain neurotransmitters.
   - (C) mimic neurotransmitters and block their receptor sites.
   - (D) enhance the effects of certain opiates like heroin.
   - (E) make recovery from physical addiction more difficult.

2. In comparison with older people, babies
   - (A) sleep more fitfully; they tend to wake up more often.
   - (B) sleep more deeply; they spend more time in stage 3 and 4 sleep.
   - (C) spend more time in the REM stage than other sleep stages.
   - (D) spend more time in stage 1, which causes them to awaken easily.
   - (E) sleep more than young adults but less than people over 50.

3. Which of the following is the best analogy for how psychologists view consciousness?
   - (A) The on/off switch on a computer.
   - (B) A circuit breaker that controls power to a house.
   - (C) A fuse that allows electricity to pass through until a short circuit occurs.
   - (D) A dimmer switch for a light fixture.
   - (E) The ignition switch on a car.

4. During a normal night's sleep, how many times do we pass through the different stages of sleep?
   - (A) 2
   - (B) 2–3
   - (C) 4–7
   - (D) 8–11
   - (E) 11–15

5. Which of the following is evidence supporting the role theory of hypnosis?
   - (A) People with rich fantasy lives are more hypnotizable.
   - (B) People will not behave under hypnosis in ways they would not without hypnosis.
   - (C) Hilgard's experiment demonstrated the presence of a hidden observer.
   - (D) Our heart and respiration rates may differ while under hypnosis.
   - (E) Some therapists successfully use hypnosis in therapy.

6. Activation-synthesis theory tries to explain
   (A) how consciousness emerges out of neural firings.
   (B) how psychoactive drugs create euphoric effects.
   (C) the origin and function of dreams.
   (D) how our mind awakens us after we pass through all the sleep stages.
   (E) how our consciousness synthesizes all the sensory information it receives.

7. Hilgard's experiment that demonstrated the presence of a hidden observer is evidence for which theory?
   (A) role theory of hypnosis
   (B) levels theory of consciousness
   (C) recuperative theory of sleep
   (D) dissociation theory of hypnosis
   (E) state theory of hypnosis

8. Which of the following two sleep disorders occur most commonly?
   (A) insomnia and narcolepsy
   (B) apnea and narcolepsy
   (C) night terrors and apnea
   (D) somnambulism and insomnia
   (E) apnea and insomnia

9. Marijuana falls under what category of psychoactive drug?
   (A) depressant
   (B) mood elevator
   (C) hallucinogen
   (D) stimulant
   (E) mood depressant

10. Night terrors and somnambulism usually occur during which stage of sleep?
    (A) stage 1, close to wakefulness
    (B) REM sleep
    (C) REM sleep, but only later in the night when nightmares usually occur
    (D) stage 4
    (E) sleep onset

11. Which neurotransmitter is affected by opiates?
    (A) serotonin
    (B) endorphins
    (C) dopamine
    (D) GABA
    (E) acetylcholine

12. In the context of this unit, the term *tolerance* refers to
    (A) treatment of psychoactive drug addicts by peers and other members of society.
    (B) the amount of sleep a person needs to function normally.
    (C) the need for an elevated dose of a drug in order to get the same effect.
    (D) the labeling of individuals automatically produced by the level of our consciousness.
    (E) the harmful side effects of psychoactive drugs.

13. The information-processing theory says that dreams
    (A) are meaningless by-products of how our brains process information during REM sleep.
    (B) are symbolic representations of the information we encode during the day.
    (C) are processed by one level of consciousness but other levels remain unaware of the dreams.
    (D) occur as the brain deals with daily stress and events during REM sleep.
    (E) occur only after stressful events, explaining why some people never dream.

14. Which level of consciousness controls involuntary body processes?
    (A) preconscious level
    (B) subconscious level
    (C) unconscious level
    (D) autonomic level
    (E) nonconscious level

15. Professor Bohkle shows a group of participants a set of geometric shapes for a short period of time. Later, Professor Bohlke shows the same group a larger set of shapes that includes the first set of geometric shapes randomly distributed among the other new images. When asked which shapes they prefer, the participants choose shapes from the first group more often than the new images, even though they cannot remember which images they had seen previously. This experiment demonstrates which concept?
    (A) priming
    (B) mere-exposure effect
    (C) shaping
    (D) primary-attribution error
    (E) primacy

Answers to Practice Questions

1. **(B)** Agonists fit into receptor sites for specific neurotransmitters and produce similar results. Choice C is a definition of antagonists. The other choices are incorrect distractions.

2. **(C)** Babies spend more time in REM. As we get older, the time spent in REM gradually decreases. The other choices are incorrect statements about the typical sleep patterns of infants.

3. **(D)** Psychologists define consciousness as our level of awareness of ourselves and our environment. A dimmer switch is the only analogy that implies a continuum from very dim to very bright with variations in between. Consciousness is not like an on/off switch as implied in the other choices.

4. **(C)** Most often, we cycle through the sleep stages around 5 to 6 times per night. The duration of a sleep cycle is approximately 90 minutes long.

5. **(A)** People who have richer fantasy lives are more easily hypnotizable. This finding supports role theory, the idea that people may be acting out a social role under hypnosis. Choice B is irrelevant and incorrect according to research. Hilgard's hidden observer is evidence for the dissociation theory of hypnosis. Choices D and E are true but are not evidence for role theory.

6. **(C)** Activation-synthesis theory states that dreams are a meaningless by-product of brain processes during REM sleep. The other choices do not relate to this theory.

7. **(D)** The hidden observer indicates that hypnosis might involve a dissociation of consciousness into different levels. Hilgard's experiments are evidence against the other theories of hypnosis, role and state theories. These experiments do not relate to general theories of consciousness or sleep.

8. **(E)** Research indicates that insomnia and apnea are the most common sleep disorders, even though apnea may be very underdiagnosed.

9. **(C)** Marijuana is a hallucinogen. Items B and E are not categories of psychoactive drugs.

10. **(D)** Sleepwalking and night terrors occur during stage 4 sleep and are unrelated to dreaming and REM sleep.

11. **(B)** Opiates mimic the effect of endorphins in the brain, producing the pain-killing and euphoric, dreamy state associated with these drugs.

12. **(C)** A person who uses psychoactive drugs gets an increased tolerance for the drugs, meaning they need more of the drugs to get the same effect. In this context, tolerance has nothing to do with the treatment or labeling of others or with sleep.

13. **(D)** Information-processing theory states that REM sleep and dreaming reflect the brain processing the stresses and events of our recent experience. Choice A is a definition of the activation-synthesis theory of dreams. Dreams and symbolic representations, choice B, fits Freud's theory of dreams best. Choices C and E are incorrect distractions.

14. **(E)** Automatic functions like heart rate are controlled by the nonconscious level. The levels mentioned in the other choices control other parts of consciousness, except for the autonomic level, which is a created distracter and not a correct term.

15. **(B)** The mere-exposure effect occurs when we prefer stimuli we have seen before over novel stimuli, even if we do not consciously remember seeing the old stimuli. Priming refers to our ability to answer questions we have been exposed to before, even if we do not remember having seen the questions. Shaping is a concept in operant conditioning, primary-attribution error is a concept in social psychology that describes our tendency to attribute a person's behavior to his or her inner disposition rather than environment. Primacy is a concept from the memory chapter.

CHAPTER 6

Learning

Overview

Psychologists differentiate between many different types of learning, a number of which we will discuss in this chapter. Learning is commonly defined as a long-lasting change in behavior resulting from experience. Although learning is not the same as behavior, most psychologists accept that learning can best be measured through changes in behavior. Brief changes are not thought to be indicative of learning. Consider, for example, the effects of running a marathon. For a short time afterward, one's behavior might differ radically, but we would not want to attribute this change to the effects of learning. In addition, learning must result from experience rather than from any kind of innate or biological change. Thus, changes in one's behavior as a result of puberty or menopause are not considered due to learning.

Classical Conditioning

Around the turn of the twentieth century, a Russian physiologist named Ivan Pavlov inadvertently discovered a kind of learning while studying digestion in dogs. Pavlov found that the dogs learned to pair the sounds in the environment where they were fed with the food that was given to them and began to salivate simply upon hearing the sounds. As a result, Pavlov deduced the basic principle of *classical conditioning*. People and animals can learn to associate neutral stimuli (for example, sounds) with stimuli that produce reflexive, involuntary responses (for example, food) and will learn to respond similarly to the new stimulus as they did to the old one (for example, salivate).

The original stimulus that elicits a response is known as the *unconditioned stimulus* (US or UCS). The US is defined as something that elicits a natural, reflexive response. In the classic Pavlovian paradigm, the US is food. Food elicits the natural, involuntary response of salivation. This response is called the *unconditioned response* (UR or UCR). Through repeated pairings with a neutral stimulus such as a bell, animals will come to associate the two stimuli together.

Ultimately, animals will salivate when hearing the bell alone. Once the bell elicits salivation, a *conditioned response* (CR), it is no longer a neutral stimulus but rather a *conditioned stimulus* (CS).

Learning has taken place once the animals respond to the CS without a presentation of the US. This learning is also called *acquisition* since the animals have acquired a new behavior. Many factors affect acquisition. For instance, up to a point, repeated pairings of CSs and USs yield stronger CRs. The order and timing of the CS and US pairings also have an impact on the strength of conditioning. Generally, the most effective method of conditioning is to present the CS first and then to introduce the US while the CS is still evident. Now return to Pavlov's dogs. Acquisition will occur fastest if the bell is rung and, while it is still ringing, the dogs are presented with food. This procedure is known as *delayed conditioning*. Less effective methods of learning include:

- *Trace conditioning*—The presentation of the CS, followed by a short break, followed by the presentation of the US.
- *Simultaneous conditioning*—CS and US are presented at the same time.
- *Backward conditioning*—US is presented first and is followed by the CS. This method is particularly ineffective.

Of course, what can be learned can be unlearned. In psychological terminology, the process of unlearning a behavior is known as *extinction*. In terms of classical conditioning, extinction has taken place when the CS no longer elicits the CR. Extinction is achieved by repeatedly presenting the CS without the US, thus breaking the association between the two. If one rings the bell over and over again and never feeds the dogs, the dogs will ultimately learn not to salivate to the bell.

One fascinating and yet-to-be-adequately-explained part of this process is known as *spontaneous recovery*. Sometimes, after a conditioned response has been extinguished and no further training of the animals has taken place, the response briefly reappears upon presentation of the conditioned stimulus. This phenomenon is known as spontaneous recovery.

Often animals conditioned to respond to a certain stimulus will also respond to similar stimuli, although the response is usually smaller in magnitude. The dogs may salivate to a number of bells, not just the one with which they were trained. This tendency to respond to similar CSs is known as *generalization*. Subjects can be trained, however, to tell the difference, or *discriminate,* between various stimuli. To train the dogs to discriminate between bells, we would repeatedly pair the original bell with presentation of food, but we would intermix trials where we presented other bells that we did not pair with food.

Classical conditioning can also be used with humans. In one famous, albeit ethically questionable, study, John Watson and Rosalie Rayner conditioned a little boy named Albert to fear a white rat. Albert initially liked the white, fluffy rat. However, by repeatedly pairing it with a loud noise, Watson and Rayner taught baby Albert to cry when he saw the rat. In this example, the loud noise is the US because it elicits the involuntary, natural response of fear (UR) and, in Albert's case, crying. The rat is the NS that becomes the CS, and the CR is crying in response to presentation of the rat alone. Albert also generalized, crying in response to a white rabbit, a man's white beard, and a variety of other white, fluffy things.

This example is an illustration of what is known as *aversive conditioning.* Whereas Pavlov's dogs were conditioned with something pleasant (food), baby Albert was conditioned to have a negative response to the white rat. Aversive conditioning has been used in a number of more socially constructive ways. For instance, to stop biting their nails, some people paint them with truly horrible-tasting materials. Nail biting therefore becomes associated with a terrible taste, and the biting should cease.

Once a CS elicits a CR, it is possible, briefly, to use that CS as a US in order to condition a response to a new stimulus. This process is known as *second-order* or *higher-order conditioning*. By using a dog and a bell as our example, after the dog salivates to the bell (first-order conditioning), the bell can be paired repeatedly with a flash of light, and the dog will salivate to the light alone (second-order conditioning), even though the light has never been paired with the food (see Table 6.1).

Table 6.1. First-Order and Second-Order Conditioning.

First-Order Conditioning	
Training:	Presentation of bell + food = salivation
Acquisition:	Presentation of bell = salivation

Second-Order Conditioning (After First-Order Conditioning Has Occurred)	
Training:	Presentation of light + bell = salivation
Acquisition:	Presentation of light = salivation

Biology and Classical Conditioning

As is evident from its description, classical conditioning can be used only when one wants to pair an involuntary, natural response with something else. Once one has identified such a US, can a subject be taught to pair it equally easily with any CS? Not surprisingly, the answer is no. Research suggests that animals and humans are biologically prepared to make certain connections more easily than others. *Learned taste aversions* are a classic example of this phenomenon. If you ingest an unusual food or drink and then become nauseous, you will probably develop an aversion to the food or drink. Learned taste aversions are interesting because they can result in powerful avoidance responses on the basis of a single pairing. In addition, the two events (eating and sickness) are probably separated by at least several hours. Animals, including people, seem biologically prepared to associate strange tastes with feelings of sickness. Clearly, this response is adaptive (helpful for the survival of the species), because it helps us learn to avoid dangerous things in the future. Also interesting is how we seem to learn what, exactly, to avoid. Taste aversions most commonly occur with strong and unusual tastes. The food, the CS, must be *salient* in order for us to learn to avoid it. Salient stimuli are easily noticeable and therefore create a more powerful conditioned response. Sometimes taste aversions are acquired without good reason. If you were to eat some mozzarella sticks a few hours before falling ill with the stomach flu, you might develop an aversion to that popular American appetizer even though it had nothing to do with your sickness.

Garcia and Koelling performed a famous experiment illustrating how rats more readily learned to make certain associations than others. They used four groups of subjects in their experiment and exposed each to a particular combination of CS and US as illustrated in Table 6.2.

Table 6.2. Garcia and Koelling's Experiment Illustrating Biological Preparedness in Classical Conditioning.

CS	US	Learned Response
Loud noise	Shock	Fear
Loud noise	Radiation (nausea)	Nothing
Sweet water	Shock	Nothing
Sweet water	Radiation (nausea)	Avoid water

The rats learned to associated noise with shock and unusual-tasting water with nausea. However, they were unable to make the connection between noise and nausea and between unusual-tasting water and shock. Again, learning to link loud noise with shock (for example, thunder and lightning) and unusual-tasting water with nausea seems to be adaptive.

Operant Conditioning

Whereas classical conditioning is a type of learning based on association of stimuli, *operant conditioning* is a kind of learning based on the association of consequences with one's behaviors. Edward Thorndike was one of the first people to research this kind of learning.

Thorndike conducted a series of famous experiments using a cat in a puzzle box. The hungry cat was locked in a cage next to a dish of food. The cat had to get out of the cage in order to get the food. Thorndike found that the amount of time required for the cat to get out of the box decreased over a series of trials. This amount of time decreased gradually; the cat did not seem to understand, suddenly, how to get out of the cage. This finding led Thorndike to assert that the cat learned the new behavior without mental activity but rather simply connected a stimulus and a response.

Thorndike put forth the *law of effect* that states that if the consequences of a behavior are pleasant, the stimulus-response (S-R) connection will be strengthened and the likelihood of the behavior will increase. However, if the consequences of a behavior are unpleasant, the S-R connection will weaken and the likelihood of the behavior will decrease. He used the term *instrumental learning* to describe his work because he believed the consequence was instrumental in shaping future behaviors.

B. F. Skinner, who coined the term operant conditioning, is the best-known psychologist to research this form of learning. Skinner invented a special contraption, aptly named a *Skinner box,* to use in his research of animal learning. A Skinner box usually has a way to deliver food to an animal and a lever to press or disk to peck in order to get the food. The food is called a *reinforcer,* and the process of giving the food is called *reinforcement.* Reinforcement is defined by its consequences; anything that makes a behavior more likely to occur is a reinforcer. Two kinds of reinforcement exist. *Positive reinforcement* refers to the addition of something pleasant. *Negative reinforcement* refers to the removal of something unpleasant. For instance, if we give a rat in a Skinner box food when it presses a lever, we are using positive reinforcement. However, if we terminate a loud noise or shock in response to a press of the lever, we are using negative reinforcement.

Affecting behavior by using unpleasant consequences is also possible. Such an approach is known as *punishment.* By definition, punishment is anything that makes a behavior less likely. The two types of punishment are known as *positive punishment* (usually referred to simply as "punishment"), which is the addition of something unpleasant, and *omission training* or *negative punishment,* the removal of something pleasant. If we give a rat an electric shock every time it touches the lever, we are using punishment. If we remove the rat's food when it touches the lever, we are using omission training. Both procedures will result in the rat ceasing to touch the bar (see Table 6.3 and 6.4).

Table 6.3. Reinforcement = A Consequence That Increases the Likelihood of a Behavior.

Types	Effects	Examples
Positive reinforcement	Adds something pleasant	Get a dollar
Negative reinforcement	Removes something unpleasant	Excuse from household chores

Table 6.4. Punishment = A Consquence That Decreases the Likelihood of a Behavior.

Types	Effects	Examples
Positive punishment	Adds something negative	Get a spanking
Omission training (also known as negative punishment)	Removes something pleasant	No dessert

Hint: Students often confuse negative reinforcement and punishment. However, any type of reinforcement *results in the behavior being more likely to be repeated. The* negative *in negative reinforcement refers to the fact that something is taken away. The* positive *in positive punishment indicates that something is added. In negative reinforcement, the removal of an aversive stimulus is what is reinforcing.*

Punishment Versus Reinforcement

Obviously, the same ends can be achieved through punishment and reinforcement. If I want students to be on time to my class, I can punish them for lateness or reward them for arriving on time. Punishment is operant conditioning's version of aversive conditioning. Punishment is most effective if it is delivered immediately after the unwanted behavior and if it is harsh. However, harsh punishment may also result in unwanted consequences such as fear and anger. As a result, most psychologists recommend that certain kinds of punishment (for example, physical punishment) be used sparingly if at all.

Two kinds of learning that specifically have to do with punishment are *escape learning* and *avoidance learning*. Escape learning allows one to terminate an aversive stimulus, while avoidance learning enables one to avoid the unpleasant stimulus altogether. If Sammy creates a ruckus in the English class he hates and is asked to leave, he is evidencing escape learning. An example of avoidance learning would be if Sammy simply cut English class.

You might wonder how the rat in the Skinner box learns to push the lever in the first place. Rather than wait for an animal to perform the desired behavior by chance, we usually try to speed up the process by using *shaping*. Shaping reinforces the steps used to reach the desired behavior. First the rat might be reinforced for going to the side of the box with the lever. Then we might reinforce the rat for touching the lever with any part of its body. By rewarding approximations of the desired behavior, we increase the likelihood that the rat will stumble upon the behavior we want.

Subjects can also be taught to perform a number of responses successively in order to get a reward. This process is known as *chaining*. One famous example of chained behavior involved a rat named Barnabus who learned to run through a veritable obstacle course in order to obtain a food reward. Whereas the goal of shaping is to mold a single behavior (e.g., a bar press by a rat), the goal in chaining is to link together a number of separate behaviors into a more complex activity (e.g., running an obstacle course).

The terms acquisition, extinction, spontaneous recovery, discrimination, and generalization can be used in our discussion of operant conditioning, too. By using a rat in a Skinner box as our example, acquisition occurs when the rat learns to press the lever to get the reward. Extinction occurs when the rat ceases to press the lever because the reward no longer results from this action. Note that punishing the rat for pushing the lever is not necessary to extinguish the response. Behaviors that are not reinforced will ultimately stop and are said to be on an extinction schedule. Spontaneous recovery would occur if, after having extinguished the bar press response and without providing any further training, the rat began to press the bar again. Generalization would be if the rat began to press other things in the Skinner box or the bar in other boxes. Discrimination would involve teaching the rat to press only a particular bar or to press the bar only under certain conditions (for example, when a tone is sounded). In the latter example, the tone is called a *discriminative stimulus*.

Not all reinforcers are food, of course. Psychologists speak of two main types of reinforcers: primary and secondary. *Primary reinforcers* are, in and of themselves, rewarding. They include things like food, water, and rest, whose natural properties are reinforcing. *Secondary reinforcers* are things we have learned to value such as praise or the chance to play a video game. Money is a special kind of secondary reinforcer, called a *generalized reinforcer,* because it can be traded for virtually anything. One practical application of generalized reinforcers is known as a *token economy.* In a token economy, every time people perform a desired behavior, they are given a token. Periodically, they are allowed to trade their tokens for any one of a variety of reinforcers. Token economies have been used in prisons, mental institutions, and even schools.

Intuitively, you probably realize that what functions as a reinforcer for some may not have the same effect on others. Even primary reinforcers, like food, will affect different animals in different ways depending, most notably, on how hungry they are. This idea, that the reinforcing properties of something depend on the situation, is expressed in the *Premack principle.* It explains that whichever of two activities is preferred can be used to reinforce the activity that is not preferred. For instance, if Peter likes apples but does not like to practice for his piano lesson, his mother could use apples to reinforce practicing the piano. In this case, eating an apple is the preferred activity. However, Peter's brother Mitchell does not like fruit, including apples, but he loves to play the piano. In his case, playing the piano is the preferred activity, and his mother can use it to reinforce him for eating an apple.

Reinforcement Schedules

When you are first teaching a new behavior, rewarding the behavior each time is best. This process is known as *continuous reinforcement.* However, once the behavior is learned, higher response rates can be obtained using certain partial-reinforcement schedules. In addition, according to the *partial-reinforcement effect,* behaviors will be more resistant to extinction if the animal has not been reinforced continuously.

Reinforcement schedules differ in two ways:

- What determines when reinforcement is delivered—the number of responses made (ratio schedules) or the passage of time (interval schedules).
- The pattern of reinforcement—either constant (fixed schedules) or changing (variable schedules).

A fixed-ratio (FR) schedule provides reinforcement after a set number of responses. For example, if a rat is on an FR-5, it will be rewarded after the fifth bar press. A variable-ratio (VR) schedule also provides reinforcement based on the number of bar presses, but that number varies. A rat on a VR-5 might be rewarded after the second press, the ninth press, the third press, the sixth press, and so on; the average number of presses required to receive a reward will be five.

A fixed-interval (FI) schedule requires that a certain amount of time elapse before a bar press will result in a reward. In an FI-3 minute, for instance, the rat will be reinforced for the first bar press that occurs after three minutes have passed. A variable-interval (VI) schedule varies the amount of time required to elapse before a response will result in reinforcement. In a VI-3 minute schedule, the rat will be reinforced for the first response made after an average time of three minutes.

Variable schedules are more resistant to extinction than fixed schedules. Once an animal becomes accustomed to a fixed schedule (being reinforced after x amount of time or y number of responses), a break in the pattern will quickly lead to extinction. However, if the reinforcement schedule has been variable, noticing a break in the pattern is much more difficult. In effect, variable schedules encourage continued responding on the chance that just one more response is needed to get the reward.

Hint: Variable schedules are more resistant to extinction than fixed schedules.

Biology and Operant Conditioning

Just as limits seem to exist concerning what one can classically condition animals to learn, limits seem to exist concerning what various animals can learn to do through operant conditioning. Researchers have found that animals will not perform certain behaviors that go against their natural inclinations. For instance, rats will not walk backward. In addition, pigs refuse to put disks into a banklike object and tend, instead, to bury the disks in the ground. The tendency for animals to forgo rewards to pursue their typical patterns of behavior is called *instinctive drift*.

Cognitive Learning

Radical behaviorists like Skinner assert that learning occurs without thought. However, cognitive theorists argue that even classical and operant conditioning have a cognitive component. In classical conditioning, such theorists argue that the subjects respond to the CS because they develop the expectation that it will be followed by the US. In operant conditioning, cognitive psychologists suggest that the subject is cognizant that its responses have certain consequences and can therefore act to maximize their reinforcement.

The Contingency Model of Classical Conditioning

The Pavlovian model of classical conditioning is known as the *contiguity model* because it postulates that the more times two things are paired, the greater the learning that will take place. Contiguity (togetherness) determines the strength of the response. Robert Rescorla revised the Pavlovian model to take into account a more complex set of circumstances. Suppose that dog 1, Rocco, is presented with a bell paired with food ten times in a row. Dog 2, Sparky, also experiences ten pairings of bell and food. However, intermixed with those ten trials are five trials in which food is presented without the bell and five more trials in which the bell is rung but no food is presented. Once these training periods are over, which dog will have a stronger salivation response to the bell? Intuitively, you will probably see that Rocco will, even though a model based purely on contiguity would hypothesize that the two dogs would respond the same since each has experienced ten pairings of bell and food.

Rescorla's model is known as the *contingency model* of classical conditioning and clearly rests upon a cognitive view of classical conditioning. *A* is contingent upon *B* when *A* depends upon *B* and vice versa. In such a case, the presence of one predicts the presence of the other. In Rocco's case, the food is contingent upon the presentation of the bell; one does not appear without the other. In Sparky's experience, sometimes the bell rings and no snacks are served, other times snacks appear without the annoying bell, and sometimes they appear together. Sparky learns less because, in her case, the relationship between the CS and US is not as clear. The difference in Rocco's and Sparky's responses strongly suggest that their expectations or thoughts influence their learning.

In addition to operant and classical conditioning, cognitive theorists have described a number of additional kinds of learning. These include observational learning, latent learning, abstract learning, and insight learning.

Observational Learning

As you are no doubt aware, people and animals learn many things simply by observing others. Watching children play house, for example, gives us an indication of all they have learned from watching their families and the families of others. Such *observational learning* is also known as *modeling* and was studied a great deal by Albert Bandura in formulating his social-learning theory. This type of learning is said to be species-specific; it only occurs between members of the same species.

Modeling has two basic components: observation and imitation. By watching his older sister, a young boy may learn how to hit a baseball. First, he observes her playing baseball with the neighborhood children in his backyard. Next, he picks up a bat and tries to imitate her behavior. Observational learning has a clear cognitive component in that a mental representation of the observed behavior must exist in order to enable the person or animal to imitate it. A significant body of research indicates that children learn violent behaviors from watching violent television programs and violent adult models.

Latent Learning

Latent learning was studied extensively by Edward Tolman. Latent means hidden, and latent learning is learning that becomes obvious only once a reinforcement is given for demonstrating it. Behaviorists had asserted that learning is evidenced by gradual changes in behavior, but Tolman conducted a famous experiment illustrating that sometimes learning occurs but is not immediately evidenced. Tolman had three groups of rats run through a maze on a series of trials. One group got a reward each time it completed the maze, and the performance of these rats improved steadily over the trials. Another group of rats never got a reward, and their performance improved only slightly over the course of the trials. A third group of rats was not rewarded during the first half of the trials but was given a reward during the second half of the trials. Not surprisingly, during the first half of the trials, this group's performance was very similar to the group that never got a reward. The interesting finding, however, was that the third group's performance improved dramatically and suddenly once it began to be rewarded for finishing the maze.

Tolman reasoned that these rats must have learned their way around the maze during the first set of trials. Their performance did not improve because they had no reason to run the maze quickly. Tolman credited their dramatic improvement in maze-running time to this latent learning. He suggested they had made a mental representation, or cognitive map, of the maze during the first half of the trials and evidenced this knowledge once it would earn them a reward.

Abstract Learning

Abstract learning involves understanding concepts such as *tree* or *same* rather than learning simply to press a bar or peck a disk in order to secure a reward. Some researchers have shown that animals in Skinner boxes seem to be able to understand such concepts. For instance, pigeons have learned to peck pictures they had never seen before if those pictures were of chairs. In other studies, pigeons have been shown a particular shape (for example, square or triangle) and rewarded in one series of trials when they picked the same shape out of two choices and in another set of trials when they pecked at the different shapes. Such studies suggest that pigeons can understand concepts and are not simply forming S-R connections, as Thorndike and Skinner had argued.

Insight Learning

Wolfgang Kohler is well known for his studies of *insight learning* in chimpanzees. Insight learning occurs when one suddenly realizes how to solve a problem. You have probably had the experience of skipping over a problem on a test only to realize later, in an instant, (we hope before you handed the test in) how to solve it.

Kohler argued that learning often happened in this sudden way due to insight rather than because of the gradual strengthening of the S-R connection suggested by the behaviorists. He put chimpanzees into situations and watched how they solved problems. In one study, Kohler suspended a banana from the ceiling well out of reach of chimpanzees. In the room were several boxes, none of which was high enough to enable the chimpanzees to reach the banana. Kohler found the chimpanzees spent most of their time unproductively rather than slowly working toward a solution. They would run around, jump, and be generally upset about their inability to snag the snack until, all of a sudden, they would pile the boxes on top of each other, climb up, and grab the banana. Kohler believed that the solution could not occur until the chimpanzees had a cognitive insight about how to solve the problem.

Practice Questions

> *Directions:* Each of the questions or incomplete statements below is followed by five suggested answers or completions. Select the one that is best in each case.

1. Just before something scary happens in a horror film, they often play scary-sounding music. When I hear the music, I tense up in anticipation of the scary event. In this situation, the music serves as a
   (A) US.
   (B) CS.
   (C) UR.
   (D) CR.
   (E) NR.

2. Try as you might, you are unable to teach your dog to do a somersault. He will roll around on the ground, but he refuses to execute the gymnastic move you desire because of
   (A) equipotentiality.
   (B) preparedness.
   (C) instinctive drift.
   (D) chaining.
   (E) shaping.

3. Which of the following is an example of a generalized reinforcer?
   (A) chocolate cake
   (B) water
   (C) money
   (D) applause
   (E) high grades

4. In teaching your cat to jump through a hoop, which reinforcement schedule would facilitate the most rapid learning?
   (A) continuous
   (B) fixed ratio
   (C) variable ratio
   (D) fixed interval
   (E) variable interval

5. The classical conditioning training procedure in which the US is presented first is known as
   (A) backward conditioning.
   (B) forward conditioning.
   (C) simultaneous conditioning.
   (D) delayed conditioning.
   (E) regular conditioning.

6. Tina likes to play with slugs, but she can find them by the shed only after it rains. On what kind of reinforcement schedule is Tina's slug hunting?
   (A) continuous
   (B) fixed interval
   (C) fixed ratio
   (D) variable interval
   (E) variable ratio

7. Just before the doors of the elevator close, Lola, a coworker you despise, enters the elevator. You immediately leave, mumbling about having forgotten something. Your behavior results in
   (A) positive reinforcement.
   (B) a secondary reinforcer.
   (C) punishment.
   (D) negative reinforcement.
   (E) omission training.

8. Which researcher studied latent learning?
   (A) Kohler
   (B) Bandura
   (C) Tolman
   (D) Watson
   (E) Skinner

9. Many psychologists believe that children of parents who beat them are likely to beat their own children. One possible explanation for this phenomenon is
   (A) modeling.
   (B) latent learning.
   (C) abstract learning.
   (D) instrumental learning.
   (E) classical conditioning.

10. When Tito was young, his parents decided to give him a quarter every day he made his bed. Tito started to make his siblings' beds also and help with other chores. Behaviorists would say that Tito was experiencing
    (A) internal motivation.
    (B) spontaneous recovery.
    (C) acquisition.
    (D) generalization.
    (E) discrimination.

11. A rat evidencing abstract learning might learn
    (A) to clean and feed itself by watching its mother perform these activities.
    (B) to associate its handler's presence with feeding time.
    (C) to press a bar when a light is on but not when its cage is dark.
    (D) the layout of a maze without hurrying to get to the end.
    (E) to press a lever when he sees pictures of dogs but not cats.

12. With which statement would B. F. Skinner most likely agree?
    (A) Pavlov's dog learned to expect that food would follow the bell.
    (B) Baby Albert thought the white rat meant the loud noise would sound.
    (C) All learning is observable.
    (D) Pigeons peck disks knowing that they will receive food..
    (E) Cognition plays an important role in learning.

13. Before his parents will read him a bedtime story, Charley has to brush his teeth, put on his pajamas, kiss his grandmother goodnight, and put away his toys. This example illustrates
    (A) shaping.
    (B) acquisition.
    (C) generalization.
    (D) chaining.
    (E) a token economy.

14. Which of the following is an example of positive reinforcement?
    (A) Buying a child a video game after she throws a tantrum.
    (B) Going inside to escape a thunderstorm.
    (C) Assigning a student detention for fighting.
    (D) Getting a cavity filled at the dentist to halt a toothache.
    (E) Depriving a prison inmate of sleep.

15. Lily keeps poking Jared in Mr. Clayton's third-grade class. Mr. Clayton tells Jared to ignore Lily. Mr. Clayton is hoping that ignoring Lily's behavior will
    (A) punish her.
    (B) extinguish the behavior.
    (C) negatively reinforce the behavior.
    (D) cause Lily to generalize.
    (E) make the behavior latent.

Answers to Practice Questions

1. **(B)** The music before a scary event in a horror movie serves as a CS. It is something we associate with a fear-inducing event (the US). In this example, preparing to be scared is the CR and the fear caused by the event in the movie is the UR. There is no such thing as a NR.

2. **(C)** Instinctive drift limits your pet's gymnastic abilities. Instinctively, your dog will perform certain behaviors and will drift toward these rather than learning behaviors that go against his nature. Equipotentiality is the opposite position that asserts that any animal can be conditoned to do anything. Preparedness refers to a biological predisposition to learn some things more quickly than others. Preparedness explains why teaching a dog to fetch a stick is easier than teaching it to do a somersault. Chaining is when one has to perform a number of discrete steps in order to secure a reward. Shaping is the process one might use in teaching a dog any new trick. Shaping is when you begin by reinforcing steps preceding the desired response.

3. **(C)** Money is a generalized reinforcer because it can be exchanged for so many things that it is reinforcing to virtually everybody. Chocolate cake (food) and water are examples of primary reinforcers, while applause and high grades are examples of secondary reinforcers.

4. **(A)** In teaching your cat to jump through a hoop, continuous reinforcement would result in the most rapid learning. New behaviors are learned most quickly when they are rewarded every time. However, once the skill has been learned, partial reinforcement will make the behaviors more resistant to extinction.

5. **(A)** The classical conditioning training procedure in which the US is presented first is known as backward conditioning since, in most other procedures, the CS is presented first. Simultaneous conditioning, as the name suggests, is when the CS and US are presented at the same time. Delayed conditioning is when the CS is presented first and overlaps the presentation of the US.

6. **(D)** Tina's slug hunting is rewarded on a variable-interval schedule. The passage of time is a key element in when she is reinforced because the slugs appear only after it rains. Since rain does not fall on a fixed schedule (for example, every third day), she is on a VI schedule. If she were on a continuous schedule, she would find slugs whenever she looked. If the slugs appeared every three days, Tina would be on a fixed-interval schedule. If she needed to turn over three rocks to find a slug, she would be on a fixed-ratio schedule. If the number of rocks she needed to turn over varied, she would be on a variable-ratio schedule.

7. **(D)** Exiting the elevator to avoid Lola is an example of negative reinforcement. Your behavior, leaving the elevator, is reinforced by the removal of an aversive stimulus (Lola). Remember that reinforcement (including negative reinforcement) always increases the likelihood of a behavior as opposed to punishment, which decreases the likelihood of a behavior.

8. **(C)** Tolman is known for his work on latent learning, learning that occurs in the absence of a reward but remains hidden until a reward is made available. Tolman's study involved three groups of rats running a maze under various contingencies of reinforcement.

9. **(A)** Many psychologists believe that children of parents who beat them are likely to beat their own children. One possible explanation for this phenomenon is modeling. Modeling, or observational learning, is the idea that people or animals can learn from watching and copying the behavior of others.

10. **(D)** Tito's new bed-making and chore-doing regime indicates that he is generalizing. Just as a rat will press other levers in other cages, Tito is performing more chores in an attempt to maximize his rewards. Behaviorists minimize the role of internal motivation; they believe that the environment motivates. Spontaneous recovery would be if Tito began making his bed again after his parents had stopped rewarding him and he had returned to his slovenly ways. Acquisition occurred when Tito initially learned to make his bed to earn the quarter. By assuming Tito's parents do not reward him for making the rest of the family's beds, he will learn ultimately to discriminate and make only his own bed.

11. **(E)** A rat evidencing abstract learning would learn to press a bar when shown pictures of dogs but not pictures of cats. In this example, the rat has learned the abstract concept of dog. Learning to clean and feed itself by watching its mother would be an example of modeling. Learning to associate a person's presence with food is classical conditioning. Learning to respond only when a light is on is an example of discrimination training. Making a cognitive map of a maze without hurrying through the maze is an example of latent learning.

12. **(C)** B. F. Skinner believed that all learning was observable. He did not believe that learning had a cognitive component but, rather, took a radical behaviorist position that behavior was all there was. All the other choices suggest learning has a cognitive component (expectation, thought, knowing, cognition), and therefore Skinner would disagree with them.

13. **(D)** Charley needs to chain together a series of behaviors in order to get a reward (the bedtime story). Shaping is reinforcing approximations of a desired behavior, usually in an effort to teach it. Acquisition, in operant conditioning, is the learning of a behavior. Generalization is when one performs similar behaviors to those that will result in reinforcement. A token economy uses generalized reinforcers to control people's behavior.

14. **(A)** Buying a child a video game after she throws a tantrum is an example of positively reinforcing a behavior you probably do not want (the tantrum). This example raises an important point: the word *positive* in positive reinforcement refers to the addition of a reinforcer and not to the goodness or badness of the act that is being reinforced. Going inside to escape a thunderstorm and getting a cavity filled at the dentist to halt a toothache are both examples of negative reinforcement (removing something unpleasant). Assigning a student detention for fighting is an example of punishment (adding something unpleasant), depriving someone of sleep is an example of omission training (removing something pleasant).

15. **(B)** Mr. Clayton is hoping that ignoring Lily's behavior will extinguish the behavior. Something that is not reinforced is put onto an extinction schedule.

CHAPTER 7

Cognition

Overview of Memory

The central question of memory research is: What causes us to remember what we remember and to forget what we forget? Memory is defined by researchers as any indication that learning has persisted over time. You might remember the bully who pushed you into the mud in second grade but forget your appointment with the school counselor. What are the processes that determine which events stick in our memories? Why and how do we lose information from memory? How accurate are our memories? Researchers do not have the final answers to any of these questions. However, models and principles of memory have emerged from the research that give us insight into how we remember.

Models of Memory

Several different models, or explanations, of how memory works have emerged from memory research. We will review two of the most important models: the three-box/information-processing model and the levels of processing model. Neither model is perfect. They describe how memory works in different ways and can describe some memory experiences better than others.

Three-Box/Information-Processing Model

The principle model of memory is the three-box model, also called the information-processing model. This model proposes the three stages that information passes through before it is stored (see Fig. 7.1).

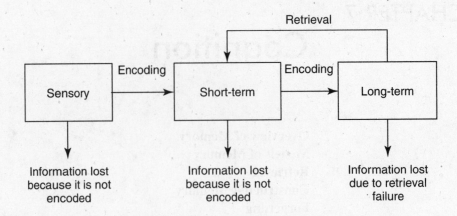

Figure 7.1. The three-box/information-processing model.

External events are first processed by our sensory memory. Then some information is encoded into our short-term (or working) memory. Some of that information is then encoded into long-term memory.

Hint: Do not take this memory model too literally. The model describes the process, not physical structures. There is not one spot in the brain that is the long-term memory spot. Memories are distributed around the cortex. Researchers use the model to describe the process rather than define how and where the brain stores memories physically.

Sensory Memory

The first stop for external events is *sensory memory*. It is a split-second holding tank for incoming sensory information. All the information your senses are processing right now is held in sensory memory for a very short period of time (less than a second). Researcher George Sperling demonstrated this in a series of experiments in which he flashed a grid of nine letters, three rows and three columns, to participants for 1/20th of a second. The participants in the study were directed to recall either the top, middle, or bottom row immediately after the grid was flashed at them. (Sperling used a high, medium, or low tone to indicate which row they should recall.) The participants could recall any of the three rows perfectly. This experiment demonstrated that the entire grid must be held in sensory memory for a split second. This type of sensory memory is called *iconic memory,* a split-second perfect photograph of a scene. Other experiments demonstrate the existence of *echoic memory,* an equally perfect split-second memory for sounds.

Most of the information in sensory memory is not encoded, however. Only some of it is encoded, or stored, in *short-term memory.* Events are encoded as visual codes (a visual image), acoustic codes (a series of sounds), or semantic codes (a sense of the meaning of the event). What determines which sensory messages get encoded? *Selective attention.* We encode what we are attending to or what is important to us. Try the following experiment. Pay attention to how your feet feel in your socks right now. You feel this now because the sensory messages from your feet are encoded from sensory memory into short-term memory. Why did you not feel your feet before? Because the messages entered sensory memory but were not encoded because you were not selectively attending to them. Sometimes selective attention is not as controlled. You have probably had the experience of speaking with one person at a party but then hearing someone say your name across the room. You were selectively attending to the person you were talking to. However, once a sensory message entered sensory memory that you knew was important (like your name or hearing someone shout "Fire!") you switched your attention to that message, and it was encoded into your short-term memory. (This is also called the *cocktail party* effect, see page 51 for more information about this phenomenon.)

Short-term/Working Memory

Short-term memory is also called working memory because these are memories we are currently working with and are aware of in our consciousness. Everything you are thinking at the current moment is held in your short-term or working memory. Short-term memories are also temporary. If we do nothing with them, they usually fade in 10 to 30 seconds. Our capacity in short-term memory is limited on average to around seven items, but this limit can be expanded through a process called *chunking*. If you want to remember a grocery list with 15 items on it, you should chunk, or group, the items into no more than seven groups. Most *mnemonic devices,* memory aids, are really examples of chunking. If you memorized the names of the planets by remembering the sentence "My very excellent mother just served us nine pizzas," you chunked the names of the planets into the first letters of the words in one sentence.

Another way to retain information in short-term memory is to *rehearse* (or repeat) it. When you look up a phone number and repeat it to yourself on the way to the phone, you are rehearsing that information. Simple repetition can hold information in short-term memory, but other strategies are more effective in ensuring short-term memories are encoded into long-term memory.

Long-term Memory

Since memories fade from sensory and short-term memory so quickly, we obviously need a more permanent way to remember events. Long-term memory is our permanent storage. As far as we know, the capacity of long-term memory is unlimited. No one reports their memory as being full and unable to encode new information. Studies show that once information reaches long-term memory, we will likely remember it for the rest of our lives. However, memories can decay or fade from long-term memory, so it is not truly permanent (see the section on forgetting, page 106). Long-term memories can be stored in three different formats:

Episodic memory	Memories of specific events, stored in a sequential series of events. Example: remembering the last time you went on a date.
Semantic memory	General knowledge of the world, stored as facts, meanings, or categories rather than sequentially. Example: What is the difference between the terms *effect* and *affect*?
Procedural memory	Memories of skills and how to perform them. These memories are sequential but might be very complicated to describe in words. Example: How to throw a curveball.

Memories can also be implicit or explicit. *Explicit memories* (also called declarative memories) are what we usually think of first. They are the conscious memories of facts or events we actively tried to remember. When you study this chapter, you try to form explicit memories about the memory theories. *Implicit memories* (also called nondeclarative memories) are unintentional memories that we might not even realize we have. For example, while your are helping your friend clean her house, you might find that you have implicit memories about how to scrub a floor properly after watching your parents do it for so many years.

Memory researchers are particularly interested in individuals who demonstrate *eidetic,* or *photographic, memory.* Psychologist Alexandra Luria studied a patient with eidetic memory who could repeat a list of 70 letters or digits. The patient could even repeat the list backward or recall it up to 15 years later! Luria and other researchers showed that these rare individuals seem to use very powerful and enduring visual images.

Hint: Some people say they have a photographic memory when what they mean is very good memory. True eidetic memory occurs very rarely. Most of us could enhance our memories through training with mnemonic devices, context, and visual imagery.

Levels of Processing Model

An alternate way to think about memory is the levels of processing model. This theory explains why we remember what we do by examining how deeply the memory was processed or thought about. Memories are neither short- nor long-term. They are *deeply* (or *elaboratively*) *processed* or *shallowly* (or *maintenance*) *processed.* If you simply repeat a fact to yourself several times and then write it on your test as quickly as you can, you have only shallowly processed that fact and you will forget it quickly. However, if you study the context and research the reasons behind the fact, you have deeply processed it and will likely recall it later. According to the levels of processing theory, we remember things we spend more cognitive time and energy processing. This theory explains why we remember stories better than a simple recitation of events and why, in general, we remember questions better than statements. When we get caught up in a story or an intriguing question, we process them deeply and are therefore more likely to remember them.

Retrieval

The last step in any memory model is retrieval, or getting information out of memory so we can use it. There are two different kinds of retrieval: recognition and recall. *Recognition* is the process of matching a current event or fact with one already in memory (for example, "Have I smelled this smell before?"). *Recall* is retrieving a memory with an external cue (for example, "What does my Aunt Beki's perfume smell like?"). Studies have identified several factors that influence why we can retrieve some memories and why we forget others.

One factor is the order in which the information is presented. Many studies demonstrate the primacy and recency effects. The *primacy effect* predicts that we are more likely to recall items presented at the beginning of a list. The *recency effect* is demonstrated by our ability to recall the items at the end of a list. Items in the middle are most often forgotten. Together the primacy and recency effect demonstrate the *serial position effect* (also called *serial position curve*). This effect is seen when recall of a list is affected by the order of items in a list.

Context is an important factor in retrieval. Have you ever tried to remember someone's name and start listing things about their appearance or personality until you finally come up with the name? This temporary inability to remember information is sometimes called the *tip-of-the-tongue-phenomenon*. One theory that explains why this might work is the *semantic network theory*. This theory states that our brain might form new memories by connecting their meaning and context with meanings already in memory. Thus, our brain creates a web of interconnected memories, each one in context tied to hundreds or thousands of other memories. So, by listing traits, you gradually get closer and closer to the name and you are finally able to retrieve it. Context also explains another powerful memory experience we all have. If you ask your parents where they were when Kennedy was shot or the shuttle Challenger exploded, they are likely to give you a detailed description of exactly what they were doing at that time. These *flashbulb memories* are powerful because the importance of the event caused us to encode the context surrounding the event. However, some studies show that flashbulb memories can be inaccurate. Perhaps we tend to construct parts of the memory to fill in gaps in our stories (see "Constructive Memory," below).

The emotional or situational context of a memory can affect retrieval in yet another way. Studies consistently demonstrate the power of *mood-congruent memory* or the greater likelihood of recalling an item when our mood matched the mood we were in when the event happened. We are likely to recall happy events when we are happy and recall negative events when we are feeling pessimistic. *State-dependent memory* refers to the phenomenon of recalling events encoded while in particular states of consciousness. If you suddenly remember an appointment while you are drowsy and about to go to sleep, you need to write it down. Very possibly, you will not remember it again until you are drowsy and in the same state of consciousness. Alcohol and other drugs affect memory in similar ways.

Constructive Memory

Maybe you have seen media coverage of the *"recovered memory"* phenomenon. Individuals claim suddenly to remember events they have "repressed" for years, often in the process of therapy. Parents have been accused of molesting and even killing children based on these recovered memories. While some of the memories can be corroborated by other means, memory researchers like Elizabeth Loftus have shown that many of these memories may be constructed or false recollections of events. A *constructed memory* can report false details of a real event or might even be a recollection of an event that never occurred. Studies show that leading questions can easily influence us to recall false details, and questioners can create an entirely new memory by repeatedly asking insistent questions. Constructed memories feel like accurate memories to the person recalling them. The only way to differentiate between a false and a real memory is through other types of evidence, such as physical evidence or other validated reports of the event. While some genuine memories may be recalled after being forgotten for years, researchers and therapists are investigating ways to ensure memories are accurate and innocent people are not accused of acts they did not commit.

Forgetting

Sometimes, despite our best efforts, we forget important events or facts that we try and want to remember. One cause of forgetting is decay, forgetting because we do not use a memory or connections to a memory for a long period of time. For example, you might memorize the state capitals for a civics test but forget many of them soon after the test because you do not need to recall them. However, your studying was not in vain! Even memories that decay do not seem to disappear completely. Many studies show an important *relearning* effect. If you have to memorize the capitals again, it will take you less time than it did the first time you studied them.

Another factor that causes forgetting is *interference*. Sometimes other information in your memory competes with what you are trying to recall. Interference can occur through two processes:

Retroactive interference	Learning new information interferes with the recall of older information. If you study your psychology at 3:00 and your sociology at 6:00, you might have trouble recalling the psychology information on a test the next day.
Proactive interference	Older information learned previously interferes with the recall of information learned more recently. If a researcher reads you a list of items in a certain order, then rereads them differently and asks you to list them in the new order, the old list proactively interferes with recall of the new list.

Hint: Some students find remembering the difference between retroactive and proactive interference difficult. Focus on which type of information is trying to be recalled. If old information is what you are searching for, retroactive (older) interference most likely applies. If you are searching for newer information, proactive (new) interference might take place.

How Memories Are Physically Stored in the Brain

Researchers know some of the brain processes and structures involved in memory, but much of this process is still a mystery. By studying patients with specific brain damage, we know that the hippocampus is important in encoding new memories. However, other brain structures are involved. Individuals with damage to the hippocampus might have *anterograde amnesia* (they cannot encode new memories), but they can recall events already in memory. They can learn new skills, although they will not remember learning them. This indicates that the memory for these skills, or procedural memory, is stored elsewhere in the brain (studies on animals indicate procedural memories are stored in the cerebellum).

At the neurological level, researchers focus on a process called *long-term potentiation*. Studies show that neurons can strengthen connections between each other. Through repeated firings, the connection is strengthened and the receiving neuron becomes more sensitive to the messages from the sending neuron. This strengthened connection might be related to the connections we make in our long-term memory.

Language

For us to conceive of thought without language is impossible. Your brain is processing the language you are reading right now. If you stop to think about the previous sentence, you think about it using language. Language is intimately connected to cognition. Some psychologists investigate how language works and how we acquire it in an attempt to understand better how we think and behave.

Elements of Language

All languages can be described with *phonemes* and *morphemes*. Phonemes are the smallest units of sound used in a language. English speakers use approximately 44 phonemes. If you have studied another language or if your primary language is not English, you have experience with other phonemes. Native Spanish speakers find the rolled *R* phoneme natural, but many English speakers have difficulty learning how to produce it since it is not used in English. Speakers of other languages have difficulty learning some English phonemes.

A morpheme is the smallest unit of meaningful sound. Morphemes can be words, such as *a* and *but,* or they can be parts of words, such as the prefixes *an-* and *pre-*. So language consists of phonemes put together to become morphemes, which make up words. These words are then spoken or written in a particular order, called syntax. Each language has its own syntax, such as where the verb is usually placed in the sentence. By examining phonemes, morphemes, and syntax (the grammar of a language), psychologists can describe different languages in detail.

Language Acquisition

Many psychologists are particularly interested in how we learn language. Often, developmental psychologists are curious about how our language learning reflects or predicts our cognitive development. These studies show that while babies are learning very different languages, they progress through the same basic stages in order to master the language. First, if you have ever been around babies, you know that babies babble. This is often cute, and it is the first stage of *language acquisition*. The babbling stage appears to be innate; even babies born completely deaf go through the babbling stage. A baby's babble represents experimentation with phonemes. They are learning what sounds they are capable of producing. Babies in this stage are capable of producing any phoneme from any language in the world. So while you may not be able to roll your *R*s, your infant sister can! As language acquisition progresses, we retain the ability to produce phonemes from our primary language (or languages) and lose the ability to make some other phonemes. This is one reason why learning more than one language starting at infancy may be advantageous. Babbling progresses into utterances of words as babies imitate the words they hear caregivers speaking.

The next language acquisition stage is *telegraphic speech*. Toddlers will combine the words they can say into simple commands. Meaning is usually clear at this stage, but syntax is absent. When your little brother shouts, "No book, movie!" you know that he means, "I do not wish to read a book at this time. I would prefer to watch a movie." Children begin to learn grammar and syntax rules during this stage, sometimes misapplying the rules. For example, they might learn that adding the suffix *-ed* signifies past tense, but they might apply it at inappropriate times, such as, "Marky hitted my head so I throwed the truck at him." Children gradually increase their abilities to combine words in proper syntax if these uses are modeled for them. This misapplication of grammar rules is called *overgeneralization*.

One important controversy in language acquisition concerns how we acquire language. Behaviorists theorized that language is learned like other learned behaviors: through operant conditioning and shaping. They thought that when children used language correctly, they got rewarded by their parents with a smile or other encouragement, and therefore they would be more likely to use language correctly in the future. More recently, cognitive psychologists challenged this theory. They point out the amazing number of words and language rules learned by children without explicit instruction by parents. Researcher Noam Chomsky theorized that humans are born with a *language acquisition device*, the ability to learn a language rapidly as children (this is also called the *nativist theory* of *language acquisition*). Chomsky pointed to the retarded development of language in cases of children deprived of exposure to language during childhood. He theorized that a critical period for learning language may exist. Most psychologists now agree that we acquire language through some combination of conditioning and an inborn propensity to learn language.

Language and Cognition

If language is central to the way we think, how does it influence what we are able to think about? Psychologist Benjamin Whorf theorized that the language we use might control, and in some ways limit, our thinking. This theory is called the *linguistic relativity hypothesis*. Many studies demonstrate the effect of labeling on how we think about people, objects, or ideas, but few studies show that the language we speak drastically changes what we can think about.

Thinking and Creativity

Describing Thought

Trying to describe thought is problematic. Descriptions are thoughts, so we are attempting to describe thought using thought itself. A global, all-inclusive definition of thought is difficult, but psychologists try to define types or categories of thoughts. *Concepts* are similar to the schemata mentioned previously. We each have cognitive rules we apply to stimuli from our environment that allow us to categorize and think about the objects, people, and ideas we encounter. These rules are concepts. Our concept of mom is different from our concept of dad, which is different from our concept of a soccer game. We may base our concepts on *prototypes* or what we think is the most typical example of a particular concept.

Another type of thought, *images,* are the mental pictures we create in our minds of the outside world. Images can be visual, such as imagining what your cat looks like. However, images can also be auditory, tactile, olfactory, or an image of a taste, such as thinking about what hot chocolate tastes like on a very cold day.

Problem Solving

Many researchers try to study thought by examining the results of thinking. Researchers can ask participants to solve problems and then investigate how the solutions were reached. This research indicates at least two different problem-solving methods we commonly use and some traps to avoid when solving a problem.

Algorithms

One way to solve a problem is to try every possible solution. An algorithm is a rule that guarantees the right solution by using a formula or other foolproof method. If you are trying to guess a computer password and you know it is a combination of only two letters, you could use an algorithm and guess pairs of letters in combination until you hit the right one. What if the password is a combination of five letters, not two? Sometimes algorithms are impractical, so a shortcut is needed to solve certain problems.

Heuristics

A heuristic is a rule of thumb—a rule that is generally, but not always, true that we can use to make a judgment in a situation. For example, if you are trying to guess the password mentioned previously, you might begin by guessing actual five-letter words rather than random combinations of letters. The password might be a meaningless combination of letters, but you know that passwords are most often actual words. This heuristic limits the possible combinations dramatically. The following shows two specific examples of heuristics.

| Availability heuristic | Judging a situation based on examples of similar situations that come to mind initially. This heuristic might lead to incorrect conclusions due to variability in personal |

Representativeness heuristic

experience. For example, a person may judge his or her neighborhood to be more dangerous than others in the city simply because that person is more familiar with violence in his or her neighborhood than in other neighborhoods. Judging a situation based on how similar the aspects are to prototypes the person holds in his or her mind. For example, a person might judge a young person more likely to commit suicide because of a prototype of the depressed adolescent when, in fact, suicide rates are not higher in younger populations.

Use of these heuristics can lead to specific problems in judgments. Overconfidence is our tendency to overestimate how accurate our judgments are. How confident we are in a judgment is not a good indicator of whether or not we are right. In studies, most people will report extreme confidence in a judgment that turns out to be wrong in a significant number of cases. Two concepts closely related to overconfidence are *belief bias* and *belief perseverance*. Both of these concepts concern our tendency not to change our beliefs in the face of contradictory evidence. Belief bias occurs when we make illogical conclusions in order to confirm our preexisting beliefs. Belief perseverance refers to our tendency to maintain a belief even after the evidence we used to form the belief is contradicted. Overall, these concepts demonstrate that humans are generally more confident in our beliefs than we should be, and we often stick with our beliefs even when presented with evidence that disproves them.

Impediments to Problem Solving

Problem-solving research identifies some common mistakes people make while trying to solve problems. *Rigidity* (also called *mental set*) refers to the tendency to fall into established thought patterns. Most people will use solutions or past experience to try to solve novel problems. Occasionally, this tendency prevents them from seeing a novel solution. One specific example of rigidity is *functional fixedness,* the inability to see a new use for an object. One of my students recently got his car stuck up to the axles in mud. Our attempts to pull him out failed until another student pointed out we could use the car jack to raise the car and put planks under the tires. Most of us thought of the jack only as a tool to help with a flat tire, not getting a car out of the mud. Another common trap in problem solving is not breaking the problem into parts. Studies show that good problem solvers identify subgoals, smaller and more manageable problems they need to solve in order to solve the whole problem. Tackling the problem in these smaller parts help good problem solvers be more successful.

Another obstacle to successful problem solving is *confirmation bias*. Many studies show that we tend to look for evidence that confirms our beliefs and ignore evidence that contradicts what we think is true. As a consequence, we may miss evidence important to finding the correct solution. For example, when I prepare my students for the AP test, I may emphasize studying techniques or information that I am familiar with and think are very important. What I think is important may be very different than what the designers of the test emphasize. My confirmation bias could hinder the students' success on the test.

Even the way a problem is presented can get in the way of solving it. *Framing* refers to the way a problem is presented. Presentation can drastically change the way we view a problem or an issue. If I tell my students, "The majority of my students have been able to solve this logic problem," they would most likely feel confident and not expect much of a challenge. However, if I tell them, "Almost half of the students in my classes never get the answer to this logic puzzle," they would most likely expect a very difficult task. In both cases I am really telling them that 51 percent of the students can solve the logic problem, but the way I frame the task changes their expectation and possibly their ability to solve the problem. Researchers must be careful about unintentionally framing questions in ways that might influence participants in their studies.

Creativity

If you thought defining thought was tough, try defining creativity! The concept itself resists categorization. Again, even though defining this concept is difficult, researchers have investigated definable aspects of creativity. Researchers investigating creative thinking find little correlation between intelligence and creativity. Studies show that while we may agree in general about specific examples that demonstrate creativity, individual criteria for creativity vary widely. Most people's criteria do involve both originality and appropriateness. When judging whether or not something is creative, we look at whether it is original or novel and somehow fits the situation. Some researchers are investigating the distinctions between *convergent thinking,* thinking pointed toward one solution, and *divergent thinking,* thinking that searches for multiple possible answers to a question. Divergent thinking is more closely associated with creativity. Creative activities usually involve thinking of new ways to use what we are all familiar with or new ways to express emotions or ideas we share. Painting by the numbers is convergent thinking, but we would probably call painting outside the lines and/or mixing your own hues creative and divergent thinking.

Practice Questions

> *Directions:* Each of the questions or incomplete statements below is followed by five suggested answers or completions. Select the one that is best in each case.

1. Mr. Krohn, a carpenter, is frustrated because he misplaced his hammer and needs to pound in the last nail in the bookcase he is building. He overlooks the fact that he could use the tennis trophy sitting above the workbench to pound in the nail. Which concept best explains why Mr. Krohn overlooked the trophy?
   (A) representativeness heuristic
   (B) retrieval
   (C) functional fixedness
   (D) belief bias
   (E) divergent thinking

2. Phonemes and morphemes refer to
   (A) elements of telegraphic speech toddlers use.
   (B) elements of language.
   (C) building blocks of concepts.
   (D) basic elements of memories stored in long-term memory.
   (E) two types of influences language has on thought according to the linguistic relativity hypothesis.

3. Which example would be better explained by the levels of processing model than the information-processing model?
   (A) Someone says your name across the room and you switch your attention away from the conversation you are having.
   (B) You forget part of a list you were trying to memorize for a test.
   (C) While visiting with your grandmother, you recall one of your favorite childhood toys.
   (D) You are able to remember verbatim a riddle you worked on for a few days before you figured out the answer.
   (E) You pay less attention to the smell of your neighbor's cologne than to the professor's lecture in your college class.

4. Contrary to what Whorf's linguistic relativity hypothesis originally predicted, what effect does recent research indicate language has on the way we think?
   (A) Since we think in language, the language we understand limits what we have the ability to think about.
   (B) Language is a tool of thought but does not limit our cognition.
   (C) The labels we apply affect our thoughts.
   (D) The relative words in each language affect our ability to think because we are restricted to the words each language uses.
   (E) The linguistic relativity hypothesis predicts that how quickly we acquire language correlates with our cognitive ability.

5. Which of the following is an example of the use of the representativeness heuristic?
    (A) Judging that a young person is more likely to be the instigator of an argument than an older person, because you believe younger people are more likely to start fights.
    (B) Breaking a math story problem down into smaller, representative parts, in order to solve it.
    (C) Judging a situation by a rule that is usually, but not always, true.
    (D) Solving a problem with a rule that guarantees the right, more representative, answer.
    (E) Making a judgment according to past experiences that are most easily recalled, therefore representative of experience.

6. Which of the following is the most complete list of elements in the three-box/information-processing model?
    (A) Sensory memory, constructive memory, working memory, and long-term memory.
    (B) Short-term memory, working memory, and long-term memory.
    (C) Shallow processing, deep processing, and retrieval.
    (D) Sensory memory, encoding, working memory, and retrieval.
    (E) Sensory memory, working memory, encoding, long-term memory, and retrieval.

7. Which of the following is an effective method for testing whether a memory is actually true or whether it is a constructed memory?
    (A) Checking to see whether it was deeply processed or shallowly processed.
    (B) Testing to see if the memory was encoded from sensory memory into working memory.
    (C) Using a PET scan to see if the memory is stored in the hippocampus.
    (D) Using other evidence, such as written records, to substantiate the memory.
    (E) There is no way to tell the difference between a true memory and a constructed one.

8. One of the ways memories are physically stored in the brain is by what process?
    (A) Deep processing, which increases levels of neurotransmitters in the hippocampus.
    (B) Encoding, which stimulates electric activity in the hippocampus.
    (C) Long-term potentiation, which strengthens connections between neurons.
    (D) Selective attention, which increases myelination of memory neurons.
    (E) Rehearsal, which causes the brain to devote more neurons to what is being rehearsed.

9. According to the nativist theory, language is acquired
   (A) by parents reinforcing correct language use.
   (B) using an inborn ability to learn language at a certain developmental stage.
   (C) best in the language and culture native to the child and parents.
   (D) only if formal language instruction is provided in the child's native language.
   (E) best through the phonics instructional method, because children retain how to pronounce all the phonemes required for the language.

10. According to the three-box/information-processing model, stimuli from our outside environment is first stored in
    (A) working memory.
    (B) the hippocampus.
    (C) the thalamus.
    (D) sensory memory.
    (E) selective attention.

11. Which of the following is the best example of the use of the availability heuristic?
    (A) Judging a situation by a rule that is usually, but not always, true.
    (B) Making a judgment according to past experiences that are most easily recalled.
    (C) Judging that a problem should be solved using a formula that guarantees the right answer.
    (D) Making a judgment according to what is usually true in your experience.
    (E) Solving a problem by breaking it into more easily available parts.

12. Which sentence most accurately describes sensory memory?
    (A) Sensory memory stores all sensory input perfectly accurately for a short period of time.
    (B) Sensory memory encodes only sensations we are attending to at the time.
    (C) Sensory memory receives memories from the working memory and decides which memories to encode in long-term memory.
    (D) Sensory memory records all incoming sensations and remembers them indefinitely.
    (E) Sensory memory records some sensations accurately, but some are recorded incorrectly, leading to constructive memory.

13. Recall is a more difficult process than recognition because
    (A) memories retrieved by recognition are held in working memory, and recalled memories are in long-term memory.
    (B) memories retrieved by recognition are more deeply processed.
    (C) the process of recall involves cues to the memory that causes interference.
    (D) memories retrieved by recognition are more recent than memories retrieved by recall.
    (E) the process of recognition involves matching a person, event, or object with something already in memory.

14. Which of the following would be the best piece of evidence for the nativist theory of language acquisition?
    (A) A child who acquires language at an extremely early age through intense instruction by her or his parents.
    (B) Statistical evidence that children in one culture learn language faster than children in another culture.
    (C) A child of normal mental ability not being able to learn language due to language deprivation at an early age.
    (D) A child skipping the babbling and telegraphic speech stages of language acquisition.
    (E) A child deprived of language at an early age successfully learning language later.

15. A friend mentions to you that she heard humans never forget anything; we remember everything that ever happens to us. What concept from memory research most directly contradicts this belief?
    (A) sensory memory
    (B) selective attention
    (C) long-term memory
    (D) constructive memory
    (E) recovered memory

Answers to Practice Questions

1. **(C)** Functional fixedness would explain that Mr. Krohn did not think of another use for the trophy, to use it as a hammer. The representativeness heuristic is a rule of thumb for making a judgment that does not apply well to this example, retrieval is a step in the memory process, and divergent thinking is associated with creative thinking. Belief bias is our tendency to stick with a belief even when presented with contrary evidence.

2. **(B)** Phonemes and morphemes are elements of language. They are not used exclusively in telegraphic speech or associated with memory, the linguistic relativity hypothesis, or concepts.

3. **(D)** The levels of processing model would predict that you would remember the riddle because it was deeply processed. Both the levels of processing model and the three-box/information-processing model could explain the other examples, but choice D best fits levels of processing.

4. **(C)** Research demonstrates that the labels we apply to objects, people, and concepts affects how we think and perceive them, but there is little evidence for other ways language influences thoughts. Whorf's hypothesis states that language restricts thought, but our cognition is not strictly limited by our vocabulary (choices A and D). The linguistic relativity hypothesis has nothing to do with language acquisition.

5. **(A)** The representativeness heuristic is judging a situation based on how similar the aspects are to prototypes the person holds in his or her mind. If a person has a prototype of young people as violent, she or he might use the representativeness heuristic to judge the situation. Breaking the problem down into smaller parts is a problem-solving technique. Judging a situation by a rule that is usually, but not always, true is a description of heuristics in general, not specifically the representativeness heuristic. An algorithm is a rule that guarantees the right answer. Making a judgment according to past experiences that are most easily recalled is the availability heuristic, not the representativeness heuristic.

6. **(E)** All five elements listed in this answer are elements in the three-box/information-processing model. Constructive memory mentioned in choice A is not part of this model (although the model can explain this phenomenon). Choice B is less complete than choice E. Choice C describes the levels of processing model. Choice D is missing long-term processing.

7. **(D)** The only way to determine if a memory is accurate or constructed is to look at other evidence for the "remembered" event. Brain scans and memory models cannot differentiate between true and false memories.

8. **(C)** Long-term potentiation strengthens neural connections by allowing them to communicate more efficiently. The other options do not describe brain processes accurately.

9. **(B)** The nativist theory states that we are born with a language acquisition device that enables us to learn language best as children. Choice A reflects a behavioristic view of language acquisition. Nativist theory has nothing to do with native languages or the phonics instructional method.

10. **(D)** Sensory memory is the split-second holding area for sensory information. Some information from sensory memory is encoded into working memory, and this process is controlled by selective attention. The three-box/information-processing model does not refer to specific brain structures like the hippocampus or the thalamus.

11. **(B)** By using the availability heuristic, we draw on examples that are the most readily recalled. Choice A is a good description of heuristics in general but not specifically the availability heuristic. Using a formula or rule that always gets the correct answer is an algorithm. Choice D more accurately describes the representativeness heuristic. Breaking a problem into more easily solved parts is a problem-solving technique, not the availability heuristic.

12. **(A)** Sensory memory holds all sensations accurately for a split second. Selective attention determines which of the memories in sensory memory we will pay attention to. Choice C is incorrect because sensory memory comes before working memory in the three-box/information-processing model. Sensory memory does not last indefinitely and does not record incorrectly, so choices D and E are incorrect.

13. **(E)** Recognition is matching a current experience with one already in memory. Choices A and B are incorrect descriptions of the process. The process of recall does not involve cues, and no difference in recency occurs between recalled and recognized memories.

14. **(C)** The critical-period hypothesis states that children need to learn language during a certain developmental period or their language may be permanently retarded. A child learning language early due to parental instruction is better evidence for the behaviorist view of language acquisition. Language-learning rates between cultures or skipping stages are irrelevant to the critical-period hypothesis. A child deprived of language early on who successfully learns language later would be evidence against the critical-period hypothesis.

15. **(B)** The concept of selective attention contradicts this statement. Selective attention determines what sensations we attend to and encode into short-term memory. Research shows that stimuli not attended to are not remembered, so we do not remember everything that happens to us. Sensory memory, long-term memory, and constructed memories do not obviously contradict the statement. The phenomenon of recovered memories might support the statement. Those who believe in recovered memories believe that we can remember an event for years or decades without being aware of it.

CHAPTER 8
Motivation and Emotion

Overview of Motivation and Emotion

In my psychology class, I often ask students at the beginning of the course why they wanted to take psychology. One of the most common replies is "Because I wanted to figure out why people do what they do." Motivation theories address this question directly. Motivations are feelings or ideas that cause us to act toward a goal. Some motivations are obvious and conscious, but some are more subtle. In this chapter, we will review the connections between physiology and motivation, general motivation theories, and specific examples of motivation in hunger and sex. Finally, we will review the psychological research and theories about emotion and stress that are closely related to motivation theory.

Theories of Motivation

If you have pets, you know that different animals are born with instincts, which are automatic behaviors performed in response to specific stimuli. Your cat did not have to learn how to clean itself, it was born with this instinct. When Darwin's theory of natural selection was published, many psychologists unsuccessfully tried to explain all human behaviors through instincts. Many ethologists, researchers who study animal behavior in a natural environment, examine the role evolution plays in human thought and behavior. They look for the evolutionary advantages of persistent human behaviors. While psychologists debate whether humans are born with any instincts, they agree that our behavior is also motivated by other biological and psychological factors.

Drive Reduction Theory

One early theory about how our physiology motivates us was drive reduction theory, the theory that our behavior is motivated by biological needs. A need is one of our requirements for survival, such as food, water, or shelter. A drive is our impulse to act in a way that satisfies this need. If, for example, you wake up late and skip breakfast, your body has a need for food that is not satisfied. This need creates a drive, hunger, and this drive causes you to get a candy bar from the vending machines in order to satisfy the need. Our body seeks *homeostasis*, a balanced internal state. When we are out of homeostasis, we have a need that creates a drive. Drives can be categorized in two ways: primary drives and secondary drives. *Primary Drives* are biological needs, like thirst. *Secondary Drives* are learned drives. For instance, we learn that resources like money can get us food and water to satisfy our primary drives. However, *drive reduction theory* cannot explain all our motivations. Sometimes, we are motivated to perform behaviors that do not seem connected with any need or drive, primary or secondary. One of my cousins has always been motivated by speed and excitement. He made sure his first car was as fast as anyone else's, he went into the Air Force for the opportunity to fly the fastest planes in the world, and he liked to drag race motorcycles in amateur races. These activities can be risky and seem to violate biological explanations for motivation. Why does anyone go skydiving or ride a roller coaster? Where do these motivations come from?

Arousal Theory

Some motivations that seem to violate biological theories of motivation can be explained by arousal theory, which states that we seek an optimum level of excitement or arousal. This arousal level can be measured by different physiological tests. Each of us has a different need for excitement or arousal, and we are motivated by activities that will help us achieve this level. People with high optimum levels of arousal might be drawn to high-excitement behaviors, while the rest of us are satisfied with less exciting and less risky activities. In general, most of us perform best with an optimum level of arousal, although this varies with different activities. We might perform well at an easy task with a very high level of arousal, but the same high level of arousal would prevent us from performing well on a difficult task (this concept is similar to *social facilitation*, see page 222). This relationship is called the *Yerkes-Dodson law* after the researchers who first investigated the concept in animals.

Incentive Theory

Sometimes, behavior is not pushed by a need, it is pulled by a desire. *Incentives* are stimuli that we are drawn to due to learning. We learn to associate some stimuli with rewards and others with punishment, and we are motivated to seek the rewards. For example, you may learn that studying with friends is fun but does not produce the desired results around test time, so you are motivated to study alone to get the reward of a good test score.

Maslow's Hierarchy of Needs

Psychologist Abraham Maslow pointed out that not all needs are created equal. He described a hierarchy of needs (see Fig. 8.1) that predicts which needs we will be motivated to satisfy first. Maslow predicted that we will act to satisfy biological needs like survival and safety. Then we will act to satisfy our emotional needs like love and self-esteem. Finally, once the previous goals have been met, we will want to attain our life goals like satisfaction and self-actualization, a need to fulfill our unique potential as a person. The more basic needs must be met before moving on to the next level. Maslow's theory makes intuitive sense, but some common human behaviors seem to violate the theory. How would the hierarchy of needs explain a student going without heat or a phone in her or his apartment in order to pay for books for school? The student who stood in front of the tank in Tiananmen Square was definitely motivated to put other needs above survival.

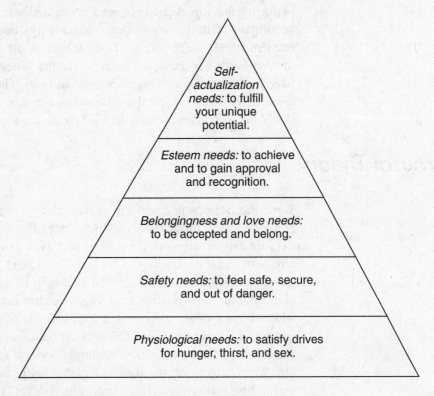

Figure 8.1. Maslow's hierarchy of needs.

Hunger Motivation

Some human behaviors appear to be deceptively simple. Why do we become hungry? Our bodies need food! However, we know the relationship is not that simple. Some people eat even when their body has enough food, and some people do not eat when their body needs nourishment. Even a seemingly simple motivation such as hunger involves several biological, psychological, and social factors.

Biological Basis of Hunger

Several biological cues create a feeling of hunger. Researchers inserted balloons into participants' stomachs. By inflating and deflating the balloons, they were able to determine that we report feeling hungry when our stomach is empty and contracts and full when our stomach feels full. Our brain also plays a role in the feeling of hunger. The hypothalamus (see Fig. 3.3, page 38) monitors and helps to control body chemistry (including the ratio of glucose and insulin) and makes us feel hungry when we need to eat. Electric stimulation of animals' brains indicates that different parts of the hypothalamus act in opposition to controlling hunger. The *lateral* hypothalamus when stimulated causes the animal to eat. Destruction of this area destroys hunger, and the animal will starve to death unless forced to eat. Another part of the hypothalamus, the *ventromedial* hypothalamus, causes the animal to stop eating when it is stimulated. If this area is destroyed, the animal will eat and gain more and more weight unless it is deprived of food. If the hypothalamus functions normally, these two areas oppose each other and signal impulses to eat and stop eating at appropriate times. *Set-point theory* describes how the hypothalamus might decide what impulse to send. This theory states that the hypothalamus wants to maintain a certain optimum body weight. When we drop below that weight, the hypothalamus tells us we should eat and lowers our *metabolic rate*—how quickly our body uses energy. The hypothalamus tells us to stop eating when that set point is reached and raises our metabolic rate to burn any excess food. Not all researchers agree that we have a set point for weight, however. They might point to psychological factors and believe that weight maintenance has more to do with learning and cognition than with the hypothalamus.

Psychological Factors in Hunger Motivation

So far, our drive to eat appears to be governed strictly by our physiology. However, some of the reasons we get hungry have little to do with our brain and body chemistry. For example, research indicates that some of us (called *externals*) are more motivated to eat by external food cues, such as attractiveness or availability of food. Others, *internals,* are less affected by the presence and presentation of food and respond more often to internal hunger cues. Everyone responds to both types of cues but to greater or lesser extents. These and other factors in eating might be learned. The *Garcia effect,* in particular, can drastically affect what foods make us hungry. You can probably think of a particular food that brings back unpleasant memories of being sick. If you eat hot dogs and then happen to get nauseous, hot dogs will probably be unappetizing to you even if you know the hot dogs did not cause your sickness. This is caused by the Garcia effect and occurs whenever nausea is paired with either food or drink. (See Chapter 6 for more information about Learned Taste Aversions and other examples of classical conditioning.)

Culture and background affect our food preferences. The foods we are raised with are most likely the foods we find most appetizing, although new preferences are acquired. Where I live in Nebraska, we eat a traditional Czechoslovakian sandwich called a Runza, which is spiced beef and cabbage inside a bread pocket.

Some of my friends who live in other parts of the country have cravings for Runza, but I am willing to bet that it sounds quite unappetizing to some of you reading this. We usually prefer foods our family, region, and culture prefer because those are the foods we learned to like.

Eating Disorders

Research into hunger motivations has at least one very important practical application—eating disorders. Many researchers seek to apply what we know about hunger and eating to treat individuals with harmful eating patterns.

The following lists the three most common eating disorders:

Bulimia	Bulimics eat large amounts of food in a short period of time (binging) and then get rid of the food (purging) by vomiting, excessive exercise, or the use of laxatives. Bulimics are obsessed with food and their weight. The majority of bulimics are women.
Anorexia nervosa	Anorexics starve themselves to below 85 percent of their normal body weight and refuse to eat due to their obsession with weight. The vast majority of anorexics are women.
Obesity	People with diagnosed obesity are severely overweight, often over 100 pounds, and the excess weight threatens their health. Obese people typically have unhealthy eating habits rather than the food obsessions of the other two disorders. Some people may also be genetically predisposed to obesity.

Many researchers are investigating the causes of eating disorders. Different cultures have drastically different rates of eating disorders, possibly due to the emphasis on body weight emphasized in the culture. Eating disorder rates are highest in the United States, possibly for this reason.

Sexual Motivation

Sexual motivations are vital for the continuation of any species. One of the primary tasks for most living organisms is reproduction. Since humans are one of the most complex living organisms, our sexual motivations are correspondingly complex. Like hunger, sex is motivated by both biological and psychological factors.

Sexual Response Cycle

The famous lab studies done by William Masters and Virginia Johnson documented the sexual response cycle in men and women. Our sexual response progresses through four stages:

Initial excitement	Genital areas become engorged with blood, penis becomes erect, clitoris swells, respiration and heart rate increase.
Plateau phase	Respiration and heart rate continue at an elevated level, genitals secrete fluids in preparation for coitus.
Orgasm	Rhythmic genital contractions that may help conception, respiration and heart rate increase further, males ejaculate, often accompanied by a pleasurable euphoria.
Resolution phase	Respiration and heart rate return to normal resting states, men experience a refractory period—a time period that must elapse before another orgasm, women do not have a similar refractory period and can repeat the cycle immediately.

Psychological Factors in Sexual Motivation

Unlike many animals, our sexual desire is not motivated strictly by hormones. Many studies demonstrate that sexual motivation is controlled to a great extent by psychological rather than biological sources. Sexual desire can be present even when the capability to have sex is lost. Accident victims who lose the ability to have sex still have sexual desires. Erotic material can inspire sexual feelings and physiological responses in men and women, including elevated levels of hormones. The interaction between our physiology and psychology creates the myriad of sexual desires we see in society and ourselves.

Sexual Orientation

As attention and controversy about sexual-orientation issues increase, so does research about homosexuality. Researchers have been able to dispel some common myths about what it means to be homosexual. Studies show that homosexuality is not related to traumatic childhood experiences, parenting styles, the quality of relationships with parents, masculinity or femininity, or whether we are raised by heterosexual or homosexual parents. Although researchers believe environmental influences probably affect sexual orientation, these factors have not yet been identified.

Researchers have identified possible biological influences, however. Some studies indicate that specific brain structures might differ in size in brains of homosexuals when compared with the same structures in heterosexuals. Twin studies indicate a genetic influence on sexual orientation since a twin is much more likely to be gay if his or her identical twin is gay. Some researchers theorize that hormones in the womb might change brain structure and influence sexual orientation. Since 3 to 10 percent (estimates vary) of the population worldwide is homosexual, research in this area will certainly continue, and the causes of sexual orientations will become more clear.

Social Motivation

So far, we have described the research regarding the motivations behind some relatively simple human behaviors such as eating and sex. What motivates the more complicated behaviors, such as taking the AP psychology test? Your attitudes and goals, the society you live in, and the people you surround yourself with also affect what you are motivated to do.

Achievement Motivation

Achievement motivation is one theory that tries to explain the motivations behind these more complex behaviors. Achievement motivation examines our desires to master complex tasks and knowledge and to reach personal goals. Humans (and some other animals) seem to be motivated to figure out our world and master skills, sometimes regardless of the benefits of the skills or knowledge.

Studies in achievement motivation find that some people have high achievement motivation and consistently feel motivated to challenge themselves more than do other people. They always set the bar a little higher and seek greater challenges. Obviously, this varies not only from person to person but from activity to activity. Not many people are motivated to achieve in every aspect of life (in fact, enough time probably is not available). However, studies that measure achievement motivation do indicate a higher-than-average achievement motivation in some people.

Hint: Achievement motivation is different than optimum arousal. Achievement motivation involves meeting personal goals and acquiring new knowledge or skills. Optimum arousal indicates the general level of arousal a person is motivated to seek, whether or not the arousal is productive in meeting a goal. The concepts might overlap in a person. (For example, a person with high achievement motivation might also have a high optimum level of arousal.) However, the concepts refer to difference aspects of motivation.

Extrinsic/Intrinsic Motivation

Another way to think about the social factors that influence motivation is by dividing them into extrinsic and intrinsic motivations. *Extrinsic motivators* are rewards that we get for accomplishments from outside ourselves (for example, grades, salary, and so on). *Intrinsic motivators* are rewards we get internally, such as enjoyment or satisfaction. Think about your own motives regarding the AP psychology test. Are you internally or externally motivated or both? Are you taking the test to get the grade and possible college credit (external) or are you internally motivated to gain the knowledge and challenge yourself by taking a difficult test? Knowing what type of motivation an individual responds best to can give managers and other leaders insight into what strategies will be most effective. Psychologists working with people managing work groups (in government, business, or other areas) might test or evaluate group members for intrinsic or extrinsic motivation and try to alter group policies accordingly. Studies show that if we want an advantageous behavior to continue, intrinsic motivation is most effective. Extrinsic motivations are very effective for a short period of time. Inevitably, though, the extrinsic motivations end and so will the desired behavior unless some intrinsic motivation continues to motivate the behavior.

Management Theory

Some research into how managers behave is closely related to extrinsic/intrinsic motivation. Studies of management styles show two basic attitudes that affect how managers do their jobs:

Theory X   Managers believe that employees will work only if rewarded with benefits or threatened with punishment.

Theory Y   Managers believe that employees are internally motivated to do good work and policies should encourage this internal motive.

Cross-cultural studies show the benefits of moving from a theory X attitude about employees to a theory Y attitude. Some companies hire consultants from other countries to teach their managers how to promote intrinsic motivation in employees.

When Motives Conflict

Sometimes what you want to do in a situation is clear to you, but at other times you no doubt find yourself conflicted about what choice to make. Psychologists discuss four major types of motivational conflicts. The first, named an *approach-approach conflict*, occurs when you must choose between two desirable outcomes. For instance, imagine that for Spring Break one of your friends invites you to spend the week in Puerto Rico and another asks you to go to San Francisco. Assuming that both choices appeal to you, you have a conflict because you can only do one. Another type of conflict, an *avoidance-avoidance conflict*, occurs when you must choose between two unattractive outcomes. If, one weekend, your parents were to give you a choice between staying home and cleaning out the garage or going on a family trip to visit some distant relatives, you might experience an avoidance-avoidance conflict. An *approach-avoidance conflict* exists when one event or goal has both attractive and unattractive features. If you were lactose-intolerant, an ice-cream cone would present such a conflict; the taste of the ice cream is appealing but its effects on you are not. Finally, people experience *multiple approach-avoidance conflicts*. In these, you must choose between two or more things, each of which has both desirable and undesirable features. You may well face such a conflict in choosing which college to attend. Of the schools at which you have been accepted, University A is the best academically, but you do not like its location. University B is close to your family and boyfriend or girlfriend but you would like to go someplace with better weather. University C has the best psychology department (hopefully one of your favorite subjects!), but you visit the campus and find it less than attractive.

Theories About Emotion

Our emotional state is closely related to our motivation. In fact, imagining one without the other is difficult. Can you imagine wanting to do a behavior without an accompanying feeling about the action? Emotion influences motivation, and motivation influences emotion. Psychologists investigate emotional states and create theories that try to explain our emotional experiences.

James-Lange Versus Cannon-Bard

One of the earliest theories about emotion was put forth by William James and Carl Lange. They theorized that we feel emotion because of biological changes caused by stress. So when the big bad wolf jumps out of the woods, Little Red Riding Hood's heart races, and this physiological change causes her to feel afraid.

Walter Cannon and Philip Bard doubted this order of events. They demonstrated that similar physiological changes correspond with drastically different emotional states. When Little Red Riding Hood's heart races, how does she know if she feels afraid, in love, embarrassed, or merely joyful? They theorized that the biological change and the cognitive awareness of the emotional state occur simultaneously. Cannon thought the thalamus is responsible for both the biological change and the cognitive awareness of emotions. Cannon believed that when the thalamus receives information about our environment, it sends signals simultaneously to our cortex and to our autonomic nervous system, creating the awareness of emotion and the physiological change at the same time. Recent research shows Cannon overestimated the role of the thalamus in this process. Many other brain structures, such as the amygdala, are also involved.

Hint: The James-Lange theory is mentioned for historical purposes. Current theories about emotion demonstrate that while biological changes are involved in emotions, they are not the sole cause of them.

Two-Factor Theory

Stanley Schacter's *two-factor theory* explains emotional experiences in a more complete way than either the James-Lange or Cannon-Bard theories do. Schacter pointed out that both our physical responses and our cognitive labels (our mental interpretations) combine to cause any particular emotional response. Schacter showed that people who are already physiologically aroused experience more intense emotions than unaroused people when both groups are exposed to the same stimuli. For example, if your heart rate is already elevated after a quick jog, you will report being more frightened by a sudden surprise than you would if you got a surprise in a resting state. Two-factor theory demonstrates that emotion depends on the interaction between two factors, biology and cognition.

Stress

You may have noticed that many of the examples used to describe emotional theories involved stressful experiences. Stress and emotion are intimately connected concepts. Psychologists study stress not only to further our understanding of motivation and emotion but also to help us with problems caused by stress. The term stress can refer to either certain life events (*stressors*) or how we react to these changes in the environment (*stress reactions*). Studies try to describe our reactions to stress and identify factors that influence how we react to stressors.

Measuring Stress

Psychologists Thomas Holmes and Richard Rahe designed one of the first instruments to measure stress. Their social readjustment rating scale (SRRS) measured stress using life-change units (LCUs). A person taking the SRRS reported changes in her or his life, such as selling a home or changing jobs. Different changes in life were assigned different LCUs; making a career change would be counted as more LCUs than moving to a new apartment. Any major life change increases the score on the SRRS. An event usually considered to be positive, like getting married, counts for as many or more LCUs as a negative event like being fired. A person who scored very high on the SRRS is more likely to have stress-related diseases than a person with a low score. Other researchers have designed more sophisticated measures of stress that take into account individual perceptions of how stressful events are and whether the stresses are pleasant or unpleasant. These more precise measures of stress show an even higher correlation with disease than the original stress measures did.

Seyle's General Adaptation Syndrome

Hans Seyle's *general adaptation syndrome (GAS)* describes the general response animals (including humans) have to a stressful event. Our response pattern to many different physical and emotional stresses is very consistent. Seyle's GAS theory describes the following stages:

Alarm reaction	Heart rate increases, blood is diverted away from other body functions to muscles needed to react. The organism readies itself to meet the challenge through activation of the sympathetic nervous system.
Resistance	The body remains physiologically ready (high heart rate, and so on). Hormones are released to maintain this state of readiness. If the resistance stage lasts too long, the body can deplete its resources.
Exhaustion	The parasympathetic nervous system returns our physiological state to normal. We can be more vulnerable to disease in this stage especially if our resources were depleted by an extended resistance stage.

Seyle's model explains some of the documented problems associated with extended periods of stress. Excessive stress can contribute to both physical diseases, such as some forms of ulcers and heart conditions, and emotional difficulties, such as depression. Our bodies can remain ready for a challenge only so long before our resources are depleted and we are vulnerable to disease due to exhaustion.

Perceived Control

Various studies show that a perceived lack of control over events exacerbates the harmful effects of stress. Rats given control over the duration of electric shocks are less likely to get ulcers than rats without this control even if both groups of rats receive the same amount of shock overall. A patient given control over the flow of morphine will report better pain control than a patient given mandated levels of morphine even though both patients get the same amount of morphine overall. Control over events tends to lessen stress, while a perceived lack of control generally makes the event more stressful.

Practice Questions

> *Directions:* Each of the questions or incomplete statements below is
> followed by five suggested answers or completions. Select the one
> that is best in each case.

1. How would drive reduction theory explain a person accepting a new job
   with a higher salary but that requires more work and responsibility?
   (A) Money is a more powerful incentive for this individual than free time.
   (B) This person seeks a higher activity level and takes the job in order to
       satisfy this drive.
   (C) For this person, money is a higher-level need than free time.
   (D) The person takes the job to satisfy the secondary drive of increased
       salary.
   (E) Humans instinctively seek greater resources and control over their
       environment.

2. Which aspects of hunger are controlled by the lateral and ventromedial
   hypothalamus?
   (A) Contraction and expansion of the stomach, indicating too much or too
       little food.
   (B) Body temperature and desire to eat.
   (C) Desire to eat and physiological processes needed for eating and
       digestion (such as salivation).
   (D) The binge and purge cycle in bulimics.
   (E) The desire to eat and the feeling of satiety, or fullness, that makes us
       stop eating.

3. All of the following are identified by researchers as important factors in the
   causes of eating disorders EXCEPT
   (A) cultural attitude toward weight.
   (B) lack of willpower.
   (C) genetic tendencies.
   (D) family history of eating disorders.
   (E) food obsessions.

4. Research is dispelling many popular myths about the so-called causes of
   homosexuality. All of the following are factors research has eliminated as
   possible causes EXCEPT
   (A) traumatic childhood experiences.
   (B) being raised by homosexual parents.
   (C) prenatal hormone levels.
   (D) parenting styles.
   (E) relationship with same-sex parent.

5. What is the principle difference between how achievement motivation theory and arousal theory explain human motivation?
   (A) Achievement motivation is a specific example of arousal motivation.
   (B) Arousal theory describes the optimum level of general arousal an individual seeks, while achievement motivation describes what goals the individual is motivated to achieve.
   (C) Arousal theory describes motivation by referring to stages in our responses to stress (the general adaptation syndrome). Achievement motivation is not used to describe motivation due to stress.
   (D) A person with a low optimum level of arousal according to arousal theory would have a high achievement motivation.
   (E) Arousal theory is an older, outdated precursor to achievement motivation theory.

6. Which of the following are reasons why intrinsic motivation might be more advantageous than extrinsic motivation?
   (A) Intrinsic motivation might be more enduring since extrinsic motivations are usually temporary.
   (B) Intrinsic motivations are easier and more convenient to provide.
   (C) Intrinsic motivations are higher on Maslow's hierarchy of needs, so we are motivated to meet them before extrinsic needs.
   (D) Intrinsic motivations are more likely to be primary drives. Extrinsic motivations are secondary drives.
   (E) Intrinsic motivations are more effective with a wider range of individuals.

7. Which sentence most closely describes the difference between theory X and theory Y types of management?
   (A) Theory X managers are more active in work groups. Theory Y managers are more hands-off, letting groups work out problems on their own.
   (B) The management theories differ in regard to what tasks they delegate to workers.
   (C) Theory Y managers regard employees as intrinsically motivated. Theory X managers see them as extrinsically motivated.
   (D) Management theory X is dominant in collectivist cultures. Theory Y is more prevalent in individualist cultures.
   (E) Theory Y is used with workers who have high optimum levels of arousal. Theory X is used with those whose arousal levels are low.

8. What does Schacter's two-factor theory state about the relationship between emotion and physiological reaction?
   (A) Emotions are caused by physiological reactions. For example, we feel excited because our heart begins to race.
   (B) Physiological reactions are caused by emotions. For example, our experience of fear causes our breathing rate to increase.
   (C) A combination of physiological reactions and our cognitive interpretation of an event produces emotion.
   (D) Physiological reactions and emotional response occur simultaneously.
   (E) Cognitive emotions occur independently of physiological states and are unrelated.

9. Excessive time spent in the resistance phase of Seyle's general adaptation syndrome can contribute to
   (A) increased time needed to adapt to new emotional situations.
   (B) decreased motivation to perform novel tasks.
   (C) stress-related diseases like ulcers or heart conditions.
   (D) a reduction in the drive to achieve goals.
   (E) resistance to learning skills needed for novel tasks.

10. Perceived control over a stressful event results in
    (A) less reported stress.
    (B) more frustration regarding the stressful event.
    (C) more motivation to solve the stressful problem.
    (D) increased arousal.
    (E) higher heart and respiration rates.

11. The balanced physiological state we are driven to attain by satisfying our needs is called
    (A) equilibrium.
    (B) homeostasis.
    (C) self-actualization.
    (D) primary satisfaction.
    (E) secondary satisfaction.

12. The Garcia effect describes
    (A) the increased motivation felt by individuals with high levels of arousal.
    (B) the increased susceptibility to illness experienced in the exhaustion phase of the stress response.
    (C) classical conditioning associating nausea with food or drink.
    (D) the effect of a theory Y management style.
    (E) the effect the hypothalamus has on perceiving hunger.

13. Which of the following factors does research indicate may influence sexual orientation?
    (A) parenting styles
    (B) degree of masculinity or femininity expressed in childhood
    (C) traumatic childhood experiences
    (D) genetic influences
    (E) being raised by homosexual parents

14. Seyle's general adaptation syndrome describes
    (A) how the central nervous system processes emotions.
    (B) the effect of low levels of arousal on emotion.
    (C) our reactions to stress.
    (D) our reactions to the different levels of Maslow's hierarchy of needs.
    (E) the sexual response cycle in humans.

15. A high score on Holmes and Rahe's social readjustment rating scale correlates with
    (A) high optimum levels of arousal.
    (B) level of need reduction.
    (C) incidence of eating disorders.
    (D) incidence of stress-related illness.
    (E) levels of perceived control.

Answers to Practice Questions

1. **(D)** Money is a secondary drive people learn to associate with primary drives. Answer A refers to incentive theory, answer B refers to arousal theory, and answer C refers to the hierarchy of needs. Not all psychologists agree that humans are born with instincts, so answer E is incorrect.

2. **(E)** The lateral part of the hypothalamus causes animals to eat when stimulated. The ventromedial hypothalamus causes animals to stop eating. The aspects described in the other answers are not controlled by these parts of the hypothalamus.

3. **(B)** All the other factors can be risk factors for the development of eating disorders, except for lack of willpower. As with most psychological disorders, the behaviors associated with eating disorders cannot be controlled by a sufferer through an act of will or by just trying harder. Most people suffering from an eating disorder need therapy, psychological help, and possible medication in order to stop their harmful behaviors.

4. **(C)** Some research indicates that hormones in the womb may influence sexual orientation. The other answers describe factors research indicates are unrelated to sexual orientation.

5. **(B)** Arousal theory says humans are motivated to seek a certain level of arousal. Achievement motivation theory describes how we are motivated to meet goals and master our environment. The rest of the answers describe the theories incorrectly.

6. **(A)** An intrinsically motivated person motivates himself or herself with internal rewards like satisfaction. Extrinsic motivators like money are usually temporary, and the individual may lose motivation for the task when the motivator stops or does not increase. Intrinsic motivations are not easier to provide. In fact, inspiring people to become intrinsically motivated may be more difficult. Intrinsic/extrinsic motivation does not relate to Maslow's hierarchy or primary and secondary drives. Both types of motivation are effective with a wide range of individuals.

7. **(C)** Theory Y managers believe workers are internally motivated. Theory X managers think workers must have external rewards in order to motivate work. Both types of managers might be equally active in work groups and might ask workers to do similar tasks. The theories might relate to types of cultures, but not the way described in answer D. Theory X and Y do not relate to optimum levels of arousal.

8. **(C)** Schacter said the cognitive label we apply to an event combined with our body's reaction creates emotion. James-Lange said biological changes cause emotion, and Cannon-Bard states that emotional reactions occur at the same time as physiological changes. No theory maintains that emotions are unrelated to biological changes.

9. **(C)** If individuals spend an excessive amount of time in the resistance phase, it may deplete their bodies' resources. They become more vulnerable to diseases in the exhaustion phase. The other answers do not relate to Seyle's general adaptation syndrome.

10. **(A)** Studies show that if people think they are in control of an event, they report the event is less stressful. Frustration might decrease, but perceived control would not increase the feeling of frustration (answer B). Perceived control does not necessarily relate to motivation, arousal, or our heart/respiration rates.

11. **(B)** Homeostasis is a balanced internal state we seek by satisfying our drives. The word equilibrium does indicate balance but is not the most correct term in this context. Self-actualization is the highest need in Maslow's hierarchy. Primary and secondary refer to drives, but the terms primary and secondary satisfaction are made-up distractions.

12. **(C)** The Garcia effect occurs when an organism associates nausea with food or drink through classical conditioning. This is a powerful form of learning that takes only one trial to establish. Pairing illness with food and drink is an adaptive response that may be hardwired in order to create a survival advantage. The other choices incorrectly describe the Garcia effect.

13. **(D)** Twin studies indicate a possible genetic influence on sexual orientation. A person whose identical twin is homosexual is more likely to be homosexual than a member of the general population. Research indicates the other factors mentioned are not environmental factors correlated with homosexuality.

14. **(C)** The GAS describes different stages in reactions to stress. The other choices do not relate to Seyle's general adaptation syndrome.

15. **(D)** The social readjustment rating scale is designed to measure stress. A high score on this instrument indicates the test taker experiences a high amount of stress, and this correlates with stress-related illnesses. The factors described in the other choices are not correlated with this test.

CHAPTER 9

Developmental Psychology

Overview

In a way, developmental psychology is the most comprehensive topic psychologists attempt to research. Developmental psychologists study how our behaviors and thoughts change over our entire lives, from birth to death (or conception to cremation). Consequently, developmental psychology involves many concepts traditionally included in other areas of psychology. For example, both personality researchers and developmental psychologists closely examine identical twins for personality similarities and differences. Some psychologists consider development psychology to be an applied, rather than pure, research topic. That is, developmental psychologists apply research from other areas of psychology to special topics involving maturation.

One way to organize the information included in the developmental psychology section is to think about one of the basic controversies: nature versus nurture. This chapter discusses influences on development from *nature* (genetic factors) first and then moves on to theories about *nurture* (environmental factors).

Research Methods

Studies in developmental psychology are usually either *cross-sectional* or *longitudinal*. Cross-sectional research uses participants of different ages to compare how certain variables may change over the life span. For example, a developmental researcher might be interested in how our ability to recall nonsense words changes as we age. The researcher might choose participants from different age groups, say 5–10, 10–20, 20–30, 30–40, and test the recall of a list of nonsense words in each group. Cross-sectional research can produce quick results, but researchers must be careful to avoid the effects of historical events and cultural trends. For example, the 30–40-year-old participant group described in the study above might have had a very different experience in school than the 5–10-year-olds are having. Perhaps memorization was emphasized in school for one group and not another. When the researcher examines the results, she or he might not know if the differences in recall between groups are due to age or different styles of education.

Longitudinal research takes place over a long period of time. Instead of sampling from various age groups as in cross-sectional research, a longitudinal study examines one group of participants over time. For example, a developmental researcher might study how a group of mentally challenged children progress in their ability to learn skills. The researcher would gather the participants and test them at various intervals of their lives (for example, every three years). Longitudinal studies have the advantage of precisely measuring the effects of development on a specific group. However, they are obviously time consuming, and the results can take years or decades to develop.

Prenatal Influences on Development

Genetics

In the chapter about biological influences on behavior, you reviewed basic information about how hereditary traits are passed on from parents to their children (see page 43 for a review). Many developmental psychologists investigate how our genes influence our development. Specifically, researchers might look at identical twins in order to determine which traits are most influenced by genetic factors (for example, review the information about the Bouchard twin study on page 43). Our genes also help determine what abilities we are born with, such as our reflexes and our process of developing motor skills.

Teratogens

Most prenatal influences on our development are strictly genetic (nature) in origin. However, the environment can also have profound influences on us before we are born. Certain chemicals or agents (called *teratogens*) can cause harm if ingested or contracted by the mother. The placenta can filter out many potentially harmful substances, but teratogens pass through this barrier and can affect the fetus in profound ways. One of the most common teratogens is alcohol. Even small amounts of alcohol can change the way the fetal brain develops. Children of alcoholic mothers who drink heavily during pregnancy are at high risk for *fetal alcohol syndrome (FAS)*. Children born with FAS have small, malformed skulls and mental retardation. Researchers are also investigating a less severe effect of moderate drinking during pregnancy, *fetal alcohol effect*. These children typically do not show all the symptoms of FAS but may have specific developmental problems later in life, such as learning disabilities or behavioral problems.

Alcohol is certainly not the only teratogen. Other psychoactive drugs, like cocaine and heroin, can cause newborns to share their parent's physical drug addiction. The serious withdrawal symptoms associated with these addictions can kill an infant. Some polluting chemicals in the environment can cause abnormal infant development. Certain bacteria and viruses are not screened by the placenta and may be contracted by the fetus.

Motor/Sensory Development

Reflexes

In the past, some philosophers and early psychologists believed that humans are born as blank slates—helpless and without any skills or reflexes. In fact, they believed this lack of reflexes or instinctual behavior was one of the factors that separated humans from animals. Researchers now know that humans are far from blank slates when we are born. All babies exhibit a set of specific *reflexes,* which are specific, inborn, automatic responses to certain specific stimuli. Some important reflexes humans are born with are listed below:

Rooting reflex	When touched on the cheek, a baby will turn his or her head to the side where he or she felt the touch and seek to put the object into his or her mouth.
Sucking reflex	When an object is placed into the baby's mouth, the infant will suck on it. (The combination of the rooting and sucking reflexes obviously helps babies eat.)
Grasping reflex	If an object is placed into a baby's palm or foot pad, the baby will try to grasp the object with his or her fingers or toes.
Moro reflex	When startled, a baby will fling his or her limbs out and then quickly retract them, making himself or herself as small as possible.
Babinski reflex	When a baby's foot is stroked, he or she will spread the toes.

Hint: *These are the reflexes we are <u>born</u> with and lose later in life. Humans have other reflexes (for example, eye blinking in response to a puff of air to the eye) that remain with us throughout our life. Humans lose the reflexes listed in this table as our brain grows and develops.*

The Newborn's Senses

In addition to inborn reflexes, humans are also born equipped with our sensory apparatus. Some of the ways that babies sense the world are identical to the way you do, but some differ greatly. Researchers know that babies can hear even before birth. Minutes after birth, a baby will try to turn his or her head toward the mother's voice. Babies have the same basic preferences in taste and smell as we do. Babies love the taste of sugar and respond to a higher concentration of sugar in foods. Preferences in tastes and smells will change as we develop (we might learn to like the smell of fish or hate it), but babies are born with the basic preferences in place. Babies' vision is different than ours in important ways, however. Sight becomes our dominant sense as we age, but when we are born, hearing is the dominant sense due to babies' poor vision. Babies are born almost legally blind. They can see well 8–12 inches in front of them, but everything beyond that range is a blur. Their vision improves quickly as they age, improving to normal vision (barring any vision problems) by the time they are about 12 months old. In addition, babies are born with certain visual preferences. Babies like to look at faces and facelike objects (symmetrical objects and shapes organized in an imitation of a face) more than any other objects. This preference and their ability to focus about 12 inches in front of them make babies well equipped to see their mother as soon as they are born.

Motor Development

Barring developmental difficulties, all humans develop the same basic motor skills in the same sequence, although the age we develop them may differ from person to person. Our motor control develops as neurons in our brain connect with one another and become *myelinated* (see page 31 for a review of neural anatomy). Research shows that most babies can roll over when they are about 5-1/2 months old, stand at about 8–9 months, and walk by themselves after about 15 months. These ages are very approximate and apply to babies all over the world. While environment and parental encouragement may have some effect on motor skills, the effect is slight.

Parenting

Attachment Theory

The influences discussed so far in this chapter have mostly been genetic or prenatal in nature. After birth, uncountable environmental influences begin to affect how we develop. Certainly one of the most important aspects of babies' early environment is the relationship between parent(s) and child. Some researchers focus on how *attachment,* or the reciprocal relationship between parent and child, affects development. Two significant researchers in this area demonstrate some of the basic findings regarding attachment.

Harry Harlow

In the 1950s, researcher Harry Harlow raised baby monkeys with two artificial wire frame figures made to resemble mother monkeys. One mother figure was fitted with a bottle the infant could eat from, and the other was wrapped in a soft material. Harlow found that infant monkeys when frightened preferred the soft mother figure even over the figure that they fed from. When the infants were surprised or stressed, they fled to the soft mother for comfort and protection. Harlow's studies demonstrated the importance of physical comfort in the formation of attachment with parents. As Harlow's infant monkeys developed, he noticed that the monkeys raised by the wire frame mothers became more stressed and frightened than monkeys raised with real mothers when put into new situations. The deprivation of an attachment with a real mother had long-term effects on these monkeys' behavior.

Mary Ainsworth

Mary Ainsworth researched the idea of attachment by placing human infants into novel situations. Ainsworth observed infants' reactions when placed into a *strange situation:* their parents left them alone for a short period of time and then returned. She divided the reactions into three broad categories:

1. Infants with *secure attachments* (about 66 percent of the participants) confidently explore the novel environment while the parents are present, are distressed when they leave, and come to the parents when they return.

2. Infants with *avoidant attachments* (about 21 percent of the participants) may resist being held by the parents and will explore the novel environment. They do not go to the parents for comfort when they return after an absence.

3. Infants with *anxious/ambivalent attachments* (also called *resistant attachments,* about 12 percent of the participants) have ambivalent reactions to the parents. They may show extreme stress when the parents leave but resist being comforted by them when they return.

Parenting Styles

So far, the developmental research and categories described focus on the behaviors of children. Parents' interaction with their children definitely has an influence on the way we develop and can be categorized in similar ways.

Authoritarian parents set strict standards for their children's behavior and apply punishments for violations of these rules. Obedient attitudes are valued more than discussions about the rationale behind the standards. Punishment for undesired behavior is more often used than reinforcement for desired behavior. If your parents were authoritarian and you came in 15 minutes after your curfew, you might be grounded from going out again the rest of the month without explanation or discussion.

Permissive parents do not set clear guidelines for their children. The rules that do exist in the family are constantly changed or are not enforced consistently. Family members may perceive that they can get away with anything at home. If your parents were permissive and you came in 15 minutes after your curfew, your parents' reaction would be unpredictable. They may not notice, not seem to mind, or threaten you with a punishment that they never follow through on.

Authoritative parents have set, consistent standards for their children's behavior, but the standards are reasonable and explained. The rationale for family rules are discussed with children old enough to understand them. Authoritative parents encourage their children's independence but not past the point of violating rules. They praise as often as they punish. In general, explanations are encouraged in an authoritative house, and the rules are reasonable and consistent. If your parents were authoritative and you came in 15 minutes after your curfew, you would already know the consequences of your action. You would know what the family rule was for breaking curfew, why the rule existed, what the consequences were, and your parents would make sure you suffered the consequences!

Hint: Some students confuse the terms authoritative *and* authoritarian. *Remember that the authoritarian style involves very strict rules without much explanation, while authoritative parents set strict rules but make sure they are reasonable and explained.*

Studies show that the authoritative style produces the most desirable and beneficial home environment. Children from authoritative homes are more socially capable and perform better academically, on average. The children of permissive parents are more likely to have emotional control problems and are more dependent. Authoritarian parents' children are more likely to distrust others and be withdrawn from peers. These studies indicate another way in which our upbringing influences our development. Researchers agree that parenting style is certainly not the whole or final answer to why we develop the way we do (and the research is correlational, not causational). However, it is a key influence along with genetic makeup, peer relationships, and other environmental influences on thought and behavior.

Stage Theories

Besides nature versus nurture, one of the other major controversies in developmental psychology is the argument about *continuity* versus *discontinuity*. Do we develop continually, at a steady rate from birth to death, or is our development discontinuous, happening in fits and starts with some periods of rapid development and some of relatively little change? Biologically, we know our development is somewhat discontinuous. We grow more as an infant and during our adolescent growth spurt than at other times in our lives. However, what about psychologically? Do we develop in our thought and behavior continuously or discontinuously? Several theorists concluded that we pass through certain stages in the development of certain psychological traits, and their theories attempt to explain these stages. You may notice that the first two stage theorists, Freud and Erikson, base their stages on psychoanalytic theories and are therefore less scientifically verifiable than the other stage theories. They are included because their stages are still often used to describe how we develop in specific areas and are of historic importance.

Hint: Each stage theory describes how different aspects of thought and behavior develop. One stage theory does not necessarily contradict another even though they may say different things about a child of the same age. Be careful when you are contrasting stage theories. Comparing one against another may be like comparing apples with oranges.

Sigmund Freud

Historically, Freud was the first to theorize that we pass though different stages in childhood. Freud said we develop through four *psychosexual* stages. Sexual to Freud meant not the act of intercourse but how we get sensual pleasure from the world. If we fail to resolve a significant conflict in our lives during one of these stages, Freud said we could become *fixated* in the stage, meaning we might remain preoccupied with the behaviors associated with that stage. (See page 155 in the chapter "Personality" for a further review of this theory.) Freud described five psychosexual stages:

Oral stage	In this stage, infants seek pleasure through their mouths. You might notice that babies tend to put everything they can grab into their mouths if they can get away with it. Freud thought that people fixated at this stage might overeat, smoke, and in general have a childlike dependence on things and people.
Anal stage	This stage develops during toilet training. If conflict around toilet training arises, a person might fixate in the stage and be overly controlling (retentive) or out of control (expulsive).
Phallic stage	During this stage, babies realize their gender and this causes conflict in the family. Freud described the process boys go through in this stage as the *Oedipus complex,* when boys resent their father's relationship with their mother. The process for girls is called the *Electra complex.* Conflict in this stage could cause later problems in relationships.
Genital stage	After the phallic stage, Freud thought children go through a short *latency stage,* or period of calm and low psychosexual anxiety, and then enter the genital stage where they remain for the rest of their lives. The focus of sexual pleasure is the genitals, and fixation in this stage is what Freud considers normal.

Hint: If Freud's psychosexual stages sound out-of-date to you, you are not alone. Many developmental psychologists would say that Freud's stage theory might have only historical importance and it is not likely to be used in scientific reseach.

Erik Erikson

Erik Erikson was a *neo-Freudian,* a theorist who believed in the basics of Freud's theory but adapted it to fit his own observations. Through his own life experiences of identity formation and his study in psychoanalysis with Anna Freud (Sigmund Freud's daughter), Erikson developed his own stage theory of development. He thought that our personality was profoundly influenced by our experiences with others, so he created the *psychosocial stage theory.* It consists of eight stages, each stage centering on a specific social conflict.

Trust versus mistrust	Babies' first social experience of the world centers on need fulfillment. Babies learn whether or not they can trust that the world provides for their needs. Erikson thought that babies need to learn that they can trust their caregivers and that their requests (crying, at first) are effective. This sense of trust or mistrust will carry throughout the rest of our lives, according to Erikson.
Autonomy versus shame and doubt	In this next stage, toddlers begin to exert their will over their own bodies for the first time. Autonomy is our control over our own body, and Erikson thought that potty training was an early effort at gaining this control. Toddlers should also learn to control temper tantrums during this stage. Childrens' most popular word during this stage might be "No!," demonstrating their attempt to control themselves and others. If we learn how to control ourselves and our environment in reasonable ways, we develop a healthy will. Erikson believes we can then control our own body and emotional reactions during the rest of the social challenges we will face.
Initiative versus guilt	In this stage, childrens' favorite word changes from "No!" to "Why?" If we trust those around us and feel in control of our bodies, we feel a natural curiosity about our surroundings. Children in this stage want to understand the world. We take the initiative in problem solving and ask many (many!) questions. If this initiative is encouraged, we will feel comfortable about expressing our curiosity through the rest of the stages. If those around us scold us for our curiosity, we might learn to feel guilty about asking questions and avoid doing so in the future.
Industry versus inferiority	This stage is the beginning of our formal education. Preschool and kindergarten were mostly about play and entertainment. In the first grade, for the first time we are asked to produce work that is evaluated. We expect to perform as well as our peers at games and school work. If we feel that we are as good at kick ball (or math problems, or singing, and so on) as the child in the next desk, we feel competent. If we realize that we are behind or cannot do as well as our peers, having an *inferiority complex,* we may feel anxious about our performance in that area throughout the rest of the stages.
Identity versus role confusion	In adolescence, Erikson felt our main social task is to discover what social identity we are

Intimacy versus isolation

Generativity versus stagnation

Integrity versus despair

most comfortable with. He thought that a person might naturally try out different roles before he or she found the one that best fit his or her internal sense of self. Adolescents try to fit into groups in order to feel confident in their identities. An adolescent should figure out a stable sense of self before moving on to the next stage or risk having an *identity crisis* later in life. Young adults who established stable identities then must figure out how to balance their ties and efforts between work (including careers, school, or self-improvement) and relationships with other people. How much time should we spend on ourselves and how much time with our families? What is the difference between a platonic and a romantic relationship? Again, the patterns established in this stage will influence the effort spent on self and others in the future. Erikson felt that by the time we reach this age, we are starting to look critically at our life path. We want to make sure that we are creating the type of life that we want for ourselves and family. We might try to seize control of our lives at this point to ensure that things go as we plan. In this stage, we try to ensure that our lives are going the way we want them to go. If they are not, we may try to change our identities or control those around us to change our lives. Toward the end of life, we look back at our accomplishments and decide if we are satisfied with them or not. Erikson thought that if we can see that our lives were meaningful, we can "step outside" the stress and pressures of society and offer wisdom and insight. If, however, we feel serious regret over how we lived our lives, we may fall into despair over lost opportunities.

Cognitive Development

Parents often focus intently on the intellectual development of their children. Intelligence is a notoriously difficult trait to assess (see Chapter 11 for more information). However, developmental researchers try to describe how children think about and evaluate the world. Jean Piaget's cognitive-development theory is the most famous theory of this type. However, some researchers now criticize parts of his theory and offer alternative explanations for the same behaviors.

Jean Piaget

Jean Piaget was working for Alfred Binet, creator of the first intelligence test, when he started to notice interesting behaviors in the children he was interviewing. Piaget noted that children of roughly the same age almost always gave similar answers to some of the questions on the intelligence test, even if the answers were wrong. He hypothesized that this was because they were all thinking in similar ways and these ways of thinking differed from the ways adults think. This hypothesis led to Piaget's theory of cognitive development. Piaget described how children viewed the world through schemata, cognitive rules we use to interpret the world. Normally, we incorporate our experiences into these existing schemata in a process called *assimilation*. Sometimes, information does not fit into or violates our schemata, so we must accommodate and change our schemata. For example, a four-year-old boy named Daniel gets a pair of cowboy boots from his parents for his birthday. He wears his cowboy boots constantly and does not see anyone else wearing them. Daniel develops a schema for cowboy boots: only little boys wear boots. Most of his experiences do not violate this schema. He sees other little boys wearing boots and assimilates this information into his schema. Then Daniel's family takes a trip to Arizona. When he gets off the plane, he sees a huge (huge to a four-year-old, at least) man wearing cowboy boots. Daniel points at the man and starts to laugh hysterically. Why is Daniel causing this scene? His schema has been violated. To Daniel, the large man is dressing like a little boy! After he stops laughing, Daniel will have to accommodate this new information and change his schema to include the fact that adults can wear cowboy boots too. By the way, this process may repeat itself the first time Daniel sees a woman in boots!

Piaget thinks humans go through this process of schema creation, assimilation, and accommodation as we develop cognitively. His cognitive development theory describes how our thinking progresses through four stages:

Sensorimotor stage (birth to approximately two years old)
> Babies start experiencing and exploring the world strictly through their senses. At the beginning of life, Piaget noted that behavior is governed by the reflexes we are born with. Soon, we start to develop our first cognitive schemata that explain the world we experience through our senses. One of the major challenges of this stage is to develop *object permanence*. Babies at first do not realize that objects continue to exist even when they are out of sensory range. When babies start to look for or somehow acknowledge that objects do exist when they cannot see them, they have object permanence and are ready to move on to the next stage.

Preoperational Stage (two to approximately seven years old)
> After we learn object permanence, we start to use symbols to represent real-world objects. This ability is the beginning of language, the most important cognitive development of this stage. We start speaking our first words and gradually learn to represent the world more completely through language. While we can refer to the world through symbols during the preoperational stage, we are still limited in the ways we can think about the relationships between objects and the characteristics of objects.

Concrete operations (eight to approximately 12 years old)

During the concrete operations stage, children learn to think more logically about complex relationships between different characteristics of objects. Piaget categorized children in the concrete-operations stage when they demonstrated knowledge of *concepts of conservation,* the realization that properties of objects remain the same even when their shapes change. These concepts demonstrate how the different aspects of objects are conserved even when their arrangment changes. See Table 9.1 for examples of the concepts:

Table 9.1. Concepts of Conservation.

Concept	Description	How to Test
Volume	The volume of a material is conserved even if the material's container or shape changes.	Pour water into differently shaped glasses and ask if the volume of the water increased, decreased, or stayed the same.
Area	Area is conserved even if objects within that area are rearranged.	Ask a child to examine two different squares of equal area, and rearrange objects within the area in order to determine if children realize the area was conserved.
Number	The number of objects stays the same when the objects are rearranged.	Take a few objects, let the child count them, rearrange the objects, and ask the child how many there are now. If the child counts them again, he or she does not understand conservation of number.

Formal operations (12 through adulthood)

This final stage of Piaget describes adult reasoning. Piaget theorized that not all of us reach formal operations in all areas of thought. Formal operational reasoning is abstract reasoning. We can manipulate objects and contrast ideas in our mind without physically seeing them or having real-world correlates. One example of abstract reasoning is *hypothesis testing.* A person in Piaget's formal-operations stage can reason from a hypothesis. To test for formal-operational thought, you might ask a child, "How would you be different if you were born on a planet that had no light?" A child in the preoperational or concrete-operational stage would have trouble answering the question because no real-world model exists to fall back on. Someone in the formal-operations stage would be able to extrapolate from this hypothesis and reason that the beings on that planet might not have eyes, would have no words for color, and might exclusively rely on other senses. Also in the formal-operations stage, we gain the ability to think about the way we think; this is called *metacognition*. We can trace our thought processes and evaluate the effectiveness of how we solved a problem.

Criticisms of Piaget: Information-Processing Model

Many developmental psychologists still value Piaget's insights about the order in which our cognitive skills develop, but most agree that he underestimated children. Many children go through the stages faster and enter them earlier than Piaget predicted. Piaget's error may be due to the way he tested children. Some psychologists wonder if some of his tests relied too heavily on language use, thus biasing the results in favor of older children with more language skills. Other theorists wonder if development does not occur more continuously than Piaget described. Perhaps our cognitive skills develop more continuously and not in discrete stages.

The *information-processing model* is a more continuous alternative to Piaget's stage theory. Information processing points out that our abilities to memorize, interpret, and perceive gradually develop as we age rather than developing in distinct stages. For example, research shows that our attention span gradually increases as we get older. This one continuous change could explain some apparent cognitive differences Piaget attributed to different cognitive stages. Maybe children's inability to understand conservation of number has more to do with their ability to focus for long periods of time than any developing reasoning ability. Developmental researchers agree that no one has the perfect model to describe cognitive development. Future research will refine our current ideas and create models that more closely describe how our thinking changes as we mature.

Moral Development

Lawrence Kohlberg

Lawrence Kohlberg's stage theory studied a completely different aspect of human development: morality. Kohlberg wanted to describe how our ability to reason about ethical situations changed over our lives. In order to do this, he asked a subject group of children to think about specific moral situations. One situation Kohlberg used is the Heinz dilemma, which describes a man named Heinz making a moral choice about whether to steal a drug he cannot afford in order to save his wife's life.

Kohlberg collected all the participants' responses and catgorized them into three stages:

Preconventional
> The youngest children in Kohlberg's sample focus on making the decison most likely to avoid punishment. Their moral reasoning is limited to how the choice affects themselves. Children in the preconventional stage might say that Heinz should not steal the drugs because he might get caught and put into prison.

Conventional

During the next stage in moral reasoning, children are able to move past personal gain or loss and look at the moral choice through others' eyes. Children in this stage make a moral choice based on how others will view them. Children learn conventional standards of what is right and wrong from their parents, peers, media, and so on. They may try to follow these standards so that other people will see them as good. Children in the conventional stage might say that Heinz should steal the drug because then he could save his wife and people would think of him as a hero.

Postconventional

The last stage Kohlberg describes is what we usually mean by *moral reasoning*. A person evaluating a moral choice using postconventional reasoning examines the rights and values involved in the choice. Kohlberg described how *universal ethical principles,* such as a personal conviction to uphold justice, might be involved in the reasoning in this stage. Those doing the reasoning might weigh the merit of altruism or limiting certain rights for the good of the group. For the first time, the morality of societal rules are examined rather than blindly accepted. Persons in the postconventional stage might say that Heinz should steal the drug because his wife's right to life outweighs the store owners' right to personal property.

Criticisms of Kohlberg

Some developmental psychologists challenge Kohlberg's conclusions. One researcher, Carol Gilligan, pointed out that Kohlberg developed the model based on the responses of boys. When girls were later tested, she continued, Kohlberg placed their responses into lower categories. Gilligan theorized that Kohlberg's assumption that boys and girls (and men and women) come to moral conclusions in the same way is incorrect. Perhaps some gender-based developmental difference occurs in how we develop our morals and ethics. According to Gilligan's research, boys have a more absolute view of what is moral while girls pay more attention to the situational factors. Boys might have moral rules that apply in every context, while girls might want to know more about the situation and relationships of the people involved before making a moral decision. Gilligan's insights about Kohlberg's theory demonstrate the importance of studying possible gender differences and how they might change as we develop. However, recent research does not support Gilligan's theory of gender differences in moral development.

Gender and Development

Another area of developmental research focuses on gender issues. Specifically, researchers are interested in how we develop our ideas about what it means to be male and female and in developmental differences between genders.

Different cultures encourage different gender roles, which are behaviors that a culture associates with a gender. Gender roles vary widely between cultures. A behavior considered feminine in one culture, such as holding hands with a friend, might be considered masculine or not gender specific in another. Different psychological perspectives provide different theories that try to explain how gender roles develop.

Biopsychological (neuropsychological) theory

Biopsychogical psychologists concentrate on the nature element in the nature/nurture combination that produces our gender role. Children learn (and are often very curious about!) the obvious biological differences between the sexes. However, biopsychologists look for more subtle biological gender differences. For the purposes of this book, going into extensive detail about all the differences between male and female brains is unnecessary. For the AP test, you should know that studies demonstrate that these differences do exist. The following is perhaps a representative example of one of the differences. One of the most significant findings is that, on average, women have larger corpus callosums (see Fig. 3.3, page 38) than men. Theoretically, this difference may affect how the right and left hemispheres communicate and coordinate tasks.

Psychodynamic theory

As noted in the chapter about psychological perspectives, some of Freud's psychodynamic perspectives are considered to have more historical value than current value. However, his views about gender role development are widely known (and sometimes referred to in the media) and so are worth mentioning. Freud viewed gender development as a competition. Young boys, unconsciously, compete with their fathers for their mothers' attention. Girls, similarly, compete with mothers for their fathers' love. Proper gender development occurs when a child realizes that she or he cannot hope to beat their same-sex parent at this competition and identifies with that person instead, girls learning to be a woman like mom or boys being a man like dad. To verify this idea empirically is difficult, if not impossible.

Social-cognitive theory

Social and cognitive psychologists concentrate on the effects society and our own thoughts about gender have on role development. Social psychologists look at how we react to boys and girls differently. For example, boys are more often encouraged in rough physical play than are girls. Cognitive psychologists focus on the internal interpretations we make about the gender message we get from our environment. *Gender-schema* theory (see page 136 for a definition of the general concept of *schema*) explains that we internalize messages about gender into cognitive rules about how each gender should behave. If a girl sees that her little brother is encouraged to wrestle with their father, she creates a rule governing how boys and girls should play.

Practice Questions

> *Directions:* Each of the questions or incomplete statements below is followed by five suggested answers or completions. Select the one that is best in each case.

1. Some researchers consider developmental psychology an applied research topic because
   (A) it is more easily applied to people's lives than research such as behaviorism.
   (B) researchers apply findings and theories from other areas of psychology to the specific topic of human development.
   (C) it is more commonly studied by a graduate student rather than an undergraduate because of the applications for other research.
   (D) doing original research in this area is difficult, so most of the research is about application.
   (E) pure research is difficult to gain support for, especially when a researcher needs to recruit children as participants.

2. You read in your philosophy class textbook that humans are born "Tabula Rasa" or "blank slates." As a student of psychology, which of the following responses would you have?
   (A) The statement is incorrect. Humans may be born without reflexes and instincts, but we are born with the ability to learn them.
   (B) The statement is correct. Humans are born without instincts or other mechanisms in place to help us survive.
   (C) The statement is correct. Humans are born with a certain number of neurons, but most develop later as we learn.
   (D) The statement is incorrect. Humans are born with a set of reflexes that help us survive.
   (E) The statement is impossible to prove since we cannot infer what babies know or do not know due to their lack of language.

3. Which of the following statements is most true about how a newborn's senses function?
   (A) A newborn's senses function the same as an adult's since the sensory apparatus develops in the womb.
   (B) All of our senses function normally when we are newborns except taste due to lack of stimulation in the womb.
   (C) All of our senses function normally when we are newborns except touch due to lack of stimulation in the womb.
   (D) A newborn's senses function at a very low level but develop very quickly with experience.
   (E) Most senses function normally, but sight develops slowly with experience.

4. Most prenatal influences on humans are genetic or hormonal in origin except for
   (A) teratogens.
   (B) stress on the mother.
   (C) parents' level of education about fetal development.
   (D) family history of mental illness.
   (E) operant conditioning occurring before birth.

5. Parental involvement can have dramatic effects on all the following human traits except
   (A) intelligence.
   (B) reading ability.
   (C) self-esteem.
   (D) motor development.
   (E) emotional development.

6. The principal difference between a longitudinal study and a cross-sectional study is
   (A) the number of participants involved.
   (B) the developmental stage of the participants.
   (C) the time span of the study.
   (D) the statistical methods employed to evaluate the data
   (E) the sampling method used to choose participants

7. Harlow's experiments with substitute mothers made of wire demonstrated the importance of what aspect of nurturing?
   (A) feeding
   (B) responsiveness to needs
   (C) imprinting
   (D) touch
   (E) stranger anxiety

8. According to research, the most advantageous parenting style for children's development is
   (A) authoritarian, because children learn boundaries quickly and appreciate consistency.
   (B) permissive, because young children need to explore the environment more than they need guidelines for behavior.
   (C) authoritarian, because it combines the best elements of the permissive and authoritative styles.
   (D) securely attached, because children are confident parents will meet their needs.
   (E) authoritative, because children have boundaries that are reasonable and justified.

9. A major difference between the psychoanalytic stage theories (Freud and Erikson) and the more cognitive or experiential stage theories (Piaget and Kohlberg) is
   (A) the psychoanalytic theories are less empirical.
   (B) the psychoanalytic theories were based exclusively on data from children with developmental disorders.
   (C) Freud and Erikson studied only young children, while Piaget and Kohlberg studied the full range of development.
   (D) only the psychoanalytic theories take parental effects into account.
   (E) the psychoanalytic theories are continuous, the others are discontinuous.

10. You have a cousin named Holden who flunked out of three expensive private schools and was arrested for wandering the streets of New York using his parents' credit card. Holden is intelligent but cannot seem to get motivated toward any career. What conflict would Erikson say Holden is struggling with?
    (A) autonomy versus authority
    (B) identity versus role confusion
    (C) integrity versus despair
    (D) industry versus inferiority
    (E) trust versus isolation

11. In which stage of cognitive development do infants learn object permanence?
    (A) preoperational
    (B) formal operations
    (C) autonomy
    (D) sensorimotor
    (E) conventional

12. According to Erikson's theory, adolescents are most primarily concerned in a search for:
    (A) career.
    (B) identity.
    (C) affection.
    (D) autonomy.
    (E) archetypes.

13. The ability to generate several alternate hypotheses in order to explain a phenomenon demonstrates cognition in which of the following Piagetian stages?
    (A) operational
    (B) hypothetical operations
    (C) syllogistic
    (D) formal operations
    (E) abstract reasoning

14. Which of the following attachment styles did Mary Ainsworth find most often in her research (in about 66% of the cases she studied)?
    (A) avoidant
    (B) authoritarian
    (C) secure
    (D) anxious/ambivalent
    (E) authoritative

15. Which of the following is the correct term for a mental rule Piaget said we use to interpret our environment?
    (A) schema
    (B) syllogism
    (C) assimilation
    (D) accommodation
    (E) hypothesis

Answers to Practice Questions

1. **(B)** Developmental psychology can be called an applied topic because many findings from other areas are applied to the topic of maturation. Many topics such as behaviorism are easily applied to our lives. It is studied at both the graduate and undergraduate levels, many original research studies are done, and pure research is still well supported even when it involves children.

2. **(D)** Humans are born with reflexes that help us nurse and find our mother. We are born with all the neurons we will ever have, and we can observe babies' behavior and infer what reflexes and abilities babies have.

3. **(E)** Most of our senses function at birth other than sight, which develops quickly as we mature. Lack of stimulation seems to have little effect on touch and taste, and most senses function at a normal level, not a low one.

4. **(A)** Teratogens are chemicals that the mother is exposed to in the environment, making them environmental influences. The rest of the answers either are not environmental in origin or do not have proven effects on a fetus.

5. **(D)** Motor development is not dramatically affected by parental involvement or encouragement since the rate of development is controlled mostly by development of the neurons in the cerebellum. The other answers are traits that might be greatly affected by parental involvement.

6. **(C)** Longitudinal studies take place over a number of years, while cross-sectional studies do not. The rest of the answers are not necessarily differences between the two types of studies.

7. **(D)** The monkeys in Harlow's experiment ran to the soft mother when frightened, demonstrating the importance of a mother's touch in attachment. The soft mothers did not feed the infant monkeys or (obviously) respond more to their needs. Stranger anxiety was present in the experiment but is not an important aspect of nurturing.

8. **(E)** The authoritative parenting style has been shown as the most advantageous in studies. The rest of the answers are incorrect because they identify the incorrect parenting style. Secure attachment is not a parenting style.

9. **(A)** The psychoanalytic theories are based on anecdotal evidence and personal inference rather than empirical research methods.

10. **(B)** Holden's inability to stay in school and decide about goals indicates a search for identity, according to Erikson.

11. **(D)** Infants learn object permanence during the sensorimotor stage, not the preoperational or formal-operations stages. Choices D and E are not stages in Piaget's theory of cognitive development.

12. **(B)** Erikson's theory places adolescents into the identity versus role confusion stage. Adolescents would very possibly be concerned with the other factors listed in the choices, but Erikson's theory identifies identity as the area of primary concern.

13. **(D)** Creating hypotheses demonstrates formal operational thought. The other choices are not stages in Piaget's theory.

14. **(C)** Most of the infants Ainsworth studied demonstrated secure attachments, rather than withering anxious/ambivalent or avoidant attachments. The terms authoritarian and authoritative refer to parenting styles, not attachment theory.

15. **(A)** A schema is a mental rule we use to interpret our environment. Assimilation and accommodation are other steps in the process of learning described by Piaget. We first try to assimilate new information into an existing schema, then accommodate the new information by changing the schema if we need to. A syllogism is a type of logical argument, and a hypothesis is an explanation for an environmental event.

Personality

Overview

Personality is a term we use all the time. When we describe people to others, we try to convey a sense of what their personalities are like. Psychologists define *personality* as the unique attitudes, behaviors, and emotions that characterize a person. As you might expect, psychologists from each of the different perspectives have different ideas about how an individual's personality is created. However, some ideas about personality do not fit neatly into one school of thought. An example is the concept of *Type A* and *Type B* personalities. *Type A* people tend to feel a sense of time pressure and are easily angered. They are competitive and ambitious; they work hard and play hard. Interestingly, research has shown that Type A people are at a higher risk for heart disease than the general population. *Type B* individuals, on the other hand, tend to be relaxed and easygoing. But these types do not fall on opposite ends of a continuum; some people fit into neither type.

Psychoanalytic Theory

Freudian Theory

Sigmund Freud believed that one's personality was essentially set in early childhood. He proposed a psychosexual stage theory of personality. *Stage theories* are ones in which development is thought to be discontinuous. In other words, the stages are qualitatively different from one another and recognizable, and people move between them in a stepwise fashion. Stage theories also posit that all people go through all the stages in the same order. Freud's theory has four stages: the oral stage, the anal stage, the phallic stage, and the adult genital stage. Between the phallic stage and the adult genital stage is a latency period that some people refer to as a stage. Freud believed that sexual urges were an important determinant of people's personality development. Each of the stages is named for the part of the body from which people derive sexual pleasure during the stage.

During the *oral stage* (birth to one year), Freud proposed that children enjoy sucking and biting because it gives them a form of sexual pleasure. During the *anal stage* (one to three years), children are sexually gratified by the act of elimination. During the *phallic stage* (three to five years), sexual gratification moves to the genitalia. The *Oedipus crisis,* in which boys sexually desire their mothers and view their fathers as rivals for their mothers' love, occurs in this stage. Some theorists have suggested that girls have a similar experience, the *Electra crisis,* in which they desire their fathers and see their mothers as competition for his love. Both the Oedipus and Electra crises are named after figures in Greek mythology who lived out these conflicts. In the phallic stage, Freud suggests that boys and girls notice their physical differences. As a result, girls come to evidence *penis envy,* the desire for a penis, and boys suffer from *castration anxiety,* the fear that if they misbehave, they will be castrated. Boys particularly fear that their fathers will castrate them to eliminate them as rivals for their mothers. To protect them against this threatening realization, Freud believed that the boys used the defense mechanism of *identification.* The purpose of defense mechanisms, in general, is to protect the conscious mind from thoughts that are too painful. Identification is when a person emulates and attaches themselves to an individual who they believe threatens them. Identification, according to Freud, serves a dual purpose. It prevents boys from fearing their fathers. It also encourages boys to break away from their attachment to their mothers (usually their primary caregivers) and learn to act like men.

After the phallic stage, children enter *latency* (six years to puberty), during which they push all their sexual feelings out of conscious awareness (repression). During latency, children turn their attention to other issues. They start school, where they learn both how to interact with others and a myriad of academic skills.

At puberty, children enter the last of Freud's stages, the *adult genital stage.* People remain in this stage for the rest of their lives and seek sexual pleasure through sexual relationships with others.

Freud suggested that children could get fixated in any one of the stages. A *fixation* could result from being either undergratified or overgratified. For instance, a child who was not fed regularly or who was overly indulged might develop an *oral fixation.* Such people, as adults, might evidence a tendency to overeat, a propensity to chew gum, an addiction to smoking, or another similar mouth-related behavior. Freud described two kinds of personalities resulting from an anal fixation due to a traumatic toilet training. Someone with an *anal expulsive personality* tends to be messy and disorganized. The term *anal retentive* is used to describe people who are meticulously neat, hyperorganized, and a bit compulsive. Fixation in the phallic stage can result in people who appear excessively sexually assured and aggressive or, alternatively, who are consumed with their perceived sexual inadequacies. These fixations result from psychic energy, the *libido,* getting stuck in one of the psychosexual stages.

Freud believed that much of people's behavior is controlled by a region of the mind he called the *unconscious.* We do not have access to the thoughts in our unconscious. In fact, Freud asserted that we spend tremendous amounts of psychic energy to keep threatening thoughts in the unconscious. Freud contrasted the unconscious mind with the *preconscious* and the *conscious*. The conscious mind contains everything we are thinking about at any one moment, while the preconscious contains everything that we could potentially summon to conscious awareness with ease. For instance, as you read these words, I hope you are not thinking about your plans for the upcoming weekend; these thoughts were in your preconscious. However, now that I have mentioned these plans, you have brought them into your conscious mind.

Hint: *Students frequently confuse the terms* subconscious *and* unconscious. *Freud wrote about the unconscious.*

Freud posited that the personality consists of three parts: the *id,* the *ego,* and the *superego.* The id contains instincts and psychic energy. Freud believed two types of instincts exist: *Eros* (the life instincts) and *Thanatos* (the death instincts). *Libido* is the energy that directs the life instincts. Eros is most often evidenced as a desire for sex, while Thanatos is seen in aggression.

The id is propelled by the *pleasure principle;* it wants immediate gratification. The id exists entirely in the unconscious mind. Babies are propelled solely by their ids. They cry whenever they desire something without regard to the external world around them. The next part of the personality to develop is the ego. The ego follows the *reality principle,* which means its job is to negotiate between the desires of the id and the limitations of the environment. The ego is partly in the conscious mind and partly in the unconscious mind. The last part of the personality to develop is the superego. Like the ego, the superego operates on both the conscious and unconscious level. Around the age of five, children begin to develop a conscience and to think about what is right and wrong. This sense of conscience, according to Freud, is their superego. Oftentimes, the ego acts as a mediator between the id and the superego. As you cram for that midterm, the id tells you to go to sleep because you are tired or to go to that party because it will be fun. The superego tells you to study because it is the right thing to do. The ego makes some kind of a compromise. You will study for two hours, drop by the party, and then go to sleep.

Part of the ego's job is to protect the conscious mind from the threatening thoughts buried in the unconscious. The ego uses defense mechanisms to help protect the conscious mind. Assume that Muffy, captain of the high school cheerleading squad, decides to leave her boyfriend of two years, Biff, the star wide receiver of the football team, for Alvin, the star of the school's chess team. Needless to say, Biff is devastated, but his ego can choose from a great variety of defense mechanisms with which to protect him. Some of these defense mechanisms are described below:

Repression

- Pushing thoughts out of conscious awareness.
- When asked how he feels about the breakup with Muffy, Biff replies, "Who? Oh, yeah, I haven't thought about her in a while."

Denial

- Not accepting the ego-threatening truth.
- Biff continues to act as if he and Muffy are still together. He waits by her locker, calls her every night, and plans their future dates.

Displacement

- Redirecting one's feeling toward another person or object. When people displace negative emotions like anger, they often displace them onto people who are less threatening than the source of the emotion. For instance, a child who is angry at his or her teacher would be more likely to displace the anger onto a classmate than onto the teacher.
- Biff could displace his feelings of anger and resentment onto his little brother, pet hamster, or football.

Projection

- Believing that the feelings one has toward someone else are actually held by the other person and directed at oneself.
- Biff insists that Muffy still cares for him.

Reaction Formation

- Expressing the opposite of how one truly feels.
- Biff claims he loathes Muffy.

Regression

- Returning to an earlier, comforting form of behavior.
- Biff begins to sleep with his favorite childhood stuffed animal, Fuzzy Kitten.

Rationalization

- Coming up with a beneficial result of an undesirable occurrence.
- Biff believes that he can now find a better girlfriend. Muffy is not really all that pretty, smart, and fun to be with.

Intellectualization

- Undertaking an academic, unemotional study of a topic.
- Biff embarks on an in-depth research project about failed teen romances.

Sublimation

- Channeling one's frustration toward a different goal. Sublimation is viewed as a particularly healthy defense mechanism.
- Biff devotes himself to writing poetry and publishes a small volume before he graduates high school.

Hint: Students frequently confuse displacement and projection. In displacement, person A has feelings about person B but redirects these feelings onto a third person or an object. In projection, person A has feelings toward person B but believes, instead, that person B has those feelings toward him or her (person A).

Criticisms of Freud

One common criticism of Freudian theory is that little empirical evidence supports it. For example, verifying the existence of many of Freud's constructs such as the unconscious, the Oedipus complex, or Thanatos is extremely difficult, if not impossible. Furthermore, psychoanalytic theory is able to interpret both

PSYCHODYNAMIC THEORIES 159

positive and negative reactions to the theory as support. For instance, both the man who is convinced by his analyst's suggestion that his difficulties stem from an unresolved attraction to his mother and the man who vociferously protests this idea can be accommodated by psychoanalytic theory. The former is compelled by the logic of the argument, while the latter's very resistance to the idea is evidence of the threatening nature of a repressed desire.

In addition, Freudian theory has little predictive power. While analysts can use the theory to create logical and often compelling explanations of why an individual acted in a certain way or developed a certain problem after the fact, psychoanalytic theory does not allow us to predict what problems an individual will develop ahead of time.

Psychoanalytic theory is also criticized for overestimating the importance of early childhood and of sex. Much contemporary research contradicts the idea that personality is essentially set by the age of three or five. Similarly, Freud's almost exclusive focus on sexual motivation led some psychologists to try to broaden the theory.

Finally, feminists find much of Freudian theory to be objectionable. One example is the concept of penis envy. Feminists such as Karen Horney and Nancy Chodorow believe that this idea grew out of Freud's assumption that men were superior to women rather than from any empirical observations. They suggested that if women were envious of men, it was probably due to all the advantages men enjoyed in society. Horney posited that men may suffer from *womb envy,* jealousy of women's reproductive capabilities. Feminists also take issue with Freud's assertion that men have stronger superegos than women.

Impact of Freudian Theory

Despite its shortcomings, Freudian theory has profoundly affected the world. Many people accept the idea that children are sexual creatures and that our behavior is shaped by unconscious thoughts. Freud's impact on culture is arguably greater than its impact on contemporary psychology. Many of the terms originally invented by Freud have crept into laypeople's language (for example, ego, unconsious, penis envy, denial). Many of Freud's ideas play a prominent role in the arts. Salvador Dali's surrealist paintings are said to depict the unconscious, and Woody Allen's films frequently feature a character undergoing psychoanalysis and playing out a Freudian drama.

Psychodynamic Theories

A number of Freud's early followers developed offshoots of psychoanalytic theory. These approaches are now usually referred to as *psychodynamic* or *neo-Freudian* approaches. Two of the best-known creators of psychodynamic theories are Carl Jung and Alfred Adler. Jung proposed that the unconscious consists of two different parts: the *personal unconscious* and the *collective unconscious.* The personal unconscious is more similar to Freud's view of the unconscious. Jung believed that an individual's personal unconscious contains the painful or threatening memories and thoughts the person does not wish to confront; he termed these *complexes.* Jung contrasted the personal unconscious with the *collective unconscious.* The collective unconscious is passed down through the species and, according to Jung, explains certain similarities we see between all cultures. The collective unconscious contains *archetypes* that Jung defined as universal concepts we all share as part of the human species. For example, the *shadow* represents the evil side of personality and the *persona* is people's creation of a public image. Jung suggested that the widespread existence of certain fears, such as fear of the dark, and the importance of the circle in many cultures, provides evidence for archetypes.

Adler is called an ego psychologist because he downplayed the importance of the unconscious and focused on the conscious role of the ego. Adler believed that people are motivated by the fear of failure, which he termed *inferiority,* and the desire to achieve, which he called *superiority*. Adler is also known for his work about the importance of birth order in shaping personality.

Trait Theories

Trait theorists believe that we can describe people's personalities by specifying their main characteristics, or traits. These characteristics (for example, honesty, laziness, ambition) are thought to be stable and to motivate behavior in keeping with the trait. In other words, when we describe someone as friendly, we mean that the person acts in a friendly manner across different situations and times.

Some trait theorists believe that the same basic set of traits can be used to describe all people's personalities. Such a belief characterizes a *nomothetic* approach. For instance, Hans Eyesenck believed that by classifying all people along an introversion-extraversion scale and a stable-unstable scale, we could describe their personalities. Raymond Cattell developed the 16 PF (personality factor) test to measure what he believed were the 16 basic traits present in all people, albeit to different degrees. A number of contemporary trait theorists believe that personality can be described using the *big five* personality traits: extraversion, agreeableness, conscientiousness, openness to experience, and emotional stability (or neuroticism).

One might wonder how psychologists can reduce the vast number of different terms we use to describe people to 16 or five basic traits. *Factor analysis* is a statistical technique used to accomplish this feat. Factor analysis allows researchers to use correlations between traits in order to see which traits cluster together as factors. If a strong correlation is found between punctuality, diligence, and neatness, for example, one could argue that these traits represent a common factor that we could name conscientiousness.

Other trait theorists, called *idiographic* theorists, assert that using the same set of terms to classify all people is impossible. Rather, they argue, each person needs to be seen in terms of what few traits best characterize his or her unique self. For example, while honesty may be a very important trait in describing one person, it may not be at all important in describing someone else.

Gordon Allport believed that although there were common traits useful in describing all people, a full understanding of someone's personality was impossible without looking at their personal traits. Allport differentiated between three different types of personal traits. He suggested that a small number of people are so profoundly influenced by one trait that it plays a pivotal role in virtually everything they do. He referred to such traits as *cardinal dispositions*. Allport posited that there are two other types of dispositions, central and secondary, that can be used to describe personality. As their names indicate, *central dispositions* have a larger influence on personality than *secondary dispositions*. Central dispositions are more often apparent and describe a more significant aspect of personality.

The main criticism of trait theories is that they underestimate the importance of the situation. Nobody is always conscientious or unfailingly friendly. Therefore, critics assert, to describe someone's personality, we need to take the context into consideration.

Biological Theories

Biological theories of personality view genes, chemicals, and body types as the central determinants of who a person is. A growing body of evidence supports the idea that human personality is shaped, in part, by genetics. Although many people associate traits with genetics, traits are not necessarily inherited. Thus far, little evidence exists for the *heritability* of specific personality traits. Heritability is a measure of the percentage of a trait that is inherited. For instance, height is highly heritable.

Conversely, much evidence suggests that genes play a role in people's *temperaments*, typically defined as their emotional style and characteristic way of dealing with the world. Psychologists and laypeople alike have long noticed that infants seem to differ immediately at birth. Some welcome new stimuli whereas others seem more fearful. Some seem extremely active and emotional while others are calmer. Psychologists believe that babies are born with different temperaments. A child's temperament, then, is thought to influence the development of his or her personality.

One of the earliest theories of personality was biological. Hippocrates believed that personality was determined by the relative levels of four humors (fluids) in the body. The four humors were blood, yellow bile, black bile, and phlegm. A cheerful person, for example, was said to have an excess of blood.

Another relatively early biological theory of personality was William Sheldon's *somatotype theory*. Sheldon identified three body types: endomorphs (fat), mesomorphs (muscular), and ectomorphs (thin). Sheldon argued that certain personality traits were associated with each of the body types. For instance, ectomorphs were shy and secretive, mesomorphs were aggressive, and endomorphs were friendly and outgoing. Sheldon's findings have not been replicated, and his methodology has been questioned. In addition, his research shows only a correlation and therefore, even if it were found to be reliable and valid, it does not show that biology shapes personality.

Behaviorist Theories

Radical behaviorists take a very different approach to personality. In fact, these theorists argue that behavior is personality and that the way most people think of the term personality is meaningless. According to this view, personality is determined by the environment. The reinforcement contingencies to which one is exposed creates one's personality. Therefore, by changing people's environments, behaviorists believe we can alter their personalities.

Social-Cognitive Theories

Many models of personality meld together behaviorists' emphasis on the importance of the environment with cognitive psychologists' focus on patterns of thought. Such models are referred to as social-cognitive or cognitive-behavioral models.

Albert Bandura suggested that personality is created by an interaction between the person (traits), the environment, and the person's behavior. His model is based on the idea of *triadic reciprocality*, also known as *reciprocal determinism*. These terms essentially mean that each of these three factors influence both of the other two in a constant looplike fashion. Look at an example. Brad is a friendly person. This personality trait influences Brad's behavior in that he talks to a lot of people. It influences the environments into which he puts himself in that he goes to a lot of parties. Brad's loquacious behavior affects his environment in that it makes the parties even more partylike. In addition, Brad's talkativeness reinforces his friendliness; the more he talks, the more friendly he thinks he is. Finally, the environment of the party reinforces Brad's outgoing nature and encourages him to strike up conversations with many people.

Bandura also posited that personality is affected by people's sense of *self-efficacy*. People with high self-efficacy are optimistic about their own ability to get things done whereas people with low self-efficacy feel a sense of powerlessness. Bandura theorized that people's sense of self-efficacy has a powerful effect on their actions. For example, assume two students of equal abilities and knowledge are taking a test. The one with higher self-efficacy would expect to do better and therefore might act in ways to make that true (e.g., spend more time on the test questions).

George Kelly proposed the *personal-construct theory* of personality. Kelly argued that people, in their attempts to understand their world, develop their own, individual systems of personal constructs. Such constructs consist of pairs of opposites such as fair-unfair, smart-dumb, and exciting-dull. People then use these constructs to evaluate their worlds. Kelly believed that people's behavior is determined by how they interpret the world. His theory is based on a *fundamental postulate* that essentially states that people's behavior is influenced by their cognitions and that by knowing how people have behaved in the past, we can predict how they will act in the future.

Some of the ideas put forth by social-cognitive theorists, including Bandura's concept of self-efficacy, are almost like traits that describe an individual's characteristic way of thinking. A final example is Julian Rotter's concept of *locus of control*. A person can be described as having either an internal or an external locus of control. People with an *internal locus of control* feel as if they are responsible for what happens to them. For instance, they tend to believe that hard work will lead to success. Conversely, people with an *external locus of control* generally believe that luck and other forces outside of their own control determine their destinies. A person's locus of control can have a large effect on how a person thinks and acts, thus impacting their personality.

A number of positive outcomes has been found to be associated with having an internal locus of control. As compared with externals, internals tend to be healthier, to be more politically active, and to do better in school. Of course, these findings are based on correlational research, so we can't conclude that locus of control causes such differences.

Humanistic Theories

Many of the other models of personality are deterministic. *Determinism* is the belief that what happens is dictated by what has happened in the past. According to psychoanalysts, personality is determined by what happened to an individual in his or her early childhood (largely during the psychosexual stages). Behaviorists assert that personality is similarly determined by the environment in which one has been raised. Neither theory supports the existence of *free will,* an individual's ability to choose his or her own destiny. Free will is an idea that has been embraced by humanistic psychology. This perspective is often referred to as the *third force* because it arose in opposition to the determinism so central to both psychoanalytic and behaviorist models.

Humanistic theories of personality view people as innately good and able to determine their own destinies through the exercise of free will. These psychologists stress the importance of people's subjective experience and feelings. They focus on the importance of a person's *self-concept* and *self-esteem.* Self-concept is a person's global feeling about himself and herself. Self-concept develops through a person's involvement with others, especially parents. Someone with a positive self-concept is likely to have high self-esteem.

Two of the most influential humanistic psychologists were Abraham Maslow and Carl Rogers. Both of these men believed that people are motivated to reach their full potential or *self-actualize.* Maslow developed the hierarchy of needs that you read about in the motivation chapter (see page 120). Self-actualization sits atop this hierarchy. Rogers created self-theory. He believed that although people are innately good, they require certain things from their interactions with others, most importantly, *unconditional positive regard,* in order to self-actualize. Unconditional positive regard is a kind of blanket acceptance. Parents that make their children feel as if they are loved no matter what provide unconditional positive regard. However, parents who make their children feel as if they will be loved only if they earn high grades or have the right kind of friends send their children the message that their love is conditional. Just as Maslow believes one needs to satisfy the needs lower on the hierarchy in order to move upward, Rogers believes that people must feel accepted in order to make strides toward self-actualization.

Assessment Techniques

Not surprisingly, psychologists' methods of assessing people's personalities differ depending upon their theoretical orientation. Some of the most common ways of measuring personality are described below along with the types of psychologists most likely to use them.

Projective tests are often used by psychoanalysts. They involve asking people to interpret ambiguous stimuli. For instance, the *Rorschach inkblot test* involves showing people a series of inkblots and asking them to describe what they see. The *thematic apperception test (TAT)* consists of a number of cards, each of which contains a picture. People are asked to describe what is happening in the pictures. Since both the inkblots and TAT cards are ambiguous, psychoanalysts reason that people's interpretations reflect their unconscious thoughts. People are thought to project their unconscious thoughts onto the ambiguous stimuli. For instance, someone who is struggling with his or her unconscious aggressive impulses may be more likely to describe violent themes. Scoring projective tests, however, is a complicated process. For instance, the Rorschach test looks not only at the content people describe but also the way they hold and turn the card and whether they focus on the whole inkblot or just a portion of it. The Rorschach test is not widely accepted as a valid measure of personality.

A far simpler and more widespread method of personality assessment is to use *self-report inventories.* Self-report inventories are essentially questionnaires that ask people to provide information about themselves. Many different kinds of psychologists, such as humanistic psychologists, trait theorists, and cognitive-behavioral psychologists, might use self-report inventories as one means by which to gather data about someone. The *Minnesota multiphasic personality inventory (MMPI)* is one of the most widely used self-report instruments.

Radical behaviorists would reject both of the above methods, arguing instead that the only way to measure people's personality is to observe their behavior. Again, a number of other kinds of psychologists, particularly cognitive-behavioral ones, would utilize observations of a person's behavior as one way to gather data.

As with any other kind of testing, *reliability* and *validity* are a concern in personality assessment. Reliability is often likened to consistency; reliable measures yield consistent, similar results even if the results are not accurate. Validity, on the other hand, means accuracy; a valid test measures what it purports to measure. See the testing chapter for a more detailed discussion of these issues.

People are naturally curious about what various personality assessments will say about them. Unfortunately, this curiosity makes people susceptible to being deceived. Research has demonstrated that people have the tendency to see themselves in vague, stock descriptions of personality. This phenomenon, the *Barnum effect,* is named after the famous circus owner P. T. Barnum, who once said "There's a sucker born every minute." Astrologers, psychics, and fortune-tellers take advantage of the Barnum effect in their work. Personality has proved difficult to define, much less measure, so be skeptical when confronted with people who offer you quick, pat descriptions of your life or future.

Practice Questions

Directions: Each of the questions or incomplete statements below is followed by five suggested answers or completions. Select the one that is best in each case.

1. According to Freud, which part of the mind acts as a person's conscience?
   (A) Eros
   (B) ego
   (C) libido
   (D) superego
   (E) id

2. Cettina fills out a personality inventory several times over the course of one year. The results of each administration of the test are extremely different. Cettina's situation suggests that this personality inventory may not be
   (A) reliable.
   (B) standardized.
   (C) normed.
   (D) projective.
   (E) fair.

3. Which approach toward personality is the least deterministic?
   (A) psychoanalytic
   (B) humanistic
   (C) trait
   (D) behaviorist
   (E) biological

4. One of your classmates remarks that "Mary is all id." What does she likely mean?
   (A) Mary uses a lot of defense mechanisms.
   (B) Mary is a highly ethical person.
   (C) Mary is a perfectionist.
   (D) Mary frequently pursues immediate gratification.
   (E) Mary is in constant conflict over the proper course of action to take.

5. The belief that personality is created by the interaction between a person, his or her behavior, and the environment is known as
   (A) combination theory.
   (B) interactionist perspective.
   (C) reciprocal determinism.
   (D) mutuality.
   (E) circular creation.

6. Juan has a huge crush on Sally, but he never admits it. Instead, he tells all who will listen that Sally is really "into him." Psychoanalysts would see Juan's bragging as an example of
   - (A) displacement.
   - (B) reaction formation.
   - (C) sublimation.
   - (D) denial.
   - (E) projection.

7. Dr. Li asks her clients to interpret ambiguous pictures of people in various settings. The method she is using is called
   - (A) the Rorschach test.
   - (B) the MMPI.
   - (C) the TAT.
   - (D) factor analysis.
   - (E) the WISC.

8. One personality trait that is thought to be highly heritable is
   - (A) generosity.
   - (B) sense of humor.
   - (C) neatness.
   - (D) inhibition.
   - (E) diligence.

9. Which psychologist(s) believed that people have free will and are motivated to self-actualize?
   - I. Carl Rogers
   - II. Sigmund Freud
   - III. Albert Bandura
   - (A) I only
   - (B) II only
   - (C) I and II
   - (D) II and III
   - (E) I, II, and III

10. Which is NOT one of the big five personality traits?
    - (A) extraversion
    - (B) openness
    - (C) agreeableness
    - (D) honesty
    - (E) conscientiousness

11. Feminist psychoanalytic critics of Freud most commonly argue that
    - (A) there is no proof that the unconscious exists.
    - (B) Freud devoted too much attention to childhood.
    - (C) women's superegos are just as strong as men's.
    - (D) men and women use different defense mechanisms.
    - (E) while women all suffer from penis envy, men all suffer from womb envy.

12. Jamal sucked his thumb until age eight. As an adult, he smokes, chews gum, and thinks constantly of food. Psychoanalysts would describe Jamal as having
    (A) an obsession.
    (B) an orally controlled libido.
    (C) an Oedipus complex.
    (D) an oral fixation.
    (E) a mother complex.

13. Someone who has an external locus of control is likely to have
    (A) a positive self-concept.
    (B) a high sense of self-efficacy.
    (C) a strong libido.
    (D) a belief in luck.
    (E) a high IQ.

14. What kind of psychologist would be most likely to use a projective personality assessment?
    (A) social cognitive
    (B) trait
    (C) behaviorist
    (D) humanistic
    (E) psychoanalytic

15. Redirecting one's unacceptable urges into more socially acceptable pursuits best defines which of the following defense mechanisms?
    (A) intellectualization
    (B) denial
    (C) sublimation
    (D) rationalization
    (E) regression

Answers to Practice Questions

1. **(D)** Freud described the superego as the part of the mind that acts as a conscience. The other two parts of the mind are the id and ego. The id acts according to the pleasure principle, while the ego acts as a buffer between the id and the demands of the external world. Eros is the life instinct, and the libido is the energy that drives Eros.

2. **(A)** A test that does not yield consistent results is not reliable. Such a test may still have been standardized and normed, both of which mean that it has been pretested on a large population and structured so that certain percentages of people answer each question in certain ways. Projective tests are used by psychoanalysts to try to see what is in a person's unconscious. Fair is not a scientific term; tests may be perceived as unfair for a variety of reasons.

3. **(B)** The humanistic model of personality arose in opposition to the determinism of earlier models. One of the fundamental precepts of humanistic psychology is that people have free will, that their behavior is not predetermined. Conversely, all of the other models listed suggest that behavior is determined, at least to an extent, rather than freely chosen.

4. **(D)** Because the id follows the pleasure principle, it pursues immediate gratification. Someone who was all id would be unlikely to need many defense mechanisms; she would just do what she wanted. Similarly, such a person would rarely be in conflict over what to do and would have little interest in the proper course of action to take. A highly ethical person would be guided by her superego. A perfectionist might also have a strong superego or, alternatively, might have an anal retentive personality.

5. **(C)** Reciprocal determinism, also known as triadic reciprocality, is Bandura's theory that personality arises out of the interaction of a person's traits, environment, and behavior. All of the remaining choices are made-up distractions.

6. **(E)** Juan is projecting. Instead of acknowledging the feelings he has toward Sally, he views Sally as having those feelings toward him. Were Juan to displace his feelings, he would express love for someone else or something else. If Juan were to use reaction formation, he would claim to hate Sally. Juan could sublimate by directing his energies toward honing his ice hockey skills or writing poetry. Finally, were Juan to deny his crush, when asked about it, he would continue to deny it.

7. **(C)** Dr. Li is using the TAT (thematic apperception test). The Rorschach test asks people to look at inkblots, not people. The MMPI is a personality inventory and therefore simply involves answering questions about oneself. Factor analysis is a statistical technique, not a personality assessment. The WISC is an intelligence test.

8. **(D)** A lot of research suggests that shyness or inhibition is inherited. Relatively little evidence exists that suggests generosity, sense of humor, neatness, or diligence is genetically predisposed. However, many psychologists persevere in looking for this evidence.

9. **(A)** Carl Rogers is a humanistic psychologist and therefore a strong proponent of the concepts of free will and self-actualization. Sigmund Freud, the father of psychoanalytic theory, had a more deterministic interpretation of human behavior. Albert Bandura is a social-cognitive

psychologist who put forth the idea of triadic reciprocality, that traits, behaviors, and environment interact to form personality. While perhaps less deterministic than the Freudian model, Bandura's theory does not ascribe a significant role to either free will or the desire to self-actualize.

10. **(D)** Honesty is not considered one of the big five personality traits. The big five are extraversion, openness, agreeableness, conscientiousness, and emotional stability.

11. **(C)** Feminist critics of Freud most commonly argue that, contrary to Freud's assertion, women's superegos are as strong as men's. Psychoanalysts, feminist or not, generally believe in the unconscious. Feminists would be no more likely than any other group of people to argue that Freud overstressed the importance of childhood. Men and women do not seem to use categorically different defense mechanisms. While Karen Horney did suggest that men might suffer from womb envy, most feminists, including Horney, make the point that women are probably more envious of the advantages that men enjoy in society than they are of men's penises.

12. **(D)** Psychoanalysts would say that Jamal has an oral fixation. They would argue that some traumatic event during the oral stage (birth to one year) caused some of his libidinal energy to become fixated in that stage. Orally controlled libido is a made-up distractor, Oedipus complex refers to boys' supposed sexual desires for their mothers, and mother complex is a term that Jung might use.

13. **(D)** Rotter's concept of locus of control has to do with how much power one feels over his or her life. Someone who has an external locus of control feels as if she or he cannot control what happens. Externals often believe their futures are in the hands of fate or luck. Someone with a positive self-concept feels good about himself or herself. Someone with a high sense of self-efficacy believes in his or her own ability to accomplish things. When we say someone has a strong libido, we usually mean she or he has a strong sex drive. Someone with a high IQ is thought to be intelligent, at least in terms of traditional measures of intelligence.

14. **(E)** A psychoanalyst would be most likely to use a projective test since such measures supposedly allow the person taking the test to project his or her unconscious thoughts onto the stimuli. Trait theorists might ask the person to fill out a personality inventory such as Cattell's 16 PF. Behaviorists would monitor the person's behavior. Social-cognitive theorists might use both self-report inventories and behavioral measures. A humanistic psychologist would also use self-report techniques and watch someone's behavior. However, this psychologist might also want to talk to the person using an unstructured interview approach in order to get a fuller sense of the person.

15. **(C)** Sublimation is when one redirects unacceptable urges into a more socially acceptable pursuit. An example would be using your sexual frustration over your attraction to your opposite-sex parent by becoming a marathon runner. Intellectualization involves distancing oneself from the threatening issue by making it into an intellectual matter. Denial is when one denies the existence of the thought or feeling. Rationalization is when one explains away a behavior or feeling by making up a plausible excuse for it. Regression is when one returns to a behavior that was common and usually comforting at an earlier stage of life.

CHAPTER 11

Testing and Individual Differences

Overview

We all take many standardized tests and receive scores that tell us how we perform. In this chapter, we will review what makes for a good test, how to interpret your scores on such tests, and what different kinds of tests exist. Then we will focus on one of the most tested characteristics of all, intelligence.

Standardization and Norms

When we say that a test is *standardized,* we mean that the test items have been piloted on a similar population of people as those who are meant to take the test and that achievement *norms* have been established. For instance, consider the scholastic achievement test (SAT), a test with which many of you are probably all too familiar. When you take the SAT, you take an experimental section, a group of questions on which you will not be evaluated. In this case, you are helping the Educational Testing Service (ETS) to standardize its future examinations. Those people taking the SAT on a particular testing date are fairly representative of the population of people taking the SAT in general. Such a group of people is known as the *standardization sample.* The psychometricians (people who make tests) at ETS use the performance of the standardization sample on the experimental sections to choose items for future tests.

The purpose of tests is to distinguish between people. Therefore, test questions that virtually everyone answers correctly as well as questions that almost no one can answer are discarded. Such items do not provide information that differentiates between the people taking the test. As you are probably aware, questions on the SAT are arranged, within a given section, in order of difficulty.

The difficulty level of the questions has been predetermined by the performance of the standardization sample. Ideally, this process of standardization yields equivalent exams, allowing a fair comparison between one person's score on the November 2002 SAT with another's on the May 2003 SAT.

Reliability and Validity

In order for us to have any faith in the meaning of a test score, we must believe the test is both reliable and valid. *Reliability* refers to the repeatability or consistency of the test as a means of measurement. For instance, if you were to take a test three times that purportedly determined what career you should pursue, and on each occasion you received radically different recommendations, you might question the reliability of the test. Similarly, if you scored 115, 92, and 133 on three different administrations of the same IQ (intelligence quotient) test, you would have little reason to believe your intelligence had been accurately measured.

The reliability of a test can be measured in several different ways. *Split-half reliability* involves randomly dividing a test into two different sections and then correlating people's performances on the two halves. The closer the correlation coefficient is to +1, the greater the split-half reliability of the test. Many tests are available in several equivalent forms. The correlation between performance on the different forms of the test is known as *equivalent-form reliability*. Finally, *test-retest reliability* refers to the correlation between a person's score on one administration of the test with the same person's score on a subsequent administration of the test.

A test is *valid* when it measures what it is supposed to measure. Validity is often referred to as the accuracy of a test. A personality test is valid if it truly measures an individual's personality, and the career inventory described above is valid only if it actually measures for what jobs a person is best suited. The latter example should serve to highlight an important point: a test cannot be valid if it is not reliable. If subsequent administrations of the career inventory yield grossly disparate results for the same person, it clearly does not accurately reflect a person's vocational strengths or interests. However, a test may be reliable without being valid. Even if someone's performance on the test repeatedly indicates that he or she should be a chef and thus is reliable, if the person hates to cook, the test is not a valid measure of his or her interest.

Just as several different kinds of reliability exist, a number of different kinds of validity exist. *Face validity* refers to a superficial measure of accuracy. A test of cake-baking ability has high face validity if you are looking for a chef but low face validity if you are in the market for a doctor. Face validity is a type of *content validity*. Content validity refers to how well a measure reflects the entire range of material it is supposed to be testing. If one really wanted to design a test to find a good chef, a test that required someone to create an entrée and whip up a salad dressing in addition to baking a cake would have greater content validity.

Another kind of validity is *criterion-related validity*. Tests may have two kinds of criterion-related validity, concurrent and predictive. *Concurrent validity* measures how much of a characteristic a person has now; is a person a good chef now? *Predictive validity* is a measure of future performance; does a person have the qualities that would enable him or her to become a good chef?

Finally, *construct validity* is thought to be the most meaningful kind of validity. If an independent measure already exists that has been established to identify those who will make fine chefs and love their work, we can correlate prospective chefs' performance on this measure with their performance on any new measure. The higher the correlation, the more construct validity the new measure has. The limitation, of course, is the difficulty in creating any measure that we believe is perfectly valid in the first place.

Hint: *Reliability and validity are important terms for you to know. The psychological meaning ascribed to these two terms may differ somewhat from how they are used by the general population. Reliability refers to a test's consistency, and validity refers to a test's accuracy.*

Types of Tests

Two common types of tests are aptitude tests and achievement tests. *Aptitude tests* measure ability or potential, while *achievement tests* measure what one has learned or accomplished. For instance, any intelligence test is supposed to be an aptitude test. These tests are made to express someone's potential, not his or her current level of achievement. Conversely, most, if not all, the tests you take in school are supposed to be achievement tests. They are supposed to indicate how much you have learned in a given subject. However, making a test that exclusively measures one of these qualities is virtually impossible. Whatever one's aptitude for a particular field or skill, one's experience affects it. Someone who has had a lot of schooling will score better on a test of mathematics aptitude than someone who might have an equally great potential to be a mathematician but who has never had any formal training in math. Similarly, two people who have achieved equally in learning biology will not necessarily score the same on an achievement test. If one has far greater test-taking aptitude, she or he will likely outscore the other.

Distinguishing between speed and power tests is also possible. *Speed tests* generally consist of a large number of questions asked in a short amount of time. The goal of a speed test is to see how quickly a person can solve problems. Therefore, the amount of time allotted should be insufficient to complete the problems. The goal of a *power test* is to gauge the difficulty level of problems an individual can solve. Power tests consist of items of increasing difficulty levels. Examinees are given sufficient time to work through as many problems as they can since the goal is to determine the ceiling difficulty level, not their problem-solving speed.

Finally, some tests are *group tests* while others are *individual tests*. Group tests are administered to a large number of people at a time. Interaction between the examiner and the people taking the test is minimal. Generally, instructions are provided to the group, and then people are given a certain amount of time to complete the various sections of the test. Group tests are less expensive to administer and are thought to be more objective than individual tests. Individual tests involve greater interaction between the examiner and examinee. Several of the IQ tests that will be discussed later in this chapter are individual tests. The Rorschach inkblot test, discussed in the personality chapter, is also an individual test. The examiner attends not only to what the person says about the inkblots but also to the process by which he or she analyzes the stimuli.

Theories of Intelligence

While *intelligence* is a commonly used term, it is an extremely difficult concept to define. Typically, intelligence is defined as the ability to gather and use information in productive ways. However, we will not present any one correct definition of intelligence because nothing that approaches a consensus has been achieved. Rather, we will present brief summaries of some of the most widely known theories of intelligence.

Many psychologists differentiate between *fluid intelligence* and *crystallized intelligence*. Fluid intelligence refers to our ability to solve abstract problems and pick up new information and skills, while crystallized intelligence involves using knowledge accumulated over time. While fluid intelligence seems to decrease as adults age, research shows that crystallized intelligence holds steady or may even increase. For instance, a 20-year-old may be able to learn a computer language more quickly than a 60-year-old, whereas the older person may well have the advantage on a vocabulary test or an exercise dependent upon wisdom.

Charles Spearman

One fundamental issue of debate is whether intelligence refers to a single ability, a small group of abilities, or a wide variety of abilities. Spearman argued that intelligence could be expressed by a single factor. He used factor analysis, a statistical technique that measures the correlations between different items, to conclude that underlying the many different specific abilities s that people regard as types of intelligence is a single factor that he named g.

L. L. Thurstone and J. P. Guilford

Thurstone's primary mental abilities theory states that intelligence is comprised of seven main abilities including reasoning, verbal comprehension, and memory. Guilford, on the other hand, posited the existence of well over 100 different mental abilities.

Howard Gardner

Gardner also subscribes to the idea of *multiple intelligences*. Unlike many other researchers, however, the kinds of intelligences that this contemporary researcher has named thus far encompass a large range of human behavior. Three of Gardner's multiple intelligences—linguistic, logical-mathematical, and spatial—fall within the bounds of qualities traditionally labeled as intelligences. To that list Gardner has added musical, bodily-kinesthetic, intrapersonal, interpersonal, and naturalist intelligence. He is working on naming others. Musical intelligence, as one might suspect, includes the ability to play an instrument or compose a symphony. A dancer or athlete would have a lot of bodily-kinesthetic intelligence as would a hunter. Intrapersonal intelligence refers to one's ability to understand oneself. People who are able to persevere without becoming discouraged or who can differentiate between situations in which they will be successful and those that may simply frustrate them have intrapersonal intelligence. Interpersonal intelligence, on the other hand, corresponds to a person's ability to get along with and be sensitive to others. Successful psychologists, teachers, and salespeople would have a lot of interpersonal intelligence. Finally, naturalist intelligence is found in people gifted at recognizing and organizing the things they encounter in the natural environment. Such people would be successful in fields such as biology and ecology.

Daniel Goleman

Recently there has been a lot of discussion of *EQ*, which is also known as *emotional intelligence*. One of the main proponents of EQ is Goleman. EQ roughly corresponds to Gardner's notions of interpersonal and intrapersonal intelligence. Researchers who argue for the importance of EQ point out that the people with the highest IQs are not always the most successful people. They contend that both EQ and IQ are needed to succeed.

Robert Sternberg

Sternberg is another contemporary researcher who has offered a somewhat nontraditional definition of intelligence. *Sternberg's triarchic theory* holds that three types of intelligence exist. Componential or analytic intelligence involves the skills traditionally thought of as reflecting intelligence. Most of what we are asked to do in school involves this type of intelligence: the ability to compare and contrast, explain, and analyze. The second type, experiential intelligence, focuses on people's ability to use their knowledge and experiences in new and creative ways. Rather than comparing the different definitions of intelligence that others have offered, someone with this type of intelligence might prefer to come up with his or her own theory of what constitutes intelligence. The third kind of intelligence Sternberg discusses is contextual or practical intelligence. People with this type of intelligence are what we consider street-smart, they are able to apply what they know to real-world situations.

This last aspect of Sternberg's theory, the idea of practical intelligence, raises another important and unresolved issue in the study of intelligence: does intelligence depend upon context? The other theories of intelligence discussed above essentially posit that intelligence is an ability, some thing or collection of things that one has or does not have. Sternberg, on the other hand, asserts that what is intelligent behavior depends on the context or situation in which it occurs. If intelligence does, indeed, depend upon context, devising an intelligence test becomes a particularly difficult task. The most common intelligence tests used (described in the next section) are based on the view of intelligence as ability based.

Intelligence Tests

Not surprisingly, the ongoing debate over what constitutes intelligence makes constructing an assessment particularly difficult. Two widely used individual tests of intelligence are the Stanford-Binet and the Weschler.

Alfred Binet was a Frenchman who wanted to design a test that would identify which children needed special attention in schools. His purpose was not to rank or track children but, rather, to improve the children's education by finding a way to tailor it better to their specific needs. Binet came up with the concept of *mental age,* an idea that presupposes that intelligence increases as one gets older. The average 10-year-old child has a mental age of 10. When this average child grows to age 12, she or he will seem more intelligent and will have a mental age of 12. By using this method, Binet created a test that would identify children who lagged behind most of their peers, were in step with their peer group, and were ahead of their peers. Binet created a standardized test using the method described earlier in this chapter. He administered questions to a standardization sample and constructed a test that would differentiate between children functioning at different levels.

Louis Terman, a Stanford professor, used this system to create the measure we know as IQ and the test known as the *Stanford-Binet IQ* test. *IQ* stands for intelligence quotient. A person's IQ score on this test is computed by dividing the person's mental age by his or her chronological age and multiplying by 100. Thus, the child described above has an IQ of 100 because $10/10 \times 100 = 100$. A child who has a mental age of 15 at age 10 would have an IQ of 150, $15/10 \times 100 = 150$. A commonly asked question about this system is how it deals with adults. While talking about a mental age of 8 or 11 or 17 makes sense, what does having a mental age of 25 or 33 or 58 mean? To address this problem, Terman assigned all adults an arbitrary age of 20.

David Weschler used a different way to measure intelligence. Although it does not involve finding a quotient, it is still known as an IQ test. Three different Weschler tests actually exist. The *Weschler adult intelligence scale (WAIS)* is used in testing adults, the *Weschler intelligence scale for children (WISC)* is given to children between the ages of six and 16, and the *Weschler preschool and primary scale of intelligence (WPPSI)* can be administered to children as young as four. The Weschler tests yield IQ scores based on what is known as *deviation IQ.* The tests are standardized so that the mean is 100, the standard deviation is 15, and the scores form a normal distribution. Remember that in a normal distribution, the percentages of scores that fall under each part of the normal curve are predetermined (see Fig. 11.1).

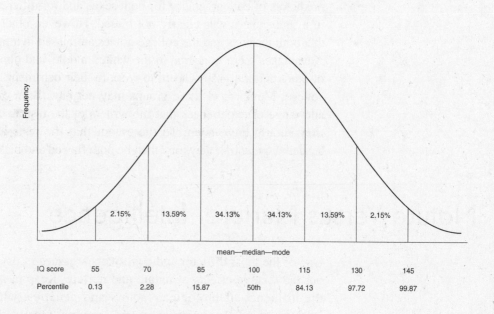

Figure 11.1. The normal distribution.

For instance, approximately 68 percent of scores fall within one standard deviation of the mean, approximately 95 percent fall within two standard deviations of the mean, and 98 to 99 percent of scores fall within three standard deviations of the mean. People's scores are determined by how many standard deviations they fall away from the mean. Thus, Peter who scores at the 15.87th percentile falls at one standard deviation below the mean and is assigned a score of 85, while Juanita who scores at the 97.72nd percentile has scored two standard deviations above the mean and has scored 130. Of course, most people do not fall exactly one or two standard deviations above the mean. However, using such an example would necessitate less obvious mathematical calculations. For more information on the normal curve, you might want to refer to the "Statistics" section in Chapter 2.

Whereas the Stanford-Binet IQ test utilizes a variety of different kinds of questions to yield a single IQ score, the Wechsler tests result in scores on a number of subscales as well as a total IQ score. For instance, the WAIS has 11 subscales. Six of them are combined to produce a verbal IQ score. Five are used to indicate performance IQ. The kinds of questions used to measure verbal IQ ask people to define words, solve mathematical word problems, and explain ways in which different items are similar. The items on the performance section involve tasks like duplicating a pattern with blocks, correctly ordering pictures so they tell a story, and identifying missing elements in pictures. Differences between a person's score on the verbal and performance sections of this exam can be used to identify learning disabilities.

Bias in Testing

Much discussion has centered on whether widely used IQ tests or the SAT are biased against certain groups. Interestingly, researchers seem to agree that although different races and sexes may score differently on these tests, the tests have the same predictive validity for all groups. In other words, SAT scores are equally good predictors of college grades for both sexes and for different racial groups and thus, in a sense, the test is clearly not biased. However, other researchers have argued that both the tests and the college grades are biased in a far more fundamental way. Advantages seem to accrue to the white, middle, and upper class. The experiences of other cultural groups seem to work to their detriment both on these tests and in college. Members of these groups may not have been exposed to the vocabulary and range of experiences that the writers of the test assume they have or believe they should have been. To the extent that the tests are supposed to identify academic potential, they may then be both flawed and biased.

Nature Versus Nurture: Intelligence

One of the most difficult and controversial issues in psychology involves sorting out the relative effects of nature and nurture. Keep in mind that nature refers to the influence of biological factors and genetics, while nurture stresses the importance of the environment and learning. One of the more hotly contested aspects of the nature-nurture debate is intelligence. Human intelligence is clearly affected by both nature and nurture. Research suggests that both genetic and environmental factors play a role in molding intelligence.

An important term that researchers use in discussing the effects of nature and nurture is *heritability*. Heritability is a measure of how much of a trait's variation is explained by genetic factors. Heritability can range from 0 to 1, where 0 indicates that the environment is totally responsible for differences in the trait and 1 means that all of the variation in the trait can be accounted for genetically. Thus, the question is how heritable is intelligence? That heritability does not apply to an individual but rather to a population is important to point out. Whatever the heritability ratio for intelligence, it will not tell us how much of any particular person's intelligence was determined by nature or nurture.

Solving this controversy once and for all is essentially impossible because we cannot ethically set up the kind of controlled experiment necessary to provide definitive answers to this question. However, many researchers have studied this issue, and some of their findings are presented below:

- Performance on intelligence tests has been increasing steadily throughout the century, a finding known as the *Flynn effect*. Since the gene pool has remained the same, this finding suggests that environmental factors such as nutrition, education, and, most interestingly, television and video games play a role in intelligence.

- Monozygotic (identical) twins, who share 100 percent of their genetic material, score much more similarly on intelligence tests than do dizygotic (fraternal) twins, who have, on average, only 50 percent of their genes in common. Nonetheless, some researchers have suggested that monozygotic twins tend to be treated more similarly than dizygotic twins, thus confounding the effects of nature with those of nurture.

- Research on identical twins separated at birth has found strong correlations in intelligence scores. However, researchers advocating more of an environmental influence point out that usually the twins are placed into similar environments, again making it difficult to sift out the relative effects of nature and nurture. For instance, if each of the twins is placed into a white, middle-class, suburban home, concluding that all their similarities are genetically based does not make sense.

- Some researchers have argued that racial differences in IQ scores provide evidence that intelligence is genetically determined. The majority of psychologists disagree, arguing that these racial differences are more likely explained by differences in environments, particularly by socioeconomic factors. For example, African Americans, as a group, tend to score 10–15 points lower on IQ tests than do whites. Many researchers argue that the greater poverty level in many minority populations, an environmental factor, is the main cause of the disparity in test scores and not a difference in genetics. Test bias is an additional factor that may contribute to the gap in test scores.

- Participation in government programs such as Head Start, meant to redress some of the disadvantages faced by impoverished groups, has been shown to correlate with higher scores on intelligence tests. However, opponents of such programs assert that these gains are limited and of short duration. Advocates of such interventions respond that expecting the gains to outlast the programs is unreasonable.

After putting the issue of cause aside, when comparing groups of people on any characteristic, keep in mind that differences within groups generally dwarf differences between groups. In other words, within any one group will be more diversity than between any two groups. Practically speaking, if we find that boys perform better on a certain test than girls do, more of a difference will exist between the highest scoring boy and the lowest scoring boy than between the average boy and the average girl. Furthermore, knowing that boys generally outperform girls on this test tells us nothing about the performance of any particular girl compared with the performance of any particular boy. Therefore, we need to be careful about how we use information about differences between groups. Essentially, we should not use it. We should ignore it and evaluate each person, regardless of group membership, as an individual.

Hint: *Within-group differences are larger than between-group differences.*

A Cautionary Note

It is often said that we live in a testing society. We like to be able to measure things and assign them a number. Therefore, keeping in mind the limitations and extraordinary labeling power of these instruments is particularly important. As we have discussed, the definition of intelligence (and many other concepts) remains hotly debated and many factors affect people's performances on tests. Thus, we need to take care not to ascribe too great a meaning to a test score. Many schools that used to measure all their students' IQs periodically have abandoned that practice. Schools that used to base admission to programs for exceptional children solely on these tests now frequently gather information in other ways as well. When IQ tests are given, the results remain confidential so as not to create expectations about how people *ought* to perform. While well-designed tests can be extremely useful, we must recognize their limitations.

Practice Questions

> *Directions:* Each of the questions or incomplete statements below is followed by five suggested answers or completions. Select the one that is best in each case.

1. Paul takes a test in the army to see if he would make a good pilot. Such a test is
   (A) a standardized test.
   (B) an aptitude test.
   (C) an intelligence test.
   (D) an achievement test.
   (E) a biased test.

2. If a test is reliable, it means that
   (A) it is given in the same way every time.
   (B) it tests what it is supposed to test.
   (C) it is a fair assessment.
   (D) it yields consistent results.
   (E) it is also valid.

3. The standardization sample is
   (A) the group of people who take the test.
   (B) a random sample of the test takers used to evaluate the performance of others.
   (C) the people used to represent the population for whom the test was intended.
   (D) all the people who might ever take the test.
   (E) the top 15 percent of scores on the test.

4. Which of the following is not one of Howard Gardner's multiple intelligences?
   (A) practical
   (B) musical
   (C) interpersonal
   (D) spatial
   (E) linguistic

5. Mrs. Cho is careful to make sure that she fairly represents the whole year's work on the final exam for her American literature class. If Mrs. Cho achieves this goal, her test will have
   (A) test-retest reliability.
   (B) construct validity.
   (C) content validity.
   (D) split-half reliability.
   (E) criterion validity.

6. Astor scores at the 84th percentile on the WISC. Which number most closely expresses his IQ?
   (A) 85
   (B) 110
   (C) 115
   (D) 120
   (E) 130

7. Spearman argued that intelligence could be boiled down to one ability known as
   (A) *s*.
   (B) *i*.
   (C) *g*.
   (D) *a*.
   (E) *x*.

8. Which of the following would provide the strongest evidence for the idea that intelligence is highly heritable?
   (A) The IQ scores of parents are positively correlated with the scores of their children.
   (B) Monozygotic twins separated at birth have extremely similar IQ scores.
   (C) Dizygotic twins score more similarly on IQ tests than do other siblings.
   (D) Adopted children's IQ scores are positively correlated with their adopted parents' scores.
   (E) Different ethnic groups have different average IQ scores.

9. All of the following people are known for their theories of intelligence except for
   (A) Thurstone.
   (B) Gardner.
   (C) Sternberg.
   (D) Flynn.
   (E) Guilford.

10. Which statement is true of power tests?
   (A) They are administered in a short amount of time.
   (B) They are an example of an individual test.
   (C) They are a pure measure of achievement.
   (D) They consist of items of varying difficulty levels.
   (E) They yield IQ scores.

11. People with high EQs would be likely to
   (A) pursue high-paying occupations.
   (B) complete college.
   (C) find jobs well suited to their individual strengths.
   (D) be creative problem solvers.
   (E) have a lot of close friends.

12. Although her score on the personality test indicated that Mary was devoid of social grace, painfully shy, and frightened of other people, she is extremely popular and outgoing. This personality test lacks
    (A) reliablity.
    (B) standardization.
    (C) consistency.
    (D) validity.
    (E) practical worth.

13. Santos is 8 years old and, according to the Stanford-Binet, he has a mental age of 10. What is his IQ?
    (A) 80
    (B) 100
    (C) 120
    (D) 125
    (E) 150

14. The Flynn effect is the finding that
    (A) intelligence seems to increase with every generation.
    (B) television has decreased intellectual performance.
    (C) linguistic skills decline with age.
    (D) within-group differences are larger than between-group differences.
    (E) the more times people take a test, the better they tend to score.

15. Desmond believes that nature is far more important in shaping personality than nurture. Desmond probably believes in the strong influence of
    (A) environment.
    (B) learning.
    (C) reinforcement.
    (D) genetics.
    (E) culture.

Answers to Practice Questions

1. **(B)** Aptitude tests aim to measure someone's ability or potential. In this case, the test is supposed to show whether Paul has the ability to be a pilot. The test may or may not be standardized or biased. The test is not attempting to measure Paul's intelligence. Since Paul has not yet been trained as a pilot, the test is not an achievement test.

2. **(D)** If a test is reliable, it yields consistent results. Standardized tests are generally given in the same way every time. A test is valid if it measures what it is supposed to measure. While valid tests are reliable, reliable tests are not necessarily valid. Whether a test is fair or biased can be evaluated in several ways as explained in the chapter. However, the fairness of a test is not synonymous with its consistency.

3. **(C)** The standardization sample represents the population for whom the test was intended and is used to construct the test. None of the other choices are referred to by any specific terminology.

4. **(A)** Practical intelligence is part of Sternberg's triarchic theory of intelligence. Gardner's multiple intelligences include linguistic, spatial, logical-mathematical, musical, bodily-kinesthetic, interpersonal, intrapersonal, and naturalist.

5. **(C)** Mrs. Cho is concerned about the content validity of her test. A test that fairly represents all the material taught in her class has content validity. Validity, in general, measures how well a test measures what it is supposed to measure. In order for Mrs. Cho's test to have construct validity, we would need to know that the test was successful in differentiating between varying levels of achievement in Mrs. Cho's class. If the test has criterion validity, we would have to know that the test successfully identified either those students who had excelled in their study of American literature (concurrent validity) or those students who would excel in the future (predictive validity). Reliability is a measure of how consistent the scores are on a test. Test-retest reliability involves giving the same test to the same population on at least two different occasions and measuring the correlation between the sets of scores. Split-half reliability is when one test is divided into two parts and the correlation between people's scores on the two halves is measured.

6. **(C)** The WISC (Weschler intelligence scale for children) yields a deviation IQ score. The mean on the WISC is set at 100. Therefore, someone who scores 100 has scored at the 50th percentile on the test. The standard deviation on the WISC is set at 15. Since approximately 34 percent of the scores in a normal distribution fall between the mean and one standard deviation above the mean, Astor's score at the 84th percentile indicates that he scored almost exactly one standard deviation above the mean. Therefore, to compute Astor's score, we simply have to add the mean (100) to one standard deviation (15).

7. **(C)** Spearman argued that intelligence could be boiled down to one ability known as g. The g stands for general intelligence. Spearman also discussed s, which stands for specific intelligences. The other letters are all simply distractions.

8. **(B)** The strongest evidence presented for intelligence to be highly heritable is that monozygotic twins separated at birth have extremely similar IQ scores. Monozygotic twins share 100 percent of their genetic material. If they are separated at birth and therefore raised in different environments, similarity in their IQ scores argues for the influence of nature or heritability. Parents' IQ scores do tend to correlate positively with those of their children, but this similarity could be explained by either genetic or environmental factors. Dizygotic twins and other siblings share the same amount of genetic material on average (50 percent). Therefore, if the former score more similarly on IQ tests, an environmental influence is suggested. For instance, dizygotic twins may be treated more similarly than other siblings and grow up during the same time period. Since adopted children do not share any genetic material with the parents who adopted them, similarities must be due to environmental factors. Differences in average IQ scores between ethnic groups could be explained by either genetic or environmental factors.

9. **(D)** While Thurstone, Gardner, Sternberg, and Guilford all tried to define intelligence, Flynn is known for his observation that intelligence is increasing.

10. **(D)** Power tests consist of items of varying levels of difficulty because their purpose is to identify the upper limit of a person's ability. Speed tests are given in a small amount of time since they seek to test how quickly someone can solve problems. Power tests could be given individually or in a group. Having a pure measure of achievement is impossible. IQ tests yield IQ scores.

11. **(C)** People with high EQs would be likely to find jobs well suited to their individual strengths. Emotional intelligence is thought to help people achieve what they want to achieve. Someone who has a high EQ will not necessarily want a high-paying job, go to college, be a creative problem solver, or have many close friends.

12. **(D)** Since the personality test does not seem to have resulted in an accurate depiction of Mary's personality, the test lacks validity. If repeated administrations of the test yielded similar results, the test could still be reliable. The test may or may not have been standardized. Consistency is generally equated with reliability. If the test lacks validity, it will not have practical worth, but the latter is not a psychological term.

13. **(D)** Scores on the Stanford-Binet IQ test are computed by dividing mental age by chronological age and multiplying by 100. Since 10 divided by 8 equals 1.25, Santos has an IQ of 125.

14. **(A)** The Flynn effect is the finding that intelligence seems to be increasing with every generation. Although television is often cast as a great social evil that rots the minds of our nation's youth, one hypothesized contribution to the Flynn effect is the exposure to the complex and rapid visual stimuli that appear on television. Linguistic skills do not decline with age. The statements in choices D and E are true but are not known as the Flynn effect.

15. **(D)** Adherents to a nature perspective often emphasize the effect of genetic makeup in shaping personality. All the other factors (environment, learning, reinforcement, and culture) are associated with a nurture perspective.

CHAPTER 12

Abnormal Psychology

Overview

Abnormal psychology is the study of people who suffer from psychological disorders. These disorders may be manifested in a person's behavior and/or thoughts. Abnormal psychology encompasses the study of relatively common problems such as depression, substance abuse, and learning difficulties, as well as the study of fairly rare, and particularly severe, disorders such as schizophrenia and bipolar disorder.

Defining Abnormality

In order to identify psychological abnormality, we must first define it. This task is surprisingly difficult. Common characteristics of abnormality include:

1. It is maladaptive (harmful) and/or disturbing to the individual. For instance, someone who has agoraphobia, fear of open spaces, and is thus unable to leave his or her home experiences something maladaptive and disturbing.

2. It is disturbing to others. Zoophilia, being sexually aroused by animals, for example, disturbs others.

3. It is unusual, not shared by many members of the population. In the United States, having visions is atypical, while in some other cultures it occurs more commonly.

4. It is irrational; it does not make sense to the average person. Feeling depressed when your family first moves away from all your friends is not seen as irrational, while prolonged depression due to virtually any situation is.

Note that people may be diagnosed with a psychological disorder even if they are not experiencing all, or even most, of the above symptoms. Another important point is that the term *insane,* often used by laypeople to describe psychological disorders in general, is not a medical term. Rather, insanity is a legal term. The reason behind the legal definition of insanity is to differentiate between those people who can be held entirely responsible for their crimes (the sane) and those people who, because of a psychological disorder, cannot be held fully responsible for their actions. When defendants plead not guilty by reason of insanity *(NGRI),* they are asking that the court acquit them due to psychological factors.

An obvious question is how psychologists determine whether or not someone has a psychological disorder. To do so, psychologists use a book called the *Diagnostic and Statistical Manual of Mental Disorders (DSM).* Periodically, this book is revised. The latest version is the *DSM-IV-TR.* The *DSM-IV-TR,* as its name suggests, provides a way for psychologists to diagnose their patients. The *DSM-IV-TR* contains the symptoms of everything currently considered to be a psychological disorder. The book's revisions have resulted in astronomical growth in the number and kinds of disorders included since the original *DSM-IV-TR.* However, sometimes behaviors classified as disorders in earlier editions, for instance homosexuality, have been removed from the definition of abnormality.

The *DSM-IV-TR* does not include any discussion of the causes (also called etiology) or treatments of the various disorders, because adherents to each of the psychological perspectives disagree. Psychoanalytic theorists locate the cause of psychological disturbances in unconscious conflicts often caused by traumatic events that occurred during the psychosexual stages (see chapter 9). Behaviorists assert that psychological problems result from the person's history of reinforcement. Cognitive theorists locate the source of psychological disorders in maladaptive ways of thinking. Humanistic psychologists view the root of such disorders in a person's feelings, self-esteem, and self-concept. One of the most recent perspectives, the sociocultural perspective, holds that social ills such as racism, sexism, and poverty lie at the heart of psychological disorders. Finally, the biomedical model sees psychological disorders as caused by biological factors such as hormonal or neurotransmitter imbalances or differences in brain structure. Biomedical psychologists believe that many psychological disorders are associated with genetic abnormalities that may lead to the physiological abnormalities described above. However, the differences do not have to occur at the genetic level.

Table 12.1. Different Perspectives on the Causes of Psychological Disorders.

Perspective	Cause of Disorder
Psychoanalytic/psychodynamic	Internal, unconscious conflicts
Humanistic	Failure to strive toward one's potential or being out of touch with one's feelings
Behavioral	Reinforcement history, the environment
Cognitive	Irrational, dysfunctional thoughts or ways of thinking
Sociocultural	Dysfunctional society
Biomedical	Organic problems, biochemical imbalances, genetic predispositions

Most clinical psychologists do not subscribe strictly to one perspective or another. Rather, most psychologists are *eclectic,* which means that they accept and use ideas from a number of different perspectives (see Table 12.1).

Categories of Disorders

The *DSM-IV-TR* lists hundreds of different psychological disorders, most of which lie beyond the scope of your introductory course. We will deal with six major kinds of disorders: anxiety disorders, somatoform disorders, dissociative disorders, mood or affective disorders, schizophrenic disorders, and personality disorders. We will also touch briefly on a few other types of disorders in order to communicate a sense of the breadth of the field. After a short explanation of each type of disorder, we will briefly discuss how psychologists from a few of the various perspectives might view the cause of some of the disorders within the category. Keep in mind that many psychologists do not strictly adhere to any one perspective. Finally, as you read about the various disorders discussed in this chapter, you may find yourself suspecting that you suffer from some of them. This phenomenon, the tendency to see in oneself the characteristics of disorders about which one is learning, is known as *intern's syndrome* and is not a psychological disorder.

Anxiety Disorders

Anxiety disorders, as their name suggests, share a common symptom of anxiety. We will discuss five anxiety disorders: phobias, generalized anxiety disorder, panic disorder, obsessive-compulsive disorder, and posttraumatic stress disorder.

A simple or *specific phobia* is an intense unwarranted fear of a situation or object such as *claustrophobia* (fear of enclosed spaces) or *arachnophobia* (fear of spiders). Two other common types of phobias are *agoraphobia* and *social phobias*. Agoraphobia is a fear of open, public spaces. People with severe agoraphobia may be afraid to venture out of their homes at all. A social phobia is a fear of a situation in which one could embarrass oneself in public, such as when eating in a restaurant or giving a lecture. Phobias are classified as anxiety disorders because contact with the feared object or situation results in anxiety.

A person who suffers from *generalized anxiety disorder,* often referred to as GAD, experiences constant, low-level anxiety. Such a person constantly feel nervous and out of sorts. On the other hand, someone with *panic disorder* suffers from acute episodes of intense anxiety without any apparent provocation. Panic attacks tend to increase in frequency, and people often suffer additional anxiety due to anticipating the attacks.

Obsessive-compulsive disorder, known as OCD, is when persistent, unwanted thoughts (obsessions) cause someone to feel the need (compulsion) to engage in a particular action. For instance, a common obsession concerns cleanliness. A man experiencing this obsession might be plagued with constant worries that his environment is dirty and full of germs. These thoughts might drive him to wash his hands and shower repeatedly, even to the extent that he is able to do virtually nothing else. Obsessions result in anxiety, and this anxiety is reduced when the person performs the compulsive behavior.

Post-traumatic stress disorder usually involves flashbacks or nightmares following a person's involvement in or observation of an extremely troubling event such as a war or natural disaster. Memories of the event cause anxiety.

Theories About the Cause of Anxiety Disorders

We will follow the discussion of the psychological disorders with a brief description of how adherents from several perspectives view the etiology of such disorders. Since many introductory psychology texts do not deal with the etiology of specific disorders at all, we will be selective and focus on the information most likely to appear on the Advanced Placement examination.

Psychoanalytic theorists see psychological disorders as caused by unresolved, unconscious conflicts. Anxiety is viewed as the result of conflicts between the desires of the id, ego, and superego. For instance, a young woman's repressed sexual attraction to her father may cause a conflict between her id, which desires the father, and her superego, which forbids such a relationship. Anxiety disorders could be the outward manifestation of this internal conflict.

Behaviorists believe all behaviors are learned. Therefore, they assert that anxiety disorders are learned. Consider acrophobia, the fear of heights, as an example. Behaviorists would say that someone who has acrophobia learned the fear response. This learning could happen through classical conditioning, operant conditioning, or some type of cognitive learning. (See the chapter "Learning" for more information about basic learning principles.) Suppose three-year-old Pablo went with his family to visit the Space Needle in Seattle. While on the observation deck, Pablo got separated from his family and was found hours later crying hysterically at the gift shop. Ever since, Pablo has been terrified of heights. In this example, behaviorists would say that Pablo learned through classical conditioning to associate heights with the fear that resulted from losing his family.

Cognitive theorists believe that disorders result from dysfunctional ways of thinking. Therefore, they would attribute an anxiety disorder to an unhealthy and irrational way of thinking and/or specific irrational thoughts. For instance, someone with GAD may have an unrealistically high standard for his or her own behavior. Since the person believes, irrationally, that she or he must always excel at everything she or he does, the person feels constant anxiety stemming from the impossibility of meeting this goal.

Somatoform Disorders

Somatoform disorders occur when a person manifests a psychological problem through a physiological symptom. In other words, such a person experiences a physical problem in the absence of any physical cause. Two somatoform disorders are hypochondriasis and conversion disorder. A person suffering from *hypochondriasis* has frequent physical complaints for which medical doctors are unable to locate the cause. In addition, such a person may believe that minor problems such as headaches or occasional shortness of breath are indicative of severe physical illness even after she or he is assured by doctors that no evidence of such physiological problems exists. .

People who have *conversion disorder* will report the existence of a severe physical problem such as paralysis or blindness, and they will, in fact, be unable to move their arms or see. However, again, no biological reason for this problem can be identified.

Theories About the Cause of Somatoform Disorders

Psychodynamic theorists would assert that somatoform disorders are merely outward manifestations of unresolved unconscious conflicts. Behaviorists would say that people with somatoform disorders are being reinforced for their behavior. For instance, someone experiencing blindness due to conversion disorder may avoid unpleasant tasks like working or someone with hypochondriasis may receive a great deal of attention.

Dissociative Disorders

Dissociative disorders involve a disruption in conscious processes. Psychogenic amnesia, fugue, and dissociative identity disorder (DID) are classified as dissociative disorders. *Psychogenic amnesia* is when a person cannot remember things and no physiological basis for the disruption in memory can be identified. Biologically induced amnesia is called *organic amnesia*. People who have *fugue* not only experience psychogenic amnesia but also find themselves in an unfamiliar environment. For example, one day Albert wakes up with no memory of who or where he is and no one else in the environment can answer that either. Albert has left friends and family, as well as his memory, behind.

Dissociative identity disorder (DID), formerly known as multiple personality disorder, is when a person has several personalities rather than one integrated personality. Someone with DID will have no set number of personalities. The different personalities can represent many different ages and both sexes. Often, two of the personalities will be the opposite of each other. People with DID commonly have a history of sexual abuse or some other terrible childhood trauma.

Theories About the Cause of Dissociative Disorders

Psychoanalytic theorists believe that dissociative disorders result when an extremely traumatic event has been so thoroughly repressed that a split in consciousness results. Behaviorists posit that people who have experienced trauma simply find not thinking about it to be rewarding, thus producing amnesia or, in extreme cases, DID.

Interestingly, cases of DID are rare outside of the United States, where the number increased dramatically in the last century as cases became more publicized. Coupled with the growing belief on the part of many psychologists that people do not engage in repression, these facts have led many to question whether DID is a legitimate psychological disorder. Critics suggest that some people diagnosed with DID may have been led to role-play the disorder inadvertently as a result of their therapists' questions (e.g., "Is there a part of you that feels differently?") and media portrayals.

Mood or Affective Disorders

Someone with a mood or affective disorder experiences extreme or inappropriate emotions. *Major depression,* also known as unipolar depression, is the most common mood disorder and is often referred to as the common cold of all psychological disorders. While we all feel unhappy now and again, most of us do not suffer from major depression. The *DSM-IV-TR* outlines the symptoms that must be present for such a diagnosis. One key factor is the length of the depressive episode. People who are clinically depressed remain unhappy for more than two weeks in the absence of a clear reason. Other common symptoms of depression include loss of appetite, fatigue, change in sleeping patterns, lack of interest in normally enjoyable activities, and feelings of worthlessness. Some people experience depression but only during certain times of the year, usually winter, when there is less sunlight. *Seasonal affective disorder* (SAD) is the resulting diagnosis. SAD is often treated with light therapy.

Unlike unipolar depression, *bipolar disorder,* formerly known as *manic depression,* usually involves both depressed and manic episodes. The depressed episodes involve all of the symptoms just discussed. People experience manic episodes in different ways but they usually involve feelings of high energy. While some sufferers will feel a heightened sense of confidence and power, others simply feel anxious and irritable. Even though some people feel an inflated sense of well-being during the manic period, they usually engage in excessively risky and poorly thought out behavior that ultimately has negative consequences for them.

Theories About the Cause of Mood Disorders

Psychoanalysts commonly view depression as the product of anger directed inward, loss during the early psychosexual stages, or an overly punitive superego. Learning theorists view the mood disorder as bringing about some kind of reinforcement such as attention or sympathy.

Aaron Beck, a cognitive theorist, believes that depression results from unreasonably negative ideas that people have about themselves, their world, and their futures. Beck calls these three components the *cognitive triad.* Another way that cognitive psychologists look at the cause of depression is by exploring the kind of attributions that people make about their experiences. An attribution is an explanation of cause. For instance, if Jonas fails a math test, he may attribute his failure to lack of studying, stupidity, his teacher, or a host of other causes. Certain attributional styles seem more likely to promote depression. Jonas may attribute his failure to an internal (I am bad at math) or an external (the class is difficult) cause. He may attribute his failure to a global (I am bad at all subjects) or a specific (I have trouble with trigonometry) cause. Finally, Jonas may attribute his failure to a stable (I will always be bad at math) or to an unstable (I had a bad day) cause. People who tend to make internal, global, and stable attributions for bad events are more likely to be depressed. Often, these same people tend to make external, specific, and unstable attributions when good things happen to them.

Many theories about the cause of depression combine a cognitive and a behavioral component. An example of these sociocognitive or cognitive-behavioral theories is Martin Seligman's idea of *learned helplessness.* Depression has been found to correlate positively with feelings of learned helplessness. Learned helplessness is when one's prior experiences have caused that person to view himself or herself as unable to control aspects of the future that are controllable. This belief, then, may result in passivity and depression. When undesirable things occur, that individual feels unable to improve the situation and therefore becomes depressed.

A growing body of evidence suggests that a biological component to affective disorders exists. Low levels of serotonin, a neurotransmitter, have been linked with unipolar depression. People who suffer from bipolar disorder have more receptors for acetylcholine, also a neurotransmitter, in their brains and skin. Other researchers have suggested that low levels of norepinephrine are associated with depression. Both unipolar depression and bipolar disorder often respond to somatic therapies (see the chapter "Treatment of Psychological Disorders"). This suggests that these disorders are caused, at least partially, by biological factors. In addition, both major depression and bipolar disorder seem to run in families, a finding that can also be interpreted as indicative of a genetic component to their etiology.

Schizophrenic Disorders

Schizophrenia is probably the most severe and debilitating of the psychological disorders. It tends to strike people as they enter young adulthood. The fundamental symptom of schizophrenia is disordered, distorted thinking often demonstrated through delusions and/or hallucinations. *Delusions* are beliefs that have no basis in reality. If I believed that I was going to win a Nobel prize in literature for writing this book, I would be experiencing a delusion. Common delusions include:

- Delusions of persecution—the belief that people are out to get you.
- Delusions of grandeur—the belief that you enjoy greater power and influence than you do, that you are the president of the United States or a Nobel prize-winning author.

Hint: People often confuse schizophrenia with DID. Schizophrenics DO NOT have split personalities. Schism does mean break, but the break referred to in the term schizophrenia is a break from reality and not a break within a person's consciousness.

Hallucinations are perceptions in the absence of any sensory stimulation. If I keep thinking I see newspaper headlines, "Weseley Wins Nobel," and hordes of autograph seekers outside my window, then I am suffering from hallucinations.

Four kinds of schizophrenia are disorganized schizophrenia, paranoid schizophrenia, catatonic schizophrenia, and undifferentiated schizophrenia. Each of these will be described briefly.

Disorganized schizophrenics evidence some odd uses of language. They may make up their own words (*neologisms*) or string together series of nonsense words that rhyme (*clang associations*). In addition, people with disorganized schizophrenia often evidence *inappropriate affect*. For instance, they might laugh in response to hearing someone has died. Alternatively, they may consistently have essentially no emotional response at all (*flat affect*).

The key symptom in *paranoid schizophrenia* is delusions of persecution. A man suffering from delusions of persecution would believe that others are trying to hurt him or out to get him.

People who suffer from *catatonic schizophrenia* engage in odd movements. They may remain motionless in strange postures for hours at a time, move jerkily and quickly for no apparent reason, or alternate between the two. When motionless, catatonic schizophrenics usually evidence *waxy flexibility.* That is, they allow their body to be moved into any alternative shape and will then hold that new pose. Catatonic schizophrenia is an increasingly rare form of schizophrenia in the United States.

Finally, people are diagnosed with *undifferentiated schizophrenia* if they exhibit disordered thinking but no symptoms of one of the other types of schizophrenia.

Schizophrenic symptoms are often divided into two types: positive and negative. *Positive symptoms* refer to excesses in behavior, thought, or mood such as neologisms and hallucinations whereas *negative symptoms* correspond to deficits such as flat affect or catatonia.

Theories About the Cause of Schizophrenic Disorders

One of the most popular ideas about the cause of schizophrenia is biological and is called the *dopamine hypothesis.* The basic idea behind the dopamine hypothesis is that high levels of dopamine seem to be associated with schizophrenia. The evidence for this link includes the findings detailed below:

- Antipsychotic drugs used to treat schizophrenia result in lower dopamine levels and a decrease in the disordered thought and behavior that is the hallmark of schizophrenia. However, extensive use of these drugs may also cause negative side effects: muscle tremors and stiffness, a problem known as *tardive dyskinesia.*
- Parkinson's disease, characterized by muscle stiffness and tremors not unlike tardive dyskinesia, is treated with a drug called L-dopa that acts to increase dopamine levels. When given in excess, L-dopa causes schizophrenic-like distortions in thought.

More evidence suggests a biological basis for schizophrenia as well. Enlarged brain ventricles are associated with schizophrenia, as are brain asymmetries. Furthermore, a genetic predisposition seems to exist for schizophrenia. Some research suggests that an abnormality on the fifth chromosome is associated with schizophrenia. Both monozygotic (identical) twins are significantly more likely to have schizophrenia than are dizygotic (fraternal) twins. People whose parents are schizophrenic are more likely to have schizophrenia than people whose parents do not have the disorder. Some research has suggested that negative symptoms are linked to genetic factors while positive symptoms tend to be related to abnormalities in dopamine levels.

Not surprisingly, not all psychologists agree that schizophrenia has a biological basis. Some people believe that certain kinds of environments may cause or increase the likelihood of developing schizophrenia. One commonly suggested cognitive-behavioral cause is the existence of *double binds*. A double bind is when a person is given contradictory messages. If when growing up, Sally is continually cautioned by her parents against acting promiscuously while they give her revealing, provocative outfits as gifts, Sally would be experiencing a double bind. People who live in environments full of such conflicting messages may develop distorted ways of thinking due to the impossibility of rationally resolving their experiences.

Hint: *Do not confuse double binds, a hypothesized cause of schizophrenia, with double blinds, a way of eliminating experimenter bias.*

Personality Disorders

Personality disorders are generally less serious than the other disorders we have discussed thus far. Personality disorders are well-established, maladaptive ways of behaving that negatively affect people's ability to function. The most important personality disorder with which you should be familiar is *antisocial personality disorder*. People with antisocial personality disorder have little regard for other people's feelings. They view the world as a hostile place where people need to look out for themselves. Not surprisingly, criminals seem to manifest a high incidence of antisocial personality disorder.

Hint: Although your vocabulary will generally help you figure out what psychological terms mean, sometimes it will mislead you. For instance, many students incorrectly assume that people who suffer from antisocial personality disorder are merely unfriendly. In reality, as explained above, people with antisocial personality disorder are insensitive to others and thus often act in ways that bring pain to others.

The characteristics of many other personality disorders are deducible from the names of the disorders. For instance, people with *dependent personality disorder* rely too much on the attention and help of others, and those with *paranoid personality disorder* feel persecuted. Similarly, but based on words more difficult to define, *narcissistic personality disorder* involves seeing oneself as the center of the universe (*narcissism* means self love), and *histrionic personality disorder* connotes overly dramatic behavior (histrionics). Keep in mind that a personality disorder is a more minor form of disorder than the others we have discussed. Therefore, people with paranoid personality disorder may believe they are being persecuted, but they will not experience the distortion of thought and delusions that paranoid schizophrenics do. Likewise, people with *obsessive-compulsive personality disorder* may be overly concerned with certain thoughts and performing certain behaviors, but they will not be debilitated to the same extent that someone with obsessive-compulsive disorder would.

Other Examples of Psychological Disorders

The *DSM-IV-TR* describes a wide variety of disorders. Although this chapter certainly cannot be comprehensive, some additional problems will be briefly discussed.

Paraphilias are marked by the sexual attraction to an object, person, or activity not usually seen as sexual. For instance, attraction to children is called *pedophilia*, to animals is called *zoophilia*, and to objects, such as shoes, is called *fetishism*. Someone who becomes sexually aroused by watching others engage in some kind of sexual behavior is a *voyeur*, someone who is aroused by having pain inflicted upon them is a *masochist*, and someone who is aroused by inflicting pain on someone else is a *sadist*. Interestingly, most paraphilias occur more commonly in men than in women, however masochism is an exception.

Eating disorders are another kind of psychological problem classified in the *DSM-IV-TR*. Although we most often hear about *anorexia nervosa* and *bulimia*, obesity is also classified in the *DSM-IV-TR*. The basic symptoms that result in a diagnosis of anorexia nervosa are loss of 15 percent or more of the average body weight for one's age and size, an intense fear of fat and food, and a distorted body image. Anorexia nervosa, which predominates in girls and young women, is essentially a form of self-starvation. Bulimia shares similar features with anorexia nervosa such as a fear of food and fat and a distorted body image. However, bulimics do not lose so much of their body weight. Bulimia commonly involves a binge-purge cycle in which sufferers eat large quantities of food and then attempt to purge the food from their bodies by throwing up or using laxatives.

Another category of psychological disorders involves the use of substances such as alcohol and drugs. Use of such substances does not automatically mean one would be classified as having a disorder. *Substance use disorder* is a diagnosis made when the use of such substances regularly and negatively affects a person's life. *Substance dependence* is another term for addiction. A person whose life is disturbed by the use of chemical substances and who is unable to cut down his or her use of the substances suffers from substance dependence.

One final example of the kinds of disorders in the *DSM-IV-TR* is developmental disorders. Some developmental disorders deal with deviations from typical social development. *Autism* is one such disorder. From very early on, autistic children seek out less social and emotional contact than do other children. Autistic children are slow to develop language skills and less likely to seek out parental support when distressed.

Other developmental disorders involve difficulties in terms of developing skills. *Attention deficit/hyperactivity disorder* (ADHD) is one example. A child with ADHD may have difficulty paying attention or sitting still. This disorder occurs much more commonly in boys. Critics suggest that the kind of behavior typical of young boys (regardless of whether its cause is biological, environmental, or a combination of the two) results in an overdiagnosis of this problem.

A Cautionary Note

The *DSM-IV-TR* provides psychologists with an invaluable tool by enabling them to diagnose their clients. However, keep in mind that diagnostic labels are not always correct and have a tendency to outlast their usefulness.

The Rosenhan Study: The Influence of Labels

In 1978, David Rosenhan conducted a study in which he and a number of associates sought admission to a number of mental hospitals. All claimed that they had been hearing voices; that was the sole symptom they reported. All were admitted to the institutions as suffering from schizophrenia. At that time, they ceased reporting any unusual symptoms and behaved as they usually did. None of the researchers were exposed as imposters, and all ultimately left the institutions with the diagnosis of schizophrenia in remission. While in the institutions, the researchers' every behavior was interpreted as a sign of their disorder. The Rosenhan study, while flawed and widely critiqued, raises several important issues:

1. Should people who were once diagnosed with a psychological problem carry that diagnosis for the rest of their lives?

2. To what extent are disorders the product of a particular environment, and to what extent do they inhere in the individual?

3. What is the level of institutional care available if the imposters could go undetected for a period of days and, in some cases, weeks?

Now that we have discussed various psychological disorders, the next chapter will discuss treatment methods.

Practice Questions

> *Directions:* Each of the questions or incomplete statements below is followed by five suggested answers or completions. Select the one that is best in each case.

1. Which of the following is not an anxiety disorder?
   (A) obsessive-compulsive disorder
   (B) conversion disorder
   (C) zoophobia
   (D) post-traumatic stress disorder
   (E) panic disorder

2. All schizophrenics suffer from
   (A) depression.
   (B) multiple personalities.
   (C) flat affect.
   (D) distorted thinking.
   (E) delusions of persecution.

3. Juan hears voices that tell him to kill people. Juan is experiencing
   (A) delusions.
   (B) obsessions.
   (C) anxiety.
   (D) hallucinations.
   (E) compulsions.

4. Linda's neighbors describe her as typically shy and mild mannered. She seems to be a devoted wife and mother to her husband and three children. Unbeknownst to these neighbors, Linda sometimes dresses up in flashy, revealing clothing and goes to bars to pick up strange men. At such times, she is boisterous and overbearing. She tells everyone she meets that her name is Jen. At other times, when she is upset, Linda slips into childlike behavior and responds only to the name Sally. Linda is suffering from
   (A) a schizophrenic disorder.
   (B) a mood disorder.
   (C) a dissociative disorder.
   (D) a somatoform disorder.
   (E) a psychosexual disorder.

5. The *DSM-IV-TR* contains
   I. a description of the symptoms of mental disorders.
   II. a description of the likely causes of mental disorders.
   III. recommended methods of treatment for mental disorders.
   (A) I only
   (B) II only
   (C) III only
   (D) I and II
   (E) I, II, and III

6. All of the following are biomedical explanations for schizophrenia EXCEPT
   (A) double binds.
   (B) brain asymmetries.
   (C) the dopamine hypothesis.
   (D) a genetic predisposition.
   (E) enlarged brain ventricles.

7. Psychologists who draw from several different theoretical perspectives rather than strictly following one are known as
   (A) open-minded.
   (B) mixed.
   (C) flexible.
   (D) eclectic.
   (E) broad.

8. Depression is associated with low levels of
   (A) acetylcholine.
   (B) epinephrine.
   (C) serotonin.
   (D) dopamine.
   (E) GABA.

9. "I am the most important person in the world" is a statement that might characterize the views of someone with which of the following personality disorders?
   (A) schizoid
   (B) antisocial
   (C) histrionic
   (D) dependent
   (E) narcissistic

10. What kind of psychologist would be most likely to describe depression as the result of an unconscious process in which anger is turned inward?
    (A) biomedical
    (B) psychoanalytic
    (C) cognitive
    (D) behavioral
    (E) sociocultural

11. Women in the United States have a higher rate of depression than do men. Which kind of psychologist would be most likely to explain this higher incidence in terms of the pressures and prejudices that women suffer?
    (A) humanistic
    (B) psychoanalytic
    (C) cognitive
    (D) behavioral
    (E) sociocultural

12. The relationship between schizophrenia and Parkinson's disease is that
    (A) both are caused by too little dopamine.
    (B) both are treated by antipsychotic drugs.
    (C) both can be caused by excessive use of amphetamines.
    (D) schizophrenia is associated with too much dopamine and Parkinson's with too little.
    (E) Parkinson's is associated with too much dopamine and schizophrenia with too little.

13. Anand is unable to move his right arm. He has been to scores of physicians seeking a cure, but none have been able to find any physiological reason for his paralysis. Anand may be suffering from
    (A) conversion disorder.
    (B) fugue.
    (C) hypochondriasis.
    (D) SAD.
    (E) OCD.

14. Mary is sexually aroused by aardvarks. Mary might be diagnosed as having
    (A) pedophilia.
    (B) masochism.
    (C) sadism.
    (D) a paraphilia.
    (E) fetishism.

15. Which statement about bulimia is true?
    (A) Only women suffer from this disorder.
    (B) All bulimics use vomiting to rid their bodies of unwanted calories.
    (C) Bulimics lose in excess of 15 percent of the normal body weight for their age and size.
    (D) The main cause of bulimia is society's emphasis on thinness.
    (E) Bulimics tend to be overly concerned with their weight and body image.

Answers to Practice Questions

1. **(B)** Conversion disorder is a type of somatoform disorder in which a psychological problem manifests itself in one, often serious, physical symptom such as blindness or paralysis. All of the other disorders listed are anxiety disorders.

2. **(D)** Distortion of thought is the characteristic common to all types of schizophrenia. Schizophrenia is distinct from both depression and dissociative identity disorder, although, as discussed in the chapter, it is often confused with the latter. Although some schizophrenics manifest flat affect, particularly disorganized schizophrenics, it is not a symptom shared by all schizophrenics. Only paranoid schizophrenics experience delusions of persecution.

3. **(D)** Perceiving sensory stimulation when none exists defines a hallucination. Delusions are irrational thoughts but do not involve a belief in the existence of sensory stimulation. Obsessions are persistent, unwanted thoughts. Compulsions are unwanted, repetitive actions that people engage in to reduce anxiety.

4. **(C)** Linda is suffering from multiple personality disorder, also known as dissociative identity disorder, a type of dissociative disorder.

5. **(A)** The *DSM-IV-TR* contains only the symptoms of the various disorders. Neither causes nor treatments are addressed in the *DSM-IV-TR* since beliefs about both causes and treatments depend on the theoretical model to which one subscribes.

6. **(A)** A double bind is when someone is told to do something and then punished for doing it. While some researchers theorize that double binds cause schizophrenia, they would be an environmental cause, not a physical or medical cause. All the other choices are biological factors that theoretically play a role in schizophrenia.

7. **(D)** Psychologists who draw on various perspectives in their work are known as eclectic. The other terms have no specific psychological meaning.

8. **(C)** Depression is associated with low levels of serotonin.

9. **(E)** Narcissism is the love of oneself. People who view themselves as the focus of the world would most likely be classified as having narcissistic personality disorder.

10. **(B)** Psychoanalysts view depression as the result of anger turned inward. Biomedical psychologists would see depression as the result of some biological cause. Cognitive psychologists would locate the cause in the person's style of thinking. Behaviorists believe depression is caused by one's reinforcement history. Psychologists adhering to the sociocultural model would fault aspects of society such as racism or poverty.

11. **(E)** Sociocultural psychologists believe that mental illness is mainly caused by certain negative aspects of society such as sexism.

12. **(D)** Schizophrenia is associated with high levels of dopamine and Parkinson's disease with low levels of dopamine. Schizophrenia is often treated with antipsychotic drugs. Excessive use of amphetamines is associated with both high levels of dopamine and schizophrenic-like symptoms.

13. **(A)** Anand's symptoms suggest he has conversion disorder, a type of somatoform disorder. Fugue is a dissociative disorder which involves amnesia and relocation. Hypochondriasis is a different kind of somatoform disorder that involves constant, minor physical complaints and the belief that these minor problems are indicative of a serious, medical problem. SAD, seasonal affective disorder, is a type of affective disorder in which people become depressed during prolonged periods of bad weather. OCD, obsessive-compulsive disorder, is an anxiety disorder in which unwanted, persistent thoughts push people to perform unwanted, repetitive actions to reduce anxiety.

14. **(D)** Paraphilias involve sexual arousal and interest in people, objects, or situations not generally considered arousing. More specifically, Mary has zoophilia since she is aroused by an animal. Pedophilia is a sexual attraction to children. Masochism is when one needs to be hurt in order to be sexually aroused, and fetishism is when objects, such as shoes, are sexually arousing.

15. **(E)** Bulimics tend to be overly concerned with their weight and body image. These concerns lead them to engage in the binge-purge cycle that typifies bulimia. A growing number of men suffer from bulimia. Not all bulimics use vomiting to purge unwanted calories. Other methods include using laxatives, diuretics, and excessive exercise. Anorexics, not bulimics, lose more than 15 percent of their normal body weight. As is true of most, if not all, disorders, the cause of bulimia is a matter of some debate.

CHAPTER 13

Treatment of Psychological Disorders

Overview

Just as there are many different views about the cause of mental disorders, many different beliefs exist about the appropriate way to treat psychological illness. All the methods of treatment, however, share a common purpose: to alter the client's behavior, thoughts, and/or feelings.

History

People have always suffered from psychological problems, but the attitudes toward and treatment of these people have changed dramatically. In many early societies, the mentally ill were seen as possessed by evil spirits. Archaeologists have unearthed human skulls with regularly shaped holes that seem to have been purposefully made. Researchers theorize that the making of the holes, a process called *trephining* was an early form of treatment that was supposed to let the harmful spirits escape.

Although both Hippocrates, who lived in Ancient Greece circa 500 B.C., and Galen, who lived in Rome circa 200 A.D., posited that psychological illnesses were influenced by biological factors and could therefore be treated, Europeans during the Middle Ages returned to the belief that demons and spirits were the cause. Persecution, rather than treatment, usually resulted.

The Enlightenment led to a more sympathetic view. Leading the call to treat victims of mental illness more humanely at the turn of the nineteenth century were Philippe Pinel in France and Dorothea Dix in the United States. These reformers railed against a system that treated the mentally ill as if they were criminals, even caging and beating them. These two helped bring about the development of separate and kinder institutions for people with severe psychological disorders.

Several recent trends in the field of mental health in the United States must also be mentioned. Following the development of drugs in the 1950s that could moderate the effects of severe disorders, many people were released from mental institutions. This phenomenon, called *deinstitutionalization,* was intended to save money as well as benefit the former inpatients. Unfortunately, deinstitutionalization was far less successful than initially hoped. Once released, many of the former patients were unable to care for themselves. Their psychological needs were supposed to be met by local clinics on an outpatient basis. Many of the people released, however, were schizophrenics who ended up homeless and delusional, unable to secure the psychological or the financial care they needed.

Recently, in the United States, a growing emphasis has been placed on *preventative efforts.* If psychological problems can be treated proactively, or before they become severe, the suffering of the client as well as the cost of providing care can be reduced. Preventative efforts can be described as primary, secondary, or tertiary. *Primary prevention* efforts attempt to reduce the incidence of societal problems, such as joblessness or homelessness, that can give rise to mental health issues. *Secondary prevention* involves working with people at-risk for developing specific problems. One example would be counseling people who live in an area that has experienced a trauma such as a natural disaster or terrorist attack. Finally, *tertiary prevention* efforts aim to keep people's mental health issues from becoming more severe, for instance, working with earthquake survivors who are already suffering from an anxiety disorder in the hopes of preventing the disorder from becoming more severe.

Types of Therapy

Clearly, people's beliefs about effective treatment are grounded in their ideas about the cause of the problem. Psychoanalytic, humanistic, behavioral, and cognitive psychologists share a belief in the power of *psychotherapy* to treat mental disorders. On the other hand, psychologists who subscribe to a biomedical model assert that such problems require *somatic treatments* such as drugs. Psychotherapies, except for behavioral treatments, largely consist of talking to a psychologist. Behaviorists, as you know, believe that psychological problems result from the contingencies of reinforcement to which a person has been exposed. Therefore, behavioral therapy focuses on changing these contingencies.

Both psychologists with a biomedical orientation and psychoanalysts generally refer to the people who come to them for help as *patients.* Most other therapists prefer the term *clients.* In discussing the various types of therapy, we will follow these conventions.

Psychoanalytic Therapy

Psychoanalysis is a therapeutic technique developed by Freud. A patient undergoing psychoanalysis will usually lie on a couch while the therapist sits in a chair out of the patient's line of vision.

Psychoanalytic theorists view the cause of disorders as unconscious conflicts. As a result, their initial focus is on identifying the underlying cause of the problem. Psychoanalysts believe that other methods of therapy may succeed in ridding a client of a particular symptom but do not address the true problem. As a result, psychoanalysts assert that patients will suffer from *symptom substitution.* Symptom substitution is when, after a person is successfully treated for one psychological disorder, that person begins to experience a new psychological problem. Psychoanalytic therapists argue that a person's symptoms are the outward manifestations of deeper problems that can be cured only through analysis. Often, this approach entails a lengthy and therefore expensive course of therapy.

To delve into the unconscious minds of his patients, Freud developed a number of techniques including hypnosis, free association, and dream analysis. *Hypnosis,* as described in the chapter "States of Consciousness," is an altered state of consciousness. When in this state, psychoanalysts believe that people are less likely to repress troubling thoughts. More commonly, psychoanalysts ask patients to *free associate*—to say whatever comes to mind without thinking. This technique is based on the idea that we all constantly censor what we say, thereby allowing us to hide some of our thoughts from ourselves. If we force ourselves to say whatever pops into our minds, we are more likely to reveal clues about what is really bothering us by eluding the ego's defenses. When psychoanalysts use *dream analysis*, discussed further in chapter 5, they ask their patients to describe their dreams. Again, since the ego's defenses are relaxed during sleep, they hope the dreams will help the therapist see what is at the root of the patient's problem.

All three of these techniques rely heavily on the *interpretations* of the therapists. In dream analysis, what the patient reports is called the *manifest content* of the dream. What is really of interest to the analyst is the *latent* or hidden content. The latent content of the dream is revealed only as a result of the therapist's interpretive work.

Sometimes patients may disagree with their therapists' interpretations. Psychoanalysts may see such objections as signs of *resistance*. Since psychoanalysis can be a painful process of coming to terms with deeply repressed, troubling thoughts, people are thought to try to protect themselves through resistance. In fact, a particularly strongly voiced disagreement to an analyst's suggestion is often viewed as an indication that the analyst is closing in on the source of the problem.

One final aspect of psychoanalysis involves *transference*. Transference is when, in the course of therapy, patients begin to have strong feelings toward their therapists. Patients may think they are in love with their therapists, may view their therapists as parental figures, or may seethe with hatred toward them. Psychoanalysts believe that, in the process of therapy, patients often redirect strong emotions felt toward people with whom they have had troubling relationships (often their parents) onto their therapists. Analysts try to interpret their patients' transference as a further technique to reveal the source of the problem.

As discussed earlier in this book, while strict adherents to Freudian theory are still known as psychoanalysts, many other psychologists have been influenced by Freud's work but have significantly modified his original theory. Such psychologists are known as *psychodynamic* theorists. While psychodynamic psychologists generally still see the unconscious as an important element in understanding a person's difficulties, they will be more likely to use a variety of techniques associated with other perspectives.

Psychoanalytic/psychodynamic treatments and the humanistic therapies that will be discussed in the next section are sometimes referred to as insight therapies. *Insight therapies* highlight the importance of the patients/clients gaining an understanding of their problems.

Humanistic Therapies

Humanistic therapies focus on helping people to understand, accept themselves, and strive to *self-actualize*. Self-actualization means to reach one's highest potential. Humanistic psychologists view it as a powerful motivational goal. Humanistic therapists operate from the belief that people are innately good and also possess *free will*. A belief that people have free will means that they are capable of controlling their own destinies. *Determinism* is the opposite belief. It holds that people have no influence over what happens to them and that their choices are predetermined by forces outside of their control. Humanistic psychologists' belief in human goodness and free will leads these psychologists to assert that if people are supported and helped to recognize their goals, they will move toward self-fulfillment.

One of the best known of humanistic therapists is Carl Rogers. Rogers created *client-centered therapy*, also known as person-centered therapy. This therapeutic method hinges on the therapist providing the client with what Rogers termed *unconditional positive regard*. Unconditional positive regard is blanket acceptance and support of a person regardless of what the person says or does. Rogers believes that unconditional positive regard is essential to healthy development. People who have not experienced it may come to see themselves in the negative ways that others have made them feel. By providing unconditional positive regard, humanistic therapists seek to help their clients accept and take responsibility for themselves.

In stark contrast to the cognitive therapies to be discussed later, client-centered therapy, and humanistic therapies in general, are *non-directive*. In other words, Rogerian therapists would not tell their clients what to do but, rather, would seek to help the clients choose a course of action for themselves. Often, client-centered therapists say very little. They encourage the clients to talk a lot about how they feel and sometimes mirror back those feelings ("So what I'm hearing you say is . . .") to help clarify the feelings for the client. This technique is known as *active listening*.

Another type of humanistic therapy is *Gestalt therapy,* developed by Fritz Perls. As we have discussed, Gestalt psychologists emphasize the importance of the whole. These therapists encourage their clients to get in touch with their whole selves. For example, Gestalt therapists encourage their clients to explore feelings of which they may not be aware and emphasize the importance of body position and seemingly minute actions. These therapists want their clients to integrate all of their actions, feelings, and thoughts into a harmonious whole. Gestalt therapists also stress the importance of the present because one can best appreciate the totality of an experience as it occurs.

Existential therapies are humanistic therapies that focus on helping clients achieve a subjectively meaningful perception of their lives. Existential therapists see clients' difficulties as caused by the clients having lost or failed to develop a sense of their lives' purpose. Therefore, these therapists seek to support clients and help them formulate a vision of their lives as worthwhile.

Behavioral Therapies

Behaviorists believe that all behavior is learned. In chapter 6, we discussed various ways that people learn including classical conditioning, operant conditioning, and modeling. Behaviorists base their therapies upon these same learning principles.

One such technique is *counterconditioning,* a kind of classical conditioning developed by Mary Cover Jones in which an unpleasant conditioned response is replaced with a pleasant one. For instance, suppose Charley is afraid of going to the doctor and cries hysterically as soon as he enters the doctor's office. His mother might attempt to replace the conditioned response of crying with contentment by bringing Charley's favorite snacks and toys with them every time they go to the office.

One behaviorist method of treatment involving counterconditioning has had considerable success in helping people with anxiety disorders, especially phobias. It was developed by Joseph Wolpe and is called *systematic desensitization.* This process involves teaching the client to replace the feelings of anxiety with *relaxation.* The first step in systematic desensitization is teaching the client to relax. A variety of techniques can be used such as breathing exercises and meditation. Next the therapist and client work together to construct what is called an anxiety hierarchy. An *anxiety hierarchy* is a rank-ordered list of what the client fears, starting with the least frightening and ending with the most frightening.

Imagine that Penelope has gone to a therapist for help with her arachnophobia (fear of spiders). At the bottom of Penelope's anxiety hierarchy is a photograph of a small spider in a magazine while at the top is her thinking of a number of larger, but harmless, spiders crawling on her. Other possible steps in the anxiety hierarchy include looking at a live spider in a tank, touching a live spider while wearing gloves, and allowing one small spider to crawl on her leg. Once Penelope has learned some relaxation techniques and constructed an anxiety hierarchy with the therapist, she can begin to use *counterconditioning* to replace her fear of spiders with relaxation.

The therapist will ask Penelope to relax and then will ask her to imagine the first step on the anxiety hierarchy. In this case, she looks at a picture of a small spider in a magazine. When Penelope can accomplish this task without feeling fear, the therapist will ask her to imagine the second step on the anxiety hierarchy. Penelope will continue to climb up the hierarchy until she feels anxious. As soon as she experiences anxiety, the therapist will tell her to take a step back down on the hierarchy until she feels calm again. This process will continue throughout Penelope's sessions with the therapist until she feels no anxiety, even when reaching the top of the hierarchy. This process is effective because learning through classical conditioning is strengthened by repeated pairings. Thus, the more times relaxation is paired with the feared stimuli, the stronger the relaxation response becomes. For some people, imagining the feared stimuli is not sufficient. They need to confront the actual items on the anxiety hierarchy. Such therapy is known as *in vivo desensitization.*

Another method of treating anxiety disorders that uses classical conditioning techniques is called *implosive therapy.* Unlike the gradual process of systematic desensitization, implosive therapy involves having the client imagine the most frightening scenario first. As one might expect, this technique produces tremendous anxiety. The idea, however, is that if clients face their fears and do not back down, they will soon realize that the fear is, in fact, irrational. In Penelope's case, if she were to begin by imagining that large spiders were crawling on her but that nothing bad was happening as a result, her fear would soon be *extinguished*. Just as systematic desensitization has a counterpart in in vivo desensitization, *flooding* involves experiencing, rather than imagining, one's peak fear until the anxiety is extinguished.

Another way that classical conditioning techniques can be used to treat people is called *aversive conditioning*. This process involves pairing a habit a person wishes to break such as smoking or bed-wetting with an unpleasant stimulus such as electric shock or nausea.

Instrumental conditioning can also be used as a method of treatment. This process involves using rewards and/or punishments to modify a person's behavior. One form of instrumental conditioning used in mental institutions, schools, and even in some people's homes is called a *token economy*. In a token economy, desired behaviors are identified and rewarded with tokens. The tokens can then be exchanged for various objects or privileges.

Modeling, as you will recall from chapter 6, is a process through which one person learns by observing and then imitating the behavior of another. Unlike the other techniques described in this section, modeling is a melding of cognitive and behavioral ideas. Modeling could be used to treat Penelope's phobia by having her watch someone else interact calmly and without ill effect with various spiders and then asking her to reenact what she had witnessed. Modeling can also be used to help people with a host of other difficulties as well.

Cognitive Therapies

As cognitive therapists locate the cause of psychological problems in the way people think, their methods of therapy concentrate on changing these unhealthy thought patterns. Cognitive therapy is often quite combative as therapists challenge the irrational thinking patterns of their clients. An example of an unhealthy way of thinking is to attribute all failures to internal, global, and permanent aspects of the self. Assume Josephine fails a psychology test. She can explain this failure in many ways. A negative and unhealthy *attributional style* would involve thinking that she is an idiot who will fail all tests in all subjects all the time. A healthier attributional style would view the cause of the failure as external (the test was difficult), specific (this topic was particularly difficult), and temporary (she will do better next time).

Rational Emotive Behavior Therapy (REBT or RET) was developed by Albert Ellis. Therapists employing *REBT* look to expose and confront the dysfunctional thoughts of their clients. For instance, someone suffering from a social phobia might voice concern over being publicly embarrassed when giving a class presentation. By using REBT, a therapist would question both the likelihood of such embarrassment occurring and the impact that would result. The therapist's goal would be to show the client that not only is his or her failure an unlikely occurrence but that, even if it did occur, it would not be such a big deal.

Aaron Beck created *Cognitive Therapy,* a process most often employed in the treatment of depression. This method involves trying to get clients to engage in pursuits that will bring them success. This will alleviate the depression while also identifying and challenging the irrational ideas that cause their unhappiness. Beck explains depression using the *cognitive triad,* people's beliefs about themselves, their worlds, and their futures. People suffering from depression often have irrationally negative beliefs about all three of these areas. Cognitive therapy aims to make these beliefs more positive.

Group Therapy

Psychotherapy can involve groups of people in addition to one-on-one client-therapist interactions. Therapists running groups can have any of the orientations described above or can be eclectic, as described in the last chapter. One common use of group therapy is in treating families. This form of treatment is known as *family therapy*. Since a client's problems do not occur in a vacuum, many therapists find meeting with the whole family helpful in revealing the patterns of interaction between family members and altering the behavior of the whole family rather than just one member.

Sometimes group therapy involves meeting with a number of people experiencing similar difficulties. Such an approach is less expensive for the clients and offers them the insight and feedback of their peers in addition to that of the therapist. *Self-help groups* such as Alcoholics Anonymous (AA) are a form of group therapy that does not involve a therapist at all.

Somatic Therapies

Psychologists with a biomedical orientation, as mentioned earlier, see the cause of psychological disorders in organic causes. These include imbalances in neurotransmitters or hormones, structural abnormalities in the brain, or genetic predispositions that might underlie the other two. Therefore, these psychologists advocate the use of somatic therapies—therapies that produce bodily changes.

The most common type of somatic therapy is drug therapy or *psychopharmacology*, also known as *chemotherapy*. Drugs treat many kinds of psychological problems, ranging from anxiety disorders to mood disorders to schizophrenia. The more severe a disorder, the more likely that drugs will be used to treat it. Schizophrenia, for example, is almost always treated with drugs. A shortcoming of most kinds of psychotherapy is its limited use in dealing with patients unable to express themselves coherently. Since disordered thought is the primary symptom of schizophrenia, people suffering from this disorder overwhelmingly have difficulty communicating with others, thus rendering psychotherapy of limited use.

Schizophrenia is generally treated with *antipsychotic* drugs such as *Thorazine* or *Haldol*. These drugs generally function by blocking the receptor sites for dopamine. Their effectiveness therefore provides support for the dopamine hypothesis described in chapter 12. An unfortunate side effect of antipsychotic medication is *tardive dyskinesia*, Parkinsonian-like, chronic muscle tremors.

Mood disorders often respond well to chemotherapy. The three most common kinds of drugs used to treat unipolar depression are *tricyclic antidepressants*, *monoamine oxidase (MAO) inhibitors*, and *serotonin-reuptake-inhibitor drugs* (most notably *Prozac*). All tend to increase the activity of serotonin, although tricyclics and MAO inhibitors seem to have wider effects. *Lithium*, a metal, is often used to treat the manic phase of bipolar disorder.

Anxiety disorders are also often treated with drugs. Essentially, these drugs act by depressing the activity of the central nervous system, thus making people feel more relaxed. Two main types of antianxiety drugs are *barbiturates*, such as *Miltown*, and *benzodiazepines*, including *Xanax* and *Valium*.

Table 13.1 lists the most common kinds of drugs used to treat many of the disorders discussed in chapter 12.

Table 13.1. Chemotherapy.

Type of Disorder	Type of Drug(s)
Anxiety disorders	Barbiturates, benzodiazepines
Unipolar depression	Monoamine oxidase (MAO) inhibitors, tricyclic antidepressants, serotonin-reuptake-inhibitors
Bipolar disorder	Lithium
Schizophrenia	Antipsychotics (neuroleptics)

Another kind of somatic therapy is *electroconvulsive therapy (ECT)*. In bilateral ECT, electric current is passed through both hemispheres of the brain. Unilateral ECT involves running current through only one hemisphere. Bilateral ECT, although generally more effective, also has more significant negative side effects, most notably loss of memory. The electric shock causes patients to experience a brief seizure. Prior to administering ECT, patients are given a muscle relaxant to reduce the effects of the seizure. Usually, following the seizure, patients briefly lose consciousness. ECT is a less common treatment than chemotherapy. It is used, most often, for severe cases of depression after other methods have failed. Although the means by which ECT works is not completely understood, one theory suggests that the benefits are the result of a change in the brain's blood flow patterns.

The most intrusive and rarest form of somatic therapy is *psychosurgery*. Psychosurgery involves the purposeful destruction of part of the brain to alter a person's behavior. Clearly, such a procedure is used only as a last resort and only on people suffering to a great extent. An early, and unfortunately widespread, form of psychosurgery was the *prefrontal lobotomy*. This operation involved cutting the main neurons leading to the frontal lobe of the brain. Although this procedure often calmed the behavior of patients, it reduced their level of functioning and awareness to a vegetative state. Even today, when surgical procedures have grown much more precise, debate remains over the risks of psychosurgery, and the procedure is rarely done.

Kinds of Therapists

In addition to the different orientations discussed above, therapists have various levels and kinds of training.

- Psychiatrists are medical doctors and are therefore the only therapists permitted to prescribe medication in most U.S. states. Not surprisingly, because of their backgrounds, psychiatrists often favor a biomedical model of mental illness and are often less extensively trained in psychotherapy.
- Clinical psychologists earn doctoral degrees (Ph.D.s) that require four or more years of study. They then work in an internship overseen by a more experienced professional.
- Counseling psychologists have graduate degrees in psychology. They have generally undergone less training and deal with less severe problems than clinical psychologists do.
- Psychoanalysts are people specifically trained in Freudian methods. They may or may not hold medical degrees.

How Effective Is Therapy?

Although therapy is clearly not always successful and many people recover from a variety of disorders without any intervention, a number of studies have documented that therapy is generally effective. The success of the treatment process is also clearly affected by the relationship between client and therapist. Therefore, a person who has a bad experience with therapy with one therapist at one time might respond more positively to another practitioner in another situation.

Practice Questions

Directions: Each of the questions or incomplete statements below is followed by five suggested answers or completions. Select the one that is best in each case.

1. Which kind of therapist is most likely to analyze a client's dreams?
   (A) behaviorist
   (B) cognitive
   (C) humanistic
   (D) psychoanalytic
   (E) biomedical

2. Coretta's therapist says little during their sessions and never makes any recommendations about what she ought to do. What kind of therapy does Coretta's therapist most likely practice?
   (A) psychodynamic
   (B) behavioral
   (C) cognitive
   (D) biomedical
   (E) humanistic

3. Craig saw a behaviorist to treat his crippling test anxiety. After a few months, Craig no longer experiences any fear when taking tests, however he has developed an obsessive-compulsive disorder. According to psychoanalysts, Craig is experiencing
   (A) free association.
   (B) symptom substitution.
   (C) an anxiety hierarchy.
   (D) problem transference.
   (E) interpretation.

4. Systematic desensitization is to in vivo desensitization as
   (A) flooding is to aversion therapy.
   (B) modeling is to implosive therapy.
   (C) aversion therapy is to modeling.
   (D) implosive therapy is to flooding.
   (E) implosive therapy is to in vivo implosive therapy.

5. Who is credited with creating client-centered therapy?
   (A) Fritz Perls
   (B) Carl Rogers
   (C) Albert Ellis
   (D) Aaron Beck
   (E) John Watson

6. Which process involves counterconditioning?
   (A) RET
   (B) ECT
   (C) transference
   (D) somatic therapy
   (E) systematic desensitization

7. Which of the following is used as a somatic therapy for depression?
       I. MAO inhibitors
      II. ECT
     III. cognitive therapy
   (A) I only
   (B) III only
   (C) I and II only
   (D) II and III only
   (E) I, II, and III

8. All of the following methods of treatment are or may be based on classical conditioning principles EXCEPT
   (A) token economy.
   (B) implosive therapy.
   (C) flooding.
   (D) systematic desensitization.
   (E) aversion therapy.

9. Maria has been in analysis for over a year. Recently, she has begun to suspect that she has fallen in love with Dr. Chin, her analyst. When she confesses her feelings, Dr. Chin is likely to tell Maria that she is experiencing
   (A) resistance.
   (B) transference.
   (C) a breakthrough.
   (D) irrational expectations.
   (E) unconditional positive regard.

10. Jeb has been working for the same company for three years. While his responsibilities have increased, his salary has not. Every time he resolves to talk with his supervisor about a raise, he loses his nerve. In therapy, Dr. Flores and her assistant demonstrate how Jeb might go about asking for a raise. Then the assistant pretends to be Jeb's boss, and Jeb practices asking for a raise. This process most closely resembles
    (A) RET.
    (B) existential therapy.
    (C) modeling.
    (D) free association.
    (E) aversion therapy.

11. One difference between psychoanalytic and cognitive modes of treatment is that cognitive therapists
    (A) say little during sessions.
    (B) emphasize the primacy of behavior.
    (C) focus on the present.
    (D) view repressed thoughts about one's childhood as the root of most problems.
    (E) do not face their clients.

12. Which method of therapy is most eclectic?
    (A) psychodynamic
    (B) client centered
    (C) aversive conditioning
    (D) psychoanalytic
    (E) token economy

13. Schizophrenia is most likely to be treated with
    (A) Prozac.
    (B) lithium.
    (C) Miltown.
    (D) Haldol.
    (E) Valium.

14. A negative side effect of ECT is
    (A) tardive dyskinesia.
    (B) memory loss.
    (C) hallucinations.
    (D) hysteria.
    (E) violent episodes.

15. An unanticipated result of the deinstitutionalization movement was
    (A) an increase in the homeless population.
    (B) an increase in drug-related crime.
    (C) an increase in the incidence of catatonic schizophrenia.
    (D) a decrease in the availability of antipsychotic drugs.
    (E) a decrease in the population of mental institutions.

Answers to Practice Questions

1. **(D)** Psychoanalysts see the root of disorders in unconscious conflicts. Therefore, their initial focus is to bring the conflict into conscious awareness. Due to patients' defenses, psychoanalysts need to employ special techniques to reveal the contents of the unconscious. Dream analysis is one such technique. Behaviorists are interested only in the clients' behavior. Cognitive therapists are more likely to explore the clients' waking thoughts. Humanistic psychologists will try to help clients clarify their own thoughts and feel positively about themselves. Therapists with a biomedical orientation will be most likely to recommend somatic therapies, like drugs.

2. **(E)** Coretta's therapist is nondirective and therefore is most likely to have a humanistic orientation. An example of such a therapy is Carl Rogers' client-centered therapy.

3. **(B)** Psychoanalysts believe that disorders are caused by unconscious conflicts that are not immediately apparent. Treating the symptom is essentially pointless since it may disappear but a new one will take its place, a phenomenon known as symptom substitution. Therefore, when Craig went to a behaviorist and was cured of his test anxiety in a few months, psychoanalysts would predict the development of a new symptom. Free association is a technique used by psychoanalysts to uncover the contents of the unconscious. An anxiety hierarchy is part of systematic desensitization, a behaviorist treatment for anxiety disorders. While no such thing as problem transference exists, transference occurs when patients put feelings about significant people in their lives onto the analyst. Analysts necessarily engage in interpretation to figure out the source of their patients' difficulties.

4. **(D)** Both systematic desensitization and in vivo desensitization are treatments for phobias and other anxiety disorders. In systematic desensitization, clients imagine the different levels of the anxiety hierarchy. However, in vivo densensitization involves experiencing the anxiety-provoking situations. Similarly, implosive therapy involves imagining an intensely feared situation until the fear is extinguished, while flooding consists of experiencing the highly anxiety-provoking situation until the fear is extinguished.

5. **(B)** Carl Rogers invented client-centered therapy. Fritz Perls is associated with Gestalt therapy, Albert Ellis with REBT, and Aaron Beck with cognitive therapy. John Watson was an early behaviorist.

6. **(E)** Counterconditioning involves replacing a CR with a new CR. In systematic desensitization, clients are taught to replace fear with relaxation. None of the other therapies listed are based on learning principles.

7. **(C)** Somatic therapies, as opposed to psychotherapies, view the cause of the problem in biology and therefore involve medical treatments. Both MAO inhibitors and ECT are somatic treatments, while cognitive therapy is a form of psychotherapy. The question then becomes whether or not MAO inhibitors and ECT are used in the treatment of depression, and, in fact, they are.

8. **(A)** Classical conditioning is a kind of learning that results from associating two things, one of which is an unconditioned stimulus, together. In operant

conditioning, the consequences of one's actions lead to learning. Token economies are based on the principles of operant conditioning; people will act in certain ways to attain rewards. Implosive therapy, flooding, and systematic desensitization are all based on classical conditioning methods. Aversion therapy is a broader term that includes both classical and operant conditioning methods.

9. **(B)** Transference is when patients direct feelings toward important people in their lives onto the therapist. Resistance also commonly occurs in psychoanalysis but is when a patient rejects the therapists' interpretations or otherwise seeks to thwart the therapeutic process.

10. **(C)** Modeling consists of observation and imitation. Jeb watches someone model how to ask for a raise, and then he practices that skill himself.

11. **(C)** Psychoanalysis stresses the importance of early childhood experience. Psychoanalysts spend a lot of time exploring patients' early lives. Cognitive therapists focus on helping their clients deal with the present. Neither type of therapist is particularly reticent; humanistic therapists are. Neither psychoanalysts nor cognitive therapists emphasize the importance of behavior; that focus characterizes behaviorists. Psychoanalysts, not cognitive psychologists, do see repressed thoughts from childhood as the root of most adult problems and do not face their clients.

12. **(A)** Eclectic therapies incorporate aspects of several different models rather than strictly adhere to one theoretical orientation. Psychodynamic therapy, while based on psychoanalysis, tends to incorporate aspects of other models as well. Client-centered therapy is humanistic. Aversive conditioning and token economies are behavioral. Psychoanalytic therapy is, of course, psychoanalytic.

13. **(D)** Haldol is an antipsychotic drug. Prozac is used to treat depression, lithium to treat mania, and Miltown and Valium to treat anxiety disorders.

14. **(B)** Memory loss, although often temporary, is a common side effect of ECT. Tardive dyskinesia is a side effect of the antipsychotic medications used to treat schizophrenia.

15. **(A)** The deinstitutionalization movement occurred when many patients were released from mental hospitals in the 1960s and 1970s. Many were schizophrenics who, unable to find jobs and adequate care outside of the hospital setting, became homeless.

CHAPTER 14
Social Psychology

Overview

Social psychology is a broad field devoted to studying the way that people relate to others. Our discussion will focus on the development and expression of attitudes, people's attributions about their own behavior and that of others, the reasons why people engage in both antisocial and prosocial behavior, and how the presence and actions of others influence the way people behave.

A major influence on the first two areas we will discuss, attitude formation and attribution theory, is *social cognition*. This field applies many of the concepts you learned about in the field of cognition, such as memory and biases, to help explain how people think about themselves and others. The basic idea behind social cognition is that, as people go through their daily lives, they act like scientists, constantly gathering data and making predictions about what will happen next so that they can act accordingly.

Attitude Formation and Change

One main focus of social psychology is attitude formation and change. An *attitude* is a set of beliefs and feelings. We have attitudes about many different aspects of our environment such as groups of people, particular events, and places. Attitudes are evaluative, meaning that our feelings toward such things are necessarily positive or negative.

A great deal of research focuses on ways to affect people's attitudes. In fact, the entire field of advertising is devoted to just this purpose. How can people be encouraged to develop a favorable attitude toward a particular brand of potato chips? Having been the target audience for many such attempts, you are no doubt familiar with a plethora of strategies used to promote favorable opinions toward a product.

The *mere exposure effect* states that the more one is exposed to something, the more one will come to like it. Therefore, in the world of advertising, more is better. When you walk into the supermarket, you will be more likely to buy the brand of potato chips you have seen advertised thousands of times rather than one that you have never heard of before.

Certain characteristics of the person imparting the message, the communicator, have been found to influence the effectiveness of a message. Attractive people, famous people, and experts are among the most persuasive communicators. As a result, professional athletes and movie stars often have second careers making commercials. Certain characteristics of the audience also affect how effective a message will be. Some research suggests that more educated people are less likely to be persuaded by advertisements. Finally, the way the message is presented can also influence how persuasive it is. Research has found that when dealing with a relatively uninformed audience, presenting a one-sided message is best. However, when attempting to influence a more sophisticated audience, a communication that acknowledges and then refutes opposing arguments will be more effective. Some research suggests that messages that arouse fear are effective. However, too much fear can cause people to react negatively to the message itself.

The Relationship Between Attitudes and Behavior

Although you might think that knowing people's attitudes would tell you a great deal about their behavior, research has found that the relationship between attitudes and behaviors is far from perfect. In 1934, LaPiere conducted an early study that illustrated this difference. In the United States in the 1930s, prejudice and discrimination against Asians was pervasive. LaPiere traveled throughout the nation visiting many hotels and restaurants with an Asian couple to see how they would be treated. On only one occasion were they treated poorly due to their race. A short time later, LaPiere contacted all of the establishments they had visited and asked about their attitudes toward Asian patrons. Over 90 percent of the respondents said that they would not serve Asians. This finding illustrates that attitudes do not perfectly predict behaviors.

Hint: *Attitudes do not perfectly predict behaviors. What people say they would do and what they actually would do often differ.*

Sometimes if you can change people's behavior, you can change their attitudes. *Cognitive dissonance theory* is based on the idea that people are motivated to have consistent attitudes and behaviors. When they do not, they experience unpleasant mental tension or dissonance. For example, suppose Amira thinks that studying is only for geeks. If she then studies for 10 hours for her chemistry test, she will experience cognitive dissonance. Since she cannot, at this point, alter her behavior (she has already studied for 10 hours), the only way to reduce this dissonance is to change her attitude and decide that studying does not necessarily make someone a geek. Note that this change in attitude happens without conscious awareness.

Festinger and Carlsmith conducted the classic experiment about cognitive dissonance in the late 1950s. Their subjects performed a boring task and were then asked to lie and tell the next subject (actually a confederate[1] of the experimenter) that they had enjoyed the task. In one condition, subjects were paid $1 to lie, and in the other condition they were paid $20. Afterward, the subjects' attitudes toward the task were measured. Contrary to what reinforcement theory would predict, those subjects who had been paid $1 were found to have significantly more positive attitudes toward the experiment than those who were paid $20. According to Festinger and Carlsmith, having already said that the boring task was interesting, the subjects were experiencing dissonance. However, those subjects who had been paid $20 experienced relatively little dissonance; they had lied because they had been paid $20. On the other hand, those subjects who were paid only $1 lacked sufficient external motivation to lie. Therefore, to reduce the dissonance, they changed their attitudes and said that they actually did enjoy the experiment.

Compliance Strategies

Often people use certain strategies to get others to comply with their wishes. Such *compliance strategies* have also been the focus of much psychological research. Suppose you need to borrow $20 from a friend. Would you be better off asking him or her for $20 right away, asking the friend first for $5 and then following up this request with another for the additional $15, or asking him or her for $100 and, after the friend refuses, asking for $20? The *foot-in-the-door* phenomenon suggests that if you can get people to agree to a small request, they will become more likely to agree to a follow-up request that is larger. Thus, once your friend agrees to lend you $5, he or she becomes more likely to lend you the additional funds. After all, the friend is clearly willing to lend you money. The *door-in-the-face* strategy argues that after people refuse a large request, they will look more favorably upon a follow-up request that seems, in comparison, much more reasonable. After flat-out refusing to lend you $100, your friend might feel bad. The least he or she could do is lend you $20.

Another common strategy is known as *norms of reciprocity*. People tend to think that when someone does something nice for them, they ought to do something nice in return. Norms of reciprocity is at work when you feel compelled to send money to the charity that sent you free return address labels or when you cast your vote in the student election for the candidate that handed out those delicious chocolate chip cookies.

Attribution Theory

Attribution theory is another area of study within the field of social cognition. Attribution theory tries to explain how people determine the cause of what they observe. For instance, if your friend Charley told you he got a perfect score on his

---

[1]Many social psychology experiments use confederates to deceive participants. Confederates are people who, unbeknownst to the participants in the experiment, work with the experimenter.

math test, you might find yourself thinking that Charley is very good at math. In that case, you have made a *dispositional* or *person attribution*. Alternatively, you might attribute Charley's success to a situational factor, such as an easy test; in that case you make a *situation attribution*. Attributions can also be stable or unstable. If you infer that Charley has always been a math wizard, you have made both a person attribution and a *stable attribution,* also called a *person-stable attribution.* On the other hand, if you think that Charley studied a lot for this one test you have made a *person-unstable attribution.* Similarly, if you believe that Ms. Mahoney, Charley's math teacher, is an easy teacher, you have made a *situation-stable attribution.* If you think that Ms. Mahoney is a tough teacher who happened to give one easy test, you have made a *situation-unstable attribution.*

Harold Kelley put forth a theory that explains the kind of attributions people make based on three kinds of information: *consistency, distinctiveness,* and *consensus.* Consistency refers to how similarly the individual acts in the same situation over time. How does Charley usually do on his math tests? Distinctiveness refers to how similar this situation is to other situations in which we have watched Charley. Does Charley do well on all tests? Has he evidenced an aptitude for math in other ways? Consensus asks us to consider how others in the same situation have responded. Did many people get a perfect score on the math test?

Consensus is a particularly important piece of information to use when determining whether to make a person or situation attribution. If Charley is the only one to earn such a good score on the math test, we seem to have learned something about Charley. Conversely, if everyone earned a high score on the test, we would suspect that something in the situation contributed to that outcome. Consistency, on the other hand, is extremely useful when determining whether to make a stable or unstable attribution. If Charley always aces his math tests, then it seems more likely that Charley is particularly skilled at math than that he happened to study hard for this one test. Similarly, if everyone always does well on Ms. Mahoney's tests, we would be likely to make the situation-stable attribution that she is an easy teacher. However, if Charley usually scores low in Ms. Mahoney's class, we will be more likely to make a situation-unstable attribution such as this particular test was easy.

People often have certain ideas or prejudices about other people before they even meet them. These preconceived ideas can obviously affect the way someone acts toward another person. Even more interesting is the idea that the expectations we have about others can influence the way those others behave. Such a phenomenon is called a *self-fulfilling prophecy.* For instance, if Jon is repeatedly told that Chet, whom he has never met, is really funny, when Jon does finally meet Chet, he may treat Chet in such a way as to elicit the humorous behavior he expected.

A classic study involving self-fulfilling prophecies was Rosenthal and Jacobson's (1968) "Pygmalion in the Classroom" experiment. They administered a test to elementary school children that supposedly would identify those children who were on the verge of significant academic growth. In reality, the test was a standard IQ test. These researchers then randomly selected a group of children from the population who took the test, and they informed their teachers that these students were ripe for such intellectual progress. Of course, since the children were selected randomly, they did not differ from any other group of children in the school. At the end of the year, the researchers returned to take another measure of the students' IQ and found that the scores of the identified children had increased more than the scores of their classmates. In some way, the teachers' expectations that these students would bloom intellectually over the year actually caused the students to outperform their peers.

Attributional Biases

Although people are quite good at sifting through all the data that bombards them and then making attributions, you will probably not be surprised to learn that errors are not uncommon. Moreover, people tend to make the same kinds of errors. A few typical biases are the fundamental attribution error, false consensus effect, self-serving bias, and the just-world belief.

When looking at the behavior of others, people tend to overestimate the importance of dispositional factors and underestimate the role of situational factors. This tendency is known as the *fundamental attribution error.* Say that you go to a party where you are introduced to Claude, a young man you have never met before. Although you attempt to engage Claude in conversation, he is unresponsive. He looks past you and, soon after, seizes upon an excuse to leave. Most people would conclude that Claude is an unfriendly person. Few consider that something in the situation may have contributed to Claude's behavior. Perhaps Claude just had a terrible fight with his girlfriend, Isabelle. Maybe on the way to the party he had a minor car accident. The point is that people systematically seem to overestimate the role of dispositional factors in influencing another person's actions.

Interestingly, people do not evidence this same tendency in explaining their own behaviors. Claude knows that he is sometimes extremely outgoing and warm. Since people get to view themselves in countless situations, they are more likely to make situational attributions about themselves than about others. Everyone has been shy and aloof at times, and everyone has been friendly. Thus, people are more likely to say that their own behavior depends upon the situation.

One caveat must be added to our discussion of the fundamental attribution error. The fundamental attribution was named *fundamental* because it was believed to be so widespread. However, many cross-cultural psychologists have argued that the fundamental attribution error is far less likely to occur in *collectivist cultures* than in *individualistic cultures.* In an individualistic culture, like the American culture, the importance and uniqueness of the individual is stressed. In more collectivist cultures, like Japanese culture, a person's link to various groups such as family or company is stressed. Cross-cultural research suggests that people in collectivist cultures are less likely to commit the fundamental attribution error, perhaps because they are more attuned to the ways that different situations influence their own behavior.

The tendency for people to overestimate the number of people who agree with them is called *the false-consensus effect.* For instance, if Jamal dislikes horror movies, he is likely to think that most other people share his aversion. Conversely, Cettina, who loves a good horror flick, overestimates the number of people who share her passion.

Self-serving bias is the tendency to take more credit for good outcomes than for bad ones. For instance, a basketball coach would be more likely to emphasize her or his role in the team's championship win than in their heartbreaking first-round tournament loss.

Hint: Students often confuse self-serving bias and self-fulfilling prophecies, ostensibly because they both contain the word self. Self-serving bias is the tendency to overstate one's role in a positive venture and underestimate it in a failure. Thus, people serve themselves by making themselves look good. Self-fulfilling prophecies, on the other hand, explain how people's ideas about others can shape the behavior of those others.

Researchers have found that people evidence a bias toward thinking that bad things happen to bad people. This belief in a just world, known simply as the *just-world belief,* in which misfortunes befall people who deserve them, can be seen in the tendency to blame victims. For example, the woman was raped because she was stupidly walking alone in a dangerous neighborhood. People are unemployed because they are lazy. If the world is just in this manner, then, assuming we view ourselves as good people, we need not fear bad things happening to ourselves.

Stereotypes, Prejudice, and Discrimination

We all have ideas about what members of different groups are like, and these expectations may influence the way we interact with members of these groups. We call these ideas *stereotypes.* Stereotypes may be either negative or positive and can be applied to virtually any group of people (for example, racial, ethnic, geographic). For instance, people often stereotype New Yorkers as pushy, unfriendly, and rude and Californians as easygoing and attractive. Some cognitive psychologists have suggested that stereotypes are basically schemata about groups. People who distinguish between stereotypes and group schemata argue that the former are more rigid and more difficult to change than the latter.

Prejudice is an undeserved, usually negative, attitude toward a group of people. Stereotyping can lead to prejudice when negative stereotypes (those rude New Yorkers) are applied uncritically to all members of a group (she is from New York, therefore she must be rude) and a negative attitude results.

While prejudice is an attitude, *discrimination* involves an action. When one discriminates, one acts on one's prejudices. If I dislike New Yorkers, I am prejudiced, but if I refuse to hire New Yorkers to work in my company, I am engaging in discrimination.

Hint: Students have difficulty distinguishing between prejudice and discrimination. Remember, the former is an attitude and the latter is a behavior.

People tend to see members of their own group, the *in-group,* as more diverse than members of other groups, *out-groups.* This phenomenon is often referred to as *out-group homogeneity.* For example, as a New Yorker myself, I know that while some New Yorkers are indeed pushy and rude, most are not. I know many well-mannered and deferential New Yorkers as well as short New Yorkers, tall New Yorkers, honest New Yorkers, and dishonest New Yorkers. While we all have extensive experience with the members of our own groups, we lack that degree of familiarity with other groups and therefore tend to see them as more similar. In addition, researchers have documented a preference for members of one's own group, a kind of *in-group bias*. In-group bias is thought to stem from people's belief that they themselves are good people. Therefore, the people with whom they share group membership are thought to be good as well.

Origin of Stereotypes and Prejudice

Many different theories attempt to explain how people become prejudiced. Some psychologists have suggested that people naturally and inevitably magnify differences between their own group and others as a function of the cognitive process of categorization. By taking into account the in-group bias discussed above, this idea suggests that people cannot avoid forming stereotypes.

Social learning theorists stress that stereotypes and prejudice are often learned through modeling. Children raised by parents who express prejudices may be more likely to embrace such prejudices themselves. Conversely, this theory suggests that prejudices could be unlearned by exposure to different models.

Combating Prejudice

One theory about how to reduce prejudice is known as the *contact theory*. The contact theory, as its name suggests, states that contact between hostile groups will reduce animosity, but only if the groups are made to work toward a goal that benefits all and necessitates the participation of all. Such a goal is called a *superordinate goal*.

Sherif's (1966) camp study (also known as the Robbers Cave study) illustrates both how easily out-group bias can be created and how superordinate goals can be used to unite formerly antagonistic groups. He conducted a series of studies at a summer camp. He first divided the campers into two groups and arranged for them to compete in a series of activities. This competition was sufficient to create negative feelings between the groups. Once such prejudices had been established, Sherif staged several camp emergencies that required the groups to cooperate. The superordinate goal of solving the crises effectively improved relations between the groups.

A number of educational researchers have attempted to use the contact theory to reduce prejudices between members of different groups in school. One goal of most cooperative learning activities is to bring members of different social groups into contact with one another as they work toward a superordinate goal, the assigned task.

Aggression and Antisocial Behavior

Another major area of study for social psychologists is aggression and antisocial behavior. Psychologists distinguish between two types of aggression: *instrumental aggression* and *hostile aggression*. Instrumental aggression is when the aggressive act is intended to secure a particular end. For example, if Bobby wants to hold the doll that Carol is holding and he kicks her and grabs the doll, Bobby has engaged in instrumental aggression. Hostile aggression, on the other hand, has no such clear purpose. If Bobby is simply angry or upset and therefore kicks Carol, his aggression is hostile aggression.

Many theories exist about the cause of human aggression. Freud linked aggression to Thanatos, the death instinct. Sociobiologists suggest that the expression of aggression is adaptive under certain circumstances. One of the most influential theories, however, is known as the *frustration-aggression hypothesis*. This hypothesis holds that the feeling of frustration makes aggression more likely. Considerable experimental evidence supports it. Another common theory is that the exposure to aggressive models makes people aggressive. Bandura, Ross, and Ross's (1963) classic Bobo doll experiment illustrated this connection. Children were exposed to adults who modeled either aggressive or nonaggressive play with, among other things, an inflatable Bobo doll that would bounce back up after being hit. Later, when given the chance to play alone in a room full of toys including poor Bobo, the children who had witnessed the aggressive adult models exhibited aggressive behavior strikingly similar to that which they had observed. The children in the control group were much less likely to be aggressive toward Bobo, particularly in the ways modeled by the adults in the experimental condition.

Prosocial Behavior

While social psychologists have devoted a lot of time and effort to studying antisocial behavior, they have also studied the factors that make people more likely to help one another. Such helping behavior is termed *prosocial behavior.* Much of the research in this area has focused on *bystander intervention,* the conditions under which people nearby are more and less likely to help someone in trouble.

The vicious murder of Kitty Genovese in Kew Gardens, NY, committed within view of at least 38 witnesses, none of whom intervened, led several psychologists to explore how people decided whether or not to help others in distress. Counterintuitively, the larger the number of people who witness an emergency situation, the less likely any one is to intervene. This finding is known as *diffusion of responsibility*. The larger the group of people who witness a problem, the less responsible any one individual feels to help. People tend to assume that someone else will take action so they need not do so. Another factor influencing bystander intervention is known as *pluralistic ignorance*. People seem to decide what constitutes appropriate behavior in a situation by looking to others. Thus, if no one in a classroom seems worried by the black smoke coming through the vent, each individual concludes that taking no action is the proper thing to do.

Attraction

Social psychologists also study what factors increase the chance that people will like one another. A significant body of research indicates that we like others who are similar to us, with whom we come into frequent contact, and who return our positive feelings. These three factors are often referred to as *similarity, proximity, and reciprocal liking*. Although conventional wisdom holds that opposites attract, psychological research indicates that we are drawn to people who are similar to us, those who share our attitudes, backgrounds, and interests. Proximity means nearness. As is suggested by the mere-exposure effect, the greater the exposure one has to another person, the more one generally comes to like that person. In addition, only by talking to someone can one identify the similarities that will draw the pair closer together. Finally, every reader has probably had the misfortune to experience that liking someone who scorns you is not enjoyable. Thus, the more someone likes you, the more you will probably like that person.

Not surprisingly, people are also attracted to others who are physically attractive. In fact, the benefits of being nice-looking extend well beyond the realm of attraction. Research has demonstrated that good-looking people are perceived as having all sorts of positive attributes including better personalities and greater job competence.

Psychologists have also devoted tremendous time and attention to the concept of love. While research seems to indicate that the emotion of love qualitatively differs from liking and a number of theories about love have been proposed, the subject has proven difficult to explain adequately.

A term often employed as part of liking and loving studies is *self-disclosure*. One self-discloses when one shares a piece of personal information with another. Close relationships with friends and lovers are often built through a process of self-disclosure. On the path to intimacy, one person shares a detail of his or her life and the other reciprocates by exposing a facet of his or her own.

The Influence of Others on an Individual's Behavior

A major area of research in social psychology is how an individual's behavior can be affected by another's actions or even merely by another person's presence. A number of studies have illustrated that people perform tasks better in front of an audience than they do when they are alone. They yell louder, run faster, and reel in a fishing rod more quickly. This phenomenon, that the presence of others improves task performance, is known as *social facilitation*. Later studies, however, found that when the task being observed was a difficult one rather than a simple, well-practiced skill, being watched by others actually hurt performance, a finding known as *social impairment*.

Conformity has been an area of much research as well. Conformity is the tendency of people to go along with the views or actions of others. Solomon Asch (1951) conducted one of the most interesting conformity experiments. He brought subjects into a room of confederates and asked them to make a series of simple perceptual judgments. Asch showed the subjects three vertical lines of varying sizes and asked them to indicate which one was the same length as a different target line. All members of the group gave their answers aloud, and the subject was always the last person to speak. All of the trials had a clear, correct answer. However, on some of them, all of the confederates gave the same, obviously incorrect judgment. Asch was interested in what the subjects would do.

Would they conform to a judgment they knew to be wrong or would they differ from the group? Asch found that in approximately one-third of the cases when the confederates gave an incorrect answer, the subjects conformed. Furthermore, approximately 70 percent of the subjects conformed on at least one of the trials. In general, studies have suggested that conformity most likely occurs when a group's opinion is unanimous. Although it would seem that the larger the group, the greater conformity that would be expressed, studies have shown that groups larger than three do not significantly increase the tendency to conform.

While conformity involves following a group without being explicitly told to do so, *obedience studies* have focused on participants' willingness to do what another asks them to do. Milgram (1974) conducted the classic obedience studies. His subjects were told that they were taking part in a study about teaching and learning, and they were assigned to play the part of teacher. The learner, of course, was a confederate. As teacher, each subject's job was to give the learner an electric shock for every incorrect response. The subject sat behind a panel of buttons each labeled with the number of volts, beginning at 15 and increasing by increments of 15 up to 450. The levels of shock were also described in words ranging from *mild* up to *XXX*. In reality, no shocks were delivered; the confederate pretended to be shocked. As the level of the shocks increased, the confederate screamed in pain, said he suffered from a heart condition, and eventually fell silent. Milgram was interested in how far subjects would go before refusing to deliver any more shocks. The experimenter watched the subject and, if questioned, gave only a few stock answers, such as "Please continue." Contrary to the predictions of psychologists who Milgram polled prior to the experiment, over 60 percent of the subjects obeyed the experimenter and delivered all the possible shocks.

Milgram replicated his study with a number of interesting twists. He found that he could decrease subjects' compliance by bringing them into closer contact with the confederates. Subjects who could see the learners gave fewer shocks than subjects who could only hear the learners. The lowest shock rates of all were administered by subjects who had to force the learner's hand onto the shock plate. However, even in that last condition, approximately 30 percent delivered all of the shocks. Further studies also suggested that a key element in promoting obedience was the perception of legitimate authority on the part of the experimenter. When the experiment was conducted at Yale, higher rates of compliance were found than when it was conducted in other areas of New Haven. When the experimenter left in the middle of the experiment and was replaced by an assistant, obedience also decreased. Finally, when other confederates were present in the room and they objected to the shocks, the percentage of subjects who quit in the middle of the experiment skyrocketed.

One final note about the Milgram experiment bears mentioning. It has been severely criticized on ethical grounds, and such an experiment would surely not receive the approval of an institutional review board (IRB) today. When debriefed, many subjects learned that had the shocks been real, they would have killed the learner. Understandably, some people were profoundly disturbed by this insight.

Group Dynamics

We are all members of many different groups. The students in your school are a group, a baseball team is a group, and the lawyers at a particular firm are a group. Some groups are more cohesive than others and exert more pressure on their members. All groups have *norms,* rules about how group members should act. For example, the lawyers at the firm mentioned above may have rules governing appropriate work dress. Within groups is often a set of specific *roles.* On a baseball team, for instance, the players have different, well-defined roles such as pitcher, shortstop, and center fielder.

Sometimes people take advantage of being part of a group by *social loafing.* Social loafing is the phenomenon when individuals do not put in as much effort when acting as part of a group as they do when acting alone. One explanation for this effect is that when alone, an individual's efforts are more easily discernible than when in a group. Thus, as part of a group, a person may be less motivated to put in an impressive performance. In addition, being part of a group may encourage members to take advantage of the opportunity to reap the rewards of the group effort without taxing themselves unnecessarily.

Group polarization is the tendency of a group to make more extreme decisions than the group members would make individually. Studies about group polarization usually have participants give their opinions individually, then group them to discuss their decisions, and then have the group make a decision. Explanations for group polarization include the idea that in a group, individuals may be exposed to new, persuasive arguments they had not thought of themselves and that the responsibility for an extreme decision in a group is diffused across the group's many members.

Sometimes people get swept up by a group and do things they never would have done if on their own such as looting or rioting. This loss of self-restraint occurs when group members feel anonymous and aroused, and this phenomenon is known as *deindividuation.*

Finally, *groupthink,* a term coined by Janis, describes the tendency for some groups to make bad decisions. Groupthink occurs when group members suppress their reservations about the ideas supported by the group. As a result, a kind of false unanimity is encouraged, and flaws in the group's decisions may be overlooked. Highly cohesive groups involved in making risky decisions seem to be at particular risk for groupthink.

Practice Questions

Directions: Each of the questions or incomplete statements below is followed by five suggested answers or completions. Select the one that is best in each case.

---

1. Which of the following suggestions is most likely to reduce the hostility felt between antagonistic groups?
    (A) Force the groups to spend a lot of time together.
    (B) Encourage the groups to avoid each other as much as possible.
    (C) Give the groups a task that cannot be solved unless they work together.
    (D) Set up a program in which speakers attempt to persuade the groups to get along.
    (E) Punish the groups whenever they treat each other badly.

2. On Monday, Tanya asked her teacher to postpone Tuesday's test until Friday. After her teacher flatly refused, Tanya asked the teacher to push the test back one day, to Wednesday. Tanya is using the compliance strategy known as
    (A) foot-in-the-door.
    (B) norms of reciprocity.
    (C) compromise.
    (D) strategic bargaining.
    (E) door-in-the-face.

3. In the Milgram studies, the dependent measure was
    (A) the highest level of shock supposedly administered.
    (B) the location of the learner.
    (C) the length of the line.
    (D) the number of people in the group.
    (E) the instructions given by the experimenter.

4. The tendency of people to look toward others for cues about the appropriate way to behave when confronted by an emergency is known as
    (A) bystander intervention.
    (B) pluralistic ignorance.
    (C) modeling.
    (D) diffusion of responsibility.
    (E) conformity.

5. Advertisements are made more effective when the communicators are
         I. attractive.
        II. famous.
       III. perceived as experts.
    (A) II only
    (B) III only
    (C) I and II
    (D) II and III
    (E) I, II, and III

6. Your new neighbor seems to know everything about ancient Greece that your social studies teacher says during the first week of school. You conclude that she is brilliant. You do not consider that she might already have learned about ancient Greece in her old school. You are evidencing
   (A) the self-fulfilling prophecy effect.
   (B) pluralistic ignorance.
   (C) confirmation bias.
   (D) the fundamental attribution error.
   (E) cognitive dissonance.

7. In Asch's conformity study, approximately what percentage of participants gave at least one incorrect response?
   (A) 30
   (B) 40
   (C) 50
   (D) 60
   (E) 70

8. Janine has always hated the color orange. However, once she became a student at Princeton, she began to wear a lot of orange Princeton Tiger clothing. The discomfort caused by her long-standing dislike of the color orange and her current ownership of so much orange-and-black-striped clothing is known as
   (A) cognitive dissonance.
   (B) contradictory concepts.
   (C) conflicting motives.
   (D) opposing cognitions.
   (E) inconsistent ideas.

9. When Pasquale had his first oboe solo in the orchestra concert, his performance was far worse than it was when he rehearsed at home. A phenomenon that helps explain Pasquale's poor performance is known as
   (A) social loafing.
   (B) groupthink.
   (C) deindividuation.
   (D) social impairment.
   (E) diffusion of responsibility.

10. Kelley's attribution theory says that people use which of the following kinds of information in explaining events?
   (A) conformity, reliability, and validity
   (B) consensus, consistency, and distinctiveness
   (C) uniqueness, explanatory power, and logic
   (D) salience, importance, and reason
   (E) distinctiveness, conformity, and salience

11. After your school's football team has a big win, students in the halls can be heard saying "*We* are awesome." The next week, after the team loses to the last-place team in the league, the same students lament that "*They* were terrible." The difference in these comments illustrates
    (A) the fundamental attribution error.
    (B) self-serving bias.
    (C) the self-fulfilling prophecy effect.
    (D) the false consensus effect.
    (E) conformity.

12. Which of the following is the best example of prejudice?
    (A) Billy will not let girls play on his hockey team.
    (B) Santiago dislikes cheerleaders.
    (C) Athena says she can run faster than anybody on the playground.
    (D) Mr. Tamp calls on boys more often than girls.
    (E) Ginny thinks all Asians are smart.

13. On their second date, Megan confides in Francisco that she still loves to watch Rugrats. He, in turn, tells her that he still cries when he watches Bambi. These two young lovers will be brought closer together through this process of
    (A) self-disclosure.
    (B) deindividuation.
    (C) in-group bias.
    (D) dual sharing.
    (E) open communication.

14. On the first day of class, Mr. Simpson divides his class into four competing groups. On the fifth day of school, Jody is sent to the principal for kicking members of the other groups. Mr. Simpson can be faulted for encouraging the creation of
    (A) group polarization.
    (B) deindividuation.
    (C) out-group bias.
    (D) superordinate goals.
    (E) groupthink.

15. Rosenthal and Jacobson's "Pygmalion in the Classroom" study showed that
    (A) people's expectations of others can influence the behavior of those others.
    (B) attitudes are not always good predictors of behavior.
    (C) contact is not sufficient to break down prejudices.
    (D) people like to think that others get what they deserve.
    (E) cohesive groups often make bad decisions.

Answers to Practice Questions

1. **(C)** A task that requires groups to cooperate is an example of a superordinate goal. Such superordinate goals are effective in breaking down hostility between groups. Contact between antagonistic groups without superordinate goals is less successful, and simply avoiding members of the other group is unlikely to decrease the intergroup hostility. While guest speakers may be able to influence the group members' attitudes, they will be less effective than the use of superordinate goals. Punishing the groups may actually increase the antagonism between them.

2. **(E)** Tanya made a large request and, when refused, came back with a smaller, more reasonable sounding request. This compliance strategy is known as door-in-the-face. Foot-in-the-door is when one makes a small request and, once that request is agreed to, follows up with a larger request. Had Tanya brought her teacher an apple and then made her request she would have been attempting to capitalize on norms of reciprocity, the idea that one good turn deserves another. Although Tanya is, in fact, attempting to broker a compromise and engage in some bargaining, the strategy she used has a more specific, psychological name.

3. **(A)** The dependent measure in the Milgram experiment was the level of shock the participants thought they were administering. While Milgram manipulated a number of independent variables including the location of the learner relative to the teacher, the dependent variable he measured was always how far the subjects would go in shocking the learners. The length of the line is a reference to the Asch conformity experiment. No groups were involved in the Milgram experiment. The experimenter's instructions did not vary between conditions.

4. **(B)** Pluralistic ignorance is defined as the tendency of people to look toward others for cues about how to act, particularly in emergency situations. Pluralistic ignorance is often tested in bystander intervention studies. Pluralistic ignorance can be seen as a kind of modeling or conformity that occurs in emergencies. However, pluralistic ignorance is a superior answer due to its clear relationship to emergency situations. Diffusion of responsibility is the finding that the more people who witness an emergency, the less likely any one is to intervene.

5. **(E)** Communications are made more effective when communicators are attractive, famous, and/or perceived as experts. All of these factors enhance the persuasiveness of an appeal.

6. **(D)** Your failure to consider the role of situational factors in explaining your new neighbor's knowledge of ancient Greece is known as the fundamental attribution error. The self-fulfilling prophecy effect is when one person's expectations affect another person's behavior. Pluralistic ignorance is the tendency to look to others for hints about how one is supposed to act in certain situations. Confirmation bias is the tendency to focus on information that supports one's initial ideas. Cognitive dissonance is the tension felt when one holds two contradictory ideas.

7. **(E)** In Asch's conformity study, approximately 70 percent of participants gave at least one incorrect answer.

8. **(A)** Janine is experiencing cognitive dissonance. The combination of her hatred of the color orange and her ownership of a lot of orange clothing results in a tension called cognitive dissonance. It will motivate her to reduce the tension by either changing her opinion of orange or radically altering her wardrobe. All of the other terms are made up.

9. **(D)** When the presence of other people inhibits someone's performance, social impairment, the opposite of social facilitation, has occurred. Social loafing is the tendency of people to exert less effort in a group than they would if they were alone. Groupthink is the idea that because group members are often loathe to express opinions different from those of the majority, some groups fall prey to poor decisions. Deindividuation is when people in a group lose their self-restraint due to arousal and anonymity and then act in antisocial ways. Diffusion of responsibility is one way to explain the inverse relationship between group size and the expression of prosocial behavior.

10. **(B)** According to Kelley, people use information about consensus, consistency, and distinctiveness when analyzing the cause of people's actions. The other terms, while related to psychology, are not generally important in attribution theory.

11. **(B)** The students in the school are evidencing self-serving bias, the tendency to take more credit for good outcomes than bad ones. When the football team wins, they want to identify with them and therefore say "We are awesome." When that same team loses, the students distance themselves from the players, explaining that "They were terrible." Fundamental attribution error is a different attributional bias. It explains that people overestimate the role of personal factors when explaining other people's behavior. The self-fulfilling prophecy effect is the finding that people's expectations about others can influence the behavior of those others. The false consensus effect is another example of an attributional bias. It says that people overestimate the number of people who share their beliefs. Finally, conformity is the tendency for people to go along with a group.

12. **(B)** A prejudice is an attitude, while discrimination involves an action. Santiago has a negative attitude or prejudice toward cheerleaders. Billy and Mr. Tamp are engaging in discrimination by acting differently toward different groups of people. Athena may be really fast or overconfident, but she is not evidencing a prejudice. Ginny's belief that all Asians are smart is a stereotype that may or may not lead her to have some kind of prejudice against Asians.

13. **(A)** Self-disclosure is the process by which two people become closer by sharing intimate details about themselves. Deindividuation is when people in a group lose their self-restraint due to arousal and anonymity and act in antisocial ways. In-group bias is the preference that people show for members of their own groups. Dual sharing is a made-up term, and open communication, while healthy in a relationship, does not describe this specific exchange.

14. **(C)** By dividing his students into groups, Mr. Simpson fostered the development of in-group and out-group bias, the belief that members of

one's own group are superior to members of other groups. While Jody's aggressive behavior cannot be fully explained by Mr. Simpson's grouping, the fact that he attacks only members of other groups suggests that outgroup bias may play a role. Group polarization is the tendency of groups to take more extreme positions than those taken by their individual members. Since Jody acts alone and not as part of a group, his aggression cannot be seen as an example of deindividuation. Superordinate goals are helpful in reducing conflict between groups by making their success contingent upon their cooperation. Groupthink is the idea that because group members are often loathe to express opinions different from those of the majority, some groups fall prey to poor decisions.

15. **(A)** Rosenthal and Jacobson's "Pygmalion in the Classroom" study illustrated the self-fulfilling prophecy effect, the ability for people's expectations about others to influence how those others behave. Attitudes do not always predict behavior well, as LaPiere's study evidenced. Contact is not usually sufficient to break down prejudice. The just-world belief tells us that people like to think that others get what they deserve. Cohesive groups sometimes engage in groupthink, resulting in bad decisions.

CHAPTER 15

Multiple-Choice Test-Taking Tips

Overview

Two-thirds of your test grade depends upon your performance on the multiple-choice questions. You will take the multiple-choice section of the test first. It is comprised of 100 questions, and you will be allotted 70 minutes in which to answer them. The questions are arranged roughly in order of difficulty. Therefore, don't be alarmed if you have more trouble answering the questions that appear later on the exam; that's just the way it should be. Below, we have summarized a few test-taking strategies that we hope will help you with the exam.

Sometime You Don't Even Need the Answer Choices!

Once you've prepared for this test you'll see that in order to answer many of the questions on the test, you don't even need to look at the answer choices. In fact, it's a good test-taking strategy to try to answer multiple-choice questions before you look at the choices. That way, once you do look at the answer choices, you have a good sense of what you are looking for.

For example, consider the following question:

Tiger is extremely concerned about doing the right thing. He feels very guilty when he even thinks about doing something immoral or illegal. According to Freud, Tiger has a strong

If you are familiar with Freud's theory of personality, you could probably guess that the answer would be "superego" without checking the answer choices. In this case, you would then have a very easy job as the choices are:

(A) id.
(B) ego.
(C) libido.
(D) superego.
(E) unconscious.

Here's another example:

A psychologist who subscribes to the biomedical perspective would be most likely to emphasize the importance of

In this case, the answer is slightly less obvious. You probably realize that it will have to do with concepts such as genetics, nature, and/or neurochemicals. Once you identify these potential answers, selecting the answer is, again, fairly simple. The choices are:

(A) the environment.
(B) hormones and neurotransmitters.
(C) repressed impulses.
(D) self-esteem.
(E) attributional style.

The correct answer is B, as hormones and neurotransmitters are examples of the kind of neurochemicals the biomedical psychologists believe influence thought and behavior.

Read All the Answer Choices

Always read all the answer choices before making your final selection. Even though it is helpful to imagine what the answer might be without reading the answer choices, it is essential that you read and carefully consider all the choices presented. Occasionally, particularly on the more difficult questions, one of the answer choices will be appealing, but another answer is superior. Remember that on a multiple-choice test you are supposed to identify the BEST possible answer.

Narrow Down the Possible Answer

Sometimes the questions on the exam are more difficult than the examples above and you will not be able to identify the correct answer before reading the answer choices. That, then, is the beauty of the multiple-choice format. As mentioned above, you should always carefully read each of the answer choices. When you decide a choice is incorrect, cross it out, and eliminate it from consideration. You will be able to use this method often to identify the correct answer.

When I Don't Know the Answer, Should I Guess?

The test is set up to correct for the impact of guessing by penalizing students a quarter point for every question they get wrong. Aware of this penalty, most students are overly cautious about guessing. Since there are five answer choices for each question, the laws of probability suggest that if you had no idea about the answer to five questions and guessed on each one, you would most likely get one correct and four wrong. Therefore you would gain a point for the one question you got right and lose a point ($4 \times \frac{1}{4}$) for the questions on which you guessed incorrectly; in other words, you would break even. However, on many questions you will be able to eliminate at least one of the answer choices. In such a situation you should definitely guess because the odds are that you'll end up with more points than if you omitted these questions.

Guess Smart

When you are not sure of the answer to a question and therefore are trying to eliminate incorrect choices, a few other suggestions about how to make good guesses on multiple-choice tests may help you.

1. *Use your common sense.*

   Don't get so caught up thinking about what you learned that you forget to use your common sense. For instance, consider the following question:

   What is the likely correlation between the amount of time students spend studying psychology and their scores on the AP Psychology exam?
   (A)   -.80
   (B)   -.25
   (C)   .18
   (D)   .62
   (E)   .97

   Assuming you know that "0" represents no correlation and that "1" is indicative of a perfect, direct relationship between the variables, your common sense can help you choose the answer. Since one would suspect that the relationship between these variables is a positive one, you are choosing between choices C, D, and E. Although you probably don't have any idea of the exact correlation, .18 seems very weak; it suggests that studying hardly has any impact at all. Conversely, .97 seems too strong; clearly some of the variation in how people do on the test is due to factors other than time spent (e.g., prior knowledge, how rested they are, and test anxiety). Therefore, common sense dictates that .62 is the best of these choices.

2. *Use your knowledge of the psychological perspectives.*

   Sometimes language used in the stem of the question can give you a clue about the right answer. Each perspective uses certain terms, and the correct answer will frequently use language from the perspective indicated in the stem of the question. For example, consider the following question:

How would a behaviorist like B.F. Skinner explain how people learn table manners?
(A) Table manners are learned by interpreting events we have observed.
(B) Table manners are learned as a result of reinforcement and punishment.
(C) Table manners are a product of repressed childhood events in the unconscious.
(D) Table manners are controlled by brain chemistry and evolutionary forces.
(E) Table manners are learned by remembering and thinking about past social events we have experienced.

   The stem of the question tells you that the correct answer must be one that a behaviorist would agree with, so you know you're looking for an answer that uses behaviorist terms and concepts. Options A and E use cognitive psychological terms (interpreting, thinking, remembering). Option C uses psychoanalytic language (repressed, unconscious), and Option D uses bio-psychological language (brain chemistry and evolutionary forces). Only Option B uses terms from the behavioral perspective (reinforcement and punishment) so it must be the right answer.

3. *Avoid extreme answer choices.* Choices that contain words like *all* or *never* or *everyone* are rarely (notice I don't say *never*) correct.

4. *Be wary of answer choices that are very similar to one another.* Remember, you're looking for the best answer. If some of the choices are so similar that one cannot be better than the other, neither can be the correct answer.

Budget Your Time

While most students find that they have enough time on the multiple choice section of the exam, you should make sure not to spend an undue amount of time on any of the questions. Wear a watch to the exam and make sure to note the time the section begins and when it is scheduled to end. Since you have 70 minutes to answer 100 questions, you have just over 2/3 of a minute for each question.

Read each question and use the techniques we have suggested. If you find yourself confused, skip the question and plan to come back to it once you have completed the section. If you are debating among several answer choices, choose one temporarily, but mark the question so that you will remember to review it once you have finished the other questions.

All These Tips Are Interesting, But How Many Questions Do I Need to Get Right to Pass?

Each exam is different. Assuming your essays are average (keep in mind that they will determine one-third of your grade), you need to earn approximately 60 points (after the guessing penalty) on the multiple-choice section to earn a "3," 70 points to earn a "4," and 80 points to earn a "5."

Finally, Remember to Apply Some of What You've Learned About Psychology

- It's better to space out your studying over many days than to cram for the same amount of time right before the exam.
- Studying is important, but so is sleep. You'll think better if you're well rested.
- According to the *Yerkes-Dodson law* (Chapter 8), a moderate level of arousal will help you perform well on the test. Although you do not want to be so anxious that you can't focus, you will want to "psych" yourself up for the test.

CHAPTER 16

Essay Writing

How to Write the AP Psychology Essay
Sample Essay Question
Rubric for Sample Question
Interpreting the Rubric
Fictional Student Essay
Grading the Fictional Response
General Hints and Tips for the Essay Portion of the Exam

How to Write the AP Psychology Essay

Every year around the beginning of June, high school and college psychology teachers gather at a university for one purpose: to grade AP psychology essays. These readers are assigned to one of the two essay questions and go through careful training to ensure they grade your writing fairly and consistently. Readers go through several reliability checks during the reading to make sure each essay is read fairly. This is a unique experience for many of them, just as writing the AP psychology essay might be a unique writing experience for you.

Writing an effective essay response on the AP psychology test may require you to modify the way you usually answer an essay question. These essays are graded in a very specific way, and your writing should take this difference into account. Essay graders strive to be very consistent and objective, so the tests are graded in a systematic way. The entire grading system is set up to ensure that every student's response is given a fair reading. Understanding how the tests are graded should give you insight as to how to use your writing time best. This chapter will provide an example of an AP-style essay question and a rubric (a guide readers use to grade student responses) similar to the ones used in the grading of the test. A fictional student response is provided with an explanation of how the rubric would be used to grade that response. Finally, some general suggestions are provided about writing AP psychology essays.

Sample Essay Question

Professor Reiman, a social psychology researcher, is interested in expanding on Solomon Asch's conformity research. Professor Reiman decides to place participants into a room with three confederates who know about the experiment. In the room, the group is asked to compare the size of geometric figures. The participants are randomly assigned to one of two conditions. In the first group, the three confederates are introduced to the participant as introductory psychology students. In the second group, two of the confederates are introduced as introductory psychology students, but one is identified as a graduate student in perception research from a prestigious college. During the experiment in both conditions, the confederates all give the same wrong answers to some of the size comparison questions. Professor Reiman keeps track of how many times the participant conforms to the incorrect answers of the rest of the group. In this experiment:

(A) Identify the independent variable, the dependent variable, the operational definition of the dependent variable, and at least one confounding variable controlled for by the experimental design.

(B) Explain the principal difference between Professor Reiman's study and Asch's original research about conformity.

(C) Predict the level of conformity in the first group relative to the level of conformity in the second group based on your knowledge of Asch's research and social psychological principles. Identify what psychological principle you base your prediction on.

After reading the question, stop and think about what it is asking you. You are allowed to make notes on the question sheet, and many students find making a simple outline at this point and organizing their thoughts helpful. All essay questions imply a certain organization for your answer. **Use** this implied organization, **do not ignore** it. You might be tempted to create a unique organization for your answer. However, your reader is not giving you points based on organization, so the time you spend on this is wasted. In addition, if you answer a question out of order, you increase the chances the reader might misunderstand what you are trying to say. In this case, the format of the question indicates you organize your essay into three main parts: A, B, and C. You do not need to label these parts A, B, and C. (In fact, make sure you do not just write your answer as an outline.) However, the question writer is giving you a hint about how best to organize your response. Write your essay in this organization. In addition, notice the essay does NOT ask you to review Asch's studies on conformity in detail. For the last two parts of the question, having a basic knowledge of Asch's study would be helpful. However, you could write a detailed description of this research and not answer this question directly. Do what is asked of you in an essay. Adding information the question does not ask for (even if it is accurate information) is a waste of time and will not get you additional points. Do not spend time writing an introduction or conclusion for your essay, since grading rubrics do not give points for introductions or conclusions. You may want to write your answer to this question before going on in this chapter to the scoring rubric for this question. When you are ready, examine the following rubric for this essay question and notice how the points are scored:

Rubric for Sample Question

This is an 8-point question. Four points are possible in part A, 1 point in part B, and 3 points in part C.

(A) Identify the independent variable, the dependent variable, the operational definition of the dependent variable, and at least one confounding variable controlled for by the experimental design.

Point 1—Independent variable—The essay should identify the different introductions of the confederates as the independent variable. In the first condition, all the confederates were introduced as psychology students. In the second condition, one of them was identified as a graduate student in perception. This was the only designed difference between the groups and is thus the variable the experimenter is trying to manipulate, the independent variable.

Point 2—Dependent variable—The student should identify conformity as the dependent variable. Professor Reiman manipulates the independent variable to see how it affects conformity, the dependent variable.

Point 3—Operational definition—Professor Reiman operationally defines conformity as the participant agreeing with the wrong answers of the confederates. Do NOT award a point if the student identifies the operational definition as conformity. Conformity is the dependent variable.

Point 4—Confounding variable—The main element of the experimental design mentioned that would control for potential confounding variables is the random assignment. Randomly assigning participants to the two conditions would control for many possible subject(participant)-relevant confounding variables (students do not need to use this term, examples are enough). A student might say "random assignment would control for the possibility that participants might misunderstand the directions" or "might be in a bad mood at the time of the study" or "might have hostile reactions to psychology students," and so on. Any example of a subject-relevant confounding variable is correct.

(B) Explain the principal difference between Professor Reiman's study and Asch's original research about conformity.

Point 5—Difference—The main difference between Professor Reiman's and Asch's study is the inclusion of this particular independent variable. In one of the conditions, Professor Reiman identifies one of the confederates as a graduate student in perception.

(C) Predict the level of conformity in the first group relative to the level of conformity in the second group based on your knowledge of Asch's research and social psychological principles. Identify what psychological principle you base your prediction on.

Point 6—Level of conformity in the first group—The student receives one point for demonstrating his or her understanding that most of the participants in the first condition would conform to the group's wrong answers. This condition is similar to Asch's original study, so the results would be similar.

Point 7—Level of conformity in the second group—The student receives another point for predicting the level of conformity in the second group, with one confederate identified as the expert. The student should predict a higher level of conformity in this group due to the addition of the authority figure.

Point 8—Social psychological principle—The student should identify obedience as the social psychological principle acting in this case in conjunction with conformity. Stanley Milgram's obedience studies demonstrate that the presence of an authority figure increases compliance, including conformity. To get the point, the essay only needs to identify obedience as the principle behind the prediction; the student does not need to cite other evidence to prove the position.

Interpreting the Rubric

Notice how the rubric directs the readers to look for points that correspond to correct answers, not mistakes you make. You might be relieved to know that you will not be penalized for saying something incorrectly or even making a factual error. Readers look for points and ignore incorrect information. This rule has one exception: Do not directly contradict yourself. Readers will not give you a point if you directly contradict something you wrote earlier. The rubric shows you how you should write your essay; it is organized in the way the question implies. If you organize your answer in this way, the reader can go through your response and look for the points in order. This is not just to be kind to the reader (although that is a nice thing to do). It increases your chances of getting points because it makes your responses more clear. The more clearly you communicate to the reader, the better your chances of getting points. In addition, providing examples and definitions increases the chances a reader will understand your explanation of a concept.

Use the sample essay question and rubric to grade the following fictional student essay.

Fictional Student Essay

Professor Reiman picked a valuable psychological topic to study. Her experimental design includes many valuable elements but also includes several problems. In this essay, I will critically examine Professor Reiman's experiment to determine the most likely results.

The independent variable in this experiment is prestige. In one condition, all the confederates are introduced as psychology students. In the other situation, one of the confederates is a graduate student in perception. This change is the independent variable. The dependent variable is whether the people change their answers or not. This is also the operational definition. One of the confounding variables in the study is the presence of the confederates. For an accurate study, Professor Reiman should not use confederates in the research, she should use a random sampling of people not familiar with her research.

The only major difference between Professor Reiman's study and Asch's research is the fact that she had one of the people in one of the groups pretend to be a graduate student in research. That is the principal difference.

I think people would conform in both groups but more in the second one than the first. Most of the people in the first group would conform to the wrong answers because speaking out against the group is hard. However, more people would conform in the second group because not only is the majority saying the wrong answer, the graduate student in psychology is saying the wrong answer too. The participants in the study would consider that person to know what he or she is talking about.

In conclusion, Professor Reiman's study is a valuable addition to the world of psychology. She proves that people are too easily swayed by experts. This can become dangerous if those experts do not know what they are talking about.

Grading the Fictional Response

You may want to use the rubric explained earlier to grade this sample response (and/or the essay you wrote for this question) on your own. Before we begin discussing individual points, notice the introduction and conclusion to this sample essay. The student does not write anything in those two sections that directly addresses the question. These two sections did not help this essay. The student could have used his or her time more effectively by just starting the essay in the second paragraph where he or she starts answering the question directly. Grading this essay using the rubric would result in the following:

Point 1—Awarded—The student correctly identifies the difference in the two groups as the independent variable:
"In one condition, all the confederates are introduced as psychology students. In the other situation, one of the confederates is a graduate student in perception. This change is the independent variable."

Point 2—Not awarded—This student is unclear about the difference between an operational definition and the dependent variable.

Point 3—Awarded—The student identifies "whether people change their answers or not" as the operational definition. The student incorrectly says this is also the dependent variable, but the point is awarded for this correct identification.

Point 4—Not awarded—The student misunderstood that the use of confederates in this study is not a confounding variable. Researchers can and often do use confederates in research. It is not in and of itself a confounding variable.

Point 5—Awarded—The student correctly explains that the difference between this study and Asch's research is the inclusion of the graduate student in perception.

Point 6—Awarded—The student states, "Most of the people in the first group would conform to the wrong answers," which corresponds with the findings in Asch's study.

Point 7—Awarded—The student predicts more of the participants exposed to the second condition would conform than those in the first condition.

Point 8—Not awarded—The student never states what psychological principle the prediction is based on. The essay explains obedience but never directly answers the question by stating the principle.

So, overall, this essay would get 5 out of 8 possible points.

General Hints and Tips for the Essay Portion of the Exam

Style/Organization Hints

1. Remember to think before you start writing and feel free to jot down a few notes. You should have timed some practice-essay responses before the test in order to have an indication of how much time you need to answer the questions. Use 2–3 minutes to organize your thoughts about each essay, but be careful not to spend so much time that you feel rushed later.

2. Do NOT write your answer in outline form. While readers do not give points for the use of full sentences, proper paragraph form, and so on, they are not allowed to give any points for an essay written as an outline. Write your essay in sentences and paragraphs. Do not label parts of your essay with letters; use paragraphs to show where you move from one point to the next.

3. Make sure you cover everything the question asks in the order it asks. Picture the likely rubric in your mind, and answer each part of the question in a clear, organized way.

4. Structure your essay so that it clearly shows you answered all parts of the question. Each paragraph should begin with a topic sentence that indicates which part of the question you are answering.

5. Do not worry about an introduction and conclusion, unless writing one helps you organize your thoughts. Remember you get points for accurate information, not style or aesthetic considerations of your essay. Do not waste time repeating the question, the reader knows it well enough by now!

6. Try to write as clearly as you can in the time you have. Readers become expert in reading difficult handwriting, but undecipherable handwriting certainly will not help you get a better score. If you have time at the end of the test, look back through your response and rewrite any particularly messy words. If you need to add text in the middle of your response, clearly indicate where the additional text should go. Some students find leaving a little space between paragraphs for this purpose effective.

7. Use all your time. If you have extra time, use it to go back and make sure you said what you wanted to, add more examples for clarification, and rewrite any confusing sections.

Content Hints

1. Keep it simple. When asked to describe several methods of experimental control, for example, the graders will want the best and therefore most common ones. Do not waste time and energy explaining unnecessarily complicated techniques. For instance, write about random sampling, not stratified sampling.

2. Use psychological terms. Readers are looking for your psychological knowledge, not what these terms mean in other contexts. In all cases, use the term, define it clearly, and give an example if possible.

3. Make sure your context is clear. Sometimes whether you get the point or not is determined by whether you are using an example in the right context. For instance, you might give a great example of retroactive interference. However, if you place it into the paragraph discussing state-dependent memory, you may not get the point if the reader is not sure you know which concept the example applies to.

4. If you feel clueless about part of an essay, do not despair. Do your best—write something, if at all possible. You might hit on what the rubric asks for. If not, you will not be penalized for trying. Do not worry—missing one part of the essay question will not doom your score.

Practice Tests

1. Ⓐ Ⓑ Ⓒ Ⓓ Ⓔ   26. Ⓐ Ⓑ Ⓒ Ⓓ Ⓔ   51. Ⓐ Ⓑ Ⓒ Ⓓ Ⓔ   76. Ⓐ Ⓑ Ⓒ Ⓓ Ⓔ
2. Ⓐ Ⓑ Ⓒ Ⓓ Ⓔ   27. Ⓐ Ⓑ Ⓒ Ⓓ Ⓔ   52. Ⓐ Ⓑ Ⓒ Ⓓ Ⓔ   77. Ⓐ Ⓑ Ⓒ Ⓓ Ⓔ
3. Ⓐ Ⓑ Ⓒ Ⓓ Ⓔ   28. Ⓐ Ⓑ Ⓒ Ⓓ Ⓔ   53. Ⓐ Ⓑ Ⓒ Ⓓ Ⓔ   78. Ⓐ Ⓑ Ⓒ Ⓓ Ⓔ
4. Ⓐ Ⓑ Ⓒ Ⓓ Ⓔ   29. Ⓐ Ⓑ Ⓒ Ⓓ Ⓔ   54. Ⓐ Ⓑ Ⓒ Ⓓ Ⓔ   79. Ⓐ Ⓑ Ⓒ Ⓓ Ⓔ
5. Ⓐ Ⓑ Ⓒ Ⓓ Ⓔ   30. Ⓐ Ⓑ Ⓒ Ⓓ Ⓔ   55. Ⓐ Ⓑ Ⓒ Ⓓ Ⓔ   80. Ⓐ Ⓑ Ⓒ Ⓓ Ⓔ
6. Ⓐ Ⓑ Ⓒ Ⓓ Ⓔ   31. Ⓐ Ⓑ Ⓒ Ⓓ Ⓔ   56. Ⓐ Ⓑ Ⓒ Ⓓ Ⓔ   81. Ⓐ Ⓑ Ⓒ Ⓓ Ⓔ
7. Ⓐ Ⓑ Ⓒ Ⓓ Ⓔ   32. Ⓐ Ⓑ Ⓒ Ⓓ Ⓔ   57. Ⓐ Ⓑ Ⓒ Ⓓ Ⓔ   82. Ⓐ Ⓑ Ⓒ Ⓓ Ⓔ
8. Ⓐ Ⓑ Ⓒ Ⓓ Ⓔ   33. Ⓐ Ⓑ Ⓒ Ⓓ Ⓔ   58. Ⓐ Ⓑ Ⓒ Ⓓ Ⓔ   83. Ⓐ Ⓑ Ⓒ Ⓓ Ⓔ
9. Ⓐ Ⓑ Ⓒ Ⓓ Ⓔ   34. Ⓐ Ⓑ Ⓒ Ⓓ Ⓔ   59. Ⓐ Ⓑ Ⓒ Ⓓ Ⓔ   84. Ⓐ Ⓑ Ⓒ Ⓓ Ⓔ
10. Ⓐ Ⓑ Ⓒ Ⓓ Ⓔ   35. Ⓐ Ⓑ Ⓒ Ⓓ Ⓔ   60. Ⓐ Ⓑ Ⓒ Ⓓ Ⓔ   85. Ⓐ Ⓑ Ⓒ Ⓓ Ⓔ
11. Ⓐ Ⓑ Ⓒ Ⓓ Ⓔ   36. Ⓐ Ⓑ Ⓒ Ⓓ Ⓔ   61. Ⓐ Ⓑ Ⓒ Ⓓ Ⓔ   86. Ⓐ Ⓑ Ⓒ Ⓓ Ⓔ
12. Ⓐ Ⓑ Ⓒ Ⓓ Ⓔ   37. Ⓐ Ⓑ Ⓒ Ⓓ Ⓔ   62. Ⓐ Ⓑ Ⓒ Ⓓ Ⓔ   87. Ⓐ Ⓑ Ⓒ Ⓓ Ⓔ
13. Ⓐ Ⓑ Ⓒ Ⓓ Ⓔ   38. Ⓐ Ⓑ Ⓒ Ⓓ Ⓔ   63. Ⓐ Ⓑ Ⓒ Ⓓ Ⓔ   88. Ⓐ Ⓑ Ⓒ Ⓓ Ⓔ
14. Ⓐ Ⓑ Ⓒ Ⓓ Ⓔ   39. Ⓐ Ⓑ Ⓒ Ⓓ Ⓔ   64. Ⓐ Ⓑ Ⓒ Ⓓ Ⓔ   89. Ⓐ Ⓑ Ⓒ Ⓓ Ⓔ
15. Ⓐ Ⓑ Ⓒ Ⓓ Ⓔ   40. Ⓐ Ⓑ Ⓒ Ⓓ Ⓔ   65. Ⓐ Ⓑ Ⓒ Ⓓ Ⓔ   90. Ⓐ Ⓑ Ⓒ Ⓓ Ⓔ
16. Ⓐ Ⓑ Ⓒ Ⓓ Ⓔ   41. Ⓐ Ⓑ Ⓒ Ⓓ Ⓔ   66. Ⓐ Ⓑ Ⓒ Ⓓ Ⓔ   91. Ⓐ Ⓑ Ⓒ Ⓓ Ⓔ
17. Ⓐ Ⓑ Ⓒ Ⓓ Ⓔ   42. Ⓐ Ⓑ Ⓒ Ⓓ Ⓔ   67. Ⓐ Ⓑ Ⓒ Ⓓ Ⓔ   92. Ⓐ Ⓑ Ⓒ Ⓓ Ⓔ
18. Ⓐ Ⓑ Ⓒ Ⓓ Ⓔ   43. Ⓐ Ⓑ Ⓒ Ⓓ Ⓔ   68. Ⓐ Ⓑ Ⓒ Ⓓ Ⓔ   93. Ⓐ Ⓑ Ⓒ Ⓓ Ⓔ
19. Ⓐ Ⓑ Ⓒ Ⓓ Ⓔ   44. Ⓐ Ⓑ Ⓒ Ⓓ Ⓔ   69. Ⓐ Ⓑ Ⓒ Ⓓ Ⓔ   94. Ⓐ Ⓑ Ⓒ Ⓓ Ⓔ
20. Ⓐ Ⓑ Ⓒ Ⓓ Ⓔ   45. Ⓐ Ⓑ Ⓒ Ⓓ Ⓔ   70. Ⓐ Ⓑ Ⓒ Ⓓ Ⓔ   95. Ⓐ Ⓑ Ⓒ Ⓓ Ⓔ
21. Ⓐ Ⓑ Ⓒ Ⓓ Ⓔ   46. Ⓐ Ⓑ Ⓒ Ⓓ Ⓔ   71. Ⓐ Ⓑ Ⓒ Ⓓ Ⓔ   96. Ⓐ Ⓑ Ⓒ Ⓓ Ⓔ
22. Ⓐ Ⓑ Ⓒ Ⓓ Ⓔ   47. Ⓐ Ⓑ Ⓒ Ⓓ Ⓔ   72. Ⓐ Ⓑ Ⓒ Ⓓ Ⓔ   97. Ⓐ Ⓑ Ⓒ Ⓓ Ⓔ
23. Ⓐ Ⓑ Ⓒ Ⓓ Ⓔ   48. Ⓐ Ⓑ Ⓒ Ⓓ Ⓔ   73. Ⓐ Ⓑ Ⓒ Ⓓ Ⓔ   98. Ⓐ Ⓑ Ⓒ Ⓓ Ⓔ
24. Ⓐ Ⓑ Ⓒ Ⓓ Ⓔ   49. Ⓐ Ⓑ Ⓒ Ⓓ Ⓔ   74. Ⓐ Ⓑ Ⓒ Ⓓ Ⓔ   99. Ⓐ Ⓑ Ⓒ Ⓓ Ⓔ
25. Ⓐ Ⓑ Ⓒ Ⓓ Ⓔ   50. Ⓐ Ⓑ Ⓒ Ⓓ Ⓔ   75. Ⓐ Ⓑ Ⓒ Ⓓ Ⓔ   100. Ⓐ Ⓑ Ⓒ Ⓓ Ⓔ

Practice Test #1

Multiple-choice Portion

Time—1 hour and 10 minutes
100 Questions

Directions: Each of the questions or incomplete statements below is followed by five suggested answers or completions. Select the one that is best in each case.

---

1. In a famous experiment, a group of factory workers was put into a special room so researchers could investigate the effects of increased lighting on productivity. Interestingly, the workers' performance was found to improve both under conditions of more and less light. This finding, that special treatment, regardless of type, can affect a group's performance, illustrates the need for a control group and is known as
   (A) the Barnum effect.
   (B) the Hawthorne effect.
   (C) the self-fulfilling prophecy effect.
   (D) confirmation bias.
   (E) sampling error.

2. The part(s) of the body with the most sensory receptors is (are) the
   (A) lips.
   (B) feet.
   (C) thighs.
   (D) neck.
   (E) wrists.

3. When Tray walked out of his algebra final, he could remember only the first question and the last few questions. Tray's recollection can best be explained by
   (A) anterograde amnesia.
   (B) retrograde amnesia.
   (C) the stress of the exam.
   (D) the serial position effect.
   (E) interference.

4. What process did researchers use to come up with the theory that five main personality traits exist?
   (A) inferential statistics
   (B) factor analysis
   (C) means-end analysis
   (D) hypothesis testing
   (E) applied research

5. Experiments differ from other types of research in that
   (A) only an experiment can prove a hypothesis.
   (B) the dependent variable is manipulated by the experimenter.
   (C) experiments attempt to show a cause-and-effect relationship.
   (D) an experiment minimizes ethical concerns.
   (E) experiments involve the collection of qualitative data.

6. Charities that send free return-address labels in the mail are hoping people will contribute money because of
   (A) social facilitation.
   (B) norms of reciprocity.
   (C) door-in-the-face.
   (D) foot-in-the-door.
   (E) deindividuation.

GO ON TO THE NEXT PAGE ➤

7. When Celie looks at the carpet directly beneath her feet, she can see that it has a black-and-white speckled pattern. When she looks at the carpet on the far side of the room, though, it looks gray. The difference in appearance of the carpet is explained by
   (A) the law of Pragnanz.
   (B) texture gradient.
   (C) summation.
   (D) binocular disparity.
   (E) motion parallax.

8. A shortage of which neurotransmitter has been linked to depression?
   (A) dopamine
   (B) epinephrine
   (C) acetylcholine
   (D) serotonin
   (E) GABA

9. The capacity of our working memories is approximately _____ items.
   (A) three
   (B) five
   (C) seven
   (D) nine
   (E) unlimited

10. Claire sat on the windy prairie contemplating how to keep her hair out of her face. She never considered using a piece of grass. This common obstacle to problem solving is known as
    (A) an algorithm.
    (B) functional fixedness.
    (C) a heuristic.
    (D) mental set.
    (E) convergent thinking.

11. REM sleep is also known as
    (A) quiet sleep.
    (B) deep sleep.
    (C) paradoxical sleep.
    (D) slow-wave sleep.
    (E) beta sleep.

12. Kohler's work with apes had to do with what type of learning?
    (A) insight
    (B) abstract
    (C) latent
    (D) observational
    (E) classical conditioning

13. In high school, Stefan could balance chemical equations faster than anyone he knew. Now when he helps his granddaughter, it takes him a little longer. This slowing of Stefan's problem-solving ability is due to a decrease in
    (A) IQ.
    (B) fluid intelligence.
    (C) creativity.
    (D) practical intelligence.
    (E) crystallized intelligence.

14. Which of the following kinds of graphs would be used to plot the correlation between people's height and weight?
    (A) frequency histogram
    (B) bar graph
    (C) frequency polygraph
    (D) pie chart
    (E) scatter plot

15. Juanita is 12 and has a mental age of 15. Her IQ is
    (A) 75
    (B) 80
    (C) 100
    (D) 125
    (E) 150

16. Siblings that are close in age are more similar in intelligence than siblings of disparate ages. The only possible conclusion to draw from this finding is that
    (A) genetics influences intelligence.
    (B) environment influences intelligence.
    (C) genetics and environment exert equally strong influences on intelligence.
    (D) older siblings tend to be smarter than younger ones.
    (E) younger siblings tend to outperform their older siblings in school.

GO ON TO THE NEXT PAGE ➤

17. A man who reports that he is seeing things that, in fact, are not there is experiencing
    (A) hallucinations.
    (B) delusions.
    (C) sensory confusion.
    (D) inappropriate adaptation.
    (E) compulsions.

18. When Jeb was rejected from the University of Michigan, his first choice, he told everyone that he did not really want to go there because Michigan is too cold. Jeb is most likely using which of the following defense mechanisms?
    (A) intellectualization
    (B) rationalization
    (C) denial
    (D) projection
    (E) reaction formation

19. What kind of psychologist would be most likely to use the TAT?
    (A) psychoanalyst
    (B) behaviorist
    (C) biomedical
    (D) humanistic
    (E) trait theorist

20. When Bobby kicks his little sister Tammy's doll under the bed, she tries to retrieve it. In Piagetian terms, Tammy has
    (A) egocentrism.
    (B) concrete operations.
    (C) animism.
    (D) object permanence.
    (E) conservation.

21. According to Erikson, a two-year-old is most likely to try to resolve which of the following conflicts?
    (A) industry versus inferiority
    (B) autonomy versus shame and doubt
    (C) initiative versus guilt
    (D) intimacy versus isolation
    (E) trust versus mistrust

22. Humanistic psychologists emphasize the importance of
    (A) free will.
    (B) observable behavior.
    (C) unconscious thoughts.
    (D) neurotransmitter levels.
    (E) attributional style.

23. At rest, the charge inside a neuron is approximately _____ millivolts.
    (A) −70
    (B) −50
    (C) 0
    (D) +50
    (E) +70

24. After confronting an emergency situation, which part of the nervous system returns the body to homeostasis?
    (A) somatic
    (B) central
    (C) sympathetic
    (D) parasympathetic
    (E) automatic

25. A negative side effect of ECT is
    (A) violent outbursts.
    (B) phobic disorders.
    (C) memory loss.
    (D) sleeplessness.
    (E) motor tremors.

26. Fredo wants to go to Craig's party because he thinks it will be fun. However, he does not want to see his ex-girlfriend, Anna, who he knows will be at the party. Fredo is experiencing
    (A) an approach-approach conflict.
    (B) an approach-avoidance conflict.
    (C) an avoidance-avoidance conflict.
    (D) a double approach-avoidance conflict.
    (E) a multiple approach-avoidance conflict.

27. Whenever Eddie goes a few hours without smoking a cigarette, he gets irritable and nervous. Eddie's need to smoke illustrates which theory of motivation?
    (A) drive reduction
    (B) cognitive consistency
    (C) evolutionary
    (D) ethology
    (E) Maslow's hierarchy of needs

28. Which is the highest level in Maslow's hierarchy of needs?
    (A) physiological needs
    (B) need for belongingness
    (C) esteem needs
    (D) self-actualization
    (E) safety needs

GO ON TO THE NEXT PAGE ➤

29. People classified as Type A are most susceptible to which of the following health problems?
    (A) cancer
    (B) heart disease
    (C) schizophrenic disorders
    (D) addictions
    (E) pulmonary disorders

30. Over which of the following functions does the right hemisphere of the brain have the most control?
    (A) language
    (B) logical reasoning
    (C) movement of the right side of the body
    (D) algebra
    (E) art and music appreciation

31. Greta wants to teach her pet bulldog, Spike, a new trick. Which schedule of reinforcement would result in the quickest learning?
    (A) variable interval
    (B) variable ratio
    (C) continuous
    (D) fixed interval
    (E) fixed ratio

32. Taking medicine to relieve a headache is an example of
    (A) positive reinforcement.
    (B) classical conditioning.
    (C) latent learning.
    (D) punishment.
    (E) negative reinforcement.

33. According to Asch's research, what is the relationship between conformity and group size?
    (A) The more people in the group, the greater the conformity shown.
    (B) Conformity increases as group size increases to nine and then drops precipitously.
    (C) There is no relationship between group size and conformity.
    (D) Conformity increases until the group has three people and then levels off.
    (E) In men, conformity increases with group size, but, in women, conformity rates stay constant.

34. The school psychologist mistakenly tells Mikey's parents that their average son is off-the-charts brilliant. Mikey's parents enroll him in extra classes, buy him a chemistry set, and take him to lots of museums. Mikey ends up valedictorian of his high school class and gets into Yale. This situation illustrates
    (A) the power of observational learning.
    (B) the self-fulfilling prophecy effect.
    (C) the fundamental attribution error.
    (D) the false-consensus effect.
    (E) the just-world bias.

35. If Ramon scored 100 on a test with a standard deviation of 10 and a mean of 80, his z score is
    (A) −2
    (B) −0.8
    (C) 0
    (D) +0.8
    (E) +2

36. A valid test of artistic ability
    (A) is normed based on the performance of a standardization sample.
    (B) yields identical results on subsequent administrations.
    (C) identifies those people who have had the best artistic training.
    (D) rewards the people who have studied art the longest.
    (E) is meant to show aptitude rather than achievement.

37. One important contribution of contemporary researchers on intelligence has been to
    (A) de-emphasize the importance of traditional components of intelligence such as mathematical and verbal abilities.
    (B) utilize more sophisticated statistical methods to identify the basic components of intelligence.
    (C) reaffirm the belief that intelligence is fixed, not changeable.
    (D) suggest that intelligence is context-free.
    (E) dismiss the study of intelligence as meaningless and counterproductive due to its susceptibility to bias.

GO ON TO THE NEXT PAGE ➤

38. The brain scan that is essentially a series of X rays is the
    (A) MRI scan.
    (B) CAT scan.
    (C) PET scan.
    (D) EEG scan.
    (E) EKG scan.

39. Which of the following chemicals would be most likely found in the synapse?
    (A) norepinephrine
    (B) insulin
    (C) estrogen
    (D) glucagon
    (E) thyroxin

40. All of the following are hallucinogens except for
    (A) angel dust.
    (B) marijuana.
    (C) LSD.
    (D) cocaine.
    (E) MDMA.

41. Billy saw the word *dophin* but read the word *dolphin*. What can explain Billy's error?
    (A) prototype-matching theory
    (B) template-matching theory
    (C) complexity
    (D) bottom-up processing
    (E) top-down processing

42. Motion pictures are actually a series of still pictures presented in rapid succession to produce the illusion of movement. This illusion of movement is called
    (A) the autokinetic effect.
    (B) the phi phenomenon.
    (C) stroboscopic motion.
    (D) light adaptation.
    (E) the false-motion effect.

43. The first step in the information-processing theory of memory is
    (A) storage.
    (B) retrieval.
    (C) interference.
    (D) encoding.
    (E) attention.

44. Loss of interest in one's daily activities is a symptom of
    (A) hypochondriasis.
    (B) depression.
    (C) borderline personality disorder.
    (D) panic disorder.
    (E) ADHD.

45. Psychogenic amnesia is classified as a
    (A) somatoform disorder.
    (B) mood disorder.
    (C) dissociative disorder.
    (D) schizophrenic disorder.
    (E) developmental disorder.

46. Groups often take more extreme positions on issues than the individuals comprising the groups. This phenomenon is known as
    (A) deindividuation.
    (B) in-group bias.
    (C) groupthink.
    (D) group polarization.
    (E) group extremism.

47. Social psychologists are the most likely group of psychologists to study
    (A) ways to increase workplace efficiency.
    (B) how memory works.
    (C) attitude formation.
    (D) the biology of learning.
    (E) the use of heuristics.

48. Kohlberg posited that the lowest level of moral development involved
    (A) consistently hurting others.
    (B) focusing on the consequences of one's action to oneself.
    (C) blindly following the law.
    (D) breaking the rules whenever one feels they are unjust.
    (E) doing whatever one's peer group advised.

49. Parents who set and enforce strict rules for their children without allowing any questioning or discussion are following what parenting style?
    (A) democratic
    (B) authoritative
    (C) totalitarian
    (D) authoritarian
    (E) neglectful

GO ON TO THE NEXT PAGE ➤

50. Gestalt psychologists emphasize the importance of
    (A) behavior.
    (B) attention.
    (C) hormones.
    (D) the whole.
    (E) projective tests.

51. Taking a random sample from a population ensures that
    (A) the sample will contain an equal number of males and females.
    (B) each member of the population has an equal chance of being selected.
    (C) the impact of confounding variables will be minimized.
    (D) experimenter bias will be eliminated.
    (E) replication will be unnecessary.

52. The most commonly employed measures of personality ask people to
    (A) keep logs of their thoughts and actions over extended periods of time.
    (B) interpret ambiguous shapes and pictures.
    (C) monitor their blood pressure, glucose levels, and other physical characteristics for several weeks.
    (D) put themselves under the surveillance of a "blind" observer for several days.
    (E) fill out questionnaires about their own personality.

53. This practice test that you are in the process of taking is an example of a(n)
    (A) standardized test.
    (B) achievement test.
    (C) power test.
    (D) speed test.
    (E) aptitude test.

54. What kind of memory is Misty using when she thinks back to the day she won the state spelling bee?
    (A) procedural
    (B) episodic
    (C) declarative
    (D) eidetic
    (E) semantic

55. "I goed to the circus" is an example of
    (A) telegraphic speech.
    (B) holophrastic speech.
    (C) babbling.
    (D) syntax.
    (E) overgeneralization.

56. Trait theorists are mainly criticized for
    (A) overemphasizing the importance of behavior.
    (B) overlooking important gender differences.
    (C) asserting that personality is fixed at birth.
    (D) underestimating the importance of situational factors.
    (E) focusing too much on negative rather than positive traits.

57. In Pavlov's classical conditioning experiments, salivation was
    I.   the US.
    II. the CR.
    III. the UR.
    (A) I only
    (B) II only
    (C) III only
    (D) I and III
    (E) II and III

58. Bandura's Bobo doll experiment is most closely associated with which of the following terms?
    (A) instincts
    (B) maturation
    (C) modeling
    (D) abstract learning
    (E) operant conditioning

59. People who suffer from antisocial personality disorder are most likely to
    (A) experience a change in their eating and sleeping habits.
    (B) view themselves as loners.
    (C) suffer from delusions.
    (D) evidence a lack of sensitivity to others.
    (E) become excessively dependent upon the opinion of others.

GO ON TO THE NEXT PAGE ➤

60. One theorized cause of eating disorders is
    (A) hypothalamic failure.
    (B) unstable set point.
    (C) the rapidly rising rate of divorce.
    (D) the societal emphasis on thinness.
    (E) dopamine levels.

61. According to the James-Lange theory of emotion, what immediately precedes recognition of the emotion?
    (A) a physiological change
    (B) cognitive appraisal
    (C) memories of similar situations
    (D) observing the stimulus
    (E) thalamic stimulation

62. What is the first stage of Hans Seyle's general adaptation syndrome?
    (A) activation
    (B) resistance
    (C) exhaustion
    (D) alarm
    (E) observation

63. Systematic desensitization is based on which principle?
    (A) counterconditioning
    (B) modeling
    (C) free will
    (D) aversive conditioning
    (E) the use of a token economy

64. What kind of therapy might involve the analysis of transference?
    (A) learning
    (B) humanistic
    (C) flooding
    (D) psychoanalysis
    (E) cognitive behavioral

65. Which of the following is a primary reinforcer?
    (A) money
    (B) water
    (C) praise
    (D) music
    (E) dolls

66. For some children, getting sent to their rooms may be a terrible punishment while others actually may see it as an opportunity to hone their video game-playing skills. That the reinforcement often depends on the individual in question is expressed by
    (A) the partial-reinforcement effect.
    (B) chaining.
    (C) the Premack principle.
    (D) outshining.
    (E) latent learning.

67. People tend to be more fearful of airplane crashes than a statistical analysis would indicate they should be due to
    (A) the availability heuristic.
    (B) the recency effect.
    (C) confirmation bias.
    (D) the framing effect.
    (E) cognitive dissonance.

68. With regard to language, Noam Chomsky proposed that
    (A) some apes can be taught to use language.
    (B) humans have a language acquisition device.
    (C) children essentially learn language through shaping.
    (D) people cannot learn new languages after a critical period has passed.
    (E) nurture has a far greater influence than nature.

69. Photoreceptors synapse with
    (A) the optic nerve.
    (B) the blind spot.
    (C) ganglion cells.
    (D) bipolar cells.
    (E) rods and cones.

70. Transduction in the ear takes place in the
    (A) ossicles.
    (B) cochlea.
    (C) tympanic membrane.
    (D) semicircular canals.
    (E) auditory canal.

GO ON TO THE NEXT PAGE ➤

71. The fatty tissue that speeds up neural transmission is known as
    (A) myelin.
    (B) astrocytes.
    (C) adipose.
    (D) nodes of Ranvier.
    (E) axolation.

72. Damage to which part of the brain would most likely result in auditory difficulties?
    (A) cerebellum
    (B) parietal lobe
    (C) amygdala
    (D) Broca's area
    (E) temporal lobe

73. Mary Ainsworth and John Bowlby are best known for their work on
    (A) parenting styles.
    (B) adult development.
    (C) attachment.
    (D) intelligence.
    (E) creativity.

74. According to Freud, an obsession with control and order might have its origin in which of the following psychosexual stages?
    (A) oral
    (B) anal
    (C) phallic
    (D) latency
    (E) adult genital

75. A common somatic treatment for depression is
    (A) RET.
    (B) prefrontal lobotomy.
    (C) MAO inhibitors.
    (D) benzodiazepines.
    (E) implosive therapy.

76. The intensity of light that needs to exist for you to first notice that the house lights are being turned on following the end of the movie is called your
    (A) just-noticeable difference.
    (B) light quotient.
    (C) absolute threshold.
    (D) stimulation tolerance.
    (E) sensitivity.

77. Which of the following is cited as evidence that hypnosis is a form of divided consciousness?
    (A) somnambulism
    (B) the hidden observer
    (C) lucid dreaming
    (D) hypnotics
    (E) free-running rhythms

78. The order of the sexual response cycle stages as described by Masters and Johnson is
    (A) excitement, plateau, orgasm, and resolution.
    (B) arousal, orgasm, plateau, and refraction.
    (C) resolution, excitement, orgasm, and plateau.
    (D) arousal, orgasm, plateau, and refraction.
    (E) plateau, excitement, orgasm, and resolution.

79. Which of the following would not characterize a person in the concrete operational stage?
    (A) using operations
    (B) understanding reversibility
    (C) believing in artificialism
    (D) appreciating conservation
    (E) solving class inclusion problems

80. In the formation of personality, humanistic psychologists are most likely to emphasize the importance of
    (A) self-esteem and self-concept.
    (B) neurochemical levels.
    (C) unconscious motivations.
    (D) attributional style.
    (E) childhood contingencies of reinforcement.

81. Ling scored 92 on a standardized test with a mean of 78 and a standard deviation of 7. At approximately what percentile did she score?
    (A) 47.5th
    (B) 50th
    (C) 68th
    (D) 95th
    (E) 97.5th

GO ON TO THE NEXT PAGE ➤

82. Interviewing 22-year-old Karen about her psychological problems is difficult because her speech lacks coherence and includes a number of made-up words. One possible cause of Karen's difficulties is
(A) bipolar disorder.
(B) an anxiety disorder.
(C) conversion disorder.
(D) autism.
(E) schizophrenia.

83. A researcher tests a group of children when they are three, six, nine, and 12 years of age. This researcher is involved in
(A) cross-sectional research.
(B) cohort-sequential research.
(C) lifespan research.
(D) longitudinal research.
(E) observational research.

84. If the results of a study are statistically significant,
(A) the results probably did not happen by chance.
(B) the methodology was probably not flawed.
(C) a perfect correlation exists between the variables.
(D) the research was done ethically.
(E) the study has been replicated at least three times.

85. Sometimes actions originally conceived of as treatments are abandoned due to lack of success and/or unintended harms. An example of such a treatment approach is
(A) ECT.
(B) trephining.
(C) chemotherapy.
(D) person-centered therapy.
(E) institutionalization.

86. Milgram found that the level of shock inflicted by subjects could be reduced by
(A) having the experimenter present during the study.
(B) introducing the subject to the learner prior to the experiment.
(C) scripting the responses of the experimenter.
(D) enabling subjects to see the learners during the experiment.
(E) using young, female subjects.

87. Studies of prosocial behavior show that bystanders are less likely to offer help to others who need it when
(A) the bystanders are alone.
(B) the weather is good.
(C) other bystanders are not helping.
(D) the person seems to be in dire need of aid.
(E) the bystanders live in small communities.

88. Which part of the brain is most instrumental in decision making?
(A) hypothalamus
(B) hippocampus
(C) frontal lobe
(D) cerebellum
(E) pons

89. In humans, brown eyes (B) is a dominant trait while blue eyes (b) is a recessive trait. What percentage of the children of Alan, homozygous for brown eyes, and Sandra, homozygous for blue eyes, will have blue eyes?
(A) 0 percent
(B) 25 percent
(C) 50 percent
(D) 75 percent
(E) 100 percent

90. Which kind of psychotherapy is criticized for having a long and expensive course of treatment?
(A) rational emotive therapy
(B) Gestalt therapy
(C) implosive therapy
(D) eclectic therapy
(E) psychoanalysis

91. Which of the following types of information is not processed by the thalamus?
(A) visual
(B) olfactory
(C) gustatory
(D) auditory
(E) touch

GO ON TO THE NEXT PAGE ➤

92. Hubel and Weisel won the Nobel prize for their work on
    (A) feature detectors in the visual cortex.
    (B) specialized taste cells on the tongue.
    (C) the influence of pheromones on human behavior.
    (D) the joints and ligaments that comprise the kinesthetic sense.
    (E) the elements of a reflex arc.

93. Sociobiologists believe that people are motivated to
    (A) maintain a peak arousal level.
    (B) ensure the survival of their genes.
    (C) surpass other members of the species.
    (D) avoid mental tension.
    (E) maximize their rewards.

94. The *DSM* is a tool psychologists use to
    (A) assess intelligence.
    (B) measure personality.
    (C) diagnose mental illness.
    (D) analyze research findings.
    (E) make sure their research meets ethical requirements.

95. Seligman's work about learned helplessness led him to propose that it was associated with which of the following psychological disorders?
    (A) mania
    (B) conversion disorder
    (C) obsessive-compulsive disorder
    (D) unipolar depression
    (E) schizophrenia

96. When you stroke a baby's cheek with your finger, the baby turns his or her head and tries to put the finger into his or her mouth. This behavior is known as the
    (A) rooting reflex.
    (B) Babinsky reflex.
    (C) plantar reflex.
    (D) feeding reflex.
    (E) pupillary reflex.

97. According to Freud, the id strives mainly to
    (A) mediate between the demands of the ego and superego.
    (B) attain gratification of its desires.
    (C) ensure the individual is acting morally.
    (D) protect the person with its defense mechanisms.
    (E) deal with reality.

98. Someone with an internal locus of control is likely to believe that
    (A) luck plays a large role in people's successes or lack thereof.
    (B) nature has determined the degree to which one will prosper in life.
    (C) not interfering with the course of fate is better.
    (D) hard work and effort result in benefits for the individual.
    (E) other people's opinions should not affect his or her own actions.

99. Light therapy is most commonly used in the treatment of
    (A) phobias.
    (B) dyslexia.
    (C) conversion disorder.
    (D) SAD.
    (E) panic disorder.

100. Aphagia (starvation) will result from continually stimulating
    (A) the ventromedial hypothalamus.
    (B) the thalamus.
    (C) the thymus.
    (D) the frontal lobe.
    (E) the lateral hypothalamus.

STOP

Answer Key

Multiple-choice Portion

1. B	21. B	41. E	61. A	81. E
2. A	22. A	42. C	62. D	82. E
3. D	23. A	43. D	63. A	83. D
4. B	24. D	44. B	64. D	84. A
5. C	25. C	45. C	65. B	85. B
6. B	26. B	46. D	66. C	86. D
7. B	27. A	47. C	67. A	87. C
8. D	28. D	48. B	68. B	88. C
9. C	29. B	49. D	69. D	89. A
10. B	30. E	50. D	70. B	90. E
11. C	31. C	51. B	71. A	91. B
12. A	32. E	52. E	72. E	92. A
13. B	33. D	53. B	73. C	93. B
14. E	34. B	54. B	74. B	94. C
15. D	35. E	55. E	75. C	95. D
16. B	36. E	56. D	76. C	96. A
17. A	37. A	57. E	77. B	97. B
18. B	38. B	58. C	78. A	98. D
19. A	39. A	59. D	79. C	99. D
20. D	40. D	60. D	80. A	100. A

Answers Explained

1. **(B)** The Hawthorne plant, where the experiment described was conducted, gave its name to the Hawthorne effect. It illustrates the need for a control group to create a baseline against which to measure the effects of an experimental treatment. The Barnum effect refers to people's tendency to believe that vague, stock descriptions of personality actually fit themselves. The self-fulfilling prophecy effect is when one person's expectations are able to elicit behavioral confirmation from another person. Confirmation bias refers to people's tendency to pay more attention to information that fits in with their initial expectations. Sampling error is the measure of the differences between a sample and the population from which it was drawn.

2. **(A)** The part(s) of the body listed that has/have the most sensory receptors are the lips. Essentially, this question is asking which is the most sensitive part of the body. As illustrated by the sensory homunculus, the other parts listed are less sensitive.

3. **(D)** The serial-position effect explains that we are better able to remember items at the beginning and end of a series (termed the primacy and recency effect, respectively). Items in the middle of a list tend to be forgotten.

4. **(B)** Factor analysis is a statistical process that uses a series of correlations to boil down many different measures into a smaller number of common factors. Inferential statistics are used to determine whether the results of research are

statistically significant. Means-end analysis is a problem-solving approach. Hypothesis testing is the cornerstone of the scientific method, the process of formulating a hypothesis, collecting data, and analyzing the results. Applied research, as opposed to basic research, has a clear, practical purpose and use.

5. **(C)** By treating the experimental and control groups the same except for the independent variable, an experiment attempts to draw a causal conclusion about the influence of the independent variable. Proving a hypothesis is impossible, regardless of what kind of research one conducts. Most research, experimental, correlational, or observational, involves linking an independent and dependent variable together in a hypothesis. Experiments raise at least as many ethical issues as do other types of research. Experiments generally involve the collection of quantitative, not qualitative, data.

6. **(B)** Norms of reciprocity means that people are inclined to treat others the same way those individuals have treated them. By giving potential donors a free gift, charities hope to trigger in them the desire to reciprocate. Door-in-the-face and foot-in-the-door are other compliance strategies discussed in the social psychology chapter. Social facilitation and deindividuation are two ways that people's behavior is affected by the presence and actions of others; both are also discussed in the social psychology chapter.

7. **(B)** Texture gradient is a depth cue that enables us to know that the more detail or texture we can see in something, the closer it is. The law of Pragnanz is one of the Gestalt principles of perception. Essentially, the law of Pragnanz is the idea that we perceive things in the simplest way possible. Summation refers to the way the retina is structured. Many photoreceptors synapse with fewer bipolar cells that, in turn, synapse with even fewer ganglion cells. Binocular disparity is a depth cue that involves comparing the images on each of our two retinas. The more similar the images, the farther the object. Motion parallax is a depth cue that lets us know that closer objects seem to move faster than faraway ones.

8. **(D)** A shortage of serotonin is thought to be one cause of depression. Too much dopamine is linked to schizophrenia, and excessive sensitivity to acetylcholine is linked to bipolar disorder.

9. **(C)** Working memory is another name for short-term memory. The average capacity of people's short-term memories is seven items.

10. **(B)** Functional fixedness is people's difficulty in seeing that objects, in this case grass, can have unusual uses. Mental set is another impediment to problem solving; people have the tendency to approach new problems in the same way that they approached old problems even when such an approach is not appropriate. An algorithm is a problem-solving strategy that ensures a correct solution, while a heuristic is an approach that provides a shortcut but may result in errors. Convergent thinking is when one correct answer is sought, often in one correct way. Divergent thinking encourages multiple answers and approaches.

11. **(C)** REM (rapid eye movement) sleep is also known as paradoxical sleep, because brain waves resemble those present when awake. However, muscle movement is suppressed and people are very difficult to wake. Quiet sleep and beta sleep do not exist. Deep sleep and slow-wave sleep are terms used to refer to stages 3 and 4 sleep.

12. **(A)** Kohler gave apes a number of problems to solve that the apes had to have an insight about how to approach. For instance, he hung a banana out of a chimpanzee's reach in a room that contained several boxes. To get the banana, the chimpanzee had to realize it needed to stack the boxes and then climb them.

13. **(B)** Fluid intelligence refers to the speed at which one is able to process information. Fluid intelligence tends to decrease with age while crystallized intelligence (for example, wisdom and vocabulary) does not. IQ, which stands for intelligence quotient, is supposed to remain fairly stable over the life span. Stefan's trouble with the equations has nothing to do with a lack of creativity or practical intelligence.

14. **(E)** Correlations show the relationship between two variables such as height and weight. In a scatter plot, one variable (height) is plotted on the x-axis and the other variable (weight) is plotted on the y-axis. The result is a series of points that show the relationship between height and weight in the sample. Frequency histograms and bar graphs are the same thing and thus cannot be the answer. Frequency polygons are line graphs. All graphs that show frequency plot the frequency on the y-axis and the variable being measured on the x-axis. Pie charts show the percentage of a sample falling into various categories.

15. **(D)** To calculate IQ, divide mental age by chronological age and multiply by 100: $15/12 \times 100 = 125$. Remember to keep in mind that if mental age is greater than chronological age, IQ will be greater than 100.

16. **(B)** The question stem does not indicate that siblings close in age are any more or less intelligent than other siblings; it simply indicates that they are more similar in terms of intelligence. No genetic difference exists between siblings that are close in age and those who are not. On average, siblings (excluding monozygotic twins) share 50 percent of their genetic material. Siblings who are close in age do have more similar environments than siblings of very different ages since they grow up in more similar circumstances.

17. **(A)** Hallucinations are when someone perceives sensory stimulation in the absence of such stimulation. Delusions are irrational beliefs (for example, aliens are controlling you) that do not involve the belief that one is sensing nonexistent stimuli. Sensory confusion and inappropriate adaptation are made-up distracters. Compulsions are unwanted, repetitive actions people engage in to reduce the anxiety associated with obsessive-compulsive disorder.

18. **(B)** Rationalization is a defense mechanism that protects a person from dealing with ego-threatening thoughts by creating a reasonable, alternative explanation for an event. In this case, rather than face the disappointment of having been rejected from his school of choice, Jeb reasons that Michigan is unpleasantly cold, and he did not want to go there anyway. The other choices are other defense mechanisms discussed in the personality chapter.

19. **(A)** The TAT, thematic apperception test, is a type of projective test. Projective tests are designed to reveal the contents of people's unconscious by asking them to explain ambiguous stimuli. Since psychoanalysts are the type of psychologists most interested in the unconscious, they are the most likely to employ projective tests.

20. **(D)** Object permanence, which develops toward the end of the first year of life, requires understanding that an object continues to exist even when you can no longer see it. Since Tammy tries to get the doll back even though it is under the bed and she can no longer see it, Tammy has object permanence. Egocentrism and animism are limitations in the thought of children in the preoperational stage. Concrete operations refers to the third stage of development in Piaget's theory in which children learn to appreciate conservation.

21. **(B)** At age two, children are being toilet trained and beginning to learn language. Erikson believed that at this age, children struggle to gain a sense of autonomy rather than be plagued by self-doubt. Industry versus inferiority characterizes the children as they begin school. Children three to five years of age struggle with the crisis of initiative versus guilt. Intimacy versus isolation is the issue for young adults to resolve as they search for a life partner. Trust versus mistrust is the first of Erikson's stages and is experienced during the first year of life.

22. **(A)** Humanistic psychologists emphasize the importance of free will. Free will refers to people's ability to make their own choices. Behaviorists stress the importance of observable behavior. Psychoanalysts focus on unconscious thoughts. Biomedical theorists emphasize the role of chemicals such as neurotransmitters. Cognitive psychologists would be most interested in attributional style.

23. **(A)** The resting potential of a neuron is –70 millivolts. The action potential of a neuron is approximately +50 millivolts.

24. **(D)** The parasympathetic nervous system calms the body after the fight or flight response has been triggered. The parasympathetic nervous system and the sympathetic nervous system are the two parts of the autonomic (not automatic) nervous system.

25. **(C)** A negative side effect of ECT is memory loss. The electric current is thought to interfere with the consolidation of new memories. This unfortunate side effect can be minimized by using unilateral, rather than bilateral, ECT.

26. **(B)** Fredo is experiencing an approach-avoidance conflict because he is attracted and repelled by different features of the same situation. An approach-approach conflict involves having to choose between two desirable alternatives, and an avoidance-avoidance conflict involves having to opt for one of two undesirable choices. No such thing as a double approach-avoidance exists. However, a multiple approach-avoidance conflict is when one is forced to choose among alternatives, each of which has both attractive and unattractive features.

27. **(A)** Hull's drive reduction theory says we are motivated to maintain homeostasis. A tissue need (lack of nicotine in Eddie's case) leads to a drive (the desire to smoke).

28. **(D)** Self-actualization, the need to strive to fill one's potential, sits atop Maslow's hierarchy of needs. Descending from there, the hierarchy includes esteem needs, love and belongingness needs, safety needs, and physiological needs.

29. **(B)** People with Type A personalities are thought to be at particular risk for heart disease.

30. **(E)** The left hemisphere is thought to control language, logic, and the right side of the body. The right hemisphere is more active in creative pursuits (for example, art and music appreciation), spatial relations, and controlling the left side of the body.

31. **(C)** When teaching someone or something a new skill, using continuous reinforcement is most efficient. A continual connection between behavior and reward is easiest to learn.

32. **(E)** Negative reinforcement is when a behavior (taking the medicine) is strengthened because it results in the removal of something unpleasant (the headache). Positive reinforcement is when a behavior is strengthened because it results in the addition of something pleasant. Classical conditioning is a whole separate type of learning that results from the pairing of an unconditioned and a conditioned stimulus. Punishment is when a behavior is weakened due to an unpleasant consequence.

33. **(D)** Asch found that increasing group size beyond three people did not appreciably increase conformity.

34. **(B)** Mikey's parents thought he was brilliant, so they treated him as if he were brilliant, and he became brilliant. This is the self-fulfilling prophecy effect.

35. **(E)** z scores measure how far a score is from the mean in units of standard deviation. Since Ramon's score is higher than the mean, his z score must be positive. To solve for the z score, one would subtract 80 from 100 and divide by 10: $100 - 80/10 = 2$.

36. **(E)** Tests that purport to show ability are aptitude tests. Valid tests do what they are supposed to do. Therefore, a valid test of artistic ability will measure artistic aptitude. A test can be valid without being normed.

37. **(A)** Contemporary researchers of intelligence such as Sternberg, Gardner, and Goleman define intelligence much more broadly than mathematical and verbal ability. They tend to believe that intelligence is changeable. Sternberg, in particular, emphasizes the importance of context. Since they have devoted considerable time to the study of intelligence, they are unlikely to dismiss such an avocation as meaningless.

38. **(B)** CAT scans basically consist of X rays taken at 180 different angles. An MRI uses magnetism to create a detailed, structural picture of the brain. PET scans use radioactive glucose to determine how active various parts of the brain are. EEGs measure brain waves, and PIG scan is a made-up distraction.

39. **(A)** Norepinephrine is both a neurotransmitter and a hormone while the other choices are only hormones. Only neurotransmitters are likely to be found in the synapse.

40. **(D)** Cocaine is a stimulant. The primary characteristic of stimulants is that they excite the central nervous system. The defining characteristic of hallucinogens is that they produce some kind of hallucinations (the perception of sensory stimulation in the absence of such stimulation).

41. **(E)** Top-down processing involves using context and expectations to help with pattern perception. Billy is used to seeing the word *dolphin* and not *dophin*. This experience affects how he processes the information. Prototype

and template matching are two theories about how bottom-up processing works. Bottom-up processing is when one uses only the stimulus to discern the pattern. Complexity is a made-up distraction.

42. **(C)** Movies are created using stroboscopic motion. The autokinetic effect is that spots of light in otherwise dark rooms may seem to move due to the combination of saccadic eye movements and the lack of context cues. The phi phenomenon explains how a series of stationary lights can produce the illusion of movement commonly seen on a movie marquee. Light adaptation refers to the process by which people adjust to seeing in bright light after having been in the dark. The false-motion effect is a distraction.

43. **(D)** The information-processing theory has three basic steps: information is encoded, then it is stored, and, finally, it can be retrieved. Interference may hinder a person's ability to retrieve information. While attention is related to memory, it is not considered a step in the information-processing theory.

44. **(B)** Loss of interest in one's daily activities is a common symptom of depression.

45. **(C)** Psychogenic amnesia is classified as a dissociative disorder. Dissociative disorders involve a break in conscious thought. Amnesia is clearly an example of such a break. Somatoform disorders are defined by the report of a physical problem in the absence of an organic cause. Mood disorders, like depression, involve a disturbance in mood. The hallmark of schizophrenic disorders is distorted thought. Developmental disorders are so named because they become evident in a particular stage of development.

46. **(D)** Group polarization is the tendency of groups to take more extreme positions than the members that make up the groups. Deindividuation is when conditions of arousal and anonymity encourage members of groups to engage in mob behavior. In-group bias is the tendency to see groups of which one is a member as superior to other groups. Groupthink is the tendency for groups to make bad decisions under stressful conditions because no one wants to disagree with what appears to be the majority's position. Group extremism is a made-up distraction.

47. **(C)** Social psychologists are most likely to study attitude formation as well as topics such as attributional theory, prejudice, and group processes. Industrial/organizational psychologists would study how to increase workplace efficiency. Cognitive psychologists would be most likely to look at how memory works. Biological theorists pay the most attention to the biology of learning, and cognitive psychologists would study the use of heuristics.

48. **(B)** Kohlberg created a three-level, six-stage model of moral development. In the lowest level, people worry about the consequences of their actions to themselves. In the second level, people usually follow social norms and laws. The highest level of moral reasoning involves creating and following one's own ethical principals.

49. **(D)** Authoritarian parents lay down the law and enforce it strictly. Democratic or authoritative parenting is viewed as the preferred method in American culture. It involves more flexibility with rules and more of an emphasis on explaining the reason behind the rules. Totalitarian is a made-up distraction. Neglectful parenting involves few rules and insensitivity to the child's needs.

50. **(D)** Gestalt psychologists emphasize the importance of the whole. Gestalt psychology, founded in Germany in the nineteenth century, has had an impact on a number of areas of psychology, such as the study of perception and treatment of disorders.

51. **(B)** Taking a random sample from a population ensures that each member of the population has an equal chance of being selected. In essence, this is the definition of random sampling. Clearly, that an unequal number of males and females will be used is still possible. Confounding variables are an issue in assignment, not in sampling. Experimenter bias can be eliminated by a double blind. Trying to replicate one's findings by using a variety of different populations is always a good idea.

52. **(E)** The most common method of collecting information about people's personalities are self-report measures such as the MMPI (Minnesota Multiphasic Personality Inventory). These measures are widely used because they are the easiest methods to use.

53. **(B)** This test measures what you have learned about psychology. Therefore, it is an achievement test. It is not standardized because people take it under different conditions, and it has not been normed based on the performance of a standardization sample. It is neither a true power test nor a true speed test. It is not an aptitude test because it does not purport to measure your innate ability to be a psychologist.

54. **(B)** Episodic memory is our memory for specific events. Procedural memory is memory for how to do things (for example, tie our shoes or ride a bicycle). Declarative and semantic memory both have to do with our memory for factual information (for example, when the American Revolution occurred and who conducted the Baby Albert experiment). Eidetic memory is another term for photographic memory.

55. **(E)** Overgeneralization refers to young children's tendency to overuse grammatical rules. Chomsky cited overgeneralization as evidence for his nativist theory of language development. Telegraphic speech is two-word speech (for example, "Go circus"). Holophrastic speech is one-word speech (for example, "Circus"). Babbling is the repetition of phonemes that precedes language (for example, "Mamamamamama"). Syntax refers to the rules of grammar used in a language.

56. **(D)** Trait theorists emphasize the importance of people's characteristic ways of acting and thinking. They do not believe that the situation has much of an influence on the individual, an idea with which many psychologists take issue.

57. **(E)** Salivation was both the CR and UR. The CR and UR are always similar. In the case of Pavlov's work, the food was the US. The food elicited the UR, salivation. By pairing the food with a bell ringing (CS), the dog came to salivate to the sound of the bell alone (CR).

58. **(C)** Bandura's Bobo doll experiment illustrated that, through the process of modeling, children will copy the aggressive behavior of adults.

59. **(D)** Antisocial personality disorder involves a lack of sensitivity to others. People with antisocial personality disorder are often callous, argumentative,

and cruel. They are not, however, antisocial in the sense that we usually use the term. They therefore do not view themselves as loners. Changes in eating and sleeping habits are common symptoms of depression. Delusions are a symptom of schizophrenia. People who depend excessively upon others may have dependent-personality disorder.

60. **(D)** One theorized cause of eating disorders is the societal emphasis on thinness. Although eating disorders have many possible causes, hypothalamic failure and unstable set point are made-up distractions. Dopamine has not been implicated in eating disorders nor has the rising rate of divorce.

61. **(A)** The James-Lange theory proposes that each emotion is triggered by a unique physiological reaction in the body that occurs after a stimulus has been observed. Schacter's two-factor theory emphasizes the role of cognition, including memories of similar situations. Cannon's theory hypothesizes that the thalamus plays a key role in simultaneously triggering both the recognition of an emotion and a physiological response.

62. **(D)** Seyle's general adaptation syndrome proposes three steps in dealing with stress. Alarm is the first stage as the person notices the stressor and prepares to grapple with it. Resistance is the second stage during which the sympathetic nervous system is aroused to fight off the stressor. Exhaustion, the last stage, is reached only if the stressor exceeds the person's ability to deal with it. During exhaustion, the parasympathetic nervous system takes over and calms the body.

63. **(A)** Systematic desensitization is based on counterconditioning. In systematic desensitization, a feared stimulus is paired with a pleasant stimulus (relaxation) until it no longer produces fear.

64. **(D)** Psychoanalysts analyze transference. Transference is when patients misdirect feelings they have toward significant people in their lives onto their analysts. By exploring transference, psychoanalysts believe they can get a window into patients' unconscious.

65. **(B)** Primary reinforcers are in and of themselves reinforcing. Primary reinforcers include food, water, and rest. Money is a generalized reinforcer because it can be traded for virtually anything. Praise, music, and dolls are secondary reinforcers, which means we have learned to value them.

66. **(C)** The Premack principle explains that something that an individual likes to do may be used to reinforce something the individual likes less. In other words, what is reinforcing depends upon the learner. The partial-reinforcement effect explains that behaviors reinforced intermittently will be more resistant to extinction than behaviors reinforced continuously. Chaining is when reinforcement depends upon the completion of a sequence of behaviors. Outshining is a phenomenon in memory where some information is more easily recalled than other information. Latent learning, studied by Tolman, is the idea that what is learned may not be made manifest until it is rewarded.

67. **(A)** In thinking about how dangerous airplanes are, people are overly influenced by what is easily accessible in their memories. Because airplane crashes get so much media attention, people overestimate their frequency and therefore feel fearful. The recency effect is the tendency to remember

information presented at the end of a series. Confirmation bias is the tendency to look for information that supports one's preexisting beliefs. The framing effect illustrates that the way a question or problem is presented affects people's processing and memories. Cognitive dissonance refers to the tension produced when someone holds two contradictory thoughts.

68. **(B)** Chomsky, a nativist, argues that people are uniquely suited to learn language because they possess a language acquisition device. He does not believe that other animals can learn language. He disputes Skinner's contention that language is learned through shaping or nurture. Although Chomsky believed that learning language during a critical period (before age seven) was easier, he did not assert that learning a language after this time was impossible.

69. **(D)** Photoreceptors are the rods and cones. The next layer of cells in the retina consists of bipolar cells. The bipolar cells then synapse with the ganglion cells, the axons of which form the optic nerve and exit the eye at the blind spot.

70. **(B)** Transduction, the process of converting one form of energy to another, takes place in the receptors. The receptors in the ear are the hair cells located in the cochlea, the part of the inner ear that looks like a shell. The ossicles are three bones (hammer, anvil, and stirrup) in the middle ear. The tympanic membrane, or eardrum, divides the auditory canal (outer ear) from the middle ear. The semicircular canals are in the inner ear and primarily function to help us keep our balance.

71. **(A)** Myelin is the fatty tissue that speeds neural transmission. Astrocytes are other structural components of the nervous system. Adipose is a name for fatty tissue, in general. The nodes of Ranvier also speed axonal transmission but they are gaps in the myelin rather than the fatty tissue itself. Axolation is a made-up distraction.

72. **(E)** The temporal lobe contains the auditory cortex. The cerebellum is mainly involved in movement and balance. The parietal lobe contains the somatosensory cortex. The amygdala is part of the limbic system and aids in processing emotion. Broca's area is found in the left, frontal lobe and is involved in language.

73. **(C)** Ainsworth and Bowlby both studied the relationship between infant and caretaker, also known as attachment.

74. **(B)** Freud believed that people whose libido became fixated in the anal state might exhibit an anal retentive or anal expulsive character as adults. Anal retentive people are compulsively neat, hyperorganized, and a little uptight, while anal expulsive people are the opposite. Freud also believed that libido could become fixated in the other psychosexual stages, resulting in other difficulties in adulthood.

75. **(C)** MAO inhibitors, a kind of drug, are commonly prescribed to treat depression. Somatic therapies involve treating the body as opposed to psychotherapies that focus on talking about one's problems. Prefrontal lobotomies are another example of a somatic treatment, but they are rarely, if ever, performed today. Benzodiazepines are another type of somatic therapy but are generally used to treat anxiety disorders. RET (rational

emotive therapy) is a common treatment for depression, but it is not a somatic therapy. Implosive therapy is most commonly used to treat phobias.

76. **(C)** Absolute threshold is a measure of how much of a stimulus is necessary for a person to perceive it 50 percent of the time. Just-noticeable difference measures how much the intensity of a stimulus must change for someone to notice it. Absolute threshold refers to only the level of stimulation necessary to perceive something initially (for example, light in a dark room or sound in a silent chamber). Just-noticeable difference or difference threshold refers to one's ability to perceive any change in stimulation level. All the other choices are made-up distractions.

77. **(B)** The hidden-observer effect, first noted by Ernest Hilgard, is the finding that while under hypnosis people are able to respond to questions that require conscious awareness. Somnambulism is another name for sleepwalking. Lucid dreaming is the ability to take control of and change the course of one's dreams. Hypnotics are a kind of drug meant to induce sleep. Free-running rhythms are the approximately 25-hour schedule that people seem to conform to when deprived of time cues.

78. **(A)** Masters and Johnson described the order of the sexual response cycle stages as excitement, plateau, orgasm, and resolution.

79. **(C)** Artificialism, the belief that everything is made by humans, characterizes the preoperational stage in Piagetian theory. Using operations, understanding reversibility, appreciating conservation, and being able to solve class-inclusion problems all describe the child in the concrete operational stage.

80. **(A)** Humanistic psychologists stress the importance of self-esteem and self-concept. Humanistic psychologists such as Rogers and Maslow emphasize the importance of people's feelings. The importance of neurochemical levels is stressed by biomedical theorists, unconscious motivations by psychoanalytic psychologists, attributional style by cognitive theorists, and contingencies of reinforcement by behaviorists.

81. **(E)** Percentile score is measured from 0. Percentile score tells you what percentage of the testing population a person outscored. On a test with a mean of 78 and a standard deviation of 7, 92 is two standard deviations above the mean ($92 - 78 = 14$; $14/7 = 2$). Someone who scores at the mean scores at the 50th percentile. The percentage of scores that falls one standard deviation above the mean in the normal curve is approximately 34 percent. An additional 13.5 percent of the scores fall between one and two standard deviations above the mean. Therefore, Ling scored at the 97.5th percentile ($50 + 34 + 13.5$).

82. **(E)** Karen is probably suffering from schizophrenia. Loose associations (lack of coherence) and neologisms (made-up words) are among the most common symptoms of disorganized schizophrenia.

83. **(D)** The researcher is conducting longitudinal research. Longitudinal research involves following a group of subjects over time to see how the members change. Cross-sectional research is when groups of different ages are tested at the same time. Cohort-sequential research combines the longitudinal and cross-sectional research by studying a number of different

groups over time. Lifespan research does not refer to any particular method, and observational research may or may not be used as part of the other methods discussed.

84. **(A)** If the results of a study are statistically significant, the results probably did not happen by chance. Inferential statistics are used to determine whether the results of a study are statistically significant. Generally, a *p* value of < .05 indicates significance.

85. **(B)** Trephining, the drilling of holes in people's skulls to allow evil spirits to escape, has been abandoned due to lack of success. All the other forms of therapy are still used today.

86. **(D)** Milgram found that the level of shock inflicted by subjects could be reduced by enabling subjects to see the learners during the experiment. The presence of the experimenter, an authority figure, was one of the factors that increased the level of shock administered.

87. **(C)** People are less likely to offer help to others who need it when other bystanders are not helping. This phenomenon is explained by diffusion of responsibility (the belief that someone else will take care of it) and pluralistic ignorance (the idea that if no one else is helping, not helping must be the right thing to do).

88. **(C)** Decision making is a high-level function and is therefore controlled by the cerebral cortex, more specifically the frontal lobe.

89. **(A)** None of the children will have blue eyes. Since each parent contributes one eye color gene to each of the children, each child will be heterozygous (Bb). Since brown eyes are the dominant trait, all the children will have brown eyes.

90. **(E)** Psychoanalysis typically takes years of multiple sessions each week. Whereas most other types of therapies focus on the clients' immediate problem(s), psychoanalysts insist that the most important job of therapy is to expose conflicts buried deep in the unconscious.

91. **(B)** The thalamus acts as a relay station for all sensory information except for smell (olfaction).

92. **(A)** Hubel and Weisel mapped the visual cortex, identifying cells that specialize in processing certain kinds of information. Some of these cells are known as simple cells, complex cells, and hypercomplex cells, names that relate to the kind of information the cells process.

93. **(B)** Sociobiologists believe that people are motivated to ensure the survival of their genes.

94. **(C)** The *DSM-IV-TR (Diagnostic Statistical Manual)* lists the symptoms of psychological disorders. Psychologists use it to diagnose their patients.

95. **(D)** Seligman proposed that one possible cause of major, or unipolar, depression was learned helplessness. Learned helplessness results from the perception that one cannot control one's life and world.

96. **(A)** The rooting reflex is the baby's response to feeling something brush against his or her cheek. The Babinsky reflex is the infant's spreading of his

or her toes in response to something contacting the foot. The plantar reflex is an adult's response of the toes curling inward when an object is dragged across a foot. A feeding reflex does not exist. The pupillary reflex refers to the pupil's change in size in response to different levels of light.

97. **(B)** The id operates according to the pleasure principle, meaning that it seeks immediate gratification. The ego follows the reality principle and mediates between the id, the superego, and the demands of the external world. The ego uses defense mechanisms to achieve this end. The superego functions as a conscience.

98. **(D)** People with internal loci of control believe that their own efforts and actions exert a powerful influence over what happens to them. Therefore, they believe that hard work and effort would pay off. People with external loci of control, on the other hand, believe that luck, fate, and forces generally out of their control significantly impact their lives.

99. **(D)** Light therapy is most commonly used to treat SAD—seasonal affective disorder. SAD is a kind of depression that seems to occur during seasons when the amount and intensity of sunlight is low.

100. **(A)** Aphagia is starvation. The ventromedial hypothalamus is known as the satiety center. If it is continually stimulated, the animal will feel satiated, will not eat, and could actually be made to starve to death. The lateral hypothalamus contains the hunger center. If stimulated repeatedly, it would cause an animal to eat excessively, a condition known as hyperaphagia.

Multiple-choice Error Analysis Sheet

After checking your answers on the practice test, you might want to gauge your areas of relative strength and weakness. This sheet will help you to classify your errors by topic area. By circling the numbers of the questions you answered incorrectly, you can get a picture of which areas you need to study the most.

CHAPTER	QUESTION NUMBERS									
History and Approaches	22	50								
Methods	1	5	14	35	51	84				
Biological Bases of Behavior	2	23	24	30	38	39	71	72	88	89
Sensation and Perception	7	42	69	70	76	91	92			
States of Consciousness	11	40	77							
Learning	12	31	32	57	58	65	66			
Cognition	3	9	10	41	43	54	55	67	68	
Motivation and Emotion	26	27	28	61	62	78	93	100		
Developmental Psychology	20	21	48	49	73	74	79	83	96	
Personality	4	19	29	52	56	80	97	98		
Testing and Individual Differences	13	15	16	36	37	53	81			
Abnormal Psychology	8	17	44	45	59	60	82	94	95	
Treatment of Psychological Disorders	25	63	64	75	85	90	99			
Social Psychology	6	18	33	34	46	47	86	87		

Essay Portion

Time—50 minutes

Directions: You have 50 minutes to answer BOTH of the following questions.

---

1. A number of the most influential psychological theories are stage theories.
    (A) What is a stage theory?
    (B) Each of the men listed below created a stage theory. Explain the main focus of each man's theory, and describe what he would identify as a major issue or concern for a seven-year-old child.
        1. Freud
        2. Erikson
        3. Piaget
        4. Kohlberg

2. All of the following are goals in any kind of psychological research.
    (A) Getting honest and accurate information.
    (B) Minimizing the effects of confounding variables.
    (C) Treating subjects ethically.

Compare and contrast laboratory experiments, naturalistic observation, and the survey method in terms of how well they meet the goals mentioned above.

Question 1 Scoring Rubric

This is a 9-point question. The definition of a stage theory is worth 1 point. The discussion of each psychologist is worth 2 points, 1 for correctly explaining the major focus of his theory and 1 for identifying what the theory would say is an important issue for a seven-year-old child.

A number of the most influential psychological theories are stage theories.

(A)   What is a stage theory?

Point 1—This point will be awarded for a description of a discontinuous theory of development. It is not enough to say that development occurs in stages but other words indicating discontinuity are acceptable.

(B)   Each of the men listed below created a stage theory. Explain the main focus of each man's theory, and describe what he would identify as a major issue or concern for a seven-year-old child.

   1. Freud
   2. Erikson
   3. Piaget
   4. Kohlberg

Point 2—Freudian or psychoanalytic theory focuses on psychosexual development that takes place over four stages and a latency period. Students need not use the term "psychosexual development" but need to express this idea.

Point 3—A seven-year-old, according to Freud, would be in latency, a time in which sexual urges are repressed and children focus on gaining social and academic competence. In order to earn the point, students need to use the term "latency" in a way that indicates they understand its meaning or refer to the repression of sexual impulses and alternative focus.

Point 4—Erikson focused on psychosocial development that takes place in an eight-stage process. While students are not required to use the term "psychosocial development," they need to indicate that Erikson broadened Freud's focus by discussing social as well as sexual development and writing about development throughout the lifespan.

Point 5—Erikson would say that a seven-year-old was in the industry versus inferiority stage. The point may be earned by describing this dichotomy in terms of the same meaning or by indicating that the child, in this stage, is striving for academic or social success in school.

Point 6—Piaget's theory is about cognitive development. Again, students may use synonyms in place of the exact term. There are four stages in the theory.

Point 7—A seven-year-old would be in the concrete operational stage, the third of the four stages, in which children become able to carry out "operations" such as addition and classification. The point may be earned by using and explaining this term or by explaining that children in this stage generally come to understand the principle of conservation.

Point 8—Kohlberg's theory is about moral development or morality. This theory has three levels, each composed of two stages.

Point 9—A seven-year-old would be in the first level, the preconventional level. In this level, decisions about right and wrong are determined by their consequences to one's self and the desire to avoid punishment.

Question 2 Scoring Rubric

This is a 9-point question. Three points can be earned in the discussion of each goal, 1 about each method.

All of the following are goals in any kind of psychological research.

(A) Getting honest and accurate information
(B) Minimizing the effects of confounding variables
(C) Treating subjects ethically

Compare and contrast laboratory experiments, naturalistic observation, and the survey method in terms of how well they meet the goals mentioned above.

(A)   Getting honest and accurate information

Point 1—Naturalistic observation is likely to get honest and accurate information since subjects are viewed in their natural habitats. However, the meaning of data depends upon interpretation by researchers. Discussion of either of these issues will earn the point.

Point 2—Using the survey method makes it difficult to get honest and accurate information due to social desirability, other response biases, or outright lying. Discussion of any of the above will earn the point.

Point 3—The artificiality of the laboratory environment impedes the researcher's ability to collect data that truly represents how subjects would behave in the world. In addition, in the laboratory, subjects may be suspicious and therefore alter their behavior. The discussion of either limitation will earn the point.

(B)   Minimizing the effects of confounding variables

Point 4—This point will be awarded for the discussion of a specific means by which to eliminate confounds in a laboratory experiment such as random assignment, using a control group, or ensuring the environments in all conditions are equivalent.

Point 5—This point will be awarded for the discussion of any specific way the survey method does or does not allow the elimination of confounds. For instance, subject-confounding variables cannot be eliminated since the experimenter does not manipulate the independent variable and randomly assign subjects. Alternatively, the student can discuss situation-relevant confounding variables. These can be eliminated if the survey is administered under controlled conditions. However, these confounds will remain if the survey is mailed or handed out to be returned at a later date.

Point 6—Naturalistic observation lacks virtually any type of control since the researcher does not influence what she or he observes.

(C)   Treating subjects ethically

Point 7—This point will be awarded for the discussion of any particular ethical concern common in an experiment such as deception or the lack of *informed* consent.

Point 8—This point will be awarded for the discussion of any particular ethical concern common in naturalistic observation such as that true consent is impossible or that it violates privacy since subjects do not know they are being observed.

Point 9—This point will be awarded for the discussion of any particular ethical concern common in the survey method such as the need to protect privacy by protecting anonymity or confidentiality or that participants need to freely choose to participate.

Calculate Your Score on Practice Test #1

Section I – Multiple Choice

$\underline{\hspace{3cm}}$ $-$ (1/4 X $\underline{\hspace{3cm}}$) $=$ $\underline{\hspace{3cm}}$

Number correct   Number wrong   Section I Score

Section II - Free Response

Question 1 $\underline{\hspace{3cm}}$ X   2.780 = $\underline{\hspace{3cm}}$

          (Maximum = 9)   Question 1 Score

Question 2 $\underline{\hspace{3cm}}$ X   2.780 = $\underline{\hspace{3cm}}$

          (Maximum = 9)   Question 2 Score

$\underline{\hspace{3cm}}$ + $\underline{\hspace{3cm}}$ = $\underline{\hspace{3cm}}$

Question 1 Score   Question 2 Score   Total Essay Score

Total Score

$\underline{\hspace{3cm}}$ + $\underline{\hspace{3cm}}$ = $\underline{\hspace{3cm}}$

Section I Score   Section II Score   Total Score (Round)

How to Convert Your Score*

      93 – 150 = 5
      72 – 92 = 4
      53 – 71 = 3
      34 – 52 = 2
      0 – 33 = 1

*Please note that this chart provides an estimate. The cutoffs between the different AP scores vary from year to year.

1. Ⓐ Ⓑ Ⓒ Ⓓ Ⓔ
2. Ⓐ Ⓑ Ⓒ Ⓓ Ⓔ
3. Ⓐ Ⓑ Ⓒ Ⓓ Ⓔ
4. Ⓐ Ⓑ Ⓒ Ⓓ Ⓔ
5. Ⓐ Ⓑ Ⓒ Ⓓ Ⓔ
6. Ⓐ Ⓑ Ⓒ Ⓓ Ⓔ
7. Ⓐ Ⓑ Ⓒ Ⓓ Ⓔ
8. Ⓐ Ⓑ Ⓒ Ⓓ Ⓔ
9. Ⓐ Ⓑ Ⓒ Ⓓ Ⓔ
10. Ⓐ Ⓑ Ⓒ Ⓓ Ⓔ
11. Ⓐ Ⓑ Ⓒ Ⓓ Ⓔ
12. Ⓐ Ⓑ Ⓒ Ⓓ Ⓔ
13. Ⓐ Ⓑ Ⓒ Ⓓ Ⓔ
14. Ⓐ Ⓑ Ⓒ Ⓓ Ⓔ
15. Ⓐ Ⓑ Ⓒ Ⓓ Ⓔ
16. Ⓐ Ⓑ Ⓒ Ⓓ Ⓔ
17. Ⓐ Ⓑ Ⓒ Ⓓ Ⓔ
18. Ⓐ Ⓑ Ⓒ Ⓓ Ⓔ
19. Ⓐ Ⓑ Ⓒ Ⓓ Ⓔ
20. Ⓐ Ⓑ Ⓒ Ⓓ Ⓔ
21. Ⓐ Ⓑ Ⓒ Ⓓ Ⓔ
22. Ⓐ Ⓑ Ⓒ Ⓓ Ⓔ
23. Ⓐ Ⓑ Ⓒ Ⓓ Ⓔ
24. Ⓐ Ⓑ Ⓒ Ⓓ Ⓔ
25. Ⓐ Ⓑ Ⓒ Ⓓ Ⓔ

26. Ⓐ Ⓑ Ⓒ Ⓓ Ⓔ
27. Ⓐ Ⓑ Ⓒ Ⓓ Ⓔ
28. Ⓐ Ⓑ Ⓒ Ⓓ Ⓔ
29. Ⓐ Ⓑ Ⓒ Ⓓ Ⓔ
30. Ⓐ Ⓑ Ⓒ Ⓓ Ⓔ
31. Ⓐ Ⓑ Ⓒ Ⓓ Ⓔ
32. Ⓐ Ⓑ Ⓒ Ⓓ Ⓔ
33. Ⓐ Ⓑ Ⓒ Ⓓ Ⓔ
34. Ⓐ Ⓑ Ⓒ Ⓓ Ⓔ
35. Ⓐ Ⓑ Ⓒ Ⓓ Ⓔ
36. Ⓐ Ⓑ Ⓒ Ⓓ Ⓔ
37. Ⓐ Ⓑ Ⓒ Ⓓ Ⓔ
38. Ⓐ Ⓑ Ⓒ Ⓓ Ⓔ
39. Ⓐ Ⓑ Ⓒ Ⓓ Ⓔ
40. Ⓐ Ⓑ Ⓒ Ⓓ Ⓔ
41. Ⓐ Ⓑ Ⓒ Ⓓ Ⓔ
42. Ⓐ Ⓑ Ⓒ Ⓓ Ⓔ
43. Ⓐ Ⓑ Ⓒ Ⓓ Ⓔ
44. Ⓐ Ⓑ Ⓒ Ⓓ Ⓔ
45. Ⓐ Ⓑ Ⓒ Ⓓ Ⓔ
46. Ⓐ Ⓑ Ⓒ Ⓓ Ⓔ
47. Ⓐ Ⓑ Ⓒ Ⓓ Ⓔ
48. Ⓐ Ⓑ Ⓒ Ⓓ Ⓔ
49. Ⓐ Ⓑ Ⓒ Ⓓ Ⓔ
50. Ⓐ Ⓑ Ⓒ Ⓓ Ⓔ

51. Ⓐ Ⓑ Ⓒ Ⓓ Ⓔ
52. Ⓐ Ⓑ Ⓒ Ⓓ Ⓔ
53. Ⓐ Ⓑ Ⓒ Ⓓ Ⓔ
54. Ⓐ Ⓑ Ⓒ Ⓓ Ⓔ
55. Ⓐ Ⓑ Ⓒ Ⓓ Ⓔ
56. Ⓐ Ⓑ Ⓒ Ⓓ Ⓔ
57. Ⓐ Ⓑ Ⓒ Ⓓ Ⓔ
58. Ⓐ Ⓑ Ⓒ Ⓓ Ⓔ
59. Ⓐ Ⓑ Ⓒ Ⓓ Ⓔ
60. Ⓐ Ⓑ Ⓒ Ⓓ Ⓔ
61. Ⓐ Ⓑ Ⓒ Ⓓ Ⓔ
62. Ⓐ Ⓑ Ⓒ Ⓓ Ⓔ
63. Ⓐ Ⓑ Ⓒ Ⓓ Ⓔ
64. Ⓐ Ⓑ Ⓒ Ⓓ Ⓔ
65. Ⓐ Ⓑ Ⓒ Ⓓ Ⓔ
66. Ⓐ Ⓑ Ⓒ Ⓓ Ⓔ
67. Ⓐ Ⓑ Ⓒ Ⓓ Ⓔ
68. Ⓐ Ⓑ Ⓒ Ⓓ Ⓔ
69. Ⓐ Ⓑ Ⓒ Ⓓ Ⓔ
70. Ⓐ Ⓑ Ⓒ Ⓓ Ⓔ
71. Ⓐ Ⓑ Ⓒ Ⓓ Ⓔ
72. Ⓐ Ⓑ Ⓒ Ⓓ Ⓔ
73. Ⓐ Ⓑ Ⓒ Ⓓ Ⓔ
74. Ⓐ Ⓑ Ⓒ Ⓓ Ⓔ
75. Ⓐ Ⓑ Ⓒ Ⓓ Ⓔ

76. Ⓐ Ⓑ Ⓒ Ⓓ Ⓔ
77. Ⓐ Ⓑ Ⓒ Ⓓ Ⓔ
78. Ⓐ Ⓑ Ⓒ Ⓓ Ⓔ
79. Ⓐ Ⓑ Ⓒ Ⓓ Ⓔ
80. Ⓐ Ⓑ Ⓒ Ⓓ Ⓔ
81. Ⓐ Ⓑ Ⓒ Ⓓ Ⓔ
82. Ⓐ Ⓑ Ⓒ Ⓓ Ⓔ
83. Ⓐ Ⓑ Ⓒ Ⓓ Ⓔ
84. Ⓐ Ⓑ Ⓒ Ⓓ Ⓔ
85. Ⓐ Ⓑ Ⓒ Ⓓ Ⓔ
86. Ⓐ Ⓑ Ⓒ Ⓓ Ⓔ
87. Ⓐ Ⓑ Ⓒ Ⓓ Ⓔ
88. Ⓐ Ⓑ Ⓒ Ⓓ Ⓔ
89. Ⓐ Ⓑ Ⓒ Ⓓ Ⓔ
90. Ⓐ Ⓑ Ⓒ Ⓓ Ⓔ
91. Ⓐ Ⓑ Ⓒ Ⓓ Ⓔ
92. Ⓐ Ⓑ Ⓒ Ⓓ Ⓔ
93. Ⓐ Ⓑ Ⓒ Ⓓ Ⓔ
94. Ⓐ Ⓑ Ⓒ Ⓓ Ⓔ
95. Ⓐ Ⓑ Ⓒ Ⓓ Ⓔ
96. Ⓐ Ⓑ Ⓒ Ⓓ Ⓔ
97. Ⓐ Ⓑ Ⓒ Ⓓ Ⓔ
98. Ⓐ Ⓑ Ⓒ Ⓓ Ⓔ
99. Ⓐ Ⓑ Ⓒ Ⓓ Ⓔ
100. Ⓐ Ⓑ Ⓒ Ⓓ Ⓔ

Practice Test #2

Multiple-choice Portion

Time—1 hour and 10 minutes
100 Questions

Directions: Each of the questions or incomplete statements below is followed by five suggested answers or completions. Select the one that is best in each case.

---

1. Kim overcomes her fear of flying by watching movies about peaceful plane trips, then talking to friends who fly often, then visiting airports. What treatment technique is Kim most likely using?
   (A) aversion therapy
   (B) systematic desensitization
   (C) generalization training
   (D) behavioral discrimination
   (E) gradual discrimination

2. Kristin conditions her fish to swim to the top of the tank whenever she turns on the light on the fish tank. In this example of classical conditioning, which of the following was most likely the unconditioned stimulus?
   (A) the light
   (B) fish food
   (C) the fish swimming to the top
   (D) the sound of the light clicking on
   (E) electric shock

3. Crystal teases a friend about her pet cat. The friend is hurt and stops speaking to Crystal. If Crystal stops teasing her friend after this experience, what type of conditioning has occurred?
   (A) classical discrimination
   (B) classical generalization
   (C) operant conditioning
   (D) classical conditioning
   (E) appetitive conditioning

4. Matthew is assigned to complete a group project with some classmates. If one of the group members lets Matt and the others do all the work, which social psychology principle is being demonstrated?
   (A) intergroup dynamics
   (B) conformity
   (C) deindividuation
   (D) group polarization
   (E) social loafing

5. A conversion disorder is a type of
   (A) mood disorder.
   (B) somatoform disorder.
   (C) dissociative disorder.
   (D) anxiety disorder.
   (E) personality disorder.

6. Which of the following is NOT part of the process of neural firing?
   (A) all or none principle
   (B) threshold
   (C) synaptic jump
   (D) neurotransmitter release
   (E) electrochemical impulse

GO ON TO THE NEXT PAGE ➤

7. Sue wakes up in the middle of the night because she suddenly realizes she forgot to feed her friends' dog yesterday while her friends are on vacation. The levels of processing theory would say Sue forgot this commitment because
   (A) her sensory memory did not encode the event into her working memory.
   (B) the memory of the event decayed in her working memory due to lack of rehearsal.
   (C) the connections in long-term memory to the event were lost.
   (D) long-term potentiation did not occur at the neural level.
   (E) she did not think about feeding the dog in an elaborate or complex way.

8. A neurotransmitter manipulated by an antidepressant medication is most likely to be
   (A) serotonin.
   (B) substance P.
   (C) acetylcholine.
   (D) adrenaline.
   (E) thyroxin.

9. A heuristic is used to
   (A) treat an anxiety disorder.
   (B) solve a problem.
   (C) prove or disprove an algorithm.
   (D) convince a skeptic as part of the foot-in-the-door technique.
   (E) memorize a long list of items.

10. If a person needs more of a psychoactive drug after the first dose in order to get the same effects, he or she has developed
   (A) a physical addiction.
   (B) tolerance.
   (C) withdrawal symptoms.
   (D) endorphin deficit.
   (E) habituation.

11. Which of the following brain structures is most involved in hunger?
   (A) amygdala
   (B) hypothalamus
   (C) motor cortex
   (D) cerebellum
   (E) corpus callosum

12. The activation-synthesis model states that dreams are
   (A) wish fulfillments.
   (B) memory integrations.
   (C) a way for the brain to deal with stress during the waking day.
   (D) the cortex's interpretation of brain processes.
   (E) activated memories being synthesized.

13. Which of the following theorists was most concerned with social development?
   (A) Erikson
   (B) Piaget
   (C) Kohlberg
   (D) Bandura
   (E) Horney

Use the following example for questions 14 and 15.

Professor Castelucci designs an experiment to test whether the presence or absence of facial hair in men affects the fear reactions of children. Professor Castelucci gathers a group of children of ages two to seven and assigns them randomly to two groups. One group of children is shown pictures of men without beards, and the other group is shown pictures of the same men with beards. The children then fill out a questionnaire designed to measure fear responses.

14. In this experiment, the presence or absence of facial hair is the
   (A) dependent variable.
   (B) control variable.
   (C) mediating variable.
   (D) independent variable.
   (E) experimental condition.

15. The score on the fear questionnaire is the
   (A) independent variable.
   (B) dependent variable.
   (C) operational definition of the dependent variable.
   (D) operational definition of the independent variable.
   (E) outcome variable.

GO ON TO THE NEXT PAGE ➤

16. Which of the following details of an experiment would NOT be required to be addressed by a committee, such as an institutional review board, examining the ethics of proposed psychological research on human participants?
    (A) informed consent
    (B) debriefing
    (C) scientific merit
    (D) proof of correlational measures
    (E) potential harm

17. Kent goes to a concert and gets caught up in the center of the dance floor where the entire group is violently dancing and slamming against one another. Soon Kent finds himself participating and slamming into those around him. Kent's behavior is an example of
    (A) autonomic sensitization.
    (B) obedience.
    (C) diffusion of responsibility.
    (D) deindividuation.
    (E) groupthink.

18. Which of the following scenarios is most likely an example of classical conditioning?
    (A) A person's fear of driving after being involved in an auto accident.
    (B) A child learning to cry if she or he wants attention.
    (C) A rat learning to run through a complex maze for food.
    (D) A student learning to study more before a test.
    (E) An adolescent learning to avoid being grounded by coming home before curfew.

19. If a sleep researcher is examining an EEG readout, which of the following would REM be most similar to?
    (A) manic state
    (B) night terrors
    (C) awake state
    (D) deep sleep
    (E) hypnotic state

20. Alan's psychiatrist notices that his behavior indicates a manic state. Alan might be diagnosed as bipolar if his behavioral symptoms also include
    (A) obvious chemical imbalances.
    (B) at least one episode of major depression.
    (C) a rapidly changing mood cycle during a 24-hour period.
    (D) impulsive behavior, such as spending sprees or promiscuity.
    (E) rapidly changing affect between the two poles of extreme happiness and extreme agitation.

21. All information coming from our senses (except olfactory sensations) pass through which brain structure?
    (A) hypothalamus
    (B) sensory cortex
    (C) brain stem
    (D) thalamus
    (E) corpus callosum

22. Nadia takes a test to determine if she learned any carpentry skills in the class she just completed. This test is an example of which type of test?
    (A) aptitude
    (B) classification
    (C) standardized
    (D) achievement
    (E) functional

23. Harvinder notices that his heart is racing and interprets this elevated heart rate as anxiety about his date tonight. This description of emotional response fits which of the following theories best?
    (A) drive reduction
    (B) James-Lange
    (C) Cannon-Bard
    (D) schema
    (E) cognitive dissonance

24. Tests like the TAT and Rorschach inkblot rely on what psychodynamic concept?
    (A) displacement
    (B) repression
    (C) subconscious mind
    (D) projection
    (E) unconscious interpretation

GO ON TO THE NEXT PAGE ➤

25. Mark is having a good time watching TV with his friends when he suddenly remembers a conversation he really enjoyed last month but had forgotten up to that moment. Which concept best explains his remembering?
    (A) state-dependent memory
    (B) mood-congruent memory
    (C) levels of processing
    (D) recovered memory
    (E) information processing

26. According to Freud, our unconscious develops primarily as a result of
    (A) childhood trauma.
    (B) neurosis.
    (C) repression.
    (D) displacement.
    (E) maturation.

27. The fovea is
    (A) the spot in the retina where the optic nerve connects with the eye.
    (B) the focal point of the lens.
    (C) the end of the cochlea that receives the sound waves.
    (D) the center of the retina containing the greatest concentration of cones.
    (E) the center of the eye where the image reverses before it reaches the retina.

28. The division of the peripheral nervous system responsible for voluntary movement is the
    (A) somatic nervous system.
    (B) sympathetic nervous system.
    (C) parasympathetic nervous system.
    (D) sensorimotor nervous system.
    (E) nonautonomic nervous system.

29. A measurement of how similar two frequencies could be before we no longer can differentiate between them is a measurement of which of the following attributes?
    (A) absolute threshold
    (B) dichotic listening
    (C) perfect pitch
    (D) auditic memory
    (E) difference threshold

30. The temporal lobes contain
    (A) the hippocampus.
    (B) the sensory cortex.
    (C) the auditory cortex.
    (D) the olfactory cortex.
    (E) the cerebral cortex.

31. According to attribution theory, Jacquetta is most likely to attribute her failure in the recent basketball tournament to:
    (A) bad luck.
    (B) poor basketball skills.
    (C) lack of preparation in her spare time.
    (D) her lack of concentration during the game.
    (E) her performance anxiety.

32. Ken attends a discussion about gun rights sponsored by the NRA and leaves the discussion more convinced than ever of his long-standing belief about the right to carry weapons. The strengthening of Ken's convictions might be due to
    (A) group polarization.
    (B) groupthink.
    (C) obedience.
    (D) mere exposure.
    (E) rigidity.

33. A teacher notices that whenever she brings chocolate chip cookies to her class, the test scores improve. She concludes that cookies increase students' scores on this test. This conclusion may be incorrect because
    (A) the independent variable was not manipulated.
    (B) the dependent variable is not operationally defined.
    (C) this is a correlational, not causational, relationship.
    (D) the test was not double blind.
    (E) the sample is not representative of the population.

GO ON TO THE NEXT PAGE ➤

34. Schemata, according to Piaget, are
    (A) rules we use to interpret the world.
    (B) problem-solving methods employed by children.
    (C) techniques we use to understand concepts of conservation.
    (D) the result of assimilation.
    (E) more influenced by our genetics than our environment.

35. A researcher interested in how children learn to understand logical relationships chooses a group of kindergartners and tests them every year for 12 years. This research method is called
    (A) cross-sectional.
    (B) descriptive.
    (C) experimental.
    (D) correlational.
    (E) longitudinal.

36. Body parts are proportionally represented in the sensory cortex according to their
    (A) range of movement.
    (B) importance to survival.
    (C) size.
    (D) sensitivity.
    (E) musculature.

37. What treatment perspective would most agree with this statement, "Depressed patients should change their negative, self-defeating attitudes"?
    (A) psychodynamic
    (B) cognitive
    (C) behavior modification
    (D) Gestalt
    (E) client centered

38. Liane and Laura start volunteering at the children's zoo. Laura volunteers because she enjoys children and wants to teach them about environmental issues. Liane volunteers because she needs volunteer experience on her resume to get into college. Laura's motivation can be called
    (A) extrinsic.
    (B) self-actualizing.
    (C) positive.
    (D) altruistic.
    (E) intrinsic.

39. Which of the following statements is the most true about the sexual response cycles of men and women?
    (A) The response cycles of men and women are the same due to biological similarities.
    (B) The response cycles of men and women differ due, in part, to the refractory period for men.
    (C) The response cycles of men and women differ due to inherited chemical differences between the genders.
    (D) The response cycles of men and women differ due to experiential factors of arousal unique to each gender.
    (E) The response cycles of men and women are largely unknown due to the difficulty of measuring arousal.

40. Obsessive-compulsive disorder is categorized in which of the following types of disorders?
    (A) dissociative
    (B) somatoform
    (C) anxiety
    (D) psychomotor
    (E) mood

41. Retinal disparity is
    (A) a monocular depth cue.
    (B) a vision condition resulting from partially detached retinas.
    (C) the slight difference in focal length between each eye.
    (D) the distance from the fovea to the optic nerve.
    (E) a binocular depth cue.

42. The term transduction refers to
    (A) neural impulses moving from the spinal cord to the rest of the brain.
    (B) the different effects of hormones in different parts of the body and brain.
    (C) neural impulses traveling from the peripheral nervous system to the central nervous system.
    (D) changing sensory stimuli from energy or chemical signals into neural impulses.
    (E) changing neurotransmitter signals into electric impulses.

GO ON TO THE NEXT PAGE ➤

43. The MMPI and other trait theory tests try to measure
    (A) environmental factors involved in personality.
    (B) personal attributions.
    (C) personality.
    (D) schemata.
    (E) motivation.

44. All of the following are types of schizophrenia except
    (A) paranoid.
    (B) disorganized.
    (C) catatonic.
    (D) dissociated.
    (E) undifferentiated.

45. In Watson's famous Little Albert experiment, the loud noise was the:
    (A) unconditioned response
    (B) punishment
    (C) unconditioned stimulus
    (D) conditioned stimulus
    (E) negative reinforcer

46. Which of the following characteristics best describes the authoritative style of parenting?
    (A) Few rules for behavior, great freedom of expression.
    (B) Many rules for behavior strictly enforced without explanation.
    (C) Close-knit family group who spends the majority of their free time together.
    (D) Consistent rules for behavior, parents explain rationale behind rules.
    (E) Rules govern behavior inside the home, but greater freedom is allowed outside the home.

47. An experiment performed by a researcher who is not aware of which participants are assigned to which condition is called (Note: Assume the participants in the study are also ignorant about which group they are assigned to)
    (A) single blind
    (B) controlled
    (C) correlational
    (D) quasi-experimental
    (E) double blind

48. Which psychologist could be called the father of operant conditioning?
    (A) John Watson
    (B) Ivan Pavlov
    (C) William James
    (D) Carl Rogers
    (E) B. F. Skinner

49. Standard deviation measures
    (A) variability.
    (B) amplitude.
    (C) frequency.
    (D) significant difference.
    (E) median.

50. An animal with only one eye would not be able to use which of the following cues for depth.
    (A) convergence
    (B) relative size
    (C) texture gradient
    (D) interposition
    (E) motion parallax

51. Schizophrenia usually manifests itself
    (A) in childhood rather than in adulthood.
    (B) in women rather than in men.
    (C) in young adulthood rather than in childhood.
    (D) in behavior rather than in cognition.
    (E) in visual rather than in auditory hallucinations.

52. Professor Guenzel wants to investigate the effect of a new video game on the development of a group of children. He hypothesizes that the video game will affect their behavior as adolescents. Which of the following research methods is most appropriate for this study?
    (A) case study
    (B) representative sample correlational study using a survey
    (C) cross-sectional study
    (D) longitudinal study
    (E) pharmacological study

GO ON TO THE NEXT PAGE ➤

53. The phrase *significant differences* in an experimental study means
    (A) the control and experimental group differ on some important variable, such as age or attitude.
    (B) the difference between the means of the control and experimental group is great enough that the researcher judges it to be significant.
    (C) the difference between the means of the groups in the experiment is probably not due to chance and is likely to result from the independent variable.
    (D) the sample the researcher chose to study is not representative and differs significantly from the general population.
    (E) the independent variable and dependent variable differ enough to make a statistical distinction between them.

54. If you are asked to determine how well a student did on a test you are not familiar with, which of the following pieces of information would be most useful to you? Assume you are also given the student's score on the test.
    (A) Mean score of the class and range of scores.
    (B) *z* score of the student's score.
    (C) Type of test and mean score of the class.
    (D) Mean score of the class and median score of the student's score.
    (E) High score in the class, low score in the class, and the mean.

55. The term *generalizability* in a research study refers to
    (A) participants' tendency to start reacting to stimuli similar to the conditioned stimuli.
    (B) whether the findings of the study can apply to the general population from which the sample was taken.
    (C) the broadening operational definitions of dependent variables as psychology becomes more sophisticated.
    (D) how the findings in the study apply to fields outside psychology.
    (E) the tendency of researchers to apply their findings beyond what the data will support.

56. The validity of a test refers to
    (A) whether people who take the test get similar scores on subsequent presentations of equivalent versions of the test.
    (B) whether the results of the test apply to the population in general.
    (C) whether the test accurately measures the characteristic it was designed to measure.
    (D) whether items on a test are interpreted in different ways by different ethnic, gender, or age groups.
    (E) how well a test predicts a change in the dependent variable due to manipulation of the independent variable.

57. Which of the following descriptions best defines the term *fluid intelligence*?
    (A) The ability to change problem-solving methods quickly as the nature of a problem changes.
    (B) Our ability to process novel information quickly.
    (C) Our ability to manipulate information already in memory.
    (D) How our intelligence changes over time in response to developmental changes.
    (E) The changing definition of intelligence over time.

GO ON TO THE NEXT PAGE ➤

58. In her memory experiment, Dr. Windle finds that familiarity with jazz music is highly correlated with performance on a memory task of word recall. Dr. Windle concludes that listening to jazz improves memory. Which of the following is a valid criticism of this conclusion based on the information given?
    (A) The sample size was too small to draw a broad conclusion.
    (B) Dr. Windle's operational definition of the independent variable is too vague.
    (C) Differences in intelligence, education, or other factors may exist between people who listen to jazz and who do not that cause the difference in memory.
    (D) The difference between the means of the control group and the experimental group are not large enough to be statistically significant.
    (E) The validity of Dr. Windle's test is appropriate, but the reliability is too low to be considered valid.

59. Most mnemonic devices, such as using acronyms, utilize which of the following concepts to enhance memory?
    (A) peg word
    (B) sensory memory
    (C) shallow processing
    (D) chunking
    (E) encoding concreteness

60. You observe a four-month-old girl pick up a stuffed animal and put part of it into her mouth. How would Piaget's cognitive development theory explain this child's action?
    (A) The child is in the oral stage of development and satisfies her libido by putting things into her mouth.
    (B) The child has been reinforced in the past for putting things into her mouth.
    (C) The child is attempting to satisfy the first level of needs: physiological.
    (D) The child instinctively puts things into her mouth in a search for food.
    (E) The child is in the sensorimotor stage and learns about objects by putting them into her mouth.

61. Dreams occur
    (A) only during REM sleep.
    (B) in any stage of sleep, but the greatest number and most vivid dreams occur during REM.
    (C) mostly during stage 4 sleep and REM sleep, depending on the individual's sleep cycle and environmental factors like diet and exercise.
    (D) more often at the beginning of your sleep cycle than at the end.
    (E) when we repress traumas during the day, according to cognitive psychologists.

62. What is one of the advantages of a noncontinuous (or partial) schedule of reinforcement, such as a variable-ratio schedule?
    (A) Conditioning the subject takes less time.
    (B) It defines the unconditioned stimulus more precisely.
    (C) The learning is more resistant to extinction.
    (D) The learning is more resistant to discrimination.
    (E) While satiation is more of a problem with a noncontinuous schedule, it can be accounted for more easily with statistics.

63. Solving a maze by starting at the end and going to the beginning is an example of
    (A) figure ground technique.
    (B) hindsight bias technique.
    (C) means-end analysis.
    (D) factor analysis.
    (E) an algorithm.

64. What stage of Piaget's cognitive-development theory would a child be in if she is able to think about concrete objects but is unable to do logical comparisons of some aspects of objects, such as area or volume?
    (A) concrete operational
    (B) preoperational
    (C) concreteness versus abstraction
    (D) preconventional
    (E) reversibility

GO ON TO THE NEXT PAGE ➤

65. Although the exact distinction between sensation and perception is debated by psychologists, which is one justifiable distinction between the two concepts?
    (A) Sensation happens in the peripheral nervous system, and perception happens in the central nervous system.
    (B) Sensation is the firing of sensory receptors, and perception is the interpretation of these impulses.
    (C) Sensations are the signals that travel to the brain, and perception is how the brain interprets these impulses.
    (D) Sensation occurs in the sensory cortex, and the rest of the cerebral cortex interprets the messages sent by the sensory cortex.
    (E) Both sensation and perception are organizations of stimuli, but sensations are less complex than fully synthesized perceptions.

66. Stanley Milgram's famous experiment in which participants thought they were involved in a study about electric shock and learning was actually investigating
    (A) conformity.
    (B) obedience.
    (C) deindividuation.
    (D) groupthink.
    (E) altruism.

67. Which of the following is most likely an example of divergent thinking?
    (A) Studying a road map to find a route between North Dakota and North Carolina.
    (B) Using a programming language to create a web page.
    (C) Following a recipe to make an Asian-style noodle soup.
    (D) Thinking of ten alternate new designs for a lightbulb.
    (E) Choosing one of three possible formulas to solve a mathematical word problem.

68. Marge is severely reprimanded at work for coming back late after lunch. When she gets home that night, she yells at her son without justification. Marge's anger might be explained best by which of the following defense mechanisms?
    (A) projection
    (B) rationalization
    (C) repression
    (D) displacement
    (E) transformation

69. Our ability to perceive the figure in a simple dot-to-dot puzzle without drawing in the lines to connect the dots is an example of which of the following Gestalt principles?
    (A) closure
    (B) proximity
    (C) continuity
    (D) similarity
    (E) linear perspective

70. Delusions, hallucinations, and disorganized speech are all categorized as what type of schizophrenic symptoms?
    (A) undifferentiated
    (B) paradoxical
    (C) diathesis stress
    (D) positive
    (E) negative

71. Kettrina goes to see a psychiatrist because recently she experienced frightening stressful episodes. Her heart begins to race and she feels as if she is about to die. Which of the following disorders best fits Kettrina's symptoms?
    (A) generalized anxiety disorder
    (B) panic disorder
    (C) bipolar disorder
    (D) heightened anxiety disorder
    (E) agoraphobia

GO ON TO THE NEXT PAGE ➤

72. The American Psychological Association is currently discussing recommending a regulation change that could eliminate which of the following differences between psychologists and psychiatrists?
    (A) Psychiatrists may be required to receive more medical training than psychologists.
    (B) Etiology training.
    (C) Prescription privileges.
    (D) Psychiatrists may now be allowed to charge for their services.
    (E) Psychiatrists may be required to receive the extra education in drug interactions psychologists have always been required to complete.

73. Which of the following is a technique a psychoanalyst from the psychodynamic perspective might use to uncover unconscious ideas or impulses?
    (A) MMPI testing
    (B) covert questioning
    (C) rational-emotive questioning
    (D) regression analysis
    (E) free association

74. A token economy might be used in which of the following types of therapy?
    (A) rational emotive
    (B) person centered
    (C) behavior therapy
    (D) modeling therapy
    (E) Gestalt therapy

75. Aphasia would most likely result from damage to which of the following parts of the brain?
    (A) sensory cortex
    (B) occipital lobe
    (C) parietal lobe
    (D) temporal lobe
    (E) corpus callosum

76. Which of the following is an important basic principle in client- or person-centered therapy?
    (A) unconditional positive regard
    (B) hierarchy of needs
    (C) behavior modification
    (D) cognitive restructuring
    (E) interpersonal therapy

77. A false first impression could easily result from which of the following errors?
    (A) self-serving bias
    (B) contact-hypothesis error
    (C) matching-hypothesis error
    (D) fundamental-attribution error
    (E) face validity mistakes

78. What is the difference between relearning and spontaneous recovery?
    (A) Relearning occurs only in humans, while spontaneous recovery can occur in either humans or animals.
    (B) Relearning refers to the rapid learning of something we learned in the past, and spontaneous recovery is the sudden reappearance of a response after a single presentation of the conditioned stimulus.
    (C) Spontaneous recovery refers to the sudden, unexplained, unpredicted increase in response after satiation, and relearning is the increase in the learning curve after the response was thought to be extinct.
    (D) Relearning refers to skills, while spontaneous recovery refers to simple reflexive responses.
    (E) Spontaneous recovery occurs in a group-learning situation involving modeling, and relearning occurs with single subjects.

GO ON TO THE NEXT PAGE ➤

79. The therapeutic effect of electro-convulsive shock therapy may be a result of which of the following?
    (A) The pharmacological effects of the drugs involved in the treatment.
    (B) The cognitive therapy required in the treatment.
    (C) The physical convulsions caused by shock.
    (D) The behavior modifications required to receive the therapy.
    (E) Electro-convulsive shock therapy is outdated and never had any effects.

80. The term *plasticity* refers to the brain's ability to
    (A) reform itself physically in response to skull trauma.
    (B) make new synaptic connections.
    (C) make neural connections in the womb while the brain forms.
    (D) use existing neural connections for multiple tasks since new synapses cannot be formed.
    (E) adapt to novel situations by rerouting neural signals from the thalamus.

81. Hope, who is four years old, is asked to draw a deer. In her mind, Hope pictures Bambi from the Disney movie and tries to draw a deer very similar to this image. Hope is using Bambi as a
    (A) heuristic.
    (B) algorithm.
    (C) prototype.
    (D) paradigm.
    (E) archetype.

82. Which of the following is an example of a primary drive?
    (A) Drive for money.
    (B) Drive for satisfying employment.
    (C) Drive of an adopted child to find her or his biological parents.
    (D) Drive for liquids when thirsty.
    (E) Drive for revenge.

83. The trait of neuroticism as described by the big five or five-factor model of personality refers to
    (A) obsessive-compulsive disorder.
    (B) energetic and extraverted behavior.
    (C) organized and productive behaviors.
    (D) repressed impulses.
    (E) emotional disturbances and excessive anxiety.

84. Which of the following is the most accurate description of the relationship between bulimia and anorexia nervosa?
    (A) Bulimia is a specific subtype of anorexia nervosa involving bingeing and purging.
    (B) Anorexia nervosa is a more serious type of bulimia because it is more often fatal.
    (C) Anorexia nervosa and bulimia are eating disorders that result from obesity.
    (D) Anorexia nervosa and bulimia are eating disorders but involve very different symptoms.
    (E) Evidence of bulimia increases the likelihood a person will develop anorexia nervosa.

85. A person who has a high optimum level of arousal might be more attracted to which of the following activities than a person with a low optimum level of arousal?
    (A) Eating foods presented in appetizing ways.
    (B) Studying material presented in a conversational, personal manner.
    (C) Drag racing high-performance motorcycles.
    (D) Watching a nature documentary about attraction.
    (E) Interpersonal interaction.

86. Which of the following types of psychologists would be most likely to use a thematic apperception test (TAT)?
    (A) behavioristic psychologist
    (B) Gestalt psychologist
    (C) psychodynamic psychologist
    (D) structuralistic psychologist
    (E) thematic psychologist

GO ON TO THE NEXT PAGE ➤

87. Which of the following are the two subscales that constitute the Wechsler adult intelligence scale (WAIS)?
    (A) aptitude and achievement
    (B) verbal and spatial
    (C) logical and analytic
    (D) verbal and performance
    (E) verbal and nonverbal

88. Young Avin protests at the dinner table because it looks like his brother got more cake than he did. In reality, they have the same amount, but Avin's brother just cut up the cake and spread it around the plate to torment Avin. Avin does not understand the concept of
    (A) sharing.
    (B) conservation of area.
    (C) conservation of number.
    (D) metacognition.
    (E) conservation of volume.

89. Robert Sternberg suggests that what we define as intelligence actually consists of which distinct types?
    (A) crystallized, fluid, and adaptive
    (B) verbal and performance
    (C) linguistic, logical, spatial, musical, kinesthetic, academic, and personal
    (D) creative, academic, and practical
    (E) convergent and divergent thinking

90. Dr. Ogden prescribes an antidepressant drug to her patient, but makes the patient promise he will attend therapy sessions three times a week. At the therapy sessions, the patient is rewarded through positive feedback for controlling his anger in various role-playing situations. In her treatment, Dr. Ogden is principally working from what two perspectives?
    (A) psychoanalytic and biopsychological
    (B) evolutionary and behavioral
    (C) humanist and eclectic
    (D) behavioral and biopsychological
    (E) eclectic and biopsychological

91. The behaviorist perspective states psychology should examine only
    (A) measurable overt behaviors because of the need for objective data.
    (B) behaviors peculiar to the species being studied in order to differentiate one species' psychology from another.
    (C) behaviors proven to indicate psychological disorders based on clinical evidence.
    (D) behaviors based on choice because free will is the defining characteristic of human thought and behavior.
    (E) reaction times to interesting aspects of consciousness like emotions involved in fight-or-flight behaviors.

92. The primacy and recency effects are demonstrated during what memory process?
    (A) deep processing
    (B) long-term potentiation
    (C) source amnesia
    (D) recall
    (E) encoding

93. Brad hypothesizes that information presented in a funny way will be remembered better than information presented in a more straightforward, traditional manner. The independent variable in Brad's research is
    (A) the information.
    (B) the amount of information recalled.
    (C) the funny presentation.
    (D) the method of presentation.
    (E) the people who present the information.

94. William Sheldon's somatotype theory relates personality and
    (A) parenting styles.
    (B) body shape.
    (C) identical twin studies.
    (D) id impulses.
    (E) observational learning.

GO ON TO THE NEXT PAGE ➤

95. You hear a young boy in your neighborhood constantly shouting "No!" at his father. What stage of Erikson's theory might the boy be going through?
    (A) autonomy versus shame and doubt
    (B) autonomy versus authority
    (C) initiative versus guilt
    (D) will versus compliance
    (E) authoritarian versus authoritative

96. Goleman's concept of emotional intelligence (EQ) corresponds to which of the following intelligences described by Gardner's multiple intelligences theory?
    (A) interpersonal and intrapersonal intelligence
    (B) empathetic intelligence
    (C) introversion
    (D) extroversion
    (E) identity versus role confusion

97. A researcher investigating whether the scores from an IQ test correlate with other measures of intelligence is investigating what aspect of IQ tests?
    (A) reliability
    (B) predictability
    (C) validity
    (D) correlation factors
    (E) adaptability

98. Some psychologists criticize Kohlberg's research and doubt the generalizability of his stage theory because
    (A) the theory is not based on empirical research.
    (B) Kohlberg did not test if the theory varied across cultures or between genders.
    (C) the moral situations he used were not realistic to young children.
    (D) the theory underestimates the age children accomplish certain developmental tasks.
    (E) Kohlberg based too much of his theory on his personal childhood experiences.

99. The cerebral cortex is
    (A) the part of the brain responsible for repressed memories.
    (B) the part of the brain responsible for sensory memory.
    (C) the dense, inner part of the brain made up of neurons and neurotransmitters.
    (D) the thin outer layer of the brain densely packed with neurons.
    (E) the section of the cortex thought to be responsible for higher thought functions.

100. A person who experiences episodes of deep depression and periods of hyperactivity might be diagnosed with which mental illness?
    (A) seasonal affective disorder
    (B) changing affect disorder or bimood disorder
    (C) schizophrenia
    (D) manic depression or bipolar disorder
    (E) bipolar personality disorder

STOP

Answer Key

Multiple-choice Portion

1. B	21. D	41. E	61. B	81. C
2. B	22. D	42. D	62. C	82. D
3. C	23. B	43. C	63. C	83. E
4. E	24. D	44. D	64. B	84. D
5. B	25. B	45. C	65. B	85. C
6. C	26. C	46. D	66. B	86. C
7. E	27. D	47. E	67. D	87. D
8. A	28. A	48. E	68. D	88. E
9. B	29. E	49. A	69. A	89. D
10. B	30. C	50. A	70. D	90. D
11. B	31. A	51. C	71. B	91. A
12. D	32. A	52. D	72. C	92. D
13. A	33. C	53. C	73. E	93. D
14. D	34. A	54. B	74. C	94. B
15. C	35. E	55. B	75. D	95. A
16. D	36. D	56. C	76. A	96. A
17. D	37. B	57. B	77. D	97. C
18. A	38. E	58. C	78. B	98. B
19. C	39. B	59. D	79. C	99. D
20. B	40. C	60. E	80. B	100. D

Answers Explained

1. **(B)** Kim is gradually getting rid of her fear by exposing herself to flying in small steps. Kim would stay at each step in the process until her anxiety stopped or was at a low level and then move on to the next step. Aversion therapy is punishing a certain response or associating it with an undesired stimulus in order to eliminate the response. The other choices are made-up distractions.

2. **(B)** Food is the only choice that could be an unconditioned stimulus, because it would naturally cause the fish to swim to the top of the tank to feed. Kristin paired food with the light (the conditioned stimulus) in this example. The fish swimming to the top is the response, and the sound of the light and electric shock are not likely to be involved in this example.

3. **(C)** Crystal stopped teasing her friend because her friend ignored the teasing. In operant conditioning, a behavior (teasing) elicits a response that either reinforces or punishes the behavior (ignoring her, a punishment). The behavior is repeated if reinforced or stopped if punished. This is not an example of classical conditioning because two stimuli are not being associated. Appetitive conditioning is not a term in learning theory.

4. **(E)** The lazy group member is socially loafing, or putting forth less effort when involved in a group than he or she would if held individually responsible. Choice A is not a term typically used in social psychology. The other terms are social psychology principles but do not relate to this example.

5. **(B)** A conversion disorder, the sudden loss of a physical ability without medical cause, is one of the somatoform disorders, which all deal with physical problems brought on by mental causes.

6. **(C)** The electricity generated within the neuron does NOT jump the gap between neurons (the synapse). When the electricity reaches the end of the axon, the terminal buttons release neurotransmitters into the synapse to be absorbed by the next cell.

7. **(E)** The levels of processing theory predicts that deeply processed events (thought about in elaborated ways and given context) are more likely to be remembered than shallowly processed events. Sue apparently processed this commitment only shallowly. Sensory memory, working memory, and long-term memory are concepts involved in the information-processing model. If long-term potentiation occurs, it occurs at the neural level by definition.

8. **(A)** Serotonin is the only chemical listed that affects mood. Selective serotonin reuptake inhibitors, such as Prozac, affect the level of serotonin in the brain in order to elevate mood. Substance P is involved in pain, and acetylcholine is involved in muscle control. Adrenaline and thyroxin are hormones released by the adrenal and thyroid glands respectively.

9. **(B)** A heuristic is a rule of thumb used to solve a problem quickly. Algorithms are also used to solve problems but take more time and guarantee the correct answer. A heuristic would not be used for the other choices.

10. **(B)** Tolerance is defined as an increased need for a substance in order to achieve the same effects. Tolerance would be involved in a physical addiction, as would withdrawal symptoms, but the terms are not synonymous. Endorphin deficit is a made-up distraction. Habituation is a related but more general concept. Habituation occurs when any response decreases to a constant stimulus, like a child losing interest in a game after playing it repeatedly.

11. **(B)** The hypothalamus helps to control both the impulse to eat and the impulse to stop eating. The other brain structures are not directly involved in hunger control.

12. **(D)** The activation-synthesis model states that dreams are the interpretation of brain activity by the cerebral cortex. Researchers know that the brain is very active during REM sleep. This activity might be interpreted by the parts of the brain that process language and higher thought as the stories, images, and emotions that make up what we call dreams. Freud thought dreams represented wish fulfillments. The other choices are similar to other explanations for dreams but do not describe the activation-synthesis model.

13. **(A)** Erikson's theory describes social development. Piaget studied cognitive development. Kohlberg studied moral development. Bandura was a cognitive behaviorist interested in observational learning. Horney was a neo-Freudian interested in identity formation.

14. **(D)** Professor Castelucci hypothesized the presence of facial hair affected fear responses, which makes facial hair the independent variable and fear the dependent variable. The questionnaire described no control or mediating variables. The experimental condition is the group that saw the pictures of men with facial hair.

15. **(C)** Fear, the dependent variable, is operationally defined as the score on this questionnaire. The independent and dependent variables have already been described. This study does not specifically identify an outcome variable.

16. **(D)** The committee may look at the statistical methods the researcher would employ but is not necessarily a factor that would apply to every proposed study. The other items listed in the choices are requirements for any study involving human participants.

17. **(D)** Deindividuation occurs when an individual gets so caught up in a group that he or she acts in ways the person normally would not. Obedience is obeying an authority figure. Diffusions of responsibility occurs when an individual fails to act because others are present and everyone relies on someone else to take the initiative. Groupthink is involved in a group decision-making process, and members of the group support each others' opinions without critical thought.

18. **(A)** A person may associate the stimulus of driving with the car accident and therefore start to fear driving. The other choices are more likely examples of operant conditioning, because in each case a behavior is either rewarded or punished.

19. **(C)** During REM sleep, our brain is nearly as active as it is when we are awake. Someone in a manic state or experiencing a night terror might have elevated brain activity, but the EEG would be distinctly different than that of someone experiencing REM sleep. Deep sleep and hypnosis would produce lowered levels of brain activity, not heightened.

20. **(B)** To be diagnosed with bipolar depression, a person must experience both a manic and a depressive episode. Chemical imbalances may be involved, but the initial diagnosis is more likely to be made based on behavior. Choice D is a description of one element of a manic state. Choices C and E are made-up distractions.

21. **(D)** All sensory information passes through the thalamus and is then directed to different parts of the brain. Olfactory information is the sole exception. The olfactory nerve directly connects to the amygdala and hippocampus.

22. **(D)** A test that determines what skills or knowledge has been learned is an achievement test. An aptitude test determines a person's potential for a certain skill or way of thinking. The other choices are made-up distractions.

23. **(B)** The James-Lange theory states that physiological changes precede emotional responses, as they do in this example. The Cannon-Bard theory says the opposite—emotional changes precede changes in the body. Drive reduction is a theory of motivation. Schema and cognitive dissonance are cognitive terms, not emotional theories.

24. **(D)** The TAT and Rorschach tests are projective tests that rely on the idea that test takers will project their unconscious ideas and impulses onto the test. Displacement and repression are also defense mechanisms like projection but are not involved in these tests. Choices C and E are terms Freud and psychodynamic theorists might use but are not as directly involved in these tests as projection is.

25. **(B)** We are more likely to remember something when we are in a similar mood as we were when we encoded the memory. This phenomenon is called mood-congruent memory. State-dependent memory is similar but involves states of consciousness rather than mood. Levels of processing and information processing are overall memory models. Recovered memory is a controversial phenomenon involving remembering "repressed" events years after they occur and does not relate to this example.

26. **(C)** Freud said we repress unacceptable ideas and impulses into our unconscious mind. Childhood trauma might be repressed, but not all repressed ideas involve childhood trauma. According to Freud, neurosis can result from fixation at a particular psychosexual stage. Displacement is a defense mechanism, and maturation is a term for development over the life span.

27. **(D)** The fovea is a depression in the retina containing the greatest concentration of cones. It is near the blind spot, where the optic nerve connects to the retina. The focal point of the lens will change when the lens changes shape to focus on different objects. Choice E is a made-up distraction.

28. **(A)** The somatic nervous system (also called the skeletal nervous system) controls voluntary muscle movements. The sympathetic and parasympathetic nervous systems are divisions of the autonomic nervous system that controls automatic body functions. Choices D and E are made-up distractions.

29. **(E)** The difference threshold is defined as how different two stimuli must be for us to notice a difference. Bringing two pitches closer and closer together in frequency would be one way to test an individual's difference threshold for pitch. The absolute threshold is the lowest level of stimuli we can detect. Dichotic listening and perfect pitch are terms involved in hearing but do not apply to this example. Auditic memory is a made-up distraction.

30. **(C)** The auditory cortices are located in the temporal lobes in both hemispheres. The hippocampus is part of the limbic system. The sensory cortex is in the parietal lobe, and the cerebral cortex is the thin layer of neurons that surrounds the brain. No location is defined for the olfactory cortex, but the olfactory nerve connects first with the amygdala and hippocampus.

31. **(A)** Attribution theory predicts, in general, we will attribute failures to forces outside our control and successes to our own effort and skill. All the other choices relate to Jacquetta's own effort or skill.

32. **(A)** Group polarization occurs when the attitudes a person enters a group discussion with are strengthened by the discussion. Groupthink is involved in a group decision-making process when members of the group support each others' opinions without critical thought. Obedience involves obeying an authority figure, not a discussion process. The mere-exposure effect affects our increased attraction to objects or people we have been previously exposed to rather than to completely novel stimuli. Rigidity is an obstacle to problem solving.

33. **(C)** The teacher noticed a correlation in her class—the presence of cookies correlated with an increase in test scores. This does not indicate that cookies

cause the change in the test scores or make the students more intelligent. Other factors might cause this change. Perhaps the teacher usually brings cookies to class later in the day when students are more alert, and the time of day is the causal factor in the test scores. Independent and dependent variables are not relevant to the mistaken conclusion. Whether the test was double blind and sampling issues are irrelevant.

34. **(A)** Piaget conceived of schemata as mental rules we use to organize incoming information. Schemata are involved in problem solving and concepts of conservation, but they are not limited to those topics. Schemata do not result from assimilation; we try to assimilate information into our schemata. Piaget's theory addresses environmental factors exclusively, not genetic ones.

35. **(E)** In a longitudinal study, researchers choose a group or groups to study and test each group periodically over a long period of time. In a cross-sectional study, a researcher would choose a sample of various select ages and test them all at once. The term *descriptive* applies to a category of statistics. Both types of research (cross-sectional and longitudinal) are experimental and could be correlational or use a different research method.

36. **(D)** The more sensory neurons located in a certain part of the body, the more sensitive it is, and the more space is devoted to it in the sensory cortex. For example, the sensory cortex contains more space for processing information from the lips than from the elbow.

37. **(B)** Cognitive therapists strive to help their patients change the way they process information, including changing negative attitudes. Psychodynamic therapists would try to uncover unconscious information. Behaviorists would use systems of reinforcement to treat patients. Client-centered therapists and Gestalt therapists help clients discover their true feelings by giving them unconditional positive regard and acknowledging the validity of their views of reality.

38. **(E)** Extrinsic motivations are external rewards like resume building. Intrinsic motivations are internal rewards, like enjoyment and satisfaction. Self-actualizing is a goal of humanistic psychology. The words *positive* and *altruistic* apply to Laura's actions but are not used in a psychological context in this way.

39. **(B)** One of the major differences between sexual response cycles is the refractory period for men, or the time delay needed between ejaculations. The other statements are incorrect generalizations about the response cycles.

40. **(C)** Obsessive-compulsive disorder is a type of anxiety disorder. Sufferers of this disorder become very anxious if they do not perform their particular compulsions.

41. **(E)** Retinal disparity is one of the clues the brain uses to perceive depth. The brain receives images from each eye. Each eye sends a slightly different image due to the gap between them. The brain uses the difference between these two images to help determine how far away something is.

42. **(D)** Transduction is the process that changes outside energy and chemicals into neural signals that are transmitted to the brain. The other statements are incorrect definitions.

43. **(C)** Trait tests like the MMPI measure different personality traits.

44. **(D)** Dissociative disorders are a category of mental illnesses. The category includes disorders like dissociative amnesia, dissociative fugue, and dissociative identity disorder. All the other choices are types of schizophrenia.

45. **(C)** Watson made a loud noise behind Little Albert, causing him to cry. The noise is the unconditional stimulus because it naturally caused the unconditioned response—crying. Albert did not have to be trained to cry in response to the noise. The noise was paired with a fuzzy white rat, the conditioned stimulus. Punishment and negative reinforcer are operant conditioning terms.

46. **(D)** Authoritative parents consistently apply rules in their families, and the rationale behind these rules is explained. Choice A best describes a permissive parenting style, and choice B is more similar to an authoritarian parenting style. Choices C and E do not correspond with any of the parenting styles.

47. **(E)** An experiment is double blind if neither the researchers nor the participants are aware of which participants are assigned to which groups. Of course, when participants are assigned to the groups, someone keeps track of which participants are in which group. However, that list is not known or available to the researchers during the study. An experiment is single blind when just the participants are not aware of which group they are assigned to. All good experiments are controlled. The correlational method is one of the research methods investigators can choose to use in a study. Quasi-experimental research is done when conducting a true experiment is impossible or impractical due to limited sample size or ethical considerations.

48. **(E)** Skinner worked his entire career investigating and popularizing operant conditioning. Watson's research involved classical conditioning, as did Pavlov's. William James wrote the first psychology textbook. Carl Rogers developed client-centered therapy, a type of humanistic therapy.

49. **(A)** A standard deviation describes how scores are arranged in a distribution, specifically the average amount each score varies from the mean. This is a measure of the variability of the scores within a distribution. Amplitude and frequency are used to measure waves. A significant difference is measured by inferential statistics. The median measures central tendency.

50. **(A)** Convergence is how far our two eyes point toward one another when looking at an object close to our face. This depth cue requires two eyes. The other choices are monocular cues for depth that could be used with only one eye.

51. **(C)** The onset of schizophrenia usually occurs in young adulthood. The other statements about schizophrenia in the other choices are incorrect.

52. **(D)** Since the video game is new, Professor Guenzel's only choice is to do a longitudinal study. Test a group of children now and then measure the effects of the video game during adolescence by comparing them with a group of children not exposed to the game. A case study would be inconclusive. Not much valuable information about this topic could be gathered with a survey. A cross-sectional study could not be done because the video game is new and no adolescents exist at this time who were

exposed to the game as children. A pharmacological study involves medication and would not be appropriate for this purpose.

53. **(C)** A difference is termed significant when the change in the variable in question is not likely to be caused by chance. Specifically, the probability of the change being due to chance has to be less than five percent ($p < .05$). The other statements are incorrect or incomplete definitions of significant difference.

54. **(B)** The z score of the student's test score will immediately tell you how well the student did on the test. The z score measures how many standard deviations away from the mean the student scored. For example, if the z score of the student's test score is 0, you know she or he scored right at the mean or average score of the test. If the z score is 2, you know she did extremely well. The information listed in the other choices might be useful but not as useful as a z score.

55. **(B)** A result is generalizable to the extent that the findings apply to the general population from which the sample was taken. Choice A describes how the term generalization is used in a learning context. The other choices are made-up distractions.

56. **(C)** A test is valid to the extent that it actually measures what it is trying to measure. Choice A is a definition of reliability. The other choices are made-up distractions.

57. **(B)** Fluid intelligence involves our ability to process new information. Choice A is similar and might involve fluid intelligence, but choice B is a more general definition. The other choices better describe crystallized intelligence.

58. **(C)** This is the only criticism that can be applied to this conclusion given the information in the question. Dr. Windle is implying a causational relationship when the data is correlational, so the conclusion may be incorrect because many other factors could actually cause the relationship. The other choices criticize the study based on information not given in the question.

59. **(D)** Most mnemonic devices use chunking as a memory aid. The devices help us remember lists of information by grouping them into smaller chunks. Acronyms are an example of this. Peg word is a specific mnemonic device. Sensory memory is part of the information-processing model of memory. Shallow processing is part of the levels of processing model. Choice E is a made-up distraction.

60. **(E)** Piaget's theory would place a four-month-old in the sensorimotor stage. One of the main ways children in this stage learn about objects is by putting them into their mouths. Choice A describes how a psychodynamic theorist would explain this action. Choice B is a behaviorist explanation. Choice C implies a humanistic orientation. Piaget did not discuss instinctive behaviors as described in choice D.

61. **(B)** As far as researchers can tell, most dreams occur during REM sleep, but they can occur at any stage of sleep. However, dreams during REM sleep are the most vivid.

62. **(C)** Responses learned with a noncontinuous schedule of reinforcement are more resistant to extinction. More time is required with this schedule, so choice

A is incorrect. Schedules of reinforcement are used in operant conditioning, not classical as implied in choice B. The schedule of reinforcement has no effect on discrimination. Satiation (the organism getting full and not wanting a food reward) could be a problem in any schedule of reinforcement.

63. **(C)** When using the means-end technique, you identify what the goal is and then work backward from there. Figure ground is a term in visual perception, and hindsight bias is a mistake in thinking. Factor analysis is a statistical technique. Algorithms are problem-solving methods, but choice C is more correct because it specifically matches the description in the question.

64. **(B)** Piaget said children in the preoperational stage know certain things about objects but do not yet understand concepts such as conservation of area or volume. A child in the concrete operational stage does understand these concepts. Choice C is a made-up distraction. Preconventional is a stage in Kohlberg's moral development theory. Reversibility is involved in the concept of conservation but is not one of Piaget's stages.

65. **(B)** Sensation happens when sensory receptors fire. Perception is the organization and interpretation of these impulses from our sensory receptors. Perception occurs in the brain, sometimes at the level of the sense, and in the retina of the eye. Choices D and E incorrectly summarize these two concepts.

66. **(B)** Milgram tested how much people will obey an authority figure. Obedience is different than conformity, which occurs when we change our behavior to bring it in line with those around us. Deindividuation and groupthink are factors that affect group situations but do not apply to Milgram's experiment. Altruism, acting for the good of others, was indirectly tested by Milgram, but the experiment directly tested obedience.

67. **(D)** Divergent thinking is the ability to think of novel solutions or explanations. All the other possible answers are examples of convergent thinking—following established methods or procedures to solve a problem.

68. **(D)** Marge knows she cannot safely become angry at work, so she is displacing her anger she feels about being reprimanded toward a safer target: her son. Projection is attributing an unacceptable thought or impulse to someone else. Rationalization is reasoning away an unacceptable impulse with excuses or reasons other than the true reason for the impulse or behavior. Repression is pushing down an unacceptable impulse into the unconscious. Transformation is a made-up distraction, not a defense mechanism as described by Freud.

69. **(A)** Closure is our ability to fill in the missing gaps in a picture, such as the gaps between the dots in a simple dot-to-dot puzzle. The other Gestalt principles mentioned—proximity, continuity, and similarity—might be indirectly involved in solving the puzzle but are not as directly involved in this example as closure is. Linear perspective is a monocular cue for depth, not a Gestalt principle.

70. **(D)** The symptoms mentioned are called positive symptoms because they are additions to a person's normal behavior. Negative symptoms of schizophrenia are withdrawal from others, flat affect, and catatonia. Undifferentiated

schizophrenia is a type of schizophrenia, not a type of symptom. The diathesis stress model attempts to explain possible causes of the disease. Choice B is a made-up distraction.

71. **(B)** Panic disorder is characterized by panic attacks similar to Kettrina's experiences described in the question. Panic disorder can be associated with generalized anxiety disorder, but not necessarily. A person with agoraphobia might experience similar attacks, but he or she would be tied to the phobia of being away from his or her home or safe environment. These attacks are not typical of bipolar disorder. Choice D is a made-up distraction, not a true psychological disorder.

72. **(C)** The only difference accurately described in these choices are prescription privileges. Currently, psychiatrists can prescribe medication and psychologists cannot. The other choices are innaccurate and do not describe differences between psychologists and psychiatrists. Choice B is a made-up distraction.

73. **(E)** Freud and other psychodynamic psychoanalysts use free association to uncover unconsious material. The MMPI is a trait theory personality test. Rational-emotive questioning would be used only in the context of rational-emotive therapy. Regression analysis is a statistical technique, and covert questioning is a made-up distraction.

74. **(C)** A behaviorist might set up a token economy and reward desired behaviors with tokens that can be exchanged for rewards. The other choices would not use this strictly behaviorist technique. Modeling is a term from the learning area. However, it is not necessarily involved in a token economy nor is it a type of therapy.

75. **(D)** Aphasia, or the inability to speak or understand language, could result from damage to Wernicke's area, which is located in the temporal lobe. The other area that could cause aphasia, Broca's area, is in the frontal lobe. The other brain areas mentioned in the choices do not deal directly with the production or understanding of speech.

76. **(A)** Unconditional positive regard, valuing a person no matter what he or she says or does, is a central principle in Carl Rogers' person-centered therapy. The other responses are not part of person-centered therapy.

77. **(D)** The fundamental attribution error occurs when we attribute a person's behavior to his or her inner disposition rather than to the situation. We could easily form an inaccurate first impression about a person's inner disposition in this way. Self-serving bias refers to our tendency to attribute success to our effort but failure to external causes. The contact hypothesis states that we will lose our bias to groups as contact with them increases. Face validity is a type of validity applied to psychological tests and instruments. Matching hypothesis concerns why people are attracted to people similar to themselves.

78. **(B)** After learning something once, we relearn it quickly even if we report having forgotten the information or skill. Spontaneous recovery occurs in both animals and humans when a response that was trained but then made extinct suddenly reoccurs after the CS is presented once more. The other choice are incorrect statements about these two concepts.

79. **(C)** Electro-convulsive shock therapy causes the body to convulse, and these convulsions may cause the benefits some people report from this treatment. This therapy does not necessarily involve drug, cognitive, or behavioral treatment, so those choices are incorrect. This treatment is still used, although it is used more carefully and humanely than in the past.

80. **(B)** When damaged, the brain can often make new synaptic connections and thus regain abilities thought to be lost due to the original damage. In this way, a person left unable to speak after a stroke can sometimes be taught to speak again. Choice A is correct in a sense since new synapatic connections are physical changes on the neural level. However, choice B is a more correct response. The other choices incorrectly define the term.

81. **(C)** Hope is using a mental image of Bambi as a perfect image, or prototype, of a deer. Heuristics and algorithms are methods of problem solving. Carl Jung described archetypes he believed people drew on from the collective unconscious. A paradigm (not strictly a psychological term) is a general view of the world or situation.

82. **(D)** Primary drives, like thirst, relate to our physical survival needs. The other drives described are secondary drives, which are learned through experience.

83. **(E)** Neuroticism is one of the big five personality dimensions that appear cross-culturally and in many personality tests. The neuroticism dimension refers to emotional instability, impulsivity, and general anxiety. Choice B corresponds to the extroversion dimension, and choice C is an aspect of the conscientiousness dimension. Obsessive-compulsive disorder is a mental illness. Repressed impulses are a part of psychodynamic theory.

84. **(D)** Bulimia and anorexia nervosa are both eating disorders but involve different symptoms and treatment. Bulimics binge, eating large amounts of food in a short period of time, and then purge the food from their system by vomiting or using laxatives. Anorexics avoid eating and can starve to death if not treated. The other descriptions of the two disorders are inaccurate comparisons.

85. **(C)** People with high optimum levels of arousal are more likely to seek out activities that heighten excitement and raise their arousal to their level of optimum performance. The other activities described would not necessarily raise their arousal levels.

86. **(C)** A TAT test relies on projection, a psychodynamic concept. The psychologist theorizes the person taking the TAT test will project his or her own unconscious feelings and impulses on to the pictures and these impulses will come out in the descriptions. Behaviorists and Gestalt psychologists would not normally use this type of projective test. Structuralism is a historic psychological theory not currently used by psychologists. Choice E is a made-up distraction.

87. **(D)** The WAIS test is measured with verbal and performance scales. Aptitude and achievement are types of tests.

88. **(E)** Children who understand conversation of volume know that the volume of the cake is preserved even though it is cut up and spread around the plate.

The brothers sharing the cake (choice A) might be nice, but it does not apply to the example given in the question. Conservation of area is a similar concept but refers to the preservation of area no mater how objects are arranged within it. Conservation of number does not apply. Metacognition is the ability to monitor our thoughts and is typical of the formal-operational stage.

89. **(D)** Sternberg's triarchic theory describes three different kinds of intelligence. Academic intelligence is measured by existing IQ tests. Practical intelligence is required to solve real-world problems. Creative intelligence is demonstrated by the creation of novel solutions or creative expressions. Crystallized and fluid intelligence describe two types of intelligence but are not part of this theory. Verbal and performance are the two subscales of the WISC test. The seven items listed in choice C are the subtypes described by Howard Gardner's multiple intelligences theory. Convergent and divergent thinking refer to different problem-solving methods but do not relate to Sternberg's theory.

90. **(D)** Dr. Ogden uses a biopsychological intervention (the antidepressant drug) and a behavioral treatment (the rewards for anger control). The other perspectives would emphasize other types of interventions.

91. **(A)** Behaviorists argued that in order to be scientific, psychology should restrict itself to measurable behaviors, not issues like free will, consciousness, or emotions. Behaviorists might study behaviors relevant to psychological disorders or species-specific behaviors, but they do not restrict research to those areas.

92. **(D)** The primacy effect, the tendency to remember the first items from a list, and the recency effect, the tendency to remember the last items on a list, are demonstrated during recall. The other terms are involved in memory but do not name processes that would demonstrate either primacy or recency.

93. **(D)** The independent variable is the one manipulated by the experimenter. Therefore, it is the way the material is presented, either in a funny way or in a straightforward way. All variables must be able to vary and, in this case, the information, the funny presentation, and the people who present the information should not vary. In an experiment, these factors must be controlled or kept the same in all the experimental conditions. The funny presentation is one level of the independent variable; it is the experimental treatment. The amount of information recalled is the dependent variable because, according to the hypothesis, the method of presentation will affect it.

94. **(B)** Sheldon's theory relates personality and body type, specifically the endomorph, ectomorph, and mesomorph types. The somatoform theory has nothing to do with parenting styles or twin studies. Id impulses would reflect a psychodynamic perspective not held by Sheldon. Observational learning would fit a behavioristic personality theory.

95. **(A)** Erikson said the autonomy versus shame and doubt stage is when we start to develop our will and sense of power over ourselves. *No* might become one of our favorite words. Choice C is one of Erikson's stages but does not fit the example given in the question. Choice E names two parenting styles, not stages of Erikson's theory. Choices B and D are made-up distractions.

96. **(A)** The interpersonal and intrapersonal intelligences described by Gardner are similar to Goleman's EQ concept. These intelligences deal with relationships between people. Choice B is a made-up distraction. Introversion and extroversion are specific personality traits. Choice D is one of Eriskon's social development stages.

97. **(C)** Checking correlations with other similar tests is one way to measure the validity of a test. Reliability is the extent to which participants get similar scores on subsequent repetitions of a test. A test score may predict a trait or behavior, but checking correlations with other tests would not concern predictability. Choices D and E are made-up distractions.

98. **(B)** Some researchers, Carol Gilligan for example, doubt that Kohlberg's stages apply across gender and culture lines since he tested mainly young boys. The theory was based on his empirical research, and the situations were designed to be understandable to children. The age ranges are not typically criticized, and he did not base his theory on personal anecdotal evidence.

99. **(D)** The cerebral cortex is a thin sheet of densely packed neurons. The other choices are incorrect descriptions of this part of the brain.

100. **(D)** Bipolar disorder (or manic depression) is marked by periods of clinical depression and manic periods of extremely elevated moods and increased activity. Seasonal affective disorder is depression tied to seasonal changes. Schizophrenia is an entirely different category of psychological disorders that involve hallucinatory or delusional symptoms. Choices B and E are made-up distractions.

Multiple-choice Error Analysis Sheet

After checking your answers on the practice test, you might want to gauge your areas of relative strength and weakness. This sheet will help you to classify your errors by topic area. By circling the numbers of the questions you answered incorrectly, you can get a picture of which areas you need to study the most.

CHAPTER	QUESTION NUMBERS										
History and Approaches	86	90									
Methods	14	15	16	33	47	49	53	54	55	58	93
Biological Bases of Behavior	6	8	11	28	30	36	75	80	99		
Sensation and Perception	21	27	29	41	42	50	65	69			
States of Consciousness	10	12	19	61							
Learning	2	3	18	45	48	62	78	91			
Cognition	7	9	25	59	63	67	81	92			
Motivation and Emotion	23	38	39	82	84	85					
Developmental Psychology	3	34	35	46	52	60	64	88	95	98	
Personality	24	26	43	68	83	94					
Testing and Individual Differences	22	56	57	87	89	96	97				
Abnormal Psychology	5	20	40	44	51	70	71	100			
Treatment of Psychological Disorders	1	37	72	73	74	76	79				
Social Psychology	4	17	31	32	66	77					

Essay Portion

Time—50 minutes

> *Directions:* You have 50 minutes to answer BOTH of the following questions.

1. A researcher is interested in investigating the relationship between temperature and aggression. Briefly describe how you would design
   (A) A correlational study to measure the relationship between these two variables. Make sure you include an explanation of how you would operationalize both variables and measure them.
   (B) An experimental study to investigate whether an increase in temperature increases rates of aggression. Make sure you include details about sampling, assignment, the independent variable, the dependent variable, operational definition of the dependent variable, and at least one method used to control for a confounding variable.
   (C) Finally, by using your knowledge of social psychology, predict what the result of these research studies would be. Identify the social psychology principle you use to predict this outcome.

2. A two-year-old child finds a piece of candy and puts it into her mouth. Later, she picks up a piece of brightly colored plastic and puts it into her mouth but quickly spits it out because it tastes bitter. Later, the parent notices the girl avoids putting plastic into her mouth but still enjoys candy. Describe how
   (A) A behaviorist would explain what learning occurred in this example. Explain how the following concepts apply to this example: positive reinforcement, punishment, generalization, and discrimination.
   (B) A cognitive psychologist would explain what learning occurred in this example using Piaget's theory of cognitive development. Explain how the following concepts apply to this example: schema, assimilation, and accommodation.
   (C) Finally, use what you wrote for parts A and B to explain what the principle difference is between the way behaviorists and cognitive psychologists view this learning situation.

Question 1 Scoring Rubric

This is a 10-point question: 2 points are possible in part A, 6 points in part B, and the final 2 points in Part C. The answers to parts A and B must be descriptions of research studies that include the required elements. The answer to the last part of the question must predict research findings based on a valid social psychological principle.

(A)   Describe a correlational study to measure the relationship between these two variables. Make sure you include an explanation of how you would operationalize both variables and measure them.

Point 1—Valid operational definition of temperature—could include validating temperature by weather service reports, tracking daily temperature using an outdoor thermometer, or other method of measuring outdoor temperature.

Point 2—Valid operational definition of aggression—could include tracking number of violent crimes that day, a naturalistic observation system where specific aggressive behaviors are identified, or another specific measurement system for aggression.

(B)   Design an experimental study to investigate whether an increase in temperature increases rates of aggression. Make sure you include details about sampling, assignment, the independent variable, the dependent variable, operational definition of the dependent variable, and at least one method used to control for a confounding variable.

Point 3—Random sampling—The student should describe a method to choose a random sample from a population. Examples might include using a random number table to choose from a list of social security numbers, obtaining a list of members of the population to be sampled and choosing randomly from the list, or using another random sampling method. Make certain that the student describes a method of random sampling, not random assignment. The student could also score a point for describing another valid sampling method, such as representative sampling.

Point 4—Random assignment—The student should describe a method to choose and randomly assign the sample to the groups involved in the experiment. Examples might include making an alphabetical list of participants and assigning every other participant to a group, randomly assigning participants to groups after all participants are present by numbering them, or using another random assignment method. Make certain that the student describes a method of random assignment, not random sampling. The student could also score a point for describing another valid sampling method, such as group matching.

Point 5—Independent variable—The student needs to identify temperature as the independent variable. Although the question does not state the researcher's hypothesis, reasonable experiments will manipulate temperature and measure its effect on aggression.

Point 6—Dependent variable—The student needs to identify aggression as the dependent variable. Make certain the student is not identifying a particular operational definition or measurement method as the dependent variable. For example, using a checklist to count aggressive behaviors during a certain period of time is an operational definition of aggression, not the dependent variable itself.

Point 7—Operational definition of dependent variable—The operational definition of the dependent variable is a valid method of measuring aggression. The student's research design can include many different measurement methods. Examples might include (but are not limited to) using a checklist to count aggressive behaviors during a certain period of time, using a self-report rating of aggressive feelings, videotaping participant behaviors and creating a system to rate the taped behaviors, direct observation of participant behaviors by researchers, and measuring physiological bodily changes related to aggression.

Point 8—Control—The student needs to point out at least one element of her or his experimental design that controls for a possible confounding variable. This could be a method of controlling bias in measurement, doing a single-blind or double-blind experiment, using deception to prevent subject bias or demand characteristics, or using another valid method of control.

(C)   Finally, by using your knowledge of social psychology, predict what the result of these research studies would be. Identify the social psychology principle you use to predict this outcome.

Point 9—Social psychology principle—The student receives one point for correctly identifying a principle from social psychology that applies to the example. The most common answer is the frustration-aggression hypothesis.

Point 10—Prediction—The student receives one point for accurately predicting how the frustration-aggression hypothesis would apply in these types of studies. The frustration-aggression hypothesis states that an increase in frustration will cause an increase in aggression. The student should describe how an increase in temperature might increase frustration, which would increase aggression, both as a correlation and in experimental conditions.

Question 2 Scoring Rubric

This is an 8-point question: 4 points are possible in part A, 3 points in part B, and the final point in Part C. Make certain the student explains the requested concepts in the proper context. That the student understands the difference between a behaviorist explanation and a cognitive explanation of the same learning situation must be evident.

(A)   A behaviorist would explain what learning occurred in this example. Explain how the following concepts apply to this example: positive reinforcement, punishment, generalization, and discrimination.

NOTE: In part A, the student needs to indicate clearly that the behavior of the toddler is evidence for positive reinforcement, punishment, and so on. It is NOT a scorable response if the student indicates the actions are performed because of something the child thinks or expects. Repeating or avoiding the behavior determines whether it is a reward or punishment. ALSO, just identifying the appropriate evidence for each concept is not enough. The question asks the student to explain how the concept applies to the example. So to score the point, the student must explain how the evidence demonstrates the concept.

Point 1—Positive reinforcement—The student should explain that the toddler was positively reinforced for putting the candy into her mouth because it was sweet. The student could explain that this reinforcement increased the likelihood the girl will repeat the behavior (she tries to put the plastic into her mouth and she continues to eat candy). The word *reward* is an acceptable synonym if the word is used in the context of positive reinforcement.

Point 2—Punishment—The essay should clearly indicate that the toddler was punished for putting the plastic into her mouth because it was bitter and/or had an unpleasant texture. The student could explain that this punishment decreased the likelihood the girl will repeat the behavior. This is proven by her later behavior (she stopped putting plastic into her mouth).

Point 3—Generalization—The essay should use as evidence for generalization the girl putting the piece of plastic into her mouth. The child was rewarded for putting the candy into her mouth. She generalized the stimulus of the candy and tried the same behavior on the similar-looking piece of plastic.

Point 4—Discrimination—The student should point out the later behavior noticed by the parent as evidence of discrimination. The child learned to respond in different ways to the candy and the plastic.

(B)   A cognitive psychologist would explain what learning occurred in this example using Piaget's theory of cognitive development. Explain how the following concepts apply to this example: schema, assimilation, and accommodation.

NOTE: In the context of part B, the student can use phrases like "the girl thought" or "the toddler figured out" or "she expected" since the cognitive theory emphasizes the role thoughts play in behavior.

Point 5—Schema—The student should describe one of the schemata the child uses in this example. Possible schemata include putting objects into her mouth to get information about them, putting things that look like candy into her mouth because they taste good, and putting candy into her mouth but not putting plastic into her mouth. Any indication that the student understands the concept of schema AND applies the concept in a valid way to the example can be scored.

Point 6—Assimilation—For this point, the student needs to point out that when the girl put the piece of plastic into her mouth, she assimilated. She was trying to apply her schema for candy to the new information, the piece of plastic.

Point 7—Accommodation—Accommodation occurred when the girl discovered her schema for candy did not apply to the plastic in a satisfactory way. She had to change her schema to cover eating candy but not eating plastic.

(C)   Finally, use what you wrote for parts A and B to explain what the principle difference is between the way behaviorists and cognitive psychologists view this learning situation.

Point 8—Difference—The student should somehow indicate that the emphasis on cognition is the difference between the way the two perspectives explain this example. The student can use many different terms for cognition—thought, expectation, what is going on inside her head, and so on. However, the student must show evidence that he or she understands that the behaviorist explanation looks strictly at behavior for evidence of the learning while the cognitive explanation emphasizes what the child is thinking in order to understand what she learned.

Calculate Your Score on Practice Test #2

Section I – Multiple Choice

_____ – (1/4 X _____) = _____
Number correct   Number wrong   Section I Score

Section II - Free Response

Question 1 _____ X 2.500 = _____
                    (Maximum = 10)   Question 1 Score

Question 2 _____ X 3.125 = _____
                    (Maximum = 8)   Question 2 Score

_____ + _____ = _____
Question 1 Score   Question 2 Score   Total Essay Score

Total Score

_____ + _____ = _____
Section I Score   Section II Score   Total Score (Round)

How to Convert Your Score*

93 – 150 = 5
72 – 92 = 4
53 – 71 = 3
34 – 52 = 2
0 – 33 = 1

*Please note that this chart provides an estimate. The cutoffs between the different AP scores vary from year to year.

Index

If this book contains CD-ROM software, you should read the following documentation before you begin to use the CD-ROM.

MINIMUM HARDWARE REQUIREMENTS

The program will run on a PC with

1. Intel Pentium® 166MHZ or equivalent processor

2. 32 MB RAM

3. MS Windows 95/98/NT/2000/XP

4. SVGA (256 Colors) Monitor

5. 8X CD-ROM drive

6. Keyboard, Mouse

The program will run on a Macintosh with

1. PowerPC 8600

2. Operating System 9.0 (or higher)

3. 32 MB RAM

4. SVGA (256 Colors) Monitor

5. 8X CD-ROM drive

6. Keyboard, Mouse

The CD-ROM includes an "autorun" feature that automatically launches the application when the CD-ROM is inserted into the CD-ROM drive. In the unlikely event that the autorun features are disabled, alternate launching instructions are provided below.

Windows 95/98/NT/2000XP:
1. Put the Barron's AP Psychology CD-ROM into the CD-ROM drive.
2. Click on the Start button and choose Run.
3. Type D:\APPsychology.EXE (assuming the CD is in drive D), then click OK.

Macintosh:
1. Put the Barron's AP Psychology CD-ROM into the CD-ROM drive.
2. Double-click the AP Psychology Installer icon.
3. Follow the onscreen instructions.